Foundations and American
Political Science

Foundations and American Political Science

The Transformation of a Discipline, 1945–1970

Emily Hauptmann

University Press of Kansas

Published by the University Press of Kansas (Lawrence, Kansas 66045), which was organized by the Kansas Board of Regents and is operated and funded by Emporia State University, Fort Hays State University, Kansas State University, Pittsburg State University, the University of Kansas, and Wichita State University.

Library of Congress Cataloging-in-Publication Data is available

Names: Hauptmann, Emily, author.
Title: Foundations and American political science : the transformation of a discipline, 1945–1970 / Emily Hauptmann.
Description: Lawrence : University Press of Kansas, 2022. | Includes bibliographical references and index.
Identifiers: LCCN 2022007364
ISBN 9780700633777 (paperback)
ISBN 9780700633784 (ebook)
Subjects: LCSH: Political science—United States—History—20th century. | Political science—Study and teaching (Higher)—United States—History—20th century. | Political science—Research—United States—History—20th century. | Endowment of research—United States—History—20th century. | Carnegie Foundation for the Advancement of Teaching. | Ford Foundation. | Rockefeller Foundation. | University of California, Berkeley. | University of Michigan.
Classification: LCC JA84.U5 H38 2022 | DDC 320.50973—dc23/eng/20220714
LC record available at https://lccn.loc.gov/2022007364.

British Library Cataloguing-in-Publication Data is available.

Printed in the United States of America

10 9 8 7 6 5 4 3 2 1

The paper used in this publication is recycled and contains 30 percent postconsumer waste. It is acid free and meets the minimum requirements of the American National Standard for Permanence of Paper for Printed Library Materials Z39.48-1992.

CONTENTS

Preface and Acknowledgments vii

List of Abbreviations xiii

Introduction 1

PART I: FOUNDATIONS

1. "Propagandists for the Behavioral Sciences": The Carnegie Corporation and the SSRC 23

2. The Ford Foundation's "Golden Eggs" and the Constitution of Behavioralism 50

3. A "Catholic" Approach: The Rockefeller Foundation's Diversified Social Science Program 78

PART II: UNIVERSITIES

4. The Transformation of Political Science at Michigan: Patronage and the Rise of Political Behavior Research 105

5. Political Science at Berkeley: Growth, Conflict, and Dispersal 134

Conclusion 168

Notes 183

Bibliography 241

Index 257

PREFACE AND ACKNOWLEDGMENTS

When I was a graduate student in the 1980s, learning to become a political theorist meant learning to read and interpret works in the "canon"—the "great books" of Western political thought. It also meant learning how others in the field had made sense of the odd-fitting, marginal place political theory occupied in late-twentieth-century political science. Some identified adversaries they held responsible for pushing political theory to the margins, often singling out behavioralism as a particularly potent foe. Others blamed weaknesses within political theory itself, while still others began to celebrate its relative autonomy within the broader discipline.[1]

But had it always been this way? That is, had political theory always been a marginal part of US political science throughout its life as an academic discipline? When I began asking such questions about the history of political theory and political science, the earliest answers I found to them were resounding negatives. Most notably, I encountered John Gunnell's argument that even before the formal founding of the American Political Science Association (APSA) in 1903 until the 1970s, "debates in and about" political theory had been "at the heart" of how political scientists thought about their discipline, "its past, and its future prospects." Hence, the marginalization of the field I took to be a given was a quite recent development driven, Gunnell argued, by a reaction against critiques of liberalism and positivism first launched by European émigré scholars in the 1940s. I found many aspects of Gunnell's account compelling, especially his insistence that some aspects of behavioralism were continuous with older patterns in the discipline.[2] Still, I wondered whether there might be other complementary historical explanations of the marginalization of political theory. I remembered my surprise when Norman Jacobson, one of my teachers in graduate school, mentioned that the Rockefeller Foundation had made some sizable grants to UC Berkeley's political science department—and that these grants were specifically for political theory. I decided to look into these, out of a desire to complement rather than echo Gunnell's historical account.

Since that time nearly two decades ago, I have spent my academic career studying academic disciplines, universities, and their sources of funding. So prolonged an examination of the branch on which I sit has been both extraordinarily illuminating and deeply unsettling. On the one hand, I gained a considerable understanding of political science as a discipline by studying the part philanthropic foundations played in its recent history—an understanding that would have remained closed to me had I continued to work within the confines of political theory as I first learned to do it. On the other hand, that understanding led me to abandon several beliefs that used to sustain me: that people who did humanistic, historical studies of politics could count on a secure if small place in political science departments and that students who wanted to pursue academic careers had a good chance of finding stable, long-term jobs. I hope this book conveys some of the understanding I have gained and trust that readers will be able to balance the illuminating against the unsettling.

This project took me a long time to conceive, redraw, and complete. Inevitably, I incurred many debts to many people along the way. Norman Jacobson first regaled me with stories of the history of Berkeley's political science department while I was a graduate student there in the 1980s. He gradually made me see that history as key to understanding the small sector of the academic world in which I have spent the past thirty years. Once my research interests moved toward studying that history, I met with, interviewed, and corresponded with Norman many times until his death in 2007. He was my first and one of my best guides. Norman also first acquainted me with Jack Gunnell's work; I was fortunate enough to get to know Jack when he spent a semester as a visiting professor at the University of Nevada, Reno, where I was teaching at the time. Jack's intellectual openness, generosity, and prodigious energy then and over the next thirty years has buoyed my own slow and halting progress. I also am grateful to Terry Ball, who was a kind and generous reader of my work for decades before we finally met in person. More recently, Arlene Saxonhouse listened to and encouraged my rough attempts to explain my interest in the recent history of political science. It was on Arlene's suggestion that I began to study the history of the Michigan department; she also made my two stints as a visiting scholar in that department possible.

My colleague at Western Michigan University, the late Bill Ritchie, brought the midcentury, open, eclectic approach to political theory I explore at many points throughout this book to life for me. A 1960 University of Michigan PhD, Bill had an expansive view of political theory; he never tired of insisting upon its centrality to political science, as he understood it. This view was initially jarring to me, given how profoundly it differed from what I had learned at Berkeley in the 1980s. I soon came to see, however, that thanks to Bill's ideas and the respectful hearing they received from his colleagues, I was being given the rare chance to teach in a 1990s department that still required all its graduate students to take several courses in political theory and offered theory as one of its three examination fields. I owe my being able to teach and mentor graduate students throughout my academic life at Western to Bill—and the idea of political theory's central place in the discipline that he learned at Michigan and made real at Western.

I was lucky that my first major foray into archival research was at the Rockefeller Archive Center. Experienced archivists Tom Rosenbaum and Mary Ann Quinn led me to see dimensions of what I was trying to understand that I never knew existed. I learned a great deal from them. When the Ford Foundation archives were still housed on the ground floor of the foundation's headquarters in Manhattan, James Moske helped me prepare for my visit, find what I needed while I was there, and make sense of it later. At Columbia University's Rare Book & Manuscript Library, Jane Gorjevsky helped me make sense of the Carnegie staff shorthand in the records of the Carnegie Corporation.

When I first returned to Berkeley as a visiting scholar at the Center for Studies in Higher Education, senior researcher Anne MacLachlan was my intellectually inspiring guide to thinking about the lives of disciplines in universities. Anya Grant in Berkeley's political science department generously allowed me access to many departmental records that had not yet made it to the university archives. Of the many people I spoke with about their experience of Berkeley in the decades before I was a student there, my conversations with the late Jeff Lustig, Joe Paff, Gene Poschman, and Peter Dale Scott were especially helpful antidotes to the "how much does this all really matter?" doldrums.

The friendly staff at the Bentley Historical Library in Ann Arbor, Michigan, made it easier to dive into yet another day of research during the two semesters I spent there. Małgorzata Myc and Dianna Bachman were especially kind, welcoming, and helpful to me. Many thanks also to the participants in the University of Michigan political science department's Political Theory Workshop—especially Lisa Disch, Arlene Saxonhouse, Liz

Wingrove, and Mariah Zeisberg—for including me in the workshop and making it possible for me to present at several sessions.

Several sabbaticals and travel grants from Western Michigan University and its political science department have supported my research over the years, as did two Rockefeller Archive Center grants in aid and a Stevens Research Travel Fellowship from the Bentley Historical Library.

Among the many conferences and workshops at which I presented earlier versions of what appears in this book, I remember a few especially fondly for encouraging me to continue pursuing this topic. In addition to the Political Theory Workshops in Ann Arbor, a 2009 conference at the École Normale Supérieure, Cachan, and another at the University of Luxembourg in 2013 helped put the wind in my sails. Thanks to Philippe Fontaine and Tom Popkowitz for inviting me to each. Special thanks to Ragnhild Barbu in Luxembourg, whose interest in what I was just beginning to say about survey research was especially encouraging.

At the University Press of Kansas, David Congdon struck just the right balance between supporting my project and explaining how I could improve it over several rounds of revisions. I am deeply grateful for his confidence and guidance. The reviewers of my manuscript each gave me new vantage points on what I was trying to say along with many helpful suggestions. I am indebted to them for the time and the care they gave my work. Thanks also to Michelle Asakawa, Derek Helms, Karl Janssen, and Erica Nicholson at Kansas for helping to turn my manuscript into a published book.

Over the course of the time that I have been working on this project, I have often stepped well outside the bounds of academic political science to study it as I thought I should. There are therefore numerous historians— historians of science and social science, especially—among the people who helped me along the way. Robert Adcock, Jessica Blatt, Thibaud Boncourt, Philippe Fontaine, Nicolas Guilhot, Tim Kaufman-Osborn, Jeff Pooley, Ted Porter, Paulo Ravecca, Joan Roelofs, Joy Rohde, Mark Solovey, Jacinda Swanson, Herb Weisberg, and Emily Zerndt all read and commented on drafts of parts of my manuscript. I am grateful to them all.

When my bad academic habits of hedging and narrowing dull my critical capacities, my partner, Erik Freye, keeps doing the hard work of sharpening them. He has also prodded me to put my sense of what happened to postwar political science in bigger historical frames. This book would not have happened without his steady encouragement. Along this long, long road, he has been my best and truest companion. I dedicate this book to him.

———

Some of the chapters in this book are revisions and, I hope, improvements of previously published articles. Chapter 1 revises and extends "'Propagandists for the Behavioral Sciences': The Overlooked Partnership between the Carnegie Corporation and the SSRC in the Mid-20th Century," which originally appeared in the *Journal of the History of the Behavioral Sciences* 52, no. 2 (2016): 167–187. Similarly, chapter 2 revises and expands "The Ford Foundation and the Rise of Behavioralism in Political Science," also published in the *Journal of the History of the Behavioral Sciences* 48, no. 2 (2012): 154–173. Chapter 3 includes some material from two shorter articles: "From Opposition to Accommodation: How Rockefeller Foundation Grants Redefined Relations between Political Theory and Social Science in the 1950s," published in the *American Political Science Review* 100, no. 4 (2006): 643–649, and "The Theorists' Gambit: Kenneth Thompson's Cultivation of Theoretical Knowledge about Politics during the Early Cold War," published in the *International History Review* 42, no. 3 (2020): 625–638. Chapter 5 includes some material from "The Evolution of Political Theory at Berkeley in a Climate of Experiment and Secession," published in *PS: Political Science & Politics* 50, no. 3 (2017): 792–796.

ABBREVIATIONS

AAUP American Association of University Professors
ANES American National Election Studies
CASBS Center for the Advanced Study of the Behavioral Sciences
CC Carnegie Corporation
CPB Committee on Political Behavior (SSRC)
FF Ford Foundation
ICPSR Inter-university Consortium for Political and Social Research
IIS Institute for International Studies (UC Berkeley)
ISR Institute for Social Research (University of Michigan)
ISS Institute for Social Science (UC Berkeley)
LAPP Legal and Political Philosophy program (Rockefeller)
NDEA National Defense Education Act
NSF National Science Foundation
ORU organized research unit
RF Rockefeller Foundation
SSRC Social Science Research Council
SRC Survey Research Center (University of Michigan)

Foundations and American Political Science

INTRODUCTION

In the fall of 2019, billionaires Tom Steyer and Michael Bloomberg self-financed their bids for the US Democratic Party's 2020 presidential nomination.[1] Despite Steyer's never having held public office and Bloomberg's long association with the Republican Party, the hundreds of millions of dollars each spent on advertising and campaign consultants had powerful if short-term effects. Both vaulted ahead of other candidates in polls taken during the early stages of the campaign; Bloomberg won fifty-five delegates in the one round of primaries in which he competed.[2] Echoes of these noisy assertions of the power of wealth were still audible long after both campaigns ended.

More often, however, the wealthy wield power more quietly and obliquely. When they exercise power quietly, they employ small armies of lawyers and accountants to defend their wealth in ways designed to avoid publicity. When the wealthy create philanthropic foundations, they exercise power obliquely. Foundations proclaim noble ideals—"a legacy of social justice" (Ford); "democracy, education and international peace" (Carnegie); "promoting the well-being of humanity around the world" (Rockefeller)—and publicize the vast amounts of money they have spent to realize them.[3] Foundations exercise great power, albeit power rebranded as philanthropy.

Private philanthropic foundations are tax-sheltered entities with public agendas, however noble some of their missions may be. Many direct a portion of what were corporate fortunes toward public ends, whether to improve the decidedly antiphilanthropic images of their founders or to advance their broader social and political aims.[4] In principle, tax exemptions come with significant constraints: the portion of their founders' wealth private philanthropies protect from the state's taxing authority can only be spent on purposes permitted by the state. To retain their tax-exempt status, private philanthropies must report on their income and expenditures annually, disburse 5 percent of their assets each year, and not engage in political advocacy.[5] Though several mid-twentieth-century congressional

1

committees investigated foundations they suspected of violating this last rule, they were ultimately unable to rein in their power. In practice, the considerable wealth channeled into foundations not only remains untaxed—it furthers the social, political, and economic ambitions of their founders, their heirs, and their current directors. Created out of the wealth amassed by industrialists, financiers, or tech giants, large foundations are private, public policy–influencing and public policy–making islands. And, for the most part, they choose what to publicize about themselves.[6]

During the past few years, there has been an uptick in public if not congressional attention to how "megadonor" philanthropists like Bill and Melinda Gates and Mark Zuckerberg and Priscilla Chan spend their considerable wealth. A number of recent studies of organized philanthropy have analyzed big foundations' explicitly political ambitions along with their capacity to influence public policy.[7] Although political scientists have studied philanthropic foundations far less frequently than have sociologists or historians, two recent symposia in PS: Political Science & Politics indicate that this may be changing. The contributors to "Why Political Scientists Should Study Organized Philanthropy" and "Advancing Philanthropic Scholarship" urge political scientists to examine the influence of private foundations on politics or, more rarely, on academic life.[8]

Such studies are long overdue. Among the many areas in which they have been active, philanthropic foundations have been powerful, hands-on patrons of higher education in the United States for over a century.[9] Yet only a few scholars—and even fewer political scientists—have paid attention to how foundations have shaped their disciplines and universities. Why?

For a start, political scientists rarely study how wealthy elites wield political power in the first place. Granted, more are writing about the politics of economic inequality today than twenty years ago. Yet most focus on the attitudes of ordinary people, the affluent upper 10 percent, or the behavior of elected officials.[10] To explain why their studies of "the new gilded age" do not zero in on those at the very top of the income distribution, some cite the "lack of sufficient data on the preferences of the truly rich." Although a few political scientists have developed a theory of how the very rich practice "wealth defense" in a variety of settings, including the contemporary United States, this approach is rare.[11]

Additionally, foundations have been remarkably successful in defining themselves as nonpolitical and nonpartisan, thereby putting a benign cast on the power they wield. Neatly occupying what they themselves have helped define as the "third sector," foundations present themselves as distinct from both the state and the corporate world. This alone places them outside the bounds of what political scientists usually study. Scholars who accept the "third sector" designation also deploy it to downplay the power of foundations. From this perspective, foundations are "incomplete institutions" unable to accomplish their goals in science, the arts, and medicine without partners; "they do not act themselves: they enable others to act."[12]

Exploring how foundations have shaped political science inevitably bumps into another unequal relationship: the discipline's fundamental dependence on institutions of higher education. The constraints built into this latter type of dependence, so central to the history of the professional social sciences in the United States, are hard for many to acknowledge, much less celebrate. Yet the ties the first generations of social scientists forged with existing educational institutions in the nineteenth century were essential professionally, promising legitimacy, longevity, and financial stability that people in these fields could not have otherwise had. As Tim Kaufman-Osborn has recently reminded us, the very ideal of academic freedom first articulated by the American Association of University Professors (AAUP) in 1915 exemplifies the constraints built into academic employment in claiming only a little island of autonomy within the much wider territory of dependence on university employers. One hundred plus years of practice has not made acknowledging this dependence or analyzing its ramifications manifestly easier.[13]

Perhaps in part to avoid confronting this dependence directly, academic professions also tend to be inward looking, giving their members strong incentives to pay attention to internal debates and initiatives rather than to the structures on which they depend. The highly specialized quality of most academic professional discourse gives it an air of a world unto itself, as if sustained by its members alone.[14] Many historical accounts of academic disciplines exhibit a similar inwardness in highlighting intramural scholarly debates as the main drivers of disciplinary change. Yet the all-too-common panics sparked by university budget cuts, government overhauls of the National Science Foundation (NSF), and the unpredictable whims of private donors periodically remind professional social scientists just how dependent they are on matters they have little power to control. There's no avoiding it: acknowledging the power of patronage over the shape and substance of academic life sets off tremors at the base of even the most securely established academic disciplines.

This book treats foundation patronage as a major force shaping the recent history of US political science. In several fundamental ways, political science became the discipline most of its current members know it to be because of the interventions of foundations in academic life. The rise of statistical analyses of cumulative sets of survey data, the proliferation and later decline of area studies programs, and the deep rifts within the discipline over which methods are best suited to understand politics each has its roots in the programs of at least one of the major midcentury foundations. This happened even though some of the most significant foundation interventions I discuss did not target political science directly. Instead, foundation allies in intermediary research councils, universities, and professional associations responded to these programs in ways that magnified their effects on the discipline. In this basic way, foundation programs often turned into collaborations between foundation officials and their academic partners— collaborations in which academics sometimes played the dominant role. These partnerships made our discipline.

Foundations and their allies in the academy sought to move the social sciences in particular directions. In some cases, they were remarkably successful in doing so. Why and how they did so—and what this meant for what political science became in the late twentieth century—are the questions that drive this book.

The Midcentury Window: Private Philanthropies Lay the Groundwork for Federal Patronage

All the recent assessments of the power of philanthropies in the twenty-first century that I mentioned above acknowledge, at least implicitly, that today's philanthropists do what they do in the wake of the contraction of large-scale federal government patronage. Moreover, some of these philanthropies have actively sought to decrease government patronage for academic research. Big philanthropies loom so large today not only because of their vast resources but also because government patronage has shrunk.

These are relatively recent developments, however. For most of the twentieth century, private philanthropies and the federal government were close allies more often than they were antagonists. Prior to World War II, federal government support for the academic social sciences was spotty; the oldest of the large foundations, including Rockefeller and Carnegie, dominated this patronage system. During World War II, however, the great volume of funds flowing from government agencies to the social sciences foreshadowed what became the postwar system of government-dominated patronage several decades later. After a brief postwar dip, government support for the social sciences again began increasing rapidly in the latter half of the 1950s. When private foundations ceded their place as the social sciences' principal patrons to federal government agencies a few years later, the hand-off was smooth and amicable.[15]

My focus in this book is on the brief but crucial transitional period between the first foundation-defined patronage system and the federal government-dominated one that succeeded it. The three big foundations I discuss were in an unusually strong position to influence political science during this time for two principal reasons: the brief but dramatic decline in federal government support after World War II and the up-for-grabs quality of midcentury political science itself. Immediately after the war, federal patronage from the military and intelligence agencies, the new National Science Foundation, or other federal agencies was at best limited and sometimes nonexistent. Many social scientists and foundation officials worried that this sudden decline signaled that government patronage in these areas might sink to or even below prewar levels. Several new postwar military or intelligence agencies did support some research in the social sciences; not surprisingly, however, these agencies favored the development of "social science weapons of war," in areas like psychological warfare, nuclear war fighting, and counterinsurgency strategies. Only social scientists specializing in a small handful of fields could plausibly contribute to such projects.[16] Prospects at the new National Science Foundation were even more limited. Though social scientists had hoped to gain some standing when the new agency began operations in 1950, all the social sciences were initially shunted into the remainder category, "the other sciences." Specific NSF programs devoted to particular social sciences came later. Political science had one of the longest waits; the NSF had no programs devoted specifically to political science until the late 1960s.[17]

In that uncertain time, the big foundations in the mid-twentieth century not only welcomed federal government agencies doing more to patronize the social sciences but also helped lay the groundwork for the federal government–dominated patronage system that began to emerge in the late 1950s. When the war ended, most of the government agencies that social scientists had served were cut back or dissolved. Thus began what Jean

Converse called "migrations to the universities."[18] Foundation programs in the social sciences, however, allowed some of these migrants to resume and expand their wartime work in their new academic homes—work for which many would later receive federal support.

Carnegie and Ford's efforts to promote what came to be called the behavioral sciences, as well as Ford and Rockefeller's programs devoted to cultivating academic expertise in international politics, all sought to make the social sciences seem more plausible as candidates for postwar federal support. Carnegie and then Ford placed their bets on fostering a practical, technically sophisticated social science—one Ford would later explicitly dub "behavioral"—that would provide policy makers synoptic analyses on key issues. Even while Rockefeller was also investing some of its social science funds in building up behavioral approaches, some of its officers argued that humanistic approaches to political issues might be even more valuable to policy makers. Despite their differences, these programs still sounded a common theme: the United States could not accomplish its strategic and ideological aims in the Cold War without the help of the social sciences. Social scientists stood to make crucial and unique contributions to the US Cold War effort, like analyzing domestic public opinion or the morale of the Soviet population, predicting the likelihood of revolution around the world, or making new substantive cases for the merits of the US political and economic system. If many now accepted that massive federal support for scientific research tied to war fighting and defense was necessary, they argued, similar commitments ought to be made to social scientific research as well. It then fell to the officials responsible for social science programs at all of the foundations to make specific versions of this argument.

As we will see in chapter 1, officers at the Carnegie Corporation as well as their allies at the Social Science Research Council (SSRC) worked hard to promote the merits of what would later be called the behavioral sciences to a number of audiences, including the federal agencies with which many had worked. Specifically, Carnegie officers sought to maintain or raise the standing of survey research after wartime programs in this area ended. As the head of the postwar SSRC, political scientist and Carnegie ally Pendleton Herring brought these initiatives to bear on his own discipline. Ford's much larger programs, discussed in chapter 2, demonstrated that sizable "start-up" funds could build significant new capacities in the academic world quickly. Though it was short-lived, Ford's Behavioral Sciences Program successfully introduced a model of a technically sophisticated, antireformist behavioral science across the social scientific disciplinary spectrum. The program also gave many academics and university administrators strong incentives to reinvent research plans and academic structures to accommodate it. While some of the Rockefeller Foundation's eclectic programs contributed to the initiatives at the heart of these Carnegie and Ford programs, others sought to direct academics' philosophical and theoretical knowledge toward Cold War ends. Rockefeller's Legal and Political Philosophy (LAPP) program, discussed in chapter 3, grew out of trustees' call for an ideological effort to shore up the image of the United States overseas. All of this nominally private patronage dispensed to social scientists during and immediately after World War II did not oppose the trend toward the nationally focused, government-dominated patronage system that succeeded it. To the contrary, it made it possible.[19]

The relationships between the philanthropic patrons and social scientists that I discuss unfolded in this active transitional period. The chapters in part 1 feature examples of each of the big midcentury foundations supporting the social sciences in focused, purposeful ways. Rockefeller, Carnegie, and Ford all made such "first move" grants, awarding substantial sums for particular social scientific approaches more on their own initiative than in response to academics' applications. Grants of this kind exemplify how actively and deliberately Rockefeller, Carnegie, and Ford sought to redirect the social sciences during this period.

Though grants of this kind are an important part of my story, they are not the whole of it. The chapters in part 2 focus on the university administrators and faculty who ultimately had to decide how to allocate and spend the funds foundation staff directed to them. Even "one-shot" grants for particular projects, like the one Carnegie made to support the University of Michigan's Survey Research Center's 1952 election study, were preceded by detailed negotiations and then repeatedly evaluated as they unfolded. Grants from multiyear foundation programs depended on an even wider web of relationships. In some cases, academics used foundation funds to further their own plans to change their departments, universities, and disciplines—plans that expressed their own ambitions more directly than those of their funders. Even in those cases in which universities and departments had no clear plans for what to do with the foundation funds they received, the process of deciding how to allocate and spend those funds took them in directions their patrons could not have anticipated and sometimes would not have endorsed. All of these dynamics are important to my story for one principal reason: the foundations most interested in what came to be called the behavioral sciences initially paid little direct attention to political science. It therefore fell largely to university administrators and academics to notice these patrons' commitment to the behavioral sciences and reorient political science accordingly. The most successful new research agendas and institutions they inaugurated during this unprecedented boom time in US higher education changed public universities and political science's place in their new research missions quickly and profoundly.

Placing Patronage in the History of Political Science

At the same time that federal patronage for all the social sciences briefly dropped off, the substance and orientation of academic political science were also up for grabs. This made it easier for foundations to affect the discipline's shape and direction. Several broad higher-education wide patterns intensified this indeterminacy. First, universities were hiring large numbers of new faculty year after year in response to the sharp increase in the number of new students in the late 1940s and 1950s. This quickly changed the composition and character of many departments. As we shall see in chapter 5, the rapid expansion of the whole University of California system built the initial momentum for the centrifugal forces that buffeted the Berkeley Political Science Department in the 1960s. Although the University of Michigan department, discussed in chapter 4, also grew quickly during this time, it changed more because of its close relationship with new research centers, especially the Survey Research Center (SRC). The proliferation of such centers, especially at large universities, changed the composition and identity not only of political science but of many other academic disciplines as well.

During that time, powerful patrons shaped all the postwar social sciences in two fundamental ways. First, they helped bring some academic fields and institutions into existence and supported their growth. Political communication studies, public opinion survey research, and international and area studies, along with the numerous university institutes and centers devoted to them, all depended on foundation patrons.[20] Second, foundations forged lasting networks linking social scientists to multiple potential clients for academic expertise. These networks linking patrons, social scientists, and their clients in government and industry during the postwar period were dense and tangled, making some crucial things about them hard to discern. Who belonged to these networks, what their members exchanged with one another, and what they produced is rarely explicit or obvious. What is more, the loyalties of the social scientists and foundation officials linked in these networks were often blurred, as were the affiliations of some institutions at their nodes.[21] Mindful of these challenges, I examine the complex networks the foundations built in the Michigan and Berkeley political science departments, what circulated through them, and what they produced.

The understanding of the history of political science I present throughout this book underscores the power of foundation patronage to shape the discipline by creating new fields and building networks through which ideas, influence, and money flowed. Once one brings foundation programs and the academics who advanced them to the fore, many familiar late-twentieth-century developments in the history of political science take on a new aspect. Important developments that changed the face of the discipline, like the steady marginalization of what was once the central field of public administration, the rise of behavioralism associated with statistical analyses of large sets of shared survey data, or the growing antagonisms between humanistic, interpretive methods and epistemologies and behavioralist, social scientific ones, were not driven by intramural debates alone. Foundation programs, directed toward the discipline by university administrators and academics who belonged to foundation-built networks, helped trigger and advance all of these changes.

To be clear, by highlighting the role of foundation patronage I do not mean to dismiss the significance of internal disciplinary debates about the relative merits of fields, analytic approaches, or epistemologies. Instead, my approach draws attention to an important material dimension of these debates. Whether they were arguing for or against a particular field, or for or against quantitative analysis or humanistic epistemologies, political scientists who engaged in such debates were keenly aware of the markedly different level of resources, prestige, and legitimacy to which they and their adversaries had access. The positions they took, the critiques they launched, and the outcomes they sought all reflected that awareness, as the conflicts in the postwar Michigan and Berkeley political science departments demonstrate.

Though patronage is rarely central to them, histories of political science written in the past few decades connect the particular intellectual commitments of political scientists with other broad currents in American society and politics.[22] For example, Robert Adcock carefully analyzes the intellectual careers of a number of nineteenth-century US political scientists while also highlighting their contributions to a much broader transatlantic debate about the meaning of liberalism. John Gunnell's history of political theory in the United States interprets a series of intramural debates about the field as attempts to bridge the gulf between academic and public discourse. Others emphasize the effect of large-scale twentieth-century political developments on political science. For instance, Ido Oren shows how political scientists have repeatedly redesigned their fundamental concepts in response to shifts in US geopolitical rivalries. Similarly, Nicolas Guilhot argues that the late-twentieth-century political scientists at the vanguard of democratization studies were often "double agents," whose shuttling between academic and policy-making circles transformed academic conceptions of democracy and human rights. And Robert Vitalis and Jessica Blatt argue that the fields of international relations and comparative politics first developed as academic supports for the nation's colonial projects to create a "white world order."[23]

I follow these scholars in situating the particular interactions between foundations and political scientists I analyze in broader social and political milieus. As the chapters in part 2 on political science at the University of Michigan and UC Berkeley demonstrate, I am especially interested in how foundations' officials and academics built and maintained their relationships in university environments. The most important of these relations unfolded over a number of years and involved a sizable number of people. Even the most robust, well-financed networks first had to work in and around a university's institutional infrastructure before they could change it. My account of the history of political science, therefore, attends not only to the discipline's foundation patrons but also to its situation in institutions of higher education.

Political Science in the University

For much of its life in the United States, the production, reproduction, and daily practice of political science has happened within colleges and universities. Of course, many people outside the academy—journalists, public officials, political consultants, pollsters, and more—"do" political science.

Still, if political science was not yet predominantly a creature of the academy when it began to form in the United States over one hundred years ago, it surely is one now. The history of political science, therefore, is in large part the history of political science in the university.

As a number of historians have noted, the social sciences did not fit easily into older conceptions of higher education that centered on classical and theological instruction. Only in the late nineteenth century, when the whole system of higher education in the United States was expanding, did the emerging political science profession begin to gain some standing as an academic discipline. Older institutions (like Columbia University) added new schools and curricula in political science at the same time that many new institutions of higher education (like Cornell, Johns Hopkins, and numerous public institutions in the middle and western United States) included them from their outsets.[24]

One could explore the links between the development of political science and the evolution of institutions of higher education beyond these beginnings, from the early twentieth century up to the present. Some notable studies have done so for the early twentieth century.[25] For the postwar period on which I focus, the most pertinent studies are those of particular universities and departments as well as analyses of political and social science done in new institutional spaces created during the Cold War.[26]

Broader studies of the recent history of US higher education that complement this more specific university- and field-focused work examine how institutions of higher education became part of the national political economy. This integration began during World War I and gained momentum during World War II. What historian of higher education Roger Geiger called the "postwar federal research economy" grew out of the organized war research economy; especially for R1 universities, federal grants and contracts have remained an important source of income ever since World War II.[27] The huge volume of federal funding that R1 universities took in from the late 1950s through the 1960s so reconfigured them that even when the rate of federal money flowing in began to fall off, these universities retained their fundamental commitment to research.[28]

The affinity between war research and the postwar university research economy was strong at the two public universities central to this book. Each had ties to research laboratories crucial to the nation's World War II effort: UC Berkeley's Lawrence Radiation Laboratory and the Ford Motor Company's wartime Willow Run plant, acquired by the University of Michigan in 1946. The presence of these labs had a transformative effect on each institution after the war. At Berkeley, the radiation laboratory served as a prototype for a number of newer scientific laboratories and, more generally, for the organized research unit (ORU), a new academic life form that thrived on the postwar Berkeley campus. After the University of Michigan acquired Willow Run, its contracts still focused on many aspects of aerial warfare, doing "more classified research in the early 1950s than all the sponsored research on the rest of the Michigan campus."[29]

Following a dramatic but brief drop immediately after the war, the federal government became the most important patron for university-based research during the postwar period. Projects focused on designing weapons, radar systems, or aircraft, funded by branches of the military, were central.[30] Other federal agencies began to support social scientific research projects linked to war, defense, or national security as well. Perhaps the best-known example of such research is Project Camelot, funded by the US Army's Special Operations Research Office (SORO). Many social scientists hoped the unclassified Project Camelot, a multi-country study of "the fundamental causes of communist revolution" and potentially their "antidotes," would prove to be "the Manhattan Project of social science." After a publicity debacle over Camelot's real aims in Latin America emboldened its opponents to criticize it more openly, the project was canceled in 1965 before it had fully begun. This very public failure, however, did not spell the end of military- and intelligence agency-funded social scientific research on university campuses. That continued, but behind new legal screens to block "public scrutiny."[31] Political scientists participated in projects of this kind that focused on counterinsurgency, psychological warfare (or its euphemized version, political communication), and nuclear war–fighting strategy. According to several recent accounts, these projects not only mattered to those who participated in them but had profound effects on the discipline as well.[32]

In addition to the constitutive role of war research ably discussed by others, I stress three broad features of the research university that were especially important to what political science became in the late twentieth century. These were its orientation toward national patrons, its growing reliance on the ORU rather than the department as a site for research and instruction, and its need for large numbers of graduate students. The "nationalization of social sciences" and the accompanying new structure of patronage registered in political science in several ways, including changing the relative prestige of its fields.[33] For example, the field of public administration had been prominent in the University of Michigan's political science department (the subject of chapter 4) from its founding in 1910 until roughly fifty years later. Yet public administration did not attract much support from foundation and federal government patrons committed to national programs. Since many in the field understood its mission to be the practical, professional one of training future public servants, it contributed little to the university's emerging research mission.[34]

By contrast, the faculty who exerted the most direct pressure to transform Michigan's political science department into a research department had already received substantial support from foundations with national programs. For example, when Warren Miller and Samuel Eldersveld proposed what became a special PhD program in political behavior, they sought to graft a research program developed outside the department at the Institute for Social Research's Survey Research Center (SRC) onto the department's graduate program. In short order, this productive and well-funded research program became the model for the rest of the department—especially when the Inter-university Consortium for Political Research (ICPR) that Miller founded in the early 1960s won early and substantial support from the NSF.[35]

In contrast to the faculty-driven reorientation at the University of Michigan, it was the University of California system's rapid postwar expansion and the accompanying intensification of its research mission that set the reorientation of the political science department at Berkeley in motion. The size of the department more than doubled in the ten years after 1945, quickly transforming it into a department with a majority of young, untenured faculty. Foundation funds, first from Ford and then from Rockefeller, accelerated the pace of its reorientation, as did the policies of ambitious administrators like Chancellor Clark Kerr. Intent on improving the national standing of Berkeley's social science departments, Kerr tasked many younger faculty with planning how the university would use the large grants foundations had made to the social sciences. Such administratively driven plans shifted the department's balance of power toward its younger, foundation-grant-conscious faculty by making them responsible for defining the department's new research priorities.[36]

Just as the big midcentury foundations reoriented the social sciences toward national aims and patrons, they also favored organized research units over departments as sites for conducting social scientific research. In the interwar period, it had been common for the oldest of the big foundations to grant unrestricted research funds to departments; after World War II, grants focused on specific projects or fostering new fields became the norm. Still, the work of departments focused primarily on teaching; most faculty tied to them, therefore, had neither the time nor the supporting staff and equipment to take on specific research projects in a short amount of time. By contrast, those affiliated with ORUs mainly did research and had few if any teaching obligations. Universities too had a number of incentives to encourage or at least tolerate the proliferation of ORUs, particularly when they attracted external funds, prestigious research faculty, and sizable cohorts of graduate students. Reinforced by multiple parties, ORUs became an important new feature of academic life in many sectors of the postwar research university.[37]

The new ORU form affected political science in different ways at Michigan and Berkeley. In its pre-university incarnation, what became Michigan's Survey Research Center had been part of a wartime federal agency. Those who worked for it then did a significant amount of contract research; once part of the university, they continued to do so. Already in the fiscal year 1951–1952, the SRC brought in grant and contract income of around $650,000. It was in large part on the strength of the SRC's substantial external financial base that researchers affiliated with it were able to influence and then ultimately redirect the University of Michigan's political science department.[38]

More than at Michigan, organized research units abounded at UC Berkeley in the postwar period in part because administrators there made early and substantial commitments to help finance a number of them. Grants from the Ford Foundation prompted the creation of two behavioral science-oriented ORUs—a Survey Research Center and a Center for the Integration of Social Science Theory—under the organizational umbrella of the Institute for Social Science (ISS).[39] Though the founding of Berkeley's Survey Research Center had more to do with Kerr's 1950s ambitions to improve the national standing of the university's sociology department than with political science, a number of political scientists would be associated with it and even direct it in the decades to come. The area and international studies centers Ford began to fund at Berkeley in the late 1950s soon overshadowed this first generation of Ford-funded ORUs. This second generation of even more generously funded ORUs quickly became more central to the department's new research identity.[40]

Individuals affiliated with such centers had more flexibility than those in departments to develop and pursue large, ongoing research projects. By the 1960s, the success of some of these projects was widely evident. The election studies conducted by Michigan's SRC had a history of foundation support; ICPR, one of SRC's spin-offs, was rapidly becoming an NSF-supported leader in archiving, distributing, and training people to use survey data. While Berkeley's SRC never matched Michigan's in size and prestige, it won NSF support to lead a project to archive international survey data. Many of the first political scientists to bring sizable outside research funds into their universities had ties to ORUs like these—survey research centers and their younger cousins, centers for area and international studies.[41]

Ultimately, those affiliated with interdisciplinary ORUs exercised considerable power within traditional disciplines. The most prominent among them produced more research, apprenticed more graduate students, and made decisions about the present and future of particular disciplines in their roles as members of editorial boards, grant reviewers, and officers of professional associations. As the career of Michigan's Warren Miller illustrates, ORU-affiliated political scientists set the rules of the disciplinary game to a greater degree than their colleagues housed in traditional departments—especially when the departments in which they were tenured allowed them to continue to vote on hiring, promotions, and policy.

Along with its new orientation toward patrons with national agendas and the advent of organized research units, graduate programs in postwar research universities also expanded dramatically. The new multi-year research contracts between federal agencies and universities depended not only on principal investigators but also on large numbers of research assistants, apprentices, and staff—all roles graduate students filled. Up to the mid-twentieth century, most graduate students had paid for their education; but in the postwar period, many secured federal support for the duration of their program. Once begun, such federal support for graduate study became an important component of the new research university. Fundamentally, the federal programs that provided this aid, including the GI Bill, the National Defense Education Act (NDEA), and the Higher Education Act, gave vast numbers of people access to higher education. At the same time, they made large-scale research possible and helped deepen the integration of universities into the national political economy.[42]

These large-scale patterns reshaped graduate education in the social sciences. Some graduate students benefited from foundation- and government-sponsored fellowships and training courses; the income research assistants received also often came from outside grants. Departments, therefore, had to compete with ORUs not only for faculty but for the labor of graduate students as well. Several Michigan ORUs outstripped its political science department in administering training courses and providing long-term research assistance opportunities; they brokered access to the NDEA's crucial federal fellowship program for graduate students as well. At Berkeley, graduate students themselves soon became aware of the disparity between the ample resources ORUs could provide compared to the meager aid they could expect from the department.

Accessing NDEA aid was crucial to making Michigan's new PhD program in political behavior program viable. With the help of several Michigan administrators, Eldersveld and Miller succeeded in convincing government officials that prospective students in political behavior should be eligible for a special graduate fellowship program authorized by the NDEA.[43] Though the NDEA program was short-lived, its fellowships provided generous support for a handful of political behavior PhD students each year from 1961 up through 1972. Many of these students worked as research assistants or as assistant directors of SRC or ICPR projects during the course of their time in graduate school. NDEA funds also supported ICPR's early education programs.[44]

A small but powerful contingent of faculty at the University of Michigan welcomed its new identity as a research university and the changes in graduate education this made possible. Not surprisingly, there were similar sympathies among some UC Berkeley faculty. Others, however, objected to how Berkeley's research university identity was affecting graduate education. For example, an Academic Senate-sponsored evaluation of Berkeley's political science department noted that graduate students received strikingly different levels of support depending on whether the fields they chose had ties to an ORU.[45] As I discuss in chapter 5, this was but one among the many factors that prompted several political theory faculty to try to leave the political science department and form a new academic department. By the early 1970s, deep differences within the department over the structure and purpose of graduate education widened into public rifts over the politics of political science, academic governance, and intellectual community in the university.

Foundation and University Records as Sources

Over a decade after he resigned from the presidency of the Carnegie Corporation, Charles Dollard remembered the heady intellectual excitement of his time with the foundation this way:

> We used to say that a foundation is one of the few neutral corners in higher education. People will come to you with stories, with problems, with dilemmas they wouldn't dare talk to anybody else about. You're not a competitor, you don't have any desire to get them off-base. More confidences are exchanged in foundation offices than anyplace I know, and more ideas paraded for the first time. . . . I used to go home from the office, lots of evenings, just intoxicated with the things that had happened during the day, with the feeling that I was right on the front edge of what was going on.[46]

One needn't accept Dollard's claim that foundations are "neutral corners in higher education" or that academics unburden themselves more fully or guilelessly in foundation offices than elsewhere. Still, foundation officers at Carnegie, Rockefeller, and Ford did hear ideas early and, for a few decades around the middle of the twentieth century, were in an especially strong position to decide which ones were worth pursuing, supporting, or redirecting.

The extensive records these foundations kept and later made available to researchers allow one to explore and document their influence on academic disciplines. In each of the chapters that follow, I use these records to show how each of the three major foundations were deeply involved in transforming twentieth-century political science. Rather than providing an overview of the large, multifaceted programs of these foundations, I focus on a few particular programs or policies pursued by each that I believe ultimately had a transformative effect on academic political science. I then pair these foundation records with the records of various institutional grantees: the SSRC, universities, research centers, and departments. Linking these records reveals the grantors, intermediaries, and grantees "bound in a web of give and take" that shaped the ideas that took root in institutional soil.[47]

The archived records of each of the three foundations I discuss are all admirably dense. They include internal communications among staff, memos written by officers for their own records, minutes of staff meetings, conference proceedings, correspondence between officers and academics, evaluations of grants, and position papers on future foundation policy. In many cases, these day-to-day materials allow one to track the gradual unfolding of a decision or the emergence of consensus or disagreement. In them, one may find the tortuous, serendipitous backstories to what became well-known scholarly orientations as well as the traces of numerous intellectual roads not taken. As I discussed earlier, even at the midcentury high-water mark of foundation patronage for the social sciences, government agency patronage was becoming increasingly significant. Many of these government-sponsored projects, however, fell under the rapidly expanding national security umbrella. Hence, during this period, foundations were the largest relatively transparent institutions outside the academy devoted to influencing what social science would become.

By contrast, universities' archived records rarely allow one to track the day-to-day evolution of a decision in the same way. As a result, the overlap of records matters more here. For instance, records pertaining to an institutional change are likely to turn up in the files of more than one of the administrative offices or academic units involved. Additionally, the personal papers of faculty members and administrators may be available in the archive of the university with which they had long-standing ties. Read together, such records constitute a rich composite source for tracking the complete arc of academic orientations, from first emergence through peak to decline.

A history of political science grounded in archival records of these kinds allows one to see approaches to the study of politics just coming into being or beginning to fade away—stages at which almost no one could have predicted their full emergence or their ultimate demise.[48] For example, how Carnegie and Ford's investments in a high-stakes redirection of the social sciences succeeded in rooting the behavioral sciences in universities and government agencies despite serious congressional challenges are essential backstories to the stunningly rapid rise of behavioralism in political science in the late 1950s. Conversely, the now seemingly old-fashioned political science that placed a premium on training future public servants and administrators had many prominent, vigorous defenders up through the mid-twentieth century. A later political science–specific manifestation of the behavioral sciences, behavioralism was no more destined for triumph than a public administration–centered political science was doomed to exile from political science's disciplinary core. Particular people, powerful patrons and academic brokers among them, made these things happen, albeit in ways they could not foresee or control.

Some readers might expect a book about the role powerful private patrons played in shaping twentieth-century political science to tell a deterministic story in which political scientists are moved to and fro by the wealthy and powerful. I have found, however, that relationships between philanthropic patrons and the recipients of their funds arise out of prolonged negotiation, not patron-issued directives (although these too do happen). These were of course negotiations between profoundly unequal parties; even the most grant-rich political scientists were keenly aware that their patrons could always withdraw, reduce, or condition their resources. Many such negotiations reached an impasse and broke down; many more never got beyond a preliminary stage. But in the tortuous unfolding of those few negotiated relationships that spanned months and years, one sees people first in foundations and then in universities bringing new approaches to political science into being.

Structure of the Book

The chapters in part 1 analyze the social science programs of each of the big three mid-twentieth-century foundations. Chapter 1 concentrates on the Carnegie Corporation's programs, the earliest to cultivate a more scientific social science. Though Carnegie's grants were small, they nevertheless successfully remade the Social Science Research Council into an enthusiastic advocate for a systematic, practical social science. Chapter 2 on the Ford Foundation's 1950s behavioral science program shows how Ford expanded Carnegie's mission by funding sweeping initiatives to create new academic institutions to support the behavioral sciences. Chapter 2 also shows that political scientists responded to this massive effort by constituting what came to be known as "behavioralism." The final chapter in part 1 focuses on the Rockefeller Foundation's complex response to these other foundations' programs. While offering significant support for the new behavioral sciences, Rockefeller concurrently designed several programs to encourage humanistic approaches in the social sciences. Each chapter in part 1 tacks back and forth between the broader social scientific ambitions of these programs and their more specific implications for political science.

The chapters in part 2 examine the reception of these foundation programs at the University of Michigan and UC Berkeley. The contrasts between how foundation grants affected the study of politics in each setting are striking, especially since these two large public research universities were similar in so many other respects. At Michigan, research centers outside the university's academic core were the principal recipients of foundation funds. People affiliated with these centers but also with the political science department were instrumental to making statistical analyses of survey data central to Michigan political science. The chapter on Berkeley focuses on the reception and aftermath of two five-year Rockefeller grants to encourage humanistic approaches to the study of political theory and international relations. These chapters consider each of these cases in the broader context of changes in the relative power of departments, professional schools, and research centers in the postwar university. They also address how these local developments affected the discipline of political science nationally.

The concluding chapter reviews the main features of the argument of the book, underscoring its historiographical contributions. It then shifts to using the book's mid-twentieth-century story to uncover some of the origins of the methodological fractures and the research ethic that persist so stubbornly in twenty-first-century political science.

PART I

FOUNDATIONS

CHAPTER ONE

"Propagandists for the Behavioral Sciences"
The Carnegie Corporation and the SSRC

I think we were, quite frankly, in the period from '46 to '50, propagandists for the behavioral sciences, and admittedly so. And God knows, we were barely in time. . . . If we'd been a generation later, I don't know what would have happened.

—Charles Dollard, Reminiscences, 1967

Carnegie Corporation does not engage in propaganda.

—Charles Dollard, "In Defense of the Social Sciences," 1954

When former Carnegie Corporation president Charles Dollard looked back on what he and his fellow officers had done for the social sciences, he commended their efforts in terms he could not—and would not—have used twenty years earlier. For one, in the late 1940s, the term "behavioral sciences" was not yet in general circulation; Dollard and his colleagues did not use it.[1] Second, though Dollard could later call himself and his closest associates "propagandists," doing so would have been wildly impolitic for a foundation officer in the first decade after World War II. Only well after Carnegie and other major foundations had survived the Cox and Reece congressional committees' scrutiny of their political influence could Dollard, in a piece of victor's wit, playfully embrace the "propagandist" charge he so flatly rejected in 1954.[2]

In this chapter, I use these two elements of Dollard's retrospective commentary to highlight Carnegie's crucial early role in promoting what came to be called the behavioral sciences as well as the close partnership the Carnegie Corporation forged with the Social Science Research Council (SSRC) to do so. Because Carnegie deliberately muted its part in it, many historians have overlooked the importance of this partnership to the postwar social sciences.[3] As early "propagandists for the behavioral sciences," senior officers at Carnegie promoted their new vision for the social sciences in different ways to different audiences, paying special attention to who delivered the message. I use Dollard's "propagandists" remark to illuminate the aims of the intense collaboration between Carnegie and the SSRC during the immediate postwar period.

Four people with multiple ties to Carnegie, the SSRC, and each other created this mid-twentieth-century partnership: Frederick Osborn, Charles Dollard, Donald Young, and Pendleton Herring. Osborn and Dollard had already been sharply critical of the prewar SSRC for what they saw as its outmoded conception of social science. The eldest of the group, Osborn published his aspirations for an integrated "science of man" in 1939 with psychology, anthropology, and sociology at its core.[4] Their experience of working in various portions of Washington's wartime bureaucracy heightened these men's ambitions for changing the character and significance of social science in the postwar period. All joined large, multidisciplinary groups working for departments of the federal state on the strength of their social scientific expertise. Osborn, a brigadier general in the US Army who was later promoted to major general, led what came to be called the army's Information and Education Division. Both Young and Dollard worked for the Research Branch of Osborn's division—Young as a consultant and Dollard first as its chief and later as deputy director of operations. Herring, the only political scientist in the group, worked as a liaison between Harvard's new school of public administration and the wartime bureaucracy. In 1941 he served as a consultant for the Bureau of the Budget. In 1945 he advised Ferdinand Eberstadt, associate secretary of the navy, on a plan to unify the armed services, a plan that contributed to the National Security Act of 1947, "which created the Department of Defense, the Joint Chiefs of Staff, the National Security Council and the Central Intelligence Agency."[5]

After the war ended, all these men worried that they and their fellow social scientists might lose what access they had gained to government policy-making. To increase that access or at least forestall its loss, all acted as "middlemen" (as Dollard called himself), working behind the scenes to burnish the image of the social sciences and forge stronger ties between social scientists and an array of patrons who might support them.[6] Although all had published some of their ideas about the new social science they hoped to foster in the immediate postwar period, the unpublished records of Carnegie and SSRC provide a better, fuller record of their aims.[7]

The projects discussed in this chapter exemplify the efforts of this group to persuade multiple audiences that the new social science they championed was practical, useful, and deserving of their support. Some projects addressed a broad public audience; others spoke principally to academics or corporate executives. I pay particular attention to those initiatives and projects Carnegie designed to persuade government policy-makers that the new social scientists ought to contribute to the policy-making process as part of a broader effort to secure long-term government patronage for them. Throughout this chapter, I consider how and why Carnegie worked with and through the SSRC to persuade each of these audiences. This partnership transformed the SSRC first; a few years later, largely due to Herring's efforts, it began to transform academic political science as well.

Carnegie was not the first foundation to work with and through the SSRC. The Rockefeller Foundation, the SSRC's first and most significant patron, had already done so for decades, initiating numerous projects the SSRC ultimately carried out.[8] Working with the not-quite-independent SSRC allowed foundations to direct many of its activities privately while publicly emphasizing its impartiality. According to Donald Fisher, the academic research mission of the SSRC made it a plausible intermediary between the foundations, the state, and the academy.[9] Internal foundation documents support Fisher's view. For example, in 1951 a monthly summary of foundation activities written for Rockefeller's Board of Trustees explained the foundation's reliance on the SSRC and other councils this way: "If these councils did not exist, it would be necessary to invent them."[10] Additionally, staff from the big foundations not only knew about each other's programs but also met and conferred often. It therefore seems plausible that Carnegie took more than a few pages from Rockefeller's book on working with and through the SSRC.[11]

Not only did the big foundations confer over how to work with the SSRC; all were also concerned with securing long-term federal patronage for the social sciences. Here too, each paid close attention to how the others pursued this aim. As Hunter Heyck has convincingly shown, the postwar patronage system for the social sciences dominated by the National Science Foundation and National Institutes of Mental Health emerged only in the latter half of the 1960s.[12] During the immediate postwar period, however, as Mark Solovey conclusively demonstrates, patronage for the social sciences rested on "shaky foundations."[13] The foundations and their academic allies remained hopeful during this uncertain time that social scientists' share of military and NSF funding would increase despite the persistent skepticism of the natural science elite and the recurring waves of criticism emanating from conservatives in Congress and public life. It was in this unstable but "thickening matrix of patronage agencies and authorities" that Carnegie engaged in what Ellen Lagemann has characterized as "strategic philanthropy" to promote a new social science. At its core, this approach invested relatively small amounts of "venture capital" in projects Carnegie officers believed other patrons—especially the federal government—might later take up and support over the longer term.[14] Transforming the SSRC into an effective partner in this effort was central to Carnegie's strategy. Under Young's leadership but especially under Herring's, that is precisely what the SSRC became.

Carnegie officials crafted their programs with an eye to making the fluid postwar patronage system more receptive to the social sciences. To accomplish that end, one pattern ran through the social science projects Carnegie supported: though Carnegie officers thoroughly designed one of them and initiated most others, all became public under the banner of the SSRC.[15] I believe Carnegie officers pursued this strategy to convince all audiences of several things: that the new social scientists they promoted knew things far beyond the reach of common sense thanks to the sophisticated quantitative techniques they had mastered, that such knowledge was useful and valuable, and, because it was scientific knowledge, it was not ideological. As "propagandists for the behavioral sciences," Carnegie officers cared just as much about who did the talking as they did about what was said. Made public by the SSRC, these projects appeared to be the fruits of the collective expertise of social scientists rather than policy-making interventions of a private foundation. To have the SSRC publicly credited with the conception, oversight, and execution of such projects would, Carnegie officers believed, enhance the image of the new social science in the eyes of an array of possible patrons.

Herring knew this strategy well, having been a Carnegie officer from 1946 to 1948. When he began his long tenure as SSRC director in 1948, he honed it to focus on a particular group of potential patrons: the agencies of the federal government. With over a decade of experience consulting with representatives of federal agencies in various capacities, Herring was ideally suited to cultivate them as patrons. At the same time, Herring was actively supporting projects to incorporate survey researchers' substantive and methodological concerns into political science to advance the study of political behavior. These projects were central to Herring's efforts to transform political science into something potential government patrons would find more "useful" and "accessible."[16]

The analysis I offer in this chapter relies on readings of archived SSRC and Carnegie Corporation documents as well as several oral histories that deal explicitly with how officers crafted these persuasive strategies. I begin by showing how the close relationship between Carnegie and the SSRC developed after a struggle between Carnegie and the Rockefeller Foundation over the direction and leadership of the SSRC in the late 1930s and early 1940s. I then examine five postwar SSRC projects that helped remake the SSRC into a major advocate for behavioral social science: Samuel Stouffer et al.'s *The American Soldier*, Stuart Chase's *The Proper Study of Mankind*, an analysis of the failure of the 1948 polls, a 1949 conference on political behavior, and the University of Michigan Survey Research Center's study of the 1952 election. Though Carnegie funded all of these projects, its officers played a much more directive role in the first three; Herring's SSRC played a more prominent part in the last two. This period of intense collaboration between Carnegie and the SSRC, I argue, constitutes an important prologue to the history of the behavioral sciences and the transformation of postwar political science as well.

Carnegie's approach differed from the Ford Foundation's well-known Behavioral Sciences Program (1951–1957) in size, style, and substance. Whereas Ford chose to publicize its desire to promote what it explicitly called the behavioral sciences widely, Carnegie preferred that the SSRC speak to various audiences about the merits of such projects. Whereas Ford used the bulk of its vast resources to make new academic space for the behavioral sciences, Carnegie used a significant portion of its more modest ones to sustain early projects that laid the groundwork for the new approach.[17] Ford's largest single expenditure to promote the behavioral sciences was the $10.35 million it spent to set up and endow the Center for the Advanced Study for the Behavioral Sciences in the mid-1950s. By this time, however, Dollard and his fellow propagandists already thought "the game . . . pretty well won." Though it spent far less to do so, by the mid-1950s Carnegie had already transformed the SSRC into an institutional support for what became the behavioral sciences of at least equal significance. Despite its smaller size and indirect methods, Carnegie's support was crucial on three counts: its timing, its transformation of the SSRC, and its early focus on securing new patrons for the social and then behavioral sciences.[18]

Carnegie and the SSRC: The Evolution of a Partnership

Before Carnegie officers began trying to improve the public standing of the social sciences, their first aim was to transform the SSRC into the right sort of partner for this effort. Remaking the SSRC into a compelling public advocate for the newly behavioral social sciences took over five years—a period that began with Carnegie officials quietly but steadily criticizing the SSRC, then issuing stern warnings of massive cuts in foundation support. After the war, two close allies of the Carnegie Corporation, Donald Young and Pendleton Herring, became leaders of the SSRC, transforming it into an effective partner in Carnegie's effort to be "propagandists for the behavioral sciences." It was under the leadership of these Carnegie allies that the SSRC became the public face of the Carnegie funded projects I discuss later in this chapter.

Carnegie and the SSRC before 1945: Grudging Support, Growing Criticism

Though Carnegie had been a significant contributor to the SSRC since the early 1930s, relations between the two were rocky just prior to the nation's entry into World War II. Under the leadership of a new cadre of senior staff, some with a special interest in its social science programs, Carnegie became an increasingly testy patron. The most important member of this group was Charles Dollard. Dollard, who joined the Carnegie staff in 1938 and became the foundation's president in 1948, had done significant graduate work in sociology.[19] On the strength of his academic background and connections, one of Dollard's first duties was to serve as Carnegie's principal liaison to the SSRC. Dollard later recalled that he took up this position in a "belligerent" mood, an assessment borne out by the tone his internal memoranda on meetings with SSRC officials.[20] Dollard's memoranda also reveal the main currents of Carnegie policy toward the SSRC.

From the late 1930s into the early 1940s, an increasingly impatient and exasperated Dollard lambasted the SSRC, then led by executive director Robert T. Crane, for getting stuck in unproductive debates and lacking intellectual ambition. The SSRC under Crane's leadership struck Dollard as an overly cautious, unimaginative organization, too set in its ways to advance a new approach to social science. What he perceived as arid squabbling among SSRC members particularly tried Dollard's patience.[21]

Though Dollard only hinted to his superiors at Carnegie that he found the SSRC too heavily dominated by older men uninterested in new trends in the social sciences, he seemed gratified that Carnegie trustee and SSRC member Osborn made these points more forcefully to Carnegie's then president, Frederick Keppel.[22] To Osborn's complaints that older men at the SSRC were not interested in publicizing the merits of the social sciences and were unfamiliar with what Osborn thought were important new trends in the social sciences, Keppel responded mildly, "The problem of pushing the affable seniors from their stools is baffling more organizations than the SSRC."[23] It was only after the long-serving Keppel retired in 1941 that Carnegie policy toward the SSRC began to reflect Dollard and Osborn's critical views.

Following Keppel's retirement, Carnegie's new president, Walter A. Jessup, signaled a desire to reevaluate Carnegie's support for the SSRC, requesting several comprehensive reports from his staff on the history of that support. Wartime belt tightening was the pretext; but even though Dollard and Osborn were both on leave for their wartime service, other Carnegie officers kept up their scrutiny of Crane's leadership. This culminated in a remarkably negative brief on Crane presented to Jessup in 1944. The report highlighted Crane's 1935 comment that because "big, expensive survey jobs do not really advance science," the SSRC ought not to undertake such projects.[24] Whether Crane still held this view in 1944 was not the issue; his having held it at one time was enough to cast significant doubt on his merits.

Critical as they were, neither Dollard, Osborn, nor Jessup ever went on record advocating Crane's removal. Still, coincidentally or not, Crane retired in 1945, shortly after they turned up the critical heat on his leadership. Following his retirement, two persons with close ties to Carnegie stepped in to lead the SSRC: Donald Young and Pendleton Herring. Only with their help did Carnegie's midcentury leaders fully become propagandists for the behavioral sciences.

The Reformation of the SSRC, 1945–1950

From the perspective of the group of Carnegie officials critical of Crane, Donald Young had the right stuff: a sociologist specializing in the study of minorities, he had worked closely with Dollard in the Research Branch in the division of the army led by Osborn, studying and surveying African American soldiers.[25] Young had also served under Crane in the SSRC prior to the war but seemed eager to leave the organization.[26] It is therefore not surprising that soon after he became the executive director of the SSRC in 1945, Young asked for more funds for several initiatives the more cautious Crane had deemed unwise: publicizing the merits of social science and increasing the SSRC's role in "research planning." The recently retired Crane expressed strong reservations about spending money in either of these areas, worrying "until social scientists . . . reach some agreement on what is known, how can our 'knowledge' impress the public?"[27] By contrast, Young was more optimistic and argued the SSRC should devote significant time and resources to each.

During Young's tenure, relations between Carnegie and the SSRC became closer and more harmonious. In an eleven-page letter to Devereux Josephs, who succeeded Jessup as president of Carnegie in 1945, Young laid out his plans for the SSRC, highlighting those activities for which significant funds would be necessary. In contrast to Crane's worry that attempts to publicize the accomplishments of social scientists might backfire, Young optimistically insisted that persuading the public of social scientists' "outstanding contributions" to the war effort should be an important part of the SSRC's mission. Additionally, Young argued that research planning ought to be "the greatest part of the Council's program." A wide range of activities fell into this category, including the SSRC identifying issues ripe for social scientific attention and making "basic social data" available to researchers. Young also argued that some research projects, like one that produced the *American Soldier*, ought to be planned and completed by an entire council committee. Significantly, it was Dollard who urged Young to send this detailed blueprint for how he would lead the SSRC to Carnegie's President Josephs.[28]

Working out relations with Carnegie was only one of Young's tasks; any leader of the SSRC had to appeal not only to Carnegie but also to Rockefeller, its largest and oldest supporter. Though Young felt certain of Carnegie's support, Rockefeller's was another matter. Concerned about his rocky relationship with Joseph Willits, head of Rockefeller's Division of Social Sciences, Young sought Dollard's advice about how best to manage it. Young was right to be concerned. Even after Crane retired from leading the SSRC, Willits solicited a long memo from him in 1947 about the future of the SSRC—a memo Willits forwarded to Dollard to express his disapproval about what was happening to the SSRC under Young.[29] Willits was upset enough about the SSRC's "rumored criticisms" of the foundations that he scheduled a meeting with Dollard to discuss them. Dollard's notes on this meeting, however, make clear that he did not share Willits's indignation—it was probably clear to both that the criticisms were aimed at Rockefeller, not Carnegie. This behind-the-scenes spat indicates that the SSRC was pulling away from Rockefeller and moving toward Carnegie.[30] Given that Rockefeller had been a steadily generous patron from the SSRC's founding in the 1920s, this was a remarkable change.

Though Young seemed to Carnegie officials to be the right person to lead the postwar SSRC, he did not stay in the position long. Young left to become the president of the Russell Sage Foundation after less than three years, a move that at least Dollard knew about well in advance and does not appear to have opposed.[31] Already by 1947, then, who would succeed Young at the SSRC had become an issue. As Dollard later recalled, a committee of people connected to the SSRC met to select Young's successor. Ultimately, that committee settled on the political scientist Pendleton Herring as "the solution" to Carnegie's concerns about the future of the SSRC—a choice its chair first cleared with Carnegie.[32]

Herring would have struck Carnegie's Dollard and Osborn as a good choice for a number of reasons. For one, by 1947, Herring was a known quantity to them. Although Herring had not been part of the Research Branch, Dollard nevertheless saw him frequently during the war, recalling that Herring was "a sort of liaison between the government and the SSRC." Indeed, Herring's multiple and long-standing ties to the federal government made him the consummate "liaison." Already in 1936, Herring, then a member of Harvard's department of government, was regularly consulting officials at a number of federal agencies on how to structure the university's new school of public administration. In 1941 he began working as an advisor for the Bureau of the Budget and multiple branches of the armed services, his work culminating in a plan for the administrative reorganization of the armed services. One of Herring's wartime supervisors, Associate Secretary of the Navy Ferdinand Eberstadt, later recommended him for a position as an associate officer at Carnegie, a position Herring held from 1946 through 1948. Herring also worked closely with Osborn during a portion of the latter's term as a US representative to the UN Committee on the Control of Atomic Energy.[33]

Such strong ties to federal government officials were a solid mark in Herring's favor. Immediately after the war, prospects for federal support for the social sciences looked bleak. It was clear to many that the legislation to establish a National Science Foundation (NSF) working its way through Congress in the late 1940s would offer little to no support for the social sciences.[34] And although many social scientists had worked for the federal government during the war, many returned to academia or the private sector by late 1945—in many cases because the offices they had served ceased to exist.[35] In this uncertain and precarious time, a person with Herring's résumé would have seemed well suited to improving social scientists' access to federal policy-making and support; already in 1945, Herring told his fellow political scientists that they should make the most of the "unparalleled opportunities for participation in government" the war had provided them.[36]

Given that the door to NSF resources appeared to be closing when he began his tenure at the SSRC, Herring pivoted toward pursuing other potential federal patrons for the social sciences. For example, less than a month after becoming president of the SSRC, Herring wrote to the chair of the Atomic Energy Commission to offer the SSRC's help with public education campaigns on atomic energy and also to request that social scientists be given a seat at the atomic energy policy-making table. More broadly, in the first few years of his presidency, Herring worked steadily on developing closer ties between the SSRC and the military and intelligence services via fellowship programs and research contracts funded by the Departments of Defense and State.[37] By the end of 1950, he assured Carnegie that under his leadership, the SSRC would be the ideal "intermediary" between academia and foundations and maintain "official consultant relationships" with an array of government agencies.[38]

At the same time, Herring was also exploring the possibility of Carnegie support for the SSRC's Committee on Political Behavior (CPB) that he had recently revived. Suggesting that this committee ought to have a budget of around $10,000 per year to do major "research planning" work on political behavior, Herring asked whether Carnegie would be interested in supporting these efforts.[39] Herring's ambitious plans in this area got a considerable boost in 1950, when the SSRC received one of the Ford Foundation's $300,000 grants for research and program development in the behavioral sciences. Though Dollard expressed concern at the news of Ford's grant to the SSRC, Herring leveraged Ford's support to make pointed bids for Carnegie to support the SSRC's work in the behavioral sciences—and for greater SSRC discretion in planning and carrying out that work.[40] By this time, then, the SSRC's commitment to what were just beginning to be called the behavioral sciences was firmly established.

A protracted and complex drama over the future of the SSRC played out between the foundations during the postwar period. Although each of the foundations had distinctive ideas about the SSRC, none seems to have tried to shut the others out completely or pursued acquiring a controlling interest in the SSRC. Instead, both Carnegie and Rockefeller officials regularly expressed the wish that the other continue its support.[41] This balancing act became more complex in the 1950s when the Ford Foundation entered the arena. But even Ford, perceived by officials of the older foundations as an inexperienced and ham-handed young giant, had no desire to take over the lion's share of the SSRC's funding.[42] As Bernard Berelson, the director of Ford's Behavioral Sciences Program, put it to another Ford officer: "The [Ford] Foundation should not buy more than, say, half of SSRC. SSRC is a good place to keep pressure on the other foundations to maintain their activities in the social sciences."[43]

Its patrons' competitive collaboration notwithstanding, the SSRC was no mere pawn to be moved wherever a particular foundation wished. Its leaders and members had their own visions for what the organization ought to do.[44] Short of being able to act on these with their own funds, SSRC officials allied themselves with one of their numerous patrons for specific projects. And under Herring's more ambitious leadership, the SSRC sought to interest not only the foundations but also government agencies in projects of their own devising. An elaborate tug-of-war, played not for conclusive victory but for consistent advantage, continued among the foundations as well as between the foundations and the SSRC—but with one major change. By 1950, owing largely to Carnegie's earlier efforts, the SSRC had been transformed into an important advocate for the new behavioral sciences.

Five Collaborations between Carnegie and the SSRC, 1945–1952

Carnegie joined Rockefeller as one of the SSRC's principal funders in the 1930s. Though its support never equaled that of the SSRC's original patron, Carnegie contributed enough on a regular basis—$25,000 per annum from 1937 to 1942 for administrative expenses alone—to influence the SSRC's projects and direction.[45] The interest both foundations took in the SSRC undeniably expanded the SSRC's operations. Still, because the SSRC depended on the foundations for its entire budget, its directors sometimes felt too tightly controlled, a mere "tail of a kite" with little power to decide what the organization would do.[46] Carnegie and Rockefeller were hands-on patrons; their officers attended major SSRC policy-making meetings, weighing in on what sorts of fellowships it should offer and what sorts of projects it should undertake. After decades in which Rockefeller had done most of the steering, unequal collaborations in which Carnegie played a strong, directive role took center stage during the immediate postwar period.[47]

Beginning in the late 1930s, Carnegie began working steadily to reform the SSRC into an energetic ally that would promote the new social sciences. I turn now to five midcentury collaborations between Carnegie and the SSRC that proved crucial to bringing the behavioral approach to political science. These were the aforementioned Samuel Stouffer et al.'s multivolume *The American Soldier*, Stuart Chase's 1948 *The Proper Study of Mankind*, and an assessment of the shortcomings of pollsters' forecasts for the 1948 presidential election. I also consider two projects that unfolded under the aegis of the SSRC Committee on Political Behavior that Herring had revived—a 1949 Ann Arbor conference on political behavior research and the University of Michigan Survey Research Center's study of voting behavior in the 1952 presidential election. In different ways, each project aimed to bolster the credibility of polling and survey research as part of a broader mission to promote the social sciences. Taken together, they made up the earliest foundation and SSRC initiatives that ultimately moved political science into the behavioral sciences.

The American Soldier

The biggest of these five Carnegie-SSRC projects was also its first: the Carnegie-financed and the subsequent SSRC-sponsored drafting of Samuel Stouffer et al.'s four-volume work, widely known as *The American Soldier*, the title of its first two volumes.[48] The books analyzed the large volume of survey data that Stouffer, Young, Dollard, and others had collected for the Research Branch in Osborn's division and discussed the methodological underpinnings of these analyses. The SSRC was not only the official sponsor of the work; a special SSRC committee oversaw its publication as well. Osborn chaired that SSRC committee, having been a trustee of the Carnegie Corporation since 1936 as well as brigadier general of the army's Information and Education Division during the war. Its duration and expense as well as the involvement of numerous Carnegie and SSRC officials makes this project a significant example of the partnership between Carnegie and the SSRC to promote survey research and what became the behavioral sciences.

Important as Osborn was to facilitating the completion of Stouffer et al.'s four-volume work, the creation, financing, and staffing of the Research Branch that designed the surveys on which it was based were even more his doing. Just prior to the nation's entry into World War II, negotiations were already underway between Carnegie and military officials to work out some way that Carnegie could finance at least some of what Osborn, as chief of the Information and Education Division, planned to do. As a private philanthropic foundation, Carnegie could not legally give money directly to the US government, though in this case that was precisely what its officers wished to do. The agreed-upon solution to this problem was to create what foundation officials called a "buffer state"—an entity not part of the government—that would be the recipient of the Carnegie grant.[49] That entity, called the Committee of Trustees on Defense, Welfare, and Recreation Experimental Programs (formed in October of 1941), then disbursed its funds directly to Osborn's division. Carnegie officials informally referred to the recipient of these grants not as the cumbersomely named Committee of Trustees; instead, they called it what it was: "the Osborn fund." After all, it was Osborn, by virtue of his enthusiasm for the new social science and his strong ties to Carnegie, who made this money flow into his division.[50]

Osborn later affirmed he had also been central to staffing the Research Branch and giving it a secure institutional home in the War Department. He remembered this project, he said, "with more pride than almost anything I've ever done. I got together the group of these scientists under Sam Stouffer of Chicago. . . . I took over a research branch which had been organized for G-2, Intelligence. It was transferred to my division when they were thrown out of Intelligence."[51] In mid-1945 when the Committee of Trustees presented its overall account of how it had expended the $100,000 Carnegie grant, its current chair, John M. Russell, noted that $23,000 had gone to "research." Around the same time, Russell also informed Carnegie that $20,000 of the grant remained unspent, offering that this money might "be used in greasing the wheels of various undertakings." The sole beneficiary of these unspent funds turned out to be Stouffer and his team (which included Charles Dollard and Donald Young), in addition to another 1945 Carnegie grant of $50,000 specifically earmarked for their work.[52]

But to whom should these funds be granted? At the end of the war, the

Research Branch along with the Committee of Trustees prepared to "dis-band"; thereafter, the SSRC became the entity entrusted with overseeing the next phase of the project.[53] In a flurry of correspondence in the fall of 1945, Young, Osborn, and an official with the Committee on Trustees quickly hammered out this arrangement. At the beginning of October 1945, newly appointed SSRC executive director Young wrote to Osborn asking that his division's wartime survey data be "placed on loan" to a joint committee of the SSRC and the National Research Council. Young underscored how valuable he believed this data would be to the social sciences but did not mention any particular research plans for it.[54] In a far more specific letter written less than two weeks later, Russell of the Committee of Trustees formally requested the $50,000 grant from Carnegie to finance what is clearly a rough draft of *The American Soldier* project. After outlining what each of the proposed four volumes of the work would cover, Russell added, "The Social Science Research Council will direct the project if that is desired." This cryptic comment suggests that Russell had probably already conferred with Young about the matter but was also inquiring what sort of arrangement Carnegie "desired" in this case.[55] The matter was settled around a month later: Russell wrote Young to announce the new Carnegie grant and to inquire how the SSRC would take over responsibility for the project from the Committee of Trustees. After Young sent him a list identifying who would serve on the SSRC committee overseeing the project (a list that included both Osborn and Russell), Russell wrote back to say that in the future this SSRC committee should report on its activities directly to Carnegie.[56] The hand-off complete, the project now formally became the responsibility of the SSRC.

Many of the people involved in what became *The American Soldier* project wore a number of different hats.[57] Because that was so, the transfer of responsibility for the project was more a strategy to allow it to continue than an infusion of new blood; many of those associated with the Research Branch during the war continued to work on the project in the coming years. What changed, therefore, was not so much who worked on the project but the audiences it addressed.

Most importantly, the military was no longer to be the project's sole audience. During the war, Stouffer and his team of researchers were disappointed that the military left them with a "nearly complete lack of autonomy in deciding which issues to investigate."[58] It was only after the war ended, then, that Stouffer and numerous other former Research Branch employees were able to comb through the data they had collected guided by their own interests. As Stouffer recalled shortly after the books were published, he and his team did most of the analytic work that appeared in them after the war, not during it.[59] So when several military officers insisted they be allowed to produce their own abridged versions of the volumes without paying any royalties to Princeton University Press, its publisher, the press pushed back. Though the press's director conceded that the original data had been the property of the US Army, he insisted they had since been extensively "processed" in a "non-governmental research" effort and therefore now belonged to the SSRC and to the publisher.[60]

After the war, Stouffer and his team were no longer primarily interested in addressing the military audience they had found so unreceptive.[61] When Osborn sent the first volume of the work to one high-ranking military officer, the testy response he received indicates that the military leadership was still far from won over by the social scientists in the Research Branch. The officer, General Brehon Somervell, predicted that many career military officers would be put off by the "very apparent intellectual snobbery exhibited by the authors towards the regular army." Somervell went on: "As an engineer I resent and I think all other engineers will resent reference to work of this type as engineering." The general's most stinging put-down compared Stouffer and his team to "a maiden, without previous experience" making pronouncements "on sex and marriage." "Her education and I.Q. may be very high," Somervell quipped, "her sincerity beyond question, but a little experience does help." Somervell took umbrage at what he saw as civilian social scientists' claims to expert knowledge about how to run the US Army. Who were they to tell him, a four-star general, about the army?[62] Tellingly, Osborn was more amused than upset by this response. He forwarded a copy of Somervell's letter to Dollard with a mordant note; Dollard responded in kind.[63] That Stouffer's book had ruffled a prominent general's feathers neither surprised nor worried them. They had wider ambitions for the book than impressing four-star generals.

Less than a year after returning to Carnegie following his wartime service in the Research Branch, Dollard presented a substantial statement of his plans for the foundation's social science program to Carnegie's Board of Trustees. The best way of "putting social science to work," Dollard argued, would be for social scientists to have greater responsibility for policy-making—a responsibility they deserved, given their contributions to various federal government agencies during the war. Carnegie could help realize this general aim by investing in developing the social scientific backbone of opinion polling. "To leave this field to those who see it only as a source of profit seems a highly questionable policy," Dollard warned. He argued that Carnegie should invest in "the encouragement of attitude studies which will be scientific in the best sense of the word. . . . Such studies will offer one of the best interdisciplinary meeting grounds which can be devised and will pave the way for more sensible work in all the social disciplines."[64] Though the postwar work on *The American Soldier* was just beginning at the time Dollard wrote this policy paper, this project exemplified Dollard's ideas about the kind of social science Carnegie ought to be supporting.

Carnegie's support for *The American Soldier* aimed to bolster the prestige of social scientific expertise. In the case of this project, the intended audiences were social scientists themselves along with an array of elites inside and outside the military who might employ them. Dollard's warm congratulatory letter to Stouffer, written shortly after the publication of volume 1, predicted the book "just can't help being a landmark in American sociology." Stouffer responded in the same vein, complimenting Dollard for all he had done "to help promote the future of the social sciences."[65] In addition to praising the work as an academic contribution, Dollard had portions of it distributed to academic and corporate leaders and even vetted a review of the work prior to its appearance in an academic journal.[66]

So why did *The American Soldier* come into being as an SSRC project? Both timing and practical considerations clearly mattered. By the fall of 1945, under newly appointed Executive Director Young, the SSRC was finally poised to become the kind of ally Carnegie officials interested in the social sciences wanted to advance their ambitious program. Like Dollard, Young had worked under Osborn for the Research Branch; Young was also an established academic sociologist well-versed in statistical research methods and interdisciplinary work. Dollard also later recalled that he felt he ought to help the young academics who had been part of the Research Branch publish some of their work after the war.[67]

Additionally, the interdisciplinary nature of the SSRC was at least as important as Young's professional background and Dollard's commitment to academic social science. Making *The American Soldier* grant to it underscored that this was a truly interdisciplinary project, done by a team of scholars from a range of academic backgrounds. Practically, too, the number of authors involved in the four-volume project was large—there were fifteen in all, a number of whom were affiliated neither with Harvard nor with Stouffer's Laboratory of Social Relations there. Given these circumstances, the SSRC may have seemed the most practical entity to administer a grant involving so many persons at different institutions. These volumes ultimately elicited nearly as much academic criticism as praise; still, they were widely reviewed and discussed.[68] Even if most members of the academic audience did not applaud *The American Soldier*, they were at least paying attention.

Chase's The Proper Study of Mankind

Some day when the work of social scientists is neatly collated in the storehouse, no government department, large corporation, big national union, or benevolent enterprise, no powerful community leader, will think of making important decisions without consulting social scientists or their findings.

—Stuart Chase[69]

Young had pledged that under his leadership, the SSRC would devote more time to making a case for the merits of the social sciences to the general public. This signaled an important shift in SSRC priorities. With Young now in charge of the SSRC, Dollard, as Carnegie's vice president, moved quickly to develop and direct the publication of a book written for a general audience about the achievements and future prospects of social science. The records Carnegie preserved for the project make clear that though Young was closely involved, he followed Dollard's lead in seeing the book through from start to finish. Carnegie wished, however, that the SSRC be the book's official sponsor.[70]

Published by Harper's in 1948, *The Proper Study of Mankind* was written by the well-known popular writer Stuart Chase. The idea for the book did not come from Chase, however. Instead, it was Dollard, with the help of Young and several others, who pitched the idea to its would-be author. And once Chase expressed an interest, it was Dollard again who organized a large group of social scientists to supply Chase (who knew little about midcentury social science) with anecdotes and explanations as well as answers to Chase's queries.[71] Dollard and Young also edited the manuscript in its entirety, recommending extensive revisions and prevailing upon a small group of academics to write up their reactions to it. Chase's book was emblematic of the postwar collaborations between Carnegie and the SSRC in which Carnegie played a strong, directive role.[72]

In an upbeat, whirlwind tour of contemporary US social science, Chase showcased social scientists doing technically sophisticated, scientifically sound, and, above all, useful things during World War II. Though wartime achievements loom large in the book, Chase took pains to explain how these achievements also had important peacetime applications. The practical value of what social scientists do was plain, Chase wrote, even to a layman like himself; moreover, he could not help but be impressed by how skilled social scientists had become. This was a rhetorically deft approach to legitimating a new kind of expertise. Coming not from the mouth of one of the new would-be experts but from a layman, Chase's endorsement of mid-twentieth-century social science was perfectly pitched to model the public deference to social scientific expertise Carnegie hoped to foster. As Chase expressed this perspective in a preliminary overview of the proposed book, "If we do not encourage social scientists to undertake the task [of answering the great unanswered questions regarding democracy, education, the international order, etc.], then we will have to leave it to the quacks, the politicians, the crystal ball gazers and the players of hunches. Which in this atomic age is not nearly good enough."[73]

The published book included similar paeans to social scientific expertise. For example, in the chapter "The Future of the Polls," Chase enthused about the technical sophistication of polling operations and the efficiency of government planning informed by them. He also gleefully imagined how scientifically conducted polls might trump the pronouncements of politicians and other nonexperts with verifiable claims about citizens' views:

> Ever since 1776—and probably long before that—statesmen, editors, politicians, and parsons have been telling us all about Americans with the utmost confidence. They could be as brash as they liked because there was no way to check up on them. . . . At last there is a scientific way for checking up on them, and from here on these intuitive geniuses had better know what they are talking about or keep quiet.[74]

Dollard consistently imagined the final product as an accessibly written general audience book. Shortly after pitching the project to Chase, Dollard made a case for the "translation" of academic social science for the general public and especially for policy-makers to Carnegie's Board of Trustees. Dollard argued that although "to translate what the professors know" was essential to "putting social science to work," the professors would not do this project well themselves. Ideally, the book would be directed not just to the general public but to corporate and policy-making elites: "If the leaders in industry, labor and government can be made more literate in the social sciences, the country will be better off."[75] Later, Dollard even ventured the hope that Chase's book would "correct some of the appalling ignorance revealed in the debate" in Congress over legislation to create a National Science Foundation. The sociologist Louis Wirth was less sanguine, noting that given Chase's well-known leftish sympathies, his book would not move many in Congress already skeptical of social science. Though Dollard readily conceded this point, he reasserted his earlier view that Chase's book was ultimately intended for a general audience and "the mine run of business men and industrialists." Other Carnegie-SSRC projects could address congressional and academic audiences.[76]

Dollard ultimately concluded that the book he had done so much to shape worked: it spoke to the right audiences in the right voice. After seeing the close-to-final draft, a delighted Dollard praised Chase's writing, commenting that one of the book's virtues was that it did not read like a "dissertation." The book proved much more successful than Dollard had hoped—so successful, in fact, that the SSRC would later use its substantial royalties to finance the early activities of its Committee on Political Behavior.[77]

SSRC Committee on 1948 Polls

Shortly after the publication of Chase's book, Carnegie officers found another occasion for close collaboration with the SSRC. Chase's book had heaped lavish praise on the latest advances in public opinion polling; but just a few months after its publication in the fall of 1948, widely publicized preelection forecasts by commercial pollsters fell flat. Each of the three major firms (Crossley, Gallup, and Roper) predicted Thomas Dewey would win the US presidency, forecasting vote totals for President Harry Truman between 4 percent and 12 percent lower than he ultimately received.[78] Just days after the election, foundation officials swung into action and organized a group of scholars under the auspices of the SSRC to craft a response to what Dollard called "the Gallup-Roper fiasco." Dollard and Leland DeVinney, a member of Stouffer's research team and now an associate officer in the Division of Social Sciences at the Rockefeller Foundation, agreed that "initiative should come from SSRC." And so another project not only financed but initiated by the foundations unfolded under the official banner of the SSRC.[79]

By the fall of 1948, Pendleton Herring was the SSRC's new head, Donald Young having left earlier in the year for a position with the Russell Sage Foundation. Carnegie's records show that though Herring was involved in conversations about this project from the outset, he was not the one pitching the idea to Dollard. Instead, Dollard's notes indicate that he, not Herring, suggested the SSRC take the public lead on the project and then proposed a specific sum that the SSRC should request from Carnegie to finance it.[80] As with Chase's book, once again the SSRC (in this case its specially designated Committee on Analysis of Pre-Election Polls and Forecasts) was the public face of this project, not Carnegie.

The project aimed to publish as quickly as possible a thorough analysis explaining why the commercial pollsters had all been wrong. As Chase had done in his book, the SSRC committee addressed its findings not primarily to other social scientists but to the general public as well as to those in government and industry who might hire pollsters or survey researchers. Completing its initial report less than two months after the presidential election, the committee released it "to newspapers and press services" in the last days of 1948. The report also appeared in the final 1948 issue of *Public Opinion Quarterly*, where Herring had long been an associate editor.[81] A dozen luminaries in social science, polling, and broadcasting contributed to this report, designed to shore up its target audiences' perception of polling in several ways.[82] First, its authors argued that even if pollsters had used the best methods available, they should have been more modest than the commercial firms (especially Roper) had been about their ability to predict electoral outcomes. Second, they took the commercial pollsters' sampling and interviewing methods to task, arguing that these were probably most to blame for the dramatic shortfall in the estimated Truman vote. Finally, the committee concluded, all commercial pollsters had wrongly assumed that most voters would not change their minds in the final weeks or months of the campaign. In sum, the SSRC committee argued that polls could be considerably less prone to error if pollsters were both more cautious about their forecasts and more scrupulous about using the best procedures available.[83]

Throughout their report, the authors took pains to distinguish social scientific approaches to surveying public opinion from commercial polling firms' practices. Though the missteps of the commercial firms were undeniable, the authors insisted that public opinion polls could still be important and valuable. Moreover, the authors strongly recommended that drawing on the expertise of social scientists was the best approach to improving the performance of polls in the future. Specifically, they recommended more research on every step in the polling process, more work on understanding the bases of voter behavior, and more social scientific contributions to improving the public's understanding of polls.[84] Not only was the article a demonstration of social scientific expertise in the area of polling; it was also an appeal for that expertise to be more widely recognized and used. Carnegie initiated this project and Chase's book for the same basic purpose: to convince not only the public but especially government and business elites that social scientific knowledge was useful and reliable.[85] In both cases, Carnegie officials apparently concluded this argument might be more successful if the SSRC, not the foundation, looked like its main architect.

1949 Ann Arbor Conference on Political Behavior

The accomplishments of the Committee [on Political Behavior] are a prime example of wise foundation strategy. For an average annual expenditure of less than $70,000, the Carnegie Corporation and the Ford Foundation over a period of fifteen years made possible the restructuring of a major discipline. ... These foundations helped to accomplish that end with minimal overhead costs and with something approaching maximal direct impact upon the perspectives and the activities of active political scientists throughout the country.

—David Truman, "A Report on Activities of the Committees"[86]

Early in Pendleton Herring's tenure as the SSRC's executive director, he began to promote projects of his own design. Stepping outside the supporting role he had played to facilitate Carnegie's plans for the SSRC Committee on the 1948 Election Polls, Herring was soon pitching his own ideas for projects concerned with political behavior. He not only requested Carnegie support for a 1949 conference on political behavior in Ann Arbor, Michigan, but, more ambitiously, asked for an ongoing commitment from Carnegie to the SSRC Committee on Political Behavior (CPB) he had revived.[87] It was chiefly Herring, therefore, who directed Carnegie resources specifically toward developing a behavioral political science.

Herring had multiple goals for the 1949 conference. For one, he wanted accomplished behavioral scientists—sociologists, anthropologists, or psychologists—to instruct interested political scientists on methodological issues; the sociologist Paul Lazarsfeld, the social anthropologist George

Murdock, and the social psychologists Rensis Likert and Angus Campbell of the University of Michigan's Institute for Social Research (ISR) were among those invited. Herring also wanted political scientists to discuss recent exemplary works in their own discipline, especially V. O. Key's forthcoming *Southern Politics*. As David Truman noted in retrospect, the conference also finalized Herring's relaunch of the CPB and began to plot the committee's future course.[88] Many clearly found the meeting inspiring, among them Avery Leiserson, who wrote to Herring to express his post-conference enthusiasm for "the 'missionary' work that we need to do in our own Political Science Association with respect both to the methodological developments in the other social sciences." Leiserson went on to say that he could "see already how the Conference may have considerable impact in promoting our schemes here [University of Chicago] for improving the facilities for research training in the graduate curriculum."[89] Such enthusiasm bode well for similar initiatives, including Carnegie's commitment to another Michigan project—the 1952 election study.[90]

In reactivating the SSRC's CPB in 1949, Herring built sturdy institutional scaffolding for a range of projects. Working with the members of the CPB, Herring secured significant behavioral science–friendly foundation funds for political science. These supported numerous additional conferences, multiyear research programs on state politics and American governmental and legal processes, and new "spin-off" SSRC committees, like the Committee on Comparative Politics.[91] Another discipline-changing project that benefited from connections to Carnegie and the SSRC's CPB was the 1952 election study carried out by the University of Michigan Survey Research Center, to which I now turn.

The 1952 Election Study

You may very properly regard [The American Voter*] as the ultimate product of an investment you made in us back in 1952.*

—Angus Campbell to John Gardner, president of the Carnegie Corporation[92]

Though *The American Soldier* was the largest and longest-lasting social science project Carnegie partnered with the SSRC to support, the foundation's support for a study of the 1952 presidential election has arguably had the most enduring impact. That study formed part of the basis for Angus Campbell, Philip Converse, Warren Miller, and Donald Stokes's *The American Voter* (1960), a definitive work on American political behavior still widely cited today.[93] Beyond that influential work, the surveys done by Campbell and others on successive elections preserved a common core of questions with the aim of collecting data on voting behavior over time. In the 1970s, this expanding data set became known as the American National Election Studies (ANES); it is overseen by a national board and has been supported by the National Science Foundation for over forty years.[94] Carnegie's "investment" in the 1952 election study therefore yielded not only *The American Voter* but also the ANES.

The impressive staying power of both *The American Voter* and the ANES stands in marked contrast to the precarious circumstances surrounding the first major survey out of which they arose. In the spring of 1952, Carnegie made a $90,000 grant to the SSRC's Committee on Political Behavior for a nationwide survey of a sample of eligible voters in advance of the November elections. Several years later, Carnegie officers made clear that their support would not extend past the 1952 election.[95] Significantly, Carnegie made the grant to the SSRC's CPB, even though the research on the 1952 election was to be conducted not by it but by the University of Michigan's Survey Research Center. Except for the study's director, the social psychologist Angus Campbell, most of the researchers involved did not belong to the committee that was the official grantee. Nevertheless, John Gardner, who would succeed Dollard as Carnegie's president in 1955, formally proposed the CPB be the grantee—a proposal that surprised and mystified CPB chair V. O. Key.[96] Initially, Gardner explained that Carnegie preferred to make the grant to the CPB because of its impressive track record.[97] When Herring explained the arrangement to the executive committee of the SSRC, he took a slightly different line, saying that Carnegie wanted to stress "the interdisciplinary character of the undertaking" so that "the committee's interest in political behavior would receive primary attention."[98] But even if it was not entirely clear to everyone involved *why* Carnegie preferred that the grant go to the SSRC's CPB, *that* this was the foundation's preference was clear enough.[99] In effect, this arrangement made a committee of the SSRC rather than Carnegie the most visible grantor and overseer of the project.

The ominous political climate no doubt contributed to Carnegie's decision to make the SSRC responsible for this grant. In the spring of 1952, the US Congress had voted to authorize the Cox Committee's investigation of tax-exempt foundations. This was not the first time this issue had come up before Congress; for at least a year, the foundations had had some forewarning that political momentum to investigate them was building.[100] Shortly after Carnegie's Board of Trustees approved the grant and just four days after Congress authorized the Cox Committee's investigation, Gardner wrote to Herring to urge extra discretion on everyone involved in the project. He warned that "particularly in an election year, such research might readily become the subject of political charges and countercharges" and that the project would most likely be "subjected to unusually rigorous—and perhaps unfriendly—scrutiny." He went on to urge Herring to make sure that the study was done "in a thoroughly non-partisan fashion . . . to keep to a minimum any possible misapprehensions."[101] Gardner's warning echoed the tortuous language Carnegie chose to describe what it was funding—"non-political and non-partisan research on political behavior."[102]

It seems likely, therefore, that concerns about the political scrutiny the foundation might face fueled Gardner's insistence that the announcement of the grant for the 1952 national election study be made in the most cautious language possible and that the SSRC rather than Carnegie oversee it. A few years later, such precautions would no longer seem necessary. After the political storms that had threatened the foundations had blown over, the Rockefeller Foundation made its grant to support the 1956 election study directly to Michigan's Survey Research Center.

Additionally, Herring along with those most directly involved in the project had their own reasons for highlighting the SSRC's role. For one, the Survey Research Center and the Institute for Social Research of which it was a part were new postwar entities operating without any annual budgetary commitment from the University of Michigan. Though the Survey Research Center had completed a variety of projects since its move to Michigan in 1946, its prestige could not match that of an SSRC committee of prominent academics under the guidance of a former Carnegie officer.[103] Second, because the Survey Research Center did not have a secure institutional foothold at Michigan, it was unusually vulnerable to the whims of others at the university. Indeed, before the project had even begun, the chair of Michigan's political science department and former APSA president, James Pollock, was already fuming that he and his political science colleagues were not guaranteed prominent parts in it.[104] In the early 1950s, however, political science was widely considered the most underdeveloped of the new behavioral sciences, a view Carnegie officers shared. "Research in the field of political science has been altogether too confined to libraries and bookish speculations, undisciplined by systematic factual observation," a Carnegie staff member wrote. "In recent years, a group of younger social scientists, inspired by recent achievements in other social science fields, have been interested in systematic quantitative studies of political behavior based on field observations and interviews."[105] Ideally, the 1952 election study would bring the greater behavioral sophistication of sociology and psychology to bear on political science. Moreover, making the grant to the SSRC's CPB put control over the project out of an older generation of political scientists like Pollock's reach—something Gardner, Campbell, and Herring all agreed was desirable.[106]

In addition to these considerations, Carnegie officials may have thought that the academic audience to whom they wished this project to speak would be more likely to listen if it were associated with a committee of the SSRC. Campbell praised the "arrangement" between the CPB and his team for similar reasons, stressing that it had "helped to broaden the interest of social scientists generally in the study" and gave "a prestigeful [sic] sponsorship" it would not have had on its own.[107] Lest these comments seem excessively self-effacing today, it should be stressed that in the early 1950s, survey research was still a newcomer to the academic world—one which many of its established denizens still regarded as unacceptably commercial. Perhaps mindful of these suspicions, Campbell took some pains in his final report to the SSRC to emphasize that the data he and his team had gathered would be treated as a public good within the academic community, widely distributed to other academics and used to train graduate students.[108] Having this project unfold under the auspices of the SSRC helped spread the word about this project, its methods, and its data among academic social scientists.

Conclusion

The rocky relationship between Carnegie and the SSRC in the 1930s became much smoother when new men who shared a commitment to a new social science became leaders of both institutions immediately after World War II. I have used Dollard's retrospective comment that he and others had been "propagandists for the behavioral sciences" to highlight how the postwar projects I discussed expressed their commitment to bring a new social science into being. Carnegie officers cared not only about the message of these projects but also about who delivered it and to whom. This concern, I believe, helps make sense of Carnegie's insistence that the SSRC be the public face of these projects—even in the case of those projects that were, like Chase's book, not only funded but also conceived and overseen from start to finish by Carnegie. If established academic social scientists were the messengers for these projects, Carnegie officers hoped, the public and especially a range of potential patrons might find the messages more compelling than if they came directly from the foundation. Once former Carnegie staff member Herring began his twenty-plus-year tenure as the head of the SSRC, he and many of its committees designed their own projects to further Carnegie's commitment to what were now beginning to be called the behavioral sciences. The projects cosponsored by Carnegie and Herring's SSRC set the stage for the behavioral revolution in political science. They also made political scientists' access to more significant federal patronage possible.

Unlike the Ford Foundation's Behavioral Sciences Program, the projects I have discussed were never bundled into an explicit program that Carnegie publicly promoted. This makes it more difficult to discern what those who made the partnership between Carnegie and the SSRC wanted to achieve. Still, the transformation of the SSRC and the projects Carnegie undertook with it do reveal the broad outlines of this group's ideas for a new social science. Everyone in the group agreed that the new social science they hoped to foster should have an integrated and a quantitatively sophisticated sociology and psychology at its core and that it should be done in settings that resembled the large multidisciplinary wartime projects in which they had participated. In the uncertain and politically volatile years immediately after World War II, this group sought to cultivate allies and patrons for what they saw as a newly powerful, practically useful social science. Moreover, these men all sought to expand social scientists' access to federal policy-making.

Carnegie's first crucial step was transforming the SSRC into the right kind of partner to promote a new kind of social science. This objective was effectively secured when Carnegie helped its allies Donald Young and Pendleton Herring become its postwar leaders. Once Young and then Herring were in place, Carnegie either initiated or funded phases of the five projects I discussed in the body of this chapter, stipulating in each case that the SSRC be its most publicly visible sponsor. In each of the projects examined, Osborn, Dollard, and finally Gardner insisted that Young or Herring's SSRC do the talking, no matter who the audiences might be. From Carnegie's perspective, this approach had a number of virtues: not only did it help establish the postwar SSRC as an advocate for the new social sciences;

it also promised to legitimize these sciences while limiting the foundation's exposure to any political scrutiny these projects might invite at the same time. When Herring began to direct the resources of this quiet program toward a not-quite-yet-behavioral political science, he sowed the seeds of what would soon become the behavioral revolution.

Carnegie's significance as a patron for what became the behavioral sciences is easy to miss. For the array of reasons I have discussed, even those senior staff who strongly supported these new approaches deliberately muted the foundation's public role in promoting these projects. Ford's Behavioral Sciences Program overshadowed what Carnegie had done not only because of its much larger budget but also because its leaders publicized it so aggressively. Though Carnegie's support was smaller and more discretely given, it was crucial in three ways. First, it began early, supporting several research teams during and immediately after the war. Second, it remade the SSRC into a close ally and public voice for what became the behavioral sciences. Finally, it put the behavioral sciences in a good position to secure substantial patronage from the NSF and other federal agencies—patronage that underwrote their further development. Saying in 1967 that the work he and his fellow "propagandists for the behavioral sciences" had been done "barely in time," Dollard recalled both the precarious early life of the would-be behavioral sciences and how much the support of the foundations and the SSRC mattered in sustaining it.

CHAPTER TWO

The Ford Foundation's "Golden Eggs" and the Constitution of Behavioralism

Once the Ford Foundation began its nationwide philanthropic program in 1950, it quickly grew to three times the size of the Carnegie and Rockefeller philanthropies combined. From 1959 to 1964, Ford funds for political science exceeded Carnegie and Rockefeller's by 20 to 1.[1] By the late 1950s, Ford was committing millions of dollars annually to fields ranging from international and area studies to US legislative studies. Central as these programs were to late twentieth-century political science, the Ford Foundation's influence on the discipline began earlier. From 1950 until 1957, Ford invested $24 million to develop what it called "the behavioral sciences." Political scientists were by no means the principal beneficiaries of this program; nevertheless, it had a profound effect on the discipline.[2] For one, behavioral approaches to the study of politics would surely not have become so prominent so quickly without Ford's well-publicized interest in this area. Even more importantly, Ford's program helped constitute the very substance of what "behavioralism" came to mean in political science.

When political scientists and historians of the discipline have commented on the emergence of the behavioral approach, some have presented it primarily as an intellectual revolution launched by political scientists, determined to reject the muddle-headed deficiencies of their predecessors. Such accounts of the "behavioral revolution" have become part of the discipline's common sense. Versions of this story appear not only in retrospective analyses like memoirs and oral histories; many accounts of the history of political science also echo it. By contrast, others have argued that behavioralism was not thoroughly revolutionary but instead continuous with some currents in early twentieth-century political science. As much as these accounts differ, all are more concerned with assessing the novelty of the behavioral approach than they are with explaining its rise. And for each, the discipline is the principal object and frame of analysis.[3]

Particularly from the postwar period on, I believe there are good historical reasons to look for agents of academic change outside of disciplinary
and even academic frames. Universities in the United States had long had
ties to powerful political and economic entities; but by the mid-twentieth
century, those ties multiplied and became stronger. By the 1960s, major research universities in the United States were actively contributing to the national political economy, their faculty competing for and working on grants
from industry, government, and private foundations.[4] When externally
funded research becomes crucial to universities and to individual academics, asking whether and how the entities that supply it influence academic
disciplines become important questions. To answer them, as Peter Seybold
has suggested, one must first identify the channels through which external
funds flow to understand how they reconfigure the terrain of academic disciplines.[5] That is what I do here.

The Behavioral Sciences in Political Science: The Rise of Behavioralism

For supporters and critics alike, behavioralism stands out as one of the most
important orientations in twentieth-century political science. Many of its
early defenders called it revolutionary; some argued it had changed the discipline irreversibly. Even though one of its architects announced the end
of the behavioral era in 1969, behavioralism still has many adherents in
political science today. In the study of public opinion, public officials, interest groups, and political beliefs, as well as in the research methods used by
many political scientists, behavioralism is still a powerful presence.[6]

Behavioral political scientists focused on recent trends in public opinion, political parties, and interest groups; in the main, they were less interested in the historical development of formal governmental and legal
structures than their predecessors had been. As Robert Adcock has per-
suasively argued, it was not so much *what* behavioralists studied, however,
than *how* they studied it that set them apart. Some political scientists had
already been studying public opinion and informal political processes in the
first half of the twentieth century. When behavioralists approached these
topics, however, they did so in several new ways. First, rather than crafting fine-grained case studies based on qualitative analyses of documents
and in-depth interviews, most behavioralists relied on statistical analyses

of large bodies of data, like public opinion surveys, censuses, and electoral records. Second, many early behavioralists in the 1950s and 1960s began appealing to neopositivist ideas about scientific explanation. The most ambitious among them aspired to develop a unified theory of behavior and "systems" that would reveal regularities underlying all human processes. These distinctive methodological and theoretical commitments reinforced one another—general theories of human behavior informed data gathering and analysis, and vice versa. They distinguished behavioralists not only from their predecessors but from many of their contemporaries as well, the most skeptical of whom argued that behavioralists neglected the historical, normative, and critical dimensions of the study of politics.[7]

These important developments in the history of political science appear in a markedly different light once one examines the role of philanthropic foundations and university administrators played in encouraging them. For one, compared to their appearance in sociology and psychology, behavioral approaches in political science developed later. Second, given when and where political scientists first pursued these approaches, there is ample evidence that they did so as *responses* to external funding opportunities made available through universities or intermediary academic organizations. By contrast, accounts that present behavioralism principally as one position in a debate among political scientists as well as those that emphasize the continuity between mid-twentieth-century behavioralism and the scientism of the early twentieth century underplay both these important aspects of its rise. Some miss or suppress them entirely.

Important as the behavioral approach became to postwar political science, psychologists and sociologists in the United States began focusing on behavior far earlier. Indeed, historian of psychology Kurt Danziger argues that a discourse of behavior had already become hegemonic in US psychology as early as the 1910s. Most first-generation behavioralists in political science were keenly aware of this and acknowledged their considerable intellectual debts to their colleagues in the other social sciences. These debts, however, were not to Skinnerian behaviorism with its conviction that experiments in tightly controlled laboratory settings were key to understanding behavior, but to the interdisciplinary, methodologically sophisticated, and eminently practical behavioral sciences. Like many behavioral scientists, behavioralists in political science disclaimed any grand visions of social reform; their ambitions focused instead on developing something analogous to what Danziger termed "a practical science of social control."[8] The story of the rise of behavioralism in political science, therefore, is best understood as a subplot in the bigger story of the rise of the behavioral sciences—a story in which the Ford Foundation played a major part.

As we saw in chapter 1, Ford was not alone in supporting the behavioral approach—the Carnegie Corporation had already made some strategic grants in this area in the 1940s and early 1950s. As I discuss in chapter 3, the Rockefeller Foundation added some significant grants of its own in this area later in the 1950s. In addition to the crucial support of these three big midcentury foundations, the Russell Sage Foundation and numerous agencies in the federal government also underwrote behavioral science projects. Finally, the Social Science Research Council (SSRC) under Donald Young and Pendleton Herring's leadership acted as an important facilitator for them all.[9] Many of the largest funded projects in this area (like Stouffer et al.'s *American Soldier*, discussed in chapter 1) involved interdisciplinary groups of psychologists, sociologists, and anthropologists as well as political scientists.

Early advocates of the behavioral approach in political science not only learned from and imported a great deal from other social sciences but also had strong connections to institutions that received substantial grants—and in some cases had even worked for foundations themselves. The earliest postwar behavioralists clustered around foundation-dependent institutions: many served on the SSRC's Committee on Political Behavior or Committee on Comparative Politics; others had closer affiliations with a foundation-funded research institute or center than with an academic department. Some political scientists at the center of these nodes, like Herring, V. O. Key, and David Truman, brokered numerous connections between their behaviorally inclined colleagues, prospective patrons, and publishers. Others, like the University of Michigan's Warren Miller, capitalized on their existing connections to well-funded interdisciplinary research institutes to build other institutions that carried the behavioral project forward. Within political science, foundation-linked figures like these played outsized roles in constituting, promoting, and institutionalizing behavioralism.[10]

To tell the story of the rise of behavioralism in political science, I begin by discussing Ford's program in the behavioral sciences, both because of its great size (around $24 million disbursed from 1951 to 1957) and because of the early and explicit commitment of its staff to steering the social sciences in a behavioral direction.[11] After summarizing the aims of the major architects of this program, I show how a range of scholars and universities tried to respond to them and then assess the program's effects on political science. I conclude by reviewing how behavioralists in political science as well as historians of the discipline have analyzed the Ford Foundation and other entities' roles in the rise of the behavioral approach.

The Ford Foundation's Behavioral Sciences Program

Ford Foundation documents make clear how central the foundation was to the initiation and ultimate institutionalization of behavioral approaches across a range of disciplines, including political science. Of course, one would expect such documents to highlight Ford's role, and perhaps even exaggerate it. Still, these documents reveal not only the great interest some officials at the Ford Foundation took in the behavioral sciences but also what Ford did to aid them. Reading these documents along with records from universities that received a significant portion of these funds makes the ways Ford's program reshaped the academic world more visible.

How Ford's Behavioral Sciences Program (Area V) influenced political science, however, is harder to discern, principally because those who designed and ran this program paid relatively little attention to the discipline.[12] Other Ford programs, such as those in Area I (World Peace) and Area II (Strengthening Free Institutions) and its spin-off, the Fund for the Republic, had stronger links to political science and public administration. For instance, political scientists who specialized in area studies or oversaw public administration projects overseas received support from Area I. Area II was perhaps even more significant, given that Peter Odegard, who was also chair of political science at UC Berkeley, had been a member of Ford's Study Committee and served as a consultant to the foundation for Area II. Many of Area II's early grants supported the National Municipal League, the National Civil Service League, and the Public Administration Clearing House—all organizations that counted many political scientists among their members.[13] By contrast, political science was not the primary focus of Area V, in part because Bernard Berelson, the Behavioral Sciences Program's director, along with other program staff, thought political science was lagging well behind the more advanced behavioral sciences of psychology or sociology. The grant record of the Behavioral Sciences Program is consistent with this view: the majority of its funds supported research by psychologists and sociologists, not political scientists.[14]

Despite all this, I believe that the influence of the Ford Foundation's program on political science was nevertheless profound. In the immediate postwar period, Ford's multimillion-dollar programs were by far the biggest private source of extramural funds for the social sciences, especially since federal government funding for the social sciences had fallen off significantly. Some of Ford's officers expressed concern about this dearth of funds for social scientific research and argued that the foundation should try to remedy it—ideally, in a way that would encourage government and industry to spend more on the social sciences in the future.[15] It was in service of this end that Ford's behavioral sciences program spent a significant portion of its money on new initiatives rather than on existing projects or academic units. Indeed, the program's most significant grants demonstrated that, with a substantial enough investment, government and industry could also build entirely new institutions in the academic world to further their aims. This was one of the ways Ford played a crucial role in "creating the Cold War university," in which research careers and academic institutions were geared toward the aims of their major patrons.[16]

Ford did not commission universities to build the behavioral sciences from a detailed blueprint; instead, when program officers sketched the direction in which they thought the social sciences should go, they made clear that they expected to be closely consulted over how each university fleshed out its aims. Though only a few political scientists were directly involved in these consultations, many more soon became aware that how well they fit into this emerging academic enterprise might matter to their professional future. The influence on political science was a kind of ripple effect: because political science was far from the center of where the Behavioral Sciences Program made the biggest splash, its influence was most discernible after the program had ended.

Renaming the Social Sciences: Making the Case for the Behavioral Sciences

When Berelson tried to make sense of Ford's Board of Trustees' decision to terminate the Behavioral Sciences Program he had directed, he concluded: "Perhaps [the program] made some ill will for itself . . . by being somewhat initiatory in its activity, by resisting such popular demands as those for free departmental funds, and by appearing in some quarters to have a 'line.'" Whether these factors did indeed contribute to the board's decision to end the program is not the issue here.[17] That Berelson himself offered such an assessment of the program he had led is more significant. There are, I believe, several important ways in which the program Berelson led was indeed "initiatory."

Before any grants were made, before any new centers were funded, the Ford Foundation began with a name change, opting to call the focus of its new program the "behavioral sciences" instead of the social sciences.[18] Donald Marquis, the Michigan psychologist in the group charged with planning the foundation's programs on the eve of its national debut, consciously made and justified that choice. In his report for the division Ford was still calling "Social Science," Marquis raised some concerns about this familiar label, noting that some still associated social science with "social reform" and "socialism." Marquis thought Ford's new program ought to raise a different set of expectations: instead of working toward achieving a good society akin to an "ideal body," social scientists should look to how science informs "medical practice. . . . It diagnoses particular modes of malfunctioning. . . . This is the general spirit of modern social science. It is specifically technical. It does not have a program for reconstructing the social world." Since some still associated "social science" with reformist agendas, Marquis argued that a new name should be part of an effort to move these fields in a more technical, applied direction. Such views were continuous with Marquis's work during and immediately after the war, first for the National Research Council and the wartime Office of Scientific Resource Development and, from 1947 on, as chair of the Department of Defense's Committee on Human Resources. In all of these positions, he had been responsible for linking social scientists to military patrons. This background made Marquis an ideal designer for a social science program meant to complement military patronage rather than compete with it.[19]

In an oral history interview more than twenty years later, Marquis discussed in greater detail why he thought Ford ought to drop the name "social science" for "behavioral sciences." In addition to shaking off any reformist associations, he pointed out that "a different label enabled us to define an area rather than accept already defined areas." Much more than a superficial rebranding, the new name announced the foundation's intention to move a set of academic disciplines in a new direction.[20] The great resources Ford had to spend allowed its officers to approach grant making much more ambitiously than the older, less well-endowed foundations had done. Starting entirely new academic programs was a real option, rather than merely "making marginal increments on top of what universities were already doing."[21]

Ford officers and consultants expressed their transformative ambitions for the Behavioral Sciences Program not only in its name but also in the substance of what they hoped the program's grantees would do: large-scale research that government and private corporations would find useful and ultimately support. A few people, like the ubiquitous Pendleton Herring, made this case to multiple foundations. Herring, who became president of the SSRC in 1948, maintained his close contacts with the Carnegie Corporation (where he had previously been an officer) while also building a close relationship with Ford, first by assisting Marquis in drafting the report for the Social Science Division and later by continuing to consult Ford on its programs. For instance, in a 1951 report to Ford's soon-to-be-president, Rowan Gaither, Herring reported that many academics welcomed Ford's grant money for "tooling up for research." "The increasing demand for applied research activity, coming from both the government and from industry in the post-war years," Herring noted, "has found some universities ill-prepared to carry their share of the burden."[22] Like Carnegie, Ford officers also believed that funding the development of social scientists' research capacities would encourage government agencies and private corporations to increase their investments in them. Demonstrating that university-based social scientists could continue to do large-scale applied research was one part of the effort; prompting social scientists themselves to adopt new attitudes toward research was another.

Looking back on the program he had led, Berelson insisted that it had done much more than paste a new, less controversial label on established ways of doing things. In his entry for "behavioral sciences" in the *International Encyclopedia of the Social Sciences*, Berelson wrote that the Behavioral Sciences Program "influenced at least the nomenclature, and probably even the conception, of an intellectual field of inquiry." Berelson also proudly noted that what Ford started had taken firm root in academic practice just a little over a decade later. Because the behavioral sciences had "survived the termination of the foundation's program . . . in 1957," he concluded, "there seems to have been a genuine need for a collective term in addition to the traditional 'social sciences.'" Scholars in psychology, sociology, and anthropology "are more or less after the same end, namely, the establishment of scientifically validated generalizations about the subject matter of human behavior—how people behave and why." In sum, Berelson believed Ford's

Behavioral Sciences Program made interdisciplinary syntheses possible that traditional disciplinary boundaries had previously blocked.[23]

Three Major Grants in Ford's Behavioral Sciences Program

Several months after Marquis finished outlining the aims of what became the Behavioral Sciences Program, the Ford Foundation launched it by making fourteen substantial, unsolicited grants "for research in individual behavior and human relations"—a dramatic gesture meant to begin and then accelerate the development of the behavioral sciences. Ford encouraged the recipients to build new programs, not supplement existing ones.[24] As correspondence between the foundation and UC Berkeley makes clear, the impetus for these grants came from the foundation rather than from the universities themselves.[25] Ford's program in this area was not a response to organized pressure or formal applications from university faculty or administrators. It was the other way around; foundation officers contacted university administrators to announce awards designed to begin new programs in the behavioral sciences. This is perhaps the most important sense in which Ford's program was initiatory.

Once Ford made these grants, most universities did not begin creating behavioral science programs quickly. When Berelson looked back on the grants made by what later became the Behavioral Sciences Program, he concluded that Ford's efforts to develop university programs in the behavioral sciences had been a mixed bag. Although he commended how later grants to the Johns Hopkins University and the Massachusetts Institute of Technology had turned out, his assessment of what happened at the institutions that received the 1950 grants was another story. Shortly after those grants were made, there were concerns that some institutions were failing to observe "the spirit of the grant," using the monies for ordinary expenses or on "research projects without primary attention to the development of resources and personnel." This less than impressive start, however, did not prevent four of these universities from getting another substantial award in 1955 to build up their capacities in the behavioral sciences; these awards included funds for graduate fellowships and research, adding faculty, supporting faculty research leave, and improving research facilities.[26] Even worse were those institutions that did nothing at all. For example, UC Berkeley, a recipient of a $300,000 grant, took no action for years, prompting some there to worry that Ford might withdraw its money at a time when they were already feeling grant poor relative to their colleagues at other research universities.[27] Still, these worries did not spur the university's leaders into immediate action. Though Berkeley's delay in making use of the Behavioral Sciences Program grant was unusually long, it helps to illustrate the challenge these grants presented all of their recipients. How were universities to develop a program in an area few faculty and administrators understood and to which fewer still had any long-standing commitment?

When Berkeley finally began to spend the 1950 grant eight years later, the money went largely toward creating the Institute for Social Science (ISS), with a Survey Research Center and a Center for the Integration of Social Science Theory under its organizational umbrella.[28] These two centers relied on faculty appointments from across the social sciences; their mission was to further the development of interdisciplinary research methods and social theory applicable to all the behavioral sciences. Practically, Ford funds allowed ISS to become a de facto internal grant-making agency responsible for disbursing small grants-in-aid to faculty from a number of departments.[29] Still, as an assistant to the chancellor made clear to ISS's director, Herbert Blumer, he would have to justify allocating these funds in an appropriately behavioral way: "The Foundation will undoubtedly request progress reports on the use of the granted funds, and we should be prepared to answer them and to defend our judgments in classing projects as 'behavioral.'" Blumer appears to have followed this advice, especially in summarizing the work done by faculty affiliated with the Survey Research Center and the Center for Social Science Theory. In a cover letter to one of his reports to Ford, he assured the foundation that the university's commitment to the behavioral sciences would continue and even increase after the terminal grant from the Behavioral Sciences Program ran out.[30]

From its inception in 1958 and well into the 1960s, ISS used Ford funds to make a number of grants to many UC faculty. Though the grants were not large, ranging from $100 to a little over $2,000, they were numerous; some individuals received multiple grants over the five years covered by the archived report.[31] At least in the first two years of the program, there were a fair number of political scientists among the grantees, even though some received support for projects with no discernible behavioral focus.[32] There are some indications that departments saw the advent of this well-funded institute as a threat to their own power within the university. For example, the chair of the political science department tried to claim a chunk of the Ford funds under ISS control to disburse among his faculty; ISS's advisory committee, however, quickly rebuffed him. Sensing that research centers like his did not need to defer to established departments, ISS director Blumer asked other research center directors whether they ought to press their advantage to secure a formal say in departmental hiring decisions.[33] These instances illustrate how this relatively new Ford-funded independent institute felt emboldened to challenge the academic preeminence of university departments.

Another smaller-scale initiatory Behavioral Sciences Program grant focused on training social scientists in statistics and higher mathematics. Berelson's plans for this grant were cheered on by other social scientists, one of whom predicted, "a relatively small investment here would pay very big dividends in the future. Can you imagine what the improvement in sociology would be if the top 20 percent of graduate students of the past generation had had a thorough training in study design and statistics?"[34] Administered by a committee of Herring's SSRC, Ford's program aimed to train people from different social-scientific disciplines and at different points in their careers. Everyone from undergraduates to tenured professors was encouraged to apply. Among the applicants were several established political scientists, including Robert Dahl, Charles Lindblom, and John Wahlke, all of whom were invited to attend the first summer workshop funded by a $120,000 grant.[35] After at least one such workshop had been held, the SSRC committee responsible for them recommended that future sessions focus more explicitly on interdisciplinary study of social-scientific problems (like group behavior) or tools broadly useful to a range of social scientists (like models of stable equilibria or stochastic models). The report's authors argued mathematics might be the key to making social science truly interdisciplinary: "Mathematics should show its advantages as a useful language, an Esperanto for the Babel's Tower of social scientists." The planning for the institute makes clear just how ambitious that goal was. The minimal entry requirement—a mere one semester of college-level mathematics—indicates the organizers of the institute expected most students would not be fluent in this "Esperanto."[36] These low expectations underscore the program's lofty ambitions: to train generations of math-deficient social scientists to work with mathematical tools. This initiative offers yet another example of the self-consciously transformative mission of Ford's Behavioral Sciences Program.

Ford's initiatives in this area got a substantial boost from the behavioral science-friendly SSRC led by Herring. Around the same time the SSRC was administering the Ford-funded workshops discussed above, its Committee on Political Behavior was also organizing Carnegie-funded summer workshops on survey research, presidential elections, and state politics geared more specifically to political scientists.[37] SSRC annual reports make clear which committees spent the most money on research planning activities. From the late 1940s through 1961, the committees most active in this area that were also sympathetic to behavioralism were Comparative Politics, followed by Mathematical Training for Social Scientists (renamed "Mathematics in Social Science Research" in 1958) and Political Behavior.

Grant programs like these not only ensured the behavioral sciences a presence in the academy but also sped up the rate at which they developed. An even more significant action taken by Berelson's division, however, was the $10.35 million spent to create and endow the Center for the Advanced Study of the Behavioral Sciences (CASBS) in Menlo Park, California. Conceived as a research center to which scholars from different disciplinary backgrounds would be invited to spend a year, the hope was that the center's fellows would devise collaborative behavioral science projects.[38] Judging by several reports from 1950s fellows, interaction among fellows from different disciplines was indeed one of the center's main attractions. More importantly, the release time the CASBS offered its fellows was a scarce resource in 1950s academic circles; many fellows used their residency to finish research projects quickly. In retrospect, Berelson expressed some disappointment that the center fell short of becoming "a seminal spearhead of new developments in the behavioral sciences"; though he thought it "very successful" as a "retreat," the CASBS did not become the hub for collaborative behavioral projects Berelson envisioned. Still, the prestige of a residency there made many established scholars pay attention to the behavioral sciences and think about whether their work could fit within this new category.[39]

It is one thing to initiate something in the academic world, as I have shown that the Ford Foundation did. It is a challenge of another order, however, to make sure that what has been initiated takes root and continues to grow. In his careful analysis of this phenomenon, Seybold argues that Ford's strategy of setting up an array of new institutions devoted to the behavioral sciences "set the agenda for social science research in the United States." Centers and institutes linked to but minimally funded by universities, like the Survey Research Centers at both Michigan and Berkeley, are among the institutions he has in mind.[40] Building on Seybold's analysis, I believe universities responded to Ford's initiatives in several ways that helped secure the endurance of the behavioral sciences. First, given the foundation's insistence that these grants be used to develop new approaches, many universities allowed entities outside of traditional academic department and college structures, like Berkeley's ISS, to administer them. Though relatively independent of university control, these entities were heavily dependent on external monies—especially in their early lives. They therefore functioned as conduits through which funders could exert influence over the shape and direction of academic research. Beginning in the 1950s, the most successful of these new entities used their foundation-derived funds to offer academics valuable scarce resources: release time, research funds and support, fellowships for their graduate students, and so on, all linked to the aims of the sponsoring foundation. Many departments simply could not offer comparable levels of support. The advent of such well-funded entities changed the internal structure of universities in ways that had important consequences for disciplines.[41] Second, at Berkeley and elsewhere, Ford officers secured pledges from university administrators to continue to support the centers their grants had created. Such alliances between the Ford Foundation and university administrations helped the behavioral approach survive the termination of Ford's program. The work of institutionalizing the behavioral sciences, therefore, went on even after Ford's Behavioral Sciences Program ended.

Ford's Influence on Political Science

The Ford Foundation's Behavioral Sciences Program influenced political science in several principal ways. First, Ford's program gave academics across the social sciences, including political scientists, strong incentives to think about what these new sciences were and how they might contribute to them. Second, because of the overall size of Ford grants, administrators and faculty began to think that research in all the social sciences, political science included, could potentially win external financial support. This in turn affected how administrators and departments evaluated the importance of different fields within the discipline. Finally, while university officials continued to puzzle over what foundation officers meant by the "behavioral sciences," at least Ford's conviction that they be interdisciplinary pursuits was clear. Despite the skepticism Ford program officers expressed about political scientists' willingness or ability to move toward behavioral science, they do not seem to have actively barred political scientists from taking part in such interdisciplinary efforts. For people across the social sciences, then, obtaining significant research funds and release time through Ford programs meant either presenting one's work as interdisciplinary and behavioral or, at the very least, paying attention to the new behavioral approach. Organizationally, an affiliation with an institute or center was a plus.

To illustrate these broad dynamics, I offer several specific examples of the effects Ford funds had on political science. First, I consider how Ford grant money accelerated the careers of a number of behaviorally oriented political scientists and helped facilitate a new emphasis on analyzing large sets of electoral data as well. I then discuss how administrators at Stanford University moved their political science department toward behavioralism in response to prospects of increased Ford funding. I conclude by considering one grant made by the Behavioral Sciences Program that appears to clash with most of the others: a grant that supported a 1962 edited volume widely regarded as a denunciation rather than a celebration of American behavioral political science.

The initial grants Ford made to universities and the SSRC in 1950 were a dramatic preview to seven more years of awards; from 1952 on, the Behavioral Sciences Program headed by Berelson designed and oversaw large grants to institutions, small grants-in-aid made directly to individual scholars, and fellowships for residencies at CASBS. Among these later institutional grants, those most relevant to political science were awards over $200,000 each to the University of Michigan and the University of North Carolina in 1955 to support faculty development and graduate study on the "behavioral aspects of politics." In the same year, Ford announced substantial awards to centers at the University of Michigan, Columbia University, and the University of Chicago devoted to "field research" and "large-scale data collection and processing."[42] As I discuss at greater length in chapters 1 and 4, support from all the major midcentury foundations allowed Michigan's Survey Research Center first to sidestep political science department control and then ultimately to change the department's orientation as well. More broadly, early foundation interest in developing universities' capacities in data collection and processing laid the groundwork for the much more substantial commitments the National Science Foundation began to make in this area in the 1960s and 1970s. Hence, Ford's support for these efforts proved to be one of its most significant contributions to the transformation of postwar political science.

In addition to these institutional grants, small grants Ford made to individual researchers also mattered. Around a year after he completed his report for the Social Science Division but before the Behavioral Sciences Program was fully underway, Marquis participated in making an early round of such grants to individuals. As was the case with the 1950 institutional grants discussed earlier, those who received these individual grants probably had not applied for them. Instead, Marquis recalled, he, Ralph Tyler (who became the first director of CASBS), and several others "got together, four or five of us, in a hotel room after dinner with bottles on the table and made up a list of fifty names."[43] One of those names was Samuel Eldersveld's, a young University of Michigan political scientist whose career Marquis believed the grant had saved. As Marquis recounted the story, Eldersveld "was a behavioral researcher in political science and was just about to be fired because the department believed that the historical approach and the theoretical analysis of power was the only thing. But he was doing and wanted to do empirical research. Well, he subsequently became mayor of Ann Arbor and is now chairman of the department. [laughter] The money kept him from being fired."[44] For his part, Eldersveld recalled that he received a $5,000 grant from Ford for "budding young scholars" of political behavior shortly after attending a 1951 summer seminar at the University of Chicago sponsored by the SSRC's Committee on Political Behavior. He was tenured in 1953.[45] Whether or not Marquis's recollection is accurate, it makes clear that he thought tipping the scales in a junior scholar's favor was an appropriate and even felicitous use of Ford funds. Additionally, Eldersveld was not the only academic to have received such an award; the Ford Foundation reported in 1952 that it had made fifty-four awards of $5,500 to support the individual research projects of behavioral scientists. In 1955 it announced that it designated $425,000 more for up to one hundred such awards. Lest these individual awards seem paltry today, $5,500 is around $56,000 in 2021 dollars—a sum most academics would consider a substantial short-term stipend for individual research. Though foundation documents include no lists of the recipients of these awards, it seems unlikely that Eldersveld was the only political scientist to have received one. This kind of direct, unlooked-for aid would have allowed any academic who received it to devote a significant portion of their time to research and writing—something most colleges and universities did not offer.[46]

Although it is not possible to know how many political scientists were among those who received grants-in-aid from Ford's Behavioral Sciences

Program, records of how many became CASBS fellows are available. Of the up to fifty fellows selected annually during CASBS's first decade, anywhere from three to seven each year were political scientists. They included prominent figures associated with behavioralism, such as Harold Lasswell (1954–1955), Robert Dahl (1955–1956), Gabriel Almond (1956–1957), Heinz Eulau (1957–1958), Eldersveld (1959–1960) and Warren Miller (1961–1962).[47] These men were already well-recognized scholars by the time of their residencies; Dahl and Miller, for example, began their residencies shortly after each had completed one of their best-known works—*Preface to Democratic Theory* and *The American Voter*, respectively. For both, however, their CASBS residencies were more than a leisurely victory lap. Dahl began developing ideas for what became *Who Governs?* during his residency; Miller laid the organizational foundations of what became ICPR during his. Eulau's CASBS residency helped advance his career in another way; he left Antioch College to take a position at Stanford University immediately afterward. Finally, nearly all of these men (with the exception of Eldersveld) would become presidents of the American Political Science Association after their residencies. As Mark Solovey has argued, Berelson wanted his program to "make the peaks higher" in all the disciplines in the behavioral sciences.[48] In political science, CASBS residencies, a few large institutional grants, and what were probably more than a handful of individual grants-in-aid did just that—even though the discipline was far from the Behavioral Sciences Program's major focus.

In her detailed account of how behavioralism rose to prominence in Stanford's political science department, Rebecca Lowen documents how an administration deeply committed to advancing Ford's program overrode the wishes of the political science faculty. As was the case at UC Berkeley, Ford officials offered Stanford administrators several grants to develop the behavioral sciences; the administration then used some of these funds to hire people already committed to the new behavioral sciences to come to Stanford. Lowen argues that Stanford's administrators worked quickly and enthusiastically to push a number of the social sciences in a behavioral direction not because of any widespread commitment to the behavioral sciences among the faculty but in response to the funding offered by Ford.[49] This general orientation had important consequences for the political science department.

When Arnaud Leavelle, the Stanford political science department's theorist, died in 1957, the department indicated its openness to a variety of approaches, recommending hiring the traditional theorist Mulford Q. Sibley along with the newly behavioralist Eulau. Provost Frederick Terman, however, initiated his own search with the intention of filling "the department's slot for a theorist . . . [with] a prominent behavioralist, such as Ithiel de Sola Pool or David Truman"; Terman ultimately "fixed upon . . . David Easton as the ideal candidate." In the short term, the department's choices prevailed. Both Sibley and Eulau were hired in 1958; but while Eulau spent the rest of his career at Stanford, Sibley's appointment was tumultuous and short-lived. There was strong and consistent departmental support for Sibley, though few of his colleagues shared his outspoken pacifist views. But to the administration, Sibley was a liability on two counts: not only was his on-campus activism in support of a nuclear test ban annoying; he was also a net financial loss to the institution since he was unlikely to win external grants.[50]

As Lowen reads this period in the Stanford political science department's history, Terman's plan to enhance the department's reputation along with its ability to win external grants culminated in 1963 and 1964 with the hiring of the behavioralists Gabriel Almond and Sidney Verba. Pleased with the results, one ebullient administrator remarked several years later: "The Almond appointment has paid off beyond my wildest expectations and hopes." Lowen stresses that the actions of university administrators were crucial to how and when behavioralism took root at Stanford. Had hiring decisions been left largely to the discretion of the faculty, the political science department would have remained more eclectic. Administrators, keen on bringing in more funds from Ford and other sources, remained focused on hiring well-established behavioralists. By the early 1970s, they had made a few such hires and denied tenure to several traditional theorists (Sibley, John Bunzel, and Joe Paff). Paff, a Berkeley PhD who had been a student of Sheldon Wolin's, taught political theory and methods of sociological analysis at Stanford beginning in the late 1960s. His open opposition to the Vietnam War brought him into conflict with Eulau and others in the department; he was denied tenure in the early 1970s. By then, the department's center of gravity had shifted decisively toward the behavioral approach.[51]

Most of the grants made by Berelson's program were designed to root behavioral approaches more firmly in the social sciences. One grant to a group of political philosophers led by Leo Strauss, however, appeared to conflict with that aim. Still regarded today as one of the most prominent critics of behavioralism in political science, Strauss's skepticism toward much of American political science was already well-known in the mid-1950s.[52] Nevertheless, Berelson approved a grant that ultimately funded *Essays on the Scientific Study of Politics*, a 1962 collection of sustained critiques of behavioralism and scientism by Strauss and several of his former students. Why would those responsible for Ford's Behavioral Sciences Program have funded such a project? And why would political philosophers best known for their criticisms of behavioral science have applied to this Ford program in the first place?

In 1952 those responsible for the behavioral sciences program decided that "improving [the behavioral sciences'] relationship" with a number of humanistic disciplines ought to be one of the program's goals. Berelson seems to have taken this objective seriously enough that when Martin Diamond, a former student of Strauss's, proposed that Ford fund summer seminars in which he, Strauss, and several others would develop sustained commentaries on American social science, Berelson responded positively and urged Strauss to submit a formal proposal.[53] Once Strauss did so, Berelson solicited evaluations of the project from Herbert Simon, Robert Dahl, and Harold Lasswell. Even though none of these was unqualifiedly positive (Lasswell's was especially curt and dismissive), Berelson recommended funding the project anyway. As it turned out, one of the commentaries in the 1962 volume focused on Simon (Storing's), and another focused on Lasswell (Robert Horwitz's).[54]

If Berelson was sincerely looking to cultivate connections with the humanities, a project led by as eminent a scholar as Strauss was a good choice. Writing to Berelson before submitting his formal application, Strauss made clear that he too was interested in forging stronger ties between political philosophy and empirical political science, evinced by his planning a joint seminar with "one of my more behaviorist colleagues" (Charles Hardin) "on the very subject of the mutual fertilization of behavioral studies and political theory." Berelson responded enthusiastically, mentioning that his sometime coauthor, Paul Lazarsfeld, "is extremely interested in precisely the kind of intellectual relationship between 'theory' and 'empirical research' that you intend to explore."[55] The formal proposal Strauss submitted a few months later did not disclose any critical aims; instead, Strauss even pitched the project as a potential aid to the behavioral sciences since "a constant re-examination of the foundation of a science is necessary to its progress." When Richard Sheldon, one of Berelson's assistants, asked Strauss a few months later whether he could be an evenhanded judge of behavioral social science, Strauss promised he and his coauthors would offer "a realistic examination of empirical works." According to Sheldon, Strauss went on to say: "No predetermined theoretical bias will be brought into the study, and although Strauss himself leans toward the metaphysical side, he feels that a check with acquaintances who know him well—for example, Grodzins and Banfield—will show that 'I am not a dogmatic fellow.'"[56] Only once most of what was to become *Essays on the Scientific Study of Politics* was complete and its unqualifiedly critical tone a fait accompli did Strauss acknowledge that it had become a sustained critique of behavioral approaches. Reporting on how he and his associates had spent the grant, Strauss then thanked the Ford Foundation for its "generous and open-minded assistance."[57]

Though it was an obvious anomaly among Behavioral Sciences Program grants, Strauss's project reveals several general things about the Ford Foundation's influence on political science. Most importantly, Ford's Behavioral Sciences Program exerted a kind of magnetic pull on political scientists and philosophers in the 1950s, drawing a wide variety of scholars to pay attention to and evaluate it. Especially since most political scientists had no prospects for NSF funding in the 1950s, Ford's programs in the behavioral sciences and other areas were the go-to sources for external funds. And since by the mid-1950s Ford was advertising its well-funded programs widely, Diamond and Strauss were surely not the only "long-shot" potential grantees to apply for support. Finally, from Berelson's perspective, opening his program to possible critique by an eminent scholar who was promising not to be "dogmatic" probably seemed a small risk to run, given the far-from-friendly criticisms the Reece Committee had recently launched against foundation-sponsored social science. On balance, having Strauss and his students pay attention to behaviorally informed approaches did more to underscore their importance than to threaten them. As Dahl had observed to Berelson, "Strauss isn't really going to stop empirical political science from moving on with its tasks."[58]

Political Scientists and Disciplinary Historians Assess the Rise of Behavioralism

The foregoing sections discussed some of the channels through which Ford behavioral science funds flowed into academic political science and began to remake its terrain. Though political science was not the primary focus of the program, the sheer volume of the funds Ford made available as well as its emphasis on interdisciplinary social science made it impossible for political scientists to ignore.

External funds for behavioral science proved crucial to political science in yet another way. Rather than merely improving the fortunes of a pre-existing research program, I believe it is more accurate to say that Ford funds helped *constitute* the behavioral approach in political science. This is a crucial historiographical point, though an elusive one to make.[59] To do so, one must pay attention to when and where foundations supported behavioral training and research relative to when behavioralism emerged in political science curricula, professional associations, and publications. As I argued in the preceding chapter, Carnegie's early commitments to what became the behavioral sciences clearly predate the emergence of the approach in political science. The Carnegie Corporation's support for the SSRC's Committee on Political Behavior (CPB) in the late 1940s was a crucial first step toward establishing a behavioral orientation in the discipline. And though Ford's much more substantial program came later than Carnegie's, it was still early enough to shape and direct what became behavioralism in political science.

There are many indications that among political scientists in the early 1950s, behavioralism was still amorphous, without clear meaning and direction.[60] For example, although the aforementioned CPB became an important institutional intermediary between foundations and the academy, it only began its activities in 1949. The 1950 survey the CPB commissioned to learn what political behavior research was being done in colleges and universities across the country turned up so little that its author, Oliver Garceau, felt compelled to speculate why so few political scientists were doing this kind of work, compared to other social scientists. Tentatively, he attributed the dearth of research in this area to political scientists' "lack of training" in statistics as well as the widespread belief that voting behavior was too small a piece of the political process to warrant focused study.[61] That political scientists were only doing a paltry amount of research in this area in the late 1940s, however, was clear.

There are other indications that behavioralism was not much of a presence in political science until the latter half of the 1950s. Until 1956, "political behavior" did not appear as a subject heading in the index of the *American Political Science Review*; there were no specific sections devoted to political behavior at the annual meetings of the American Political Science Association until 1963. Also, what became the University of Michigan's well-known special PhD program in political behavior admitted its first students only in 1960.[62] These dates suggest that 1940s and early 1950s foundation grants and programs in the behavioral sciences happened early enough to play a constitutive role in what became behavioralism in political science. Put together with what I have already discussed about the explicitly transformative aims of the Carnegie and Ford programs and their effects on political science, the case is stronger still.

By saying that external funding constituted behavioral political science, however, I do not mean to imply that those who identified with the approach had no interests or volitions of their own. Rather, when the Ford Foundation and others deliberately redesigned social science as behavioral science, a wide range of academics were moved to identify with this new venture and, as Jefferson Pooley has put it, "fashion their intellectual self-concepts" in accordance with it.[63] Many clearly experienced this as an exciting intellectual journey; but it was a guided journey all the same. By contrast, when political scientists and historians of the discipline acknowledge that the behavioral approach benefited from generous foundation support, most assume—I think untenably—that behavioralism had already gelled as an academic approach *before* Ford supported it. In what follows, I begin by presenting how several well-known early advocates of behavioralism evaluated the importance of foundation funding to it. I then consider the degree to which historians of political science have considered the part external funding played in behavioralism's rise.

Shortly after the Ford Foundation launched its nationwide program, the not-quite-yet-behavioralist Heinz Eulau commented on its potential implications for political science. In an essay entitled "Social Science at the Crossroads," he reviewed a number of works representing new and promising ways of doing social science, including the 1949 report of Ford's Study Committee. To Eulau, Ford's interest in the social sciences seemed potentially transformative: "Until now, no foundation with means comparable to those of the Ford Foundation has ventured so far as to lay all of its golden eggs into the shapeless basket of social science." Eulau was not the only social scientist to whom Ford's unexpected largesse seemed like magic. Around the same time, the psychologist Gordon Allport compared social scientists to Cinderella, stunned by the sudden appearance of Ford's "golden coach" ready to transport her to a royal ball.[64]

At the time he published this essay, Eulau's career, like social science, was also at a crossroads. After completing his PhD at Berkeley in 1941, he worked briefly as a research assistant to Harold Lasswell's War Communications Research Project, using basic codes to analyze the content of the Argentine, Brazilian, and Chilean press. When the Rockefeller-funded project Lasswell oversaw ended, Eulau did similar work for a Propaganda Analysis Section in the Department of Justice, some of which made it into the many articles he wrote for the *New Republic*. Though Eulau would later emphasize his profound intellectual debt to Lasswell, his own transformation into a self-identified behavioralist happened nearly a decade later, well after he began teaching at Antioch College in 1947. By his own account, it was during the summer of 1954 at a seminar led by the University of Michigan's Warren Miller and funded by the Carnegie Corporation that Eulau learned to analyze large sets of electoral data collected by Michigan's Survey Research Center. A year later, his published work made clear that he had chosen a behavioral path.[65]

Though Eulau stressed the significance of Ford's "golden eggs" before he fully identified as a behavioralist, foundation patronage does not come up at all in the widely read celebration of behavioralism he published in the early 1960s. Instead, Eulau chose to present behavioralists as contemporary intellectual heroes, comparing them to Socrates for their bold embrace of new ways of thinking and underscoring the many obstacles they had to overcome. Adding to this picture, Eulau represented the education of the first generation of postwar behavioralists as arduous and unsupported: "In the last fifteen years, most of those who have come to the behavioral persuasion in politics have been largely self-taught. Trained in the traditional techniques of political science, they had to develop new skills." This heroic narrative suppresses how generous government and foundation funding made the retraining of many would-be behavioralists possible. Eulau's own experience was no exception, including his stint as a wartime research assistant to Lasswell and, more significantly, his retraining in the Miller-led workshop funded by Carnegie. Though Eulau later acknowledged both these debts, the heroic narrative that elides the importance of foundation and government patronage has become a part of the discipline's common sense.[66]

Unlike Eulau's heroic narrative, one of the most frequently cited early assessments of behavioralism by the already influential Robert Dahl readily acknowledged the importance of foundation funding to the success of behavioralism. "If the foundations had been hostile to the behavioral approach," Dahl wrote, "there can be no doubt that it would have had very rough sledding indeed." Candidly, Dahl acknowledged that foundation and state support along with other "interrelated . . . powerful stimuli" helped behavioralists achieve professional success quickly: "The revolutionary sectarians have found themselves, perhaps more rapidly than they thought possible, becoming members of the establishment."[67] Put this way, behavioralists' rapid ascendance seems more a stroke of good fortune that happened *to* them rather than the result of their own arduous efforts. Eulau would make a similar point over a decade later, remarking that the "great avalanche" of behavioral work published in the 1960s was more lucky than inevitable: "It was as if a coin had been dropped into the slot machine and the jackpot had been hit."[68] In these instances, both Dahl and Eulau acknowledged, however obliquely, that they felt the wind of powerful forces from outside the discipline at their backs.

Such frankness about how foundation and government patronage affected behavioralists' fortunes still misleadingly casts behavioralists as the lucky beneficiaries of the patronage and favor of an establishment to which they did not belong. Dahl's well-known pluralist conception of power, which represents power as highly fluid and widely distributed among many groups, underwrites this view. Applying this view to the rise of behavioralism, however, veers away from focusing on how many of the people who shaped the behavioral turn in postwar social science held positions in foundations, the academy, *and* government agencies, simultaneously or in short succession.[69] Pendleton Herring, discussed in chapter 1, is one example; Donald Marquis, discussed earlier in this chapter, is another. Marquis's fellow consultant for what became Ford's Behavioral Sciences Program, Hans Speier, is yet another. Considering a complete list of the ubiquitous Speier's multiple affiliations makes the futility of highlighting just one of them clear. A faculty member at the New School for Social Research, Speier had worked for the Office of War Information during World War II, then headed the RAND Corporation's Social Science Division in the 1950s while helping to build the Ford Foundation's social science programs. No single professional tag will do for the consummate "defense intellectual" Speier; he was a government official, a foundation staff member, *and* an academic.[70] Many others, like Herring, Marquis, and Miller, had multiple, long-standing affiliations to government, foundations, and the academy that made the rise of behavioralism in political science possible. Count up the many hats these men wore, and one begins to see just how dense the network of institutional linkages that bound together private foundations, the federal government, and the academy during the postwar period was.[71]

Once one focuses on this dense network of institutional linkages, trying to draw sharp distinctions between foundation and government funding seems like a fool's errand.[72] Even when government and foundation programs were formally distinct, they often supported the same types of research. This was not a coincidence; rather, many foundation officials, Carnegie's Frederick Osborn and Ford's H. Rowan Gaither among them, linked the programs of the foundations they helped to run to particular government agencies and initiatives. So important was federal government patronage to well-known university centers and institutes, like Michigan's Institute for Social Research (ISR), MIT's Center for International Studies (CENIS), and others, that they became virtual "outposts of government."[73] Not only did the personnel of seemingly distinct institutions overlap; their aims often did as well.

By presenting academic behavioralists as a group distinct from foundations and the state, Dahl also implies that behavioralism had a coherent identity before it became so prominent—and that therefore external funds did not constitute it but merely supported it. This assessment turns up in several recent accounts by historians of political science as well. For example, James Farr's account of the rise of behavioralism emphasizes its connections to several figures in early twentieth-century political science, especially the University of Chicago's Charles Merriam. Mid-twentieth-century behavioralism in political science, in Farr's view, grew out of the "Chicago school" Merriam began to build in the 1920s, a school further developed by Harold Lasswell, V. O. Key, Herbert Simon, Gabriel Almond, and David Easton. The importance Farr assigns to the 1920s beginnings of the Chicago school bolsters his interpretation of postwar behavioralism as more of a reorientation rather than a revolution within academic political science.

If one shifts one's focus to the SSRC, an institution present in but less central to Farr's account, these local academic roots seem less important. Farr notes in passing that Merriam's important role in the SSRC's first decades was crucial to his ability to "bring in funds to [realize his vision of interdisciplinary research] and to build a department of innovative like-minded political scientists." Putting it this way, however, suggests that the SSRC was mainly an institutional vehicle for Merriam's "vision"; this downplays the crucial role of the Rockefeller Foundation in building it. More than Merriam, the Rockefeller Foundation's Beardsley Ruml was the principal architect of the SSRC. Though both were "sophisticated conservatives" who believed improving the social sciences would help "preserve the underlying structure of society," it fell to Ruml to outline the problems that would fall under this new organization's broad umbrella and plan how the $20 million the trustees of the Rockefeller Foundation allotted to the cause should be spent. Behavioralism's ancestors, therefore, include not just Chicago's Merriam but also Rockefeller's Ruml and his vision of making the social sciences effective tools for elite governance.[74]

Despite emphasizing behavioralism's early twentieth-century academic roots, Farr still presents it as a largely postwar development, identifying 1951 to 1961 as its "crucial decade." Here again, Farr briefly mentions the part the SSRC's new Committee on Political Behavior played in fostering the academic work published during the early 1950s. As discussed in chapter 1, the 1949 meeting Herring organized in Ann Arbor, Michigan, where political scientists learned from already self-identified behavioral scientists in sociology and psychology, along with the later conferences and summer seminars organized by the CPB, helped to accelerate the development of behavioralism in political science. These were all part of the major investments that first Carnegie, followed by Ford and then Rockefeller, made in the SSRC as well as other institutions to develop the behavioral sciences.[75]

Unlike Farr, John Dryzek does not emphasize behavioralism's origins in the "Chicago school," nor does he impute as much coherence to its mid-twentieth-century manifestation as Farr does. Calling behavioralism a "revolution without enemies," Dryzek remarks that despite the polemical tone many behavioralists adopted, most stopped short of identifying who exactly had practiced the political science they claimed to have overthrown. If, as Dryzek concludes, behavioralism was much less a revolution than a "selective radicalization of existing disciplinary tendencies," what motivated it? New funding opportunities, Dryzek suggests, might have played a role: "Behavioralism led to more survey research being funded and published, an increase in the relative frequency of quantitative studies in the discipline's top journals, and a relative decline in work addressed to public policy. The emphasis on science facilitated access to new funding sources such as the National Science Foundation." Though Dryzek is appropriately skeptical of discipline-specific accounts of behavioralism, this formulation is still too political science–centric. Funding for quantitatively informed survey research *preceded* the advent of behavioralism in political science, as did thoroughly scientistic arguments for NSF funding for the social sciences.[76]

The story of survey research centers and their eventual importance to political science (which I touch upon in chapter 1 and tell at greater length in chapter 4 on political science at the University of Michigan) illustrates this point more specifically. More generally, as I have argued, the timing of major foundation programs promoting the behavioral sciences relative to the emergence of behavioralism in political science suggests that the latter took shape in response to and with the encouragement of foundation programs.

Compared to Farr and Dryzek's accounts, Albert Somit and Joseph Tanenhaus's widely cited history of American political science comes closer to acknowledging the constitutive role of external funds in the immediate postwar period. For one, they present behavioralism as a decidedly postwar phenomenon, attributing less significance to its connection to earlier approaches than Farr does. Anticipating Dryzek, they do not interpret behavioralism as a substantive rejection of other orientations within political science but as "a widespread dissatisfaction with the 'state of the discipline.'" In their view, the would-be revolutionaries' awareness of how little access to governmental patronage and influence they had compared to their colleagues in the other social sciences fueled their "dissatisfaction." From Somit and Tanenhaus's perspective, therefore, the powerful patrons who favored the behavioral sciences were not tapping into existing interests as much as they were sparking new ones: "Political scientists would have been less than human were they not tempted to manifest a deep interest in the kinds of research known to be favored by Ford Foundation staff and advisers." Further, they argue that foundation and federal government patrons' decided "partiality to behavioralism" moved even some political scientists "who had private reservations about behavioralism . . . to render at least lip service to the new creed." Whereas Drzyek leaves the question of what motivated the behavioral revolution hanging, Somit and Tanenhaus answer it by highlighting the importance of both foundation and government patronage as well as the SSRC's role as a conduit for it. In doing so, they come much closer than Farr and Dryzek to saying that such patronage helped constitute behavioralism.[77]

Along with Somit and Tanenhaus, Terence Ball offers another sustained discussion of the relationship between behavioralism and external funding. Ball notes that social scientists' involvement in the World War II bureaucracy prompted many to lobby for government funding for the social sciences after the war ended. To that end, social scientists tried a number of rhetorical gambits, like asserting a deep affinity between the natural and the social sciences or the fundamentally disinterested, nonideological character of the social sciences. These arguments were more successful in convincing many social scientists to think of their fields in new ways than in winning over skeptical legislators. In effect, the pursuit of external funding already began to constitute new orientations.[78]

More specifically, Ball notes that the "bountiful" funds that became available after the war led to the emergence of "the academic entrepreneur or grantsman skilled in the art of securing governmental and foundation funding." Those adept at directing external money into their projects and institutions often shared the aims of their patrons. This, Ball argues, had significant implications for what was becoming an increasingly behavioral political science.[79] As the early history of Michigan's Survey Research Center (discussed in chapters 1 and 4) illustrates, behavioral research was too large-scale and costly to be supported by university funds alone; external support from government or foundation funders was essential to it. While Ball concludes that funders did not explicitly "predetermine the specific outcomes or findings of scholarly research, they do, however, help to shape the kinds of questions that researchers ask and answer, and the kinds of inquiries and investigations deemed worthy of support and thereby, less directly, of reporting via conferences, symposia, publications and even, eventually, pedagogy." Behavioralists' aversion to investigating the "locus, distribution and uses of power," their readiness to investigate how to "counter" ideological opponents of the United States, and their often "celebratory" stance toward the US political system leads Ball to conclude that, however "unconsciously and indirectly," the approach was shaped by its patrons.[80] In contrast to the other historians of political science discussed here, Ball stretches his historical frame well beyond the bounds of the discipline to include the social sciences, their foundation and government patrons, and their universities. That wide a view is essential to capturing the major developments outside political science's disciplinary bounds that allowed the behavioral revolution to sweep through it so quickly.

Conclusion

When the Ford Foundation's Board of Trustees decided to terminate the Behavioral Sciences Program in 1957, its deeply disappointed director chided the board's members for abandoning what he called a "major [American] intellectual invention of the twentieth century." For as much as Berelson believed Ford might have still done in this area, he could nevertheless conclude, "The behavioral sciences are here to stay."[81] The planning of the mission of the Behavioral Sciences Program and the design of its major grants not only brought the behavioral sciences to life in American universities but also helped ensure their survival. From its earliest grants to foster the behavioral sciences in universities nationwide to the endowment of the Center for the Advanced Study of the Behavioral Sciences, the division's strongly interdisciplinary initiatives reshaped many disciplines, even those like political science that were not the main concern of its staff. As the Berkeley and Stanford cases I discussed illustrate, Ford's program made administrators and faculty see that research in sociology, anthropology, psychology, political science, and economics could win substantial external support—albeit for research initiatives that came from funders rather than from universities. In the very early 1950s, Ford's Marquis and Berelson had aspirations for the behavioral sciences they wanted to bring into being: they should be interdisciplinary in both theory and method, technically sophisticated, well-suited to practical applications, and focused on understanding and managing current sociopolitical problems.

Strikingly similar visions moved many political scientists to turn toward behavioral science in the 1950s and 1960s. Speaking in the same idiom, Dahl credited behavioralists with bringing back "some unity within the social sciences"; Eulau welcomed behavioral scientists' commitment to research geared toward "action or policy."[82] More broadly, to its advocates, the postwar advent of large-scale quantitative research supported by generous funding was one of the behavioral revolution's greatest achievements.

Though behavioralism was far from wholly novel, its adherents were right to stress how much it changed political science as well as how quickly it did so. As I have argued, however, explaining the rise of behavioralism as a move in an intramural academic debate misses the crucial role of the Ford Foundation's Behavioral Sciences Program in fueling the postwar rise of behavioralism in political science. Many persistently obscure features of political science's behavioral revolution—its indeterminate origins and aims, its rapid success—begin to clear up once Ford's program, along with those of the other foundations, are drawn into the analytical frame. That the behavioral revolution in political science began shortly after Ford launched its Behavioral Sciences Program was neither a coincidence nor a manifestation of a culture-wide "mood."[83] Instead, the unusually large and directive grants Ford made sparked and fueled the behavioral revolution.

CHAPTER THREE

A "Catholic" Approach

The Rockefeller Foundation's Diversified
Social Science Program

*Too often ideas alone are given credit as the moving force in history
without recognition of the crucial role of material resources in transforming
abstractions into realties. Of course ideas are indispensable, and so is
leadership, but without money the necessary impetus for innovation is often
lacking.*

—Merle Curti and Roderick Nash, *Philanthropy and the Shaping of American Higher Education*

*If the foundations are guilty of using their power to persuade the universities
to do things they would not otherwise have done, how serious a crime is it?*

—Robert S. Morison, "Foundations and Universities"

As I argued in chapter 1, the Carnegie Corporation's enthusiastic patronage built solid footing for the emerging behavioral sciences in the immediate postwar period. Internal Carnegie documents testify to the deep commitment of Frederick Osborn, Charles Dollard, Donald Young, and Pendleton Herring to strengthening the emerging behavioral sciences. Their choice not to publicize this commitment was a strategic one. For the reasons I discussed, Carnegie officers believed their support for the behavioral sciences would be more effective if these projects were publicly associated with the Social Science Research Council. Though done quietly, Carnegie directed much of its midcentury spending in the social sciences to this one particular area its officers thought most promising.

Carnegie officers and their allies in the SSRC thought hard about how to present the behavioral social science projects they supported as new and exciting but also unimpeachably legitimate at the same time. To that end, they focused not only on publicizing the projects themselves but also on constructing hospitable institutional infrastructures in universities and academic professional associations to support this kind of work.[1] Such infrastructure building projects, including the well-known ones launched by the Ford Foundation discussed in chapter 2, are crucial parts of how foundations produce knowledge. While grants to individuals or research teams for specific projects cannot do much on their own to root broader orientations in academic life, foundation support for academic departments, research centers, and professional groups can potentially reorient a wide swath of academic work for a long time. The prolonged battle Carnegie and Rockefeller officers fought over the leadership and orientation of the SSRC recounted in chapter 1 was as fierce as it was because both believed the success of their programs depended on the cooperation of the SSRC.[2]

In this chapter, I focus on a diverse array of the Rockefeller Foundation's infrastructure building projects in the social sciences. These included several project grants that bolstered new midcentury social scientific institutions, including the SSRC's Committee on Political Behavior and the University of Michigan's Survey Research Center. Other Rockefeller programs, however, pulled in the opposite direction, notably the effort to pressure a recalcitrant SSRC into administering a fellowship program in political theory and philosophy and the investments in expanding the field of political theory in several prominent political science departments. Although the cost of these projects fell far short of the sums disbursed by Ford's Behavioral Sciences Program, they expressed Rockefeller's long-term ambitions to reorient a sector of academic political science.

The Rockefeller Foundation's wide-ranging postwar programs in the social sciences supported several markedly different approaches to the study of politics. In addition to funding political theory and philosophy, Rockefeller supported public administration, the scientific study of political behavior, and international relations.[3] Though some Rockefeller officers challenged one or more of these diverse commitments in internal program and policy debates in the 1940s and early 1950s, the eclecticism that prevailed within the Division of Social Sciences (DSS) set Rockefeller social science programs apart from Carnegie and Ford's. And unlike Carnegie and Ford's concentrated investments in the new behavioral sciences, Rockefeller funding sought to reorient some established approaches in addition to underwriting newer ones. While so diversified a grant-making strategy suggests the "scatteration" of which midcentury foundations had been accused,

Rockefeller's influence on postwar political science was still considerable and by no means weaker than that of Carnegie and Ford. For one, its officers decided not to cede the field of behavioral social science to Ford and Carnegie.[4] At the same time, they launched a program focused on the field of political theory and philosophy—a field in which Carnegie and Ford showed little interest.

Joseph Willits, the director of Rockefeller's Division of Social Sciences from 1939 to 1954, was the principal architect of this strategy. An industrial economist, Willits began his career at the Rockefeller Foundation as director of Social Sciences in 1939. He had been a professor at the University of Pennsylvania since 1919 and later served as dean at Penn's Wharton School of Finance and Commerce (1933–1939) and president (1933–1936) and executive director (1936–1939) at the National Bureau of Economic Research.[5] In contrast to the Carnegie Corporation's targeted emphasis on the behavioral sciences, Willits repeatedly insisted that Rockefeller's postwar social science program be a "catholic" one. Early in Willits's tenure, it might have been prudent for him to take this approach, given the Rockefeller Foundation's President Raymond Fosdick's skeptical attitude toward the social sciences in the late 1930s and early 1940s.[6] Yet well beyond his first years as director and even into Dean Rusk's presidency, Willits remained steadily committed to a more diversified social science program. In the late 1940s, several junior division officers argued for more focus; one wanted a program that shored up the "public philosophy" of the United States, the other, a program targeting the sciences of social relations and human behavior.[7] Willits deflected both suggestions, opting again for a broader program. Scientific approaches to the study of society were to be a significant part of it, but so were other broad categories, like "applied work" and "moral philosophy and value." Willits meant such a wide-ranging program in the social sciences to do more than place hedged bets on conflicting approaches. Instead, he maintained that Rockefeller's support for diverse approaches was the best way to "contribute toward a . . . better integrated philosophy of the social sciences." Affirming these views up to the end of his tenure as director in 1954, Willits warned those in his division not to lapse into "an 'either-or' state of mind" of supporting either humanistic or scientific approaches exclusively. "We should be catholic enough in our grasp of the complexity of social issues," he continued, "to appreciate that each enriches the other; each is essential to the other."[8]

Even after Willits stepped down as its director in 1954, Rockefeller's social science program continued to be a "catholic" one. This is puzzling, especially since the next two directors of the Division of Social Sciences, Norman S. Buchanan (1955–1958) and Kenneth W. Thompson (1960–1961), had each been pointedly critical of the merits of one of the approaches the DSS supported: the behavioral sciences. Like Willits, Buchanan was an economist; his conception of the scientific study of society was emphatically not a behavioral one. Early in his tenure as head of the DSS, Buchanan pointed out that the Ford Foundation's overly restrictive understanding of the behavioral sciences did not include "economics and political science and international relations"; the behavioral sciences, therefore, should not be thought synonymous with "the social sciences in general."[9] Thompson had been a student of the University of Chicago's Hans Morgenthau, the theorist of international politics whose critique of the excesses of "scientism" Thompson largely shared.[10] Yet despite their antipathies to the behavioral sciences, neither Buchanan nor Thompson took serious steps toward curtailing their division's support for them. Why?

For one, Rockefeller's support for what its mid-1950s annual reports began to call "the social sciences as scientific disciplines" was much broader than sociology or social psychology, the core behavioral sciences of the day. A good deal of support in this category went instead to institutions doing research in economics or demography, the kinds of social science Buchanan especially endorsed. This emphasis was not new; funding projects and research institutes devoted to economics, like the National Bureau for Economic Research, had been a central element of Rockefeller's grants in the social sciences for decades.[11]

Also, any steps to curtail funding for the behavioral sciences may have seemed impolitic to both Buchanan and Thompson, given the presence of associate director Leland C. DeVinney on their staff. When DeVinney joined the division's staff in 1948, he was also part of a large group of social scientists headed by Samuel Stouffer completing the four-volume *Studies in Social Psychology during World War II.* As I discussed in chapter 1, this project was generously supported from start to finish by the Carnegie Corporation. More commonly known by the title of its first two volumes, *The American Soldier*, the book was widely praised for its sophisticated yet practical use of survey methods and attitude measures. Once on the division's staff, DeVinney argued that Rockefeller should support this type of social science dedicated to developing "better instruments and methods for the observation, description, measurement, and analysis of human behavior."[12]

DeVinney was the strongest advocate for the behavioral sciences in the division. Given his PhD in sociology and his long association with Stouffer both during and immediately after the war, DeVinney's principal interests were in sociology and psychology rather than political science.[13] Especially for the period with which I am concerned, DeVinney focused his efforts on the fields he knew best, encouraging Rockefeller to support well-established behavioral science programs staffed principally by sociologists and psychologists.[14] Nevertheless, DeVinney's advocacy for the behavioral sciences had considerable if unintended effects on political science. As I discuss in greater detail below, it was during DeVinney's short tenure as acting director of the division from mid-1954 to mid-1955 that Angus Campbell of the University of Michigan Survey Research Center (SRC) sent Rockefeller a proposal to fund a study of the 1956 election. DeVinney's support for his fellow social psychologist proved crucial; Campbell's team secured its first major Rockefeller Foundation grant to support their 1956 election study, a grant they may well have not won if Buchanan or Thompson had been heading the division. In retrospect, such election studies appear to have been destined for success, given the prominence of survey research in late twentieth-century political science. Contemporaneous foundation documents, however, tell another story—a story in which luck and serendipity play prominent roles.

Rockefeller's midcentury social science program, considerably more diversified than Carnegie's or Ford's, appeared to be designed to pull political science in opposing directions. For the remainder of this chapter, I discuss several Rockefeller grants and fellowship programs that supported distinct modes of political knowledge that were all vying for legitimacy in mid-twentieth-century political science. Several of these grants appeared tailored to particular projects, like V. O. Key's *Southern Politics* or Angus Campbell et al.'s *The American Voter*. Support for these two projects at least indirectly also bolstered the newer institutions with which their authors were associated: the SSRC's Committee on Political Behavior, in Key's case, and the Michigan Survey Research Center, in Campbell's. By contrast, the Legal and Political Philosophy (LAPP) program was designed to repurpose an older field some foundation staff believed they and other patrons had neglected. LAPP aimed not just to aid individuals working in the field of political theory and philosophy but also to build a more hospitable institutional environment for work in this field as well as to enlist some of its scholars in

Cold War political projects. To these ends, LAPP offered fellowships for individual projects and recruited committees of prominent scholars to make these awards. LAPP also made substantial long-term grants to departments to support faculty research in theory and political philosophy and, in its final phase, linked the study of Western political ideals to Rockefeller initiatives to shape universities overseas. Taken together, the most influential Rockefeller grants in political science supported an array of approaches to political knowledge that, already in the 1950s, many in the discipline were beginning to see not just as different but as incompatible.

Support for V. O. Key's *Southern Politics*

Rockefeller's Division of Social Sciences gradually moved toward supporting behavioral political science not only because of DeVinney's indirect endorsement but also on the strength of its officers' long-standing relationship with the political scientist V. O. Key. Though often portrayed as an important figure in the rise of behavioralism, Key's role in mid-twentieth-century political science is more of a transitional one. Key's ties to Rockefeller vividly illustrate several broad trends in midcentury political science: the waning of public administration and the rise of behavioralism in the study of American politics, as well as debates over the implications of quantitative analyses of political life and the importance of theory in the discipline. Both because of the time during which Key was professionally active and because of the many roles he assumed, archived records concerning Key's ties to Rockefeller offer an excellent window on how those caught up in these trends made sense of them. Strikingly, Key's growing interest in and respect for behavioralism moved even the most skeptical Rockefeller officers to temper their criticisms of studies of political behavior. The intellectual explorations of so professionally distinguished and active a grantee ultimately influenced the attitudes of his patron.

Like many people who received advanced degrees in political science in the early decades of the twentieth century, Key had a strong grounding in public administration; his earliest published work fell squarely in that field. And although Key analyzed quantitative data, like many others who came to be identified as behavioralists, most of his best-known work relied on aggregate data, like voting returns and census data, rather than individuals' responses to opinion surveys. Reliance on electoral and demographic data, though not common in mid-twentieth-century political science, was more familiar than the construction and analysis of surveys.[15] For these reasons, I believe it was possible for social science officers at the Rockefeller Foundation to support Key without initially seeing that support as a strong endorsement of behavioralism. To flesh out these points, I discuss two crucial grants Rockefeller made to Key. The first supported the research and writing of *Southern Politics*; the second, the collection and analysis of decades of statistics on elections in states outside the South.[16]

The project that became Key's *Southern Politics* began as a proposal not from Key himself but from the director of the University of Alabama's Bureau of Public Administration, Roscoe Martin. When Martin's plans for a bureau-sponsored study of the poll tax ran aground, he approached Willits to discuss the possibility of Rockefeller funding for a broader study of the electoral process in the South. Bureaus of public administration were research organizations with a circumscribed charge: to do research in the interest of the public officials and citizens of the state or municipality to which they were attached.[17] Rockefeller made the initial grant to the Alabama bureau in early 1946; Roger F. Evans, the officer reviewing grants in public administration at the time, was also responsible for overseeing its progress. At least initially, then, the project Martin proposed was regarded as a project in public administration, an area Rockefeller had long supported, not a self-consciously novel foray into behavioral science.[18]

Once Key agreed to lead the study, he too did not emphasize the novelty of what he wished to do; instead, he said he meant to write a book addressed to a wide audience rather than just political scientists. Key's *Southern Politics* was well-received by both popular and academic reviewers. The popular press praised its "humane" and "dispassionate" analysis of the deep flaws that marred electoral politics in the southern states, while political scientists heralded it as an excellent model for the scientific study of political behavior.[19] In addition to inspiring many of the early makers of the behavioral revolution, Key's book fulfilled the hopes of the project's creator, Roscoe Martin—hopes that had more to do with changing the politics of the South than with reorienting the theory and methods that prevailed in midcentury political science.

Several years later, in 1951, Key approached the Rockefeller Foundation directly with a project of his own design to collect and analyze state election statistics. By this time, the SSRC's Committee on Political Behavior had come into being and Key was serving as its chair.[20] If Key had not appeared to be an advocate for behavioralism to Rockefeller officials in the late 1940s, his association with this new approach was impossible to miss now. How, then, did Rockefeller social science officers evaluate the merits of the research Key was now proposing?

The 1951 grant action highlighted how Key's new project was continuous with the work he had done in *Southern Politics*; in many ways, it was.[21] In the new project, Key proposed to collect and analyze fifty years of electoral data for nineteen states outside the South, using approaches similar to those of his 1949 book. Such a systematic collection of electoral data over time, Key believed, offered the best basis for answers to a range of questions about political parties, voter participation, and political machines. Notably, Key contrasted the merits of the data he proposed to collect with the shortcomings of nationwide surveys of voters during a presidential election year. He expressed his "grave doubts" about the merits of conclusions based solely on such surveys, arguing that "an analysis of many contrasting situations from state politics gives a much better base for understanding than does the usual reliance solely on presidential data."[22] Key's ideas about the best data for the study of political behavior differed considerably from those of prominent survey researchers, like Angus Campbell. In the early 1950s, political scientists and public administrators were most likely more familiar with Key's ideas than Campbell's.

Nevertheless, several Rockefeller officers found the weight Key placed on collecting and analyzing electoral data unsettling enough to ask Key to justify it. In the early months of 1951, after he had already submitted several drafts of the project but before the grant was made, Key noted that Willits had told him that some members of his staff were "a little worried by my emphasis on quantification." Key sought to assuage these concerns by pointing out that a good part of the analysis in *Southern Politics* had relied on in-depth interviews with public figures and by noting that he thought one should "regard statistical methods in political research more as a means of description and of thinking than as a means of precise measurement."[23] Apparently, the way Key addressed these concerns was convincing. Over the next few years, several members of the division's staff especially critical of the trend toward "scientism" in political science praised Key's open-mindedness on the subject. For example, Herbert Deane, a consultant for Rockefeller's legal and political philosophy program, commented approvingly that Key thought there was "plenty of room [in political science] for the 'poets' as well as the 'scientists.'" And despite Thompson's open skepticism about the behavioral sciences, he apparently wanted Key to join the advisory committee overseeing his division's new legal and political philosophy program. Key, a member of the SSRC's Committee on Political Behavior and its former chair, accepted.[24]

Support for Michigan's Survey Research Center (SRC): The 1956 and 1960 Election Studies

Besides Key's *Southern Politics*, there are few midcentury works that continue to be as celebrated and widely cited by political scientists as Campbell, Converse, Miller, and Stokes's *The American Voter*.[25] This work was the product of a formidable research infrastructure being built at Michigan with a mix of foundation and government funds. The approaches and institutions associated with Michigan political science have played so prominent a part in the discipline for the past sixty years that they now have an aura of inevitability about them—something I discuss in more detail in chapter 4 on political science at the University of Michigan. But in the 1950s, the work that Campbell and his fellow SRC researchers were doing was not yet wholly legitimate among academic social scientists. Though the Carnegie Corporation had supported the 1952 election study by a grant to the SSRC's Committee on Political Behavior (discussed in chapter 1), Campbell and his team knew they could not expect Carnegie to fund their planned 1956 study. Rockefeller support was the next option; during the short time that DeVinney was Rockefeller's acting director of the Division of Social Sciences, he gave Campbell's request a sympathetic hearing. His endorsement of Campbell's work, however, was not widely shared. The sharply critical stances other DSS officers took toward the behavioral sciences are vividly evident in the grant file devoted to the Michigan SRC's study of the 1956 presidential election.[26]

Rockefeller ultimately did provide significant support for Campbell's election studies—the 1956 grant of $110,000 for three years was followed by a $206,800 grant in 1960 for four more. Though substantial, these grants were not early investments in new lines of research. By the mid-1950s, researchers at Michigan's SRC had already completed several studies of voting behavior as well as numerous studies of consumer behavior and the attitudes of employees in large firms. A range of patrons had funded SRC projects, including Carnegie, the Office of Naval Research, the Federal Reserve

Board, and IBM.[27] Rockefeller too had made several earlier grants to the SRC for economic research and what might now be called organizational psychology. These grants supplemented existing SRC contracts with federal agencies and corporations, allowing SRC researchers to work with the data they had collected to improve their survey and data analysis techniques.[28] By contrast, their support for Campbell's research on voting behavior came a few years later and with some reservations.

Whether Campbell first broached the idea of Rockefeller support for his 1956 study or whether DeVinney invited him to do so is not clear. Some of the earliest items in the grant file, however, show Campbell making his case for support directly to his fellow social psychologist, DeVinney, when DeVinney was serving as acting director of the Division of Social Sciences from mid-1954 to mid-1955. When Campbell submitted the final proposal around a month later, he thanked DeVinney not only for suggesting revisions to an earlier draft but also for having "seen fit to take our proposal to the higher councils of the Foundation." Campbell not only knew DeVinney well but also felt sure DeVinney understood and supported the work he proposed to do.[29]

Once the economist Norman Buchanan became the new permanent director of the DSS in the summer of 1955, however, he initially took a much more skeptical view of the proposed project. Feeling that Campbell's proposal lacked a compelling justification, Buchanan wrote to DeVinney: "The immediate case for this study seems to be that there is an election in 1956. Are we to expect, then, a study in 1960, 1964, *ad infinitum*?" Further, Buchanan questioned whether Campbell and his associates believed another survey would help them "understand the political process" or whether their goal was merely "the refinement of survey techniques."[30] Although Campbell had argued explicitly in his 1955 proposal that collecting cumulative data on voting behavior in successive elections was essential to explaining trends and changes in political behavior, Buchanan apparently did not find these arguments compelling. Still, despite Buchanan's reservations, Rockefeller funded Campbell's proposal.

Buchanan's concerns eased somewhat when he assessed Campbell's work along with that of the Institute for Social Research (ISR) as a whole some two years later. He continued to worry, however, that the frenetic pace of work at ISR prevented scholars from thinking about how their work might contribute to social-scientific theory. ISR's staff, Buchanan noted, was "kept panting to find new things to do to pay the bills" because the University of

Michigan provided only 10 percent of their budget—the rest came from grants or contract research.[31]

Assistant Director Thompson was also openly skeptical of Campbell's project; records of his skepticism do not appear in the grant file until 1957, however, well after Rockefeller had made the first grant. Once Thompson began to weigh in on the project, he made his skepticism abundantly clear. First, he asked at least eleven political scientists to assess the contributions of Campbell's work to political science and political theory as well as whether they believed his work had predictive power. Few of the responses included in the file are unqualifiedly positive; the rest are lukewarm or critical.[32] Thompson and DeVinney then met with Campbell to communicate the gist of these assessments to him and to give him a chance to respond. Notes by both officers on this meeting with Campbell begin with a long list of challenges they wanted Campbell to address; many expressed Thompson's doubts about the merits of behavioral science for the study of politics rather than DeVinney's support. Both note that they asked Campbell to discuss what about his work was specifically interesting to political scientists, given its strong emphasis on "psychological variables." They also challenge Campbell to justify an assumption implicit in his emphasis on cumulative data—namely, that there are "underlying stable factors" that can explain political behavior over time, rather than "continually changing interests and motives . . . in response to continually changing historical events." In their summary of Campbell's responses to these and other criticisms, they remark that Campbell was "surprised and disappointed at the implication that a significant number of political scientists do not find this work interesting and useful."[33] Still, as with Buchanan's initial reservations, Thompson's criticism-gathering project did not undermine Rockefeller support for Campbell's work.

No aura of inevitability surrounds survey research on political attitudes in these documents. Instead, the records of Rockefeller support for the SRC's election studies discussed above make clear that survey research projects, so central to late twentieth-century political science, were far from widely accepted in the discipline in the 1950s. Nor was their claim to being legitimate social science yet secure; after all, the legitimacy of the behavioral sciences in general was not yet so. Without his professional connections to a highly placed Rockefeller Foundation officer and some lucky timing, Campbell probably would not have been able to obtain Rockefeller support for the SRC's study of the 1956 election—even despite Carnegie's support for the 1952 study. That Rockefeller opted to support these studies at all seems serendipitous. Once given, however, that support proved crucial to establishing the legitimacy of survey research as an approach to the study of politics.

The Legal and Political Philosophy (LAPP) Program

The aforementioned Rockefeller project grants helped bring two of the most celebrated scholarly works in political science of the mid-twentieth-century into being. From Rockefeller's perspective at the time, however, these grants were commitments to particular scholars for specific projects rather than parts of a larger program designed to transform political science. One of Rockefeller's social science division programs, however, did have such transformative ambitions: the program in Legal and Political Philosophy (LAPP). John B. Stewart, a political theorist who served as a consultant to the program, recalled learning that the idea for the program came from John Foster Dulles during his tenure as the chair of the foundation's Board of Trustees. As Stewart remembered it, Dulles's rationale was an explicitly ideological one: he believed Rockefeller should invest in scholarly work that explained and defended "the ideas behind the institutions and legal systems of Western society" to counter the growing appeal of Marxism during the Cold War.[34]

Inspired in broad outlines by Dulles and later supported by the foundation's president Dean Rusk, the particulars of the early 1950s LAPP program were the work of Herbert A. Deane and John B. Stewart. Both Deane and Stewart were young Columbia University political theorists serving as consultants to the Rockefeller Foundation; both were central to formulating policy for the new program with only occasional amendment from division director Willits.[35] In 1955, when he became assistant director, Thompson assumed chief responsibility for LAPP and continued to supervise the program for the remainder of its life.[36] Under Thompson's direction, the program developed another emphasis, linking political theory to foreign policy-making and international politics.

A conference convened in 1952 brought together foundation officers and a number of academics to brainstorm about what LAPP's purpose should be. Some, expressing impatience with what they saw as "pedestrian and purely descriptive" qualities of current work in the field, wanted the program to spur political theorists to address contemporary problems and "establishment of closer relations" with government officials. Others wanted the program to focus scholarly attention on the relation between theory and empirical research.[37] Despite these differences, nearly all participants agreed with Louis Hartz's assessment that compared to other more generously funded fields in the discipline, political theory and philosophy were underfunded and withering.[38]

After the conference ended, DSS staff remained at odds about how LAPP ought to fit into the foundation's broader social science program. On the one hand, DeVinney objected to launching a program designed to support only theorists and philosophers.[39] Deane took the opposite view, arguing that such a program was precisely what Rockefeller needed to counter what he thought were dangerous trends in social science. In one of his first major policy memos about the proposed program, Deane warned of the cultural damage he believed the continued neglect of "'insight,' 'wisdom' or 'theory' in its original sense" might do. Noting that some social scientists shared his concern that specialized training programs focused on social scientific technique were making deep study of philosophic traditions obsolete, Deane scolded them for being "unaware that they and their imitators bear any share of the responsibility for the rise of this new barbarism."[40] Division head Willits then stepped into this dispute, taking Deane to task for criticizing social science so harshly. Chastened, Deane replied he had not "intended to suggest that RF should abandon or curtail its efforts to promote the development of scientific studies of human behavior and social relations." He also accepted that even if Rockefeller's board gave LAPP the green light, only 10 percent of the division's budget would be allocated to it, compared to the 35 percent for "developing a science of social behavior."[41] While Deane continued to insist that a program devoted to legal and political philosophy could be an effective counter to the most dangerous strains in social science, he also tried another tack more congenial to Willits's views: "The dichotomy–science vs. philosophy–is, in my opinion, sterile, vicious, and outmoded. . . . In the most highly developed of the natural sciences, physics, the opposition between theory and research, concept and fact, has virtually disappeared." Perhaps, Deane ventured, LAPP might enhance the mutual dependence of theoretical and empirical work.[42]

These two justifications for LAPP—as a counterweight to social science or an exploration of the complementarity of theory and empirical research—were hardly compatible. Yet Rockefeller proceeded to fund the new program without ironing out these and other wrinkles. Shortly before the foundation's board approved establishing LAPP, Willits, in a memo to President Rusk, acknowledged that deep differences over its "goals and policies and program" persisted, but he insisted that these were all "evidence of wholesome vigor.... Creative conflict is our best hope." Making his case for the program in less combative terms than Deane had used, Willits stressed that while legal and political philosophy could address issues that social science could not, the two ought to be seen not as "competitive . . . but as complementary."[43] By the time he was preparing to resign from his position as consultant, Deane had gravitated toward this way of speaking about the relationship between LAPP and the social sciences as well, if only as a way to defuse tensions.[44]

These sorts of disagreements became less prominent when several officers reasserted the Cold War ideological aims first broached by Dulles. In 1955 Rusk, Thompson, and Stewart all explicitly endorsed this new focus. Rusk was the first to do so when he expressed concern about the widespread appeal of Communism to European intellectuals at a meeting of the program's Advisory Committee. Observing that few applicants to LAPP had proposed projects to address this problem thus far, Rusk wondered if this was because the foundations had acquired too much of an "empirical reputation."[45] Thompson, who had just begun to serve as the division's assistant director, agreed. He then ventured that because theorists were not focusing on a "democratic answer to Marxism," this might also be contributing to the decline of political theory in the United States. Along these lines, Thompson argued that LAPP should be broadened to include work on "the theoretical aspects of international relations" and analyses of contemporary Marxist movements.[46] Stewart, now the principal consultant for LAPP, also endorsed this ideological recasting and proposed that Rockefeller sponsor a multiauthored manifesto in defense of democracy for wide distribution.[47] This new emphasis solidified the following year when Rusk asked the Advisory Committee to think about how to align LAPP with the Board of Trustees' recent decision to allot a large portion of the foundation's budget to projects in underdeveloped countries.[48] This new ideological focus had the most profound effect on the institutional LAPP grant made to the University of California, Berkeley and remained one of the program's aims for the remainder of its life.

Over the course of its life, foundation officers and Advisory Committee members shaped different phases of LAPP to promote several distinct modes of knowledge: a humanistic political knowledge juxtaposed to empirical social science followed by an ideologically inflected theoretical knowledge to equip a new cadre of academic experts for Cold War political roles. Different though the ambitions behind promoting these modes of knowledge were, Rockefeller officers and their academic advisors found the field of political theory and philosophy to be the right staging ground for all of them. Humanistic study of the history of political thought was a familiar current in the field that even those who felt it needed refurbishing did not wish to abandon. At the same time, many felt the field needed to move toward more contemporary, relevant, politically engaged theoretical work. Political theory and philosophy had well-staked claims to territory in mid-twentieth-century political science. It is therefore not surprising that a wide variety of plans for remaking the discipline and making it more attractive to government patrons began by attempting to redesign the place and purpose of this field.

The LAPP Fellowship Programs

From 1953 to 1962 the Rockefeller Foundation made a number of grants to individual scholars under the auspices of LAPP. Awards to established scholars were made directly by the foundation; beginning in 1955, most awards made to graduate students and recent PhDs were made by the SSRC but funded by Rockefeller.

Recipients of LAPP grants to established scholars pursued a great diversity of approaches; many fell well outside the bounds of what would be considered political theory today. The projects supported included mathematical models of political choice (Gordon Tullock), a theory of international affairs (Henry Kissinger), studies of the ancient roots of modern Western values (Allan Bloom and Leo Strauss), a reconsideration of theories of public administration (Herbert Storing), an empirical study of the psychology of political extremism (Herbert McClosky), and "a basic study of the theory of politics" (Hannah Arendt).[49] This broad and inclusive conception of political theory was not merely a quirk of this particular foundation program; instead, it captured some of the breadth and formless fluidity of how political theory was understood and practiced in the 1950s.

The expansive conception of political theory that Thompson promoted once he became responsible for LAPP tapped into existing ambitions to redefine and expand the bounds of the field.[50] For instance, political scientists made numerous attempts to connect theoretical or philosophical work on politics and the empirical social sciences in the 1950s and early 1960s. Herbert McClosky's LAPP-funded project on the psychology of political extremism is a good example of such an attempt. McClosky's approach depended heavily on developing and administering psychometric tests; nonetheless, he argued that he saw himself working on "questions important for political theory." No one at the Rockefeller Foundation ruled his proposal out of LAPP's bounds. When Thompson asked Robert Dahl, then chair of Yale's political science department, to assess the merits of McClosky's proposal, Dahl responded:

> His [McClosky's] union of the basic concerns of traditional political theory with modern empirical techniques may well be unique in the field; certainly it is not common. It is a union that I have for sometime believed should be strongly encouraged and indeed I find it very difficult to see any future for political science as a key discipline without the construction of a bridge between political theory and modern social science—a bridge, moreover, that will carry vast traffic.[51]

Though Dahl praised McClosky's work for being "unique," his description of it fit the bridge-building enterprises he himself as well as other notable figures in the discipline, like David Easton, had undertaken.

Such attempts to redefine political theory by linking it more closely with empirical social science provoked considerable conflict with the SSRC during the 1950s and 1960s. Political theory's place within the larger discipline of political science was a matter of contention as well. Aware of these tensions, the academics assembled to design the standards that would govern LAPP asked, should political theory even belong to the social sciences in the first place? And, depending on one's answer to this question, what ought to be the relationship between political theory and empirical or behavioral social science? Several people within Rockefeller's Division of Social Sciences, including Willits, anticipated conflict: "When the Advisory Committee [for LAPP] met in June [1953] there was great dissent from having the SSRC administer fellowships in this area because the SSRC has shown a decided lack of sympathy in helping men in these fields of inquiry." Stewart, who was just beginning his service as a consultant for LAPP, worried: "If the Foundation goes to the SSRC and says, 'Here is so much money,' won't you, in effect, be asking them to change their view of the social sciences to accommodate the dispensing of this money. This might well be a very presumptious [sic] step for the Foundation to take." Acknowledging that he did not expect the SSRC to be enthusiastic about administering this phase of LAPP, Willits responded strategically: "There are also advantages to the theory of infiltration. There might be an advantage in pushing the SSRC and thus through infiltration an interest might be established in this area of study and research at the SSRC."[52]

The statement that accompanied the first appropriation Rockefeller made to the SSRC for the LAPP fellowship program confronted the resistance the foundation expected there head on. "Concern has been expressed by many persons, chiefly laymen, but also academicians, at the consistent spread of the assumption that the scientific study of social phenomena is enough, and at the increasing neglect by our generation of those political values on which our society was founded, attention to which is necessary if wisdom is to be realized."[53] Not surprisingly, Stewart reported a few months later that he had "learned informally that some SSRC staff members and some directors" were not happy about being saddled with this program. What sense did it make for an organization dedicated to social science to administer a program that questioned its fundamental purpose? "Some SSRC staff members and some directors were opposed to acceptance of the Foundation grant, on the grounds that philosophy and social science research were quite different things."[54] Given the strength of these rumored objections, Stewart braced himself to be bombarded with them when he attended a meeting of the SSRC's board in September 1954.

When the SSRC-appointed Advisory Committee first met in November 1954, its first task was "to obtain a sense of the standards or criteria which should provide guidance in the administration of this program." This prompted an extended discussion of the kinds of political theory the committee wished to support. Unusually, Rockefeller's archives contain two accounts of this meeting. The first account listed three distinct understandings of political theory advanced at the meeting: "(1) the history of ideas; (2) political philosophy . . . , and (3) the formulation of hypotheses about behavior which could be tested empirically." The unnamed author of this account then went on to soften the distinctions between these ideas, noting that there was enough "overlapping" between them "that it would be undesirable to assert their separateness."[55] This assessment deliberately strove to tamp down conflict by throwing the doors open to markedly different approaches to political theory.

Rockefeller Foundation consultant Stewart's account of the deliberations of this committee, however, tells a different story. Unlike the unnamed author of the first account, who did not attribute specific comments to particular people, Stewart's version mentions the participants who made particular statements. Doing so allowed Stewart to highlight disagreements within the group rather than the points on which it reached consensus.[56]

For instance, in Stewart's account, several participants express impatience with proposals to define political theory broadly. If the group's charge was to select LAPP fellowship recipients, how would a broad definition of political theory help them rule any applicant out? Along these lines, Stewart summarizes an exasperated Frederick Watkins of Yale remarking, "If behaviorism is political theory, then all political scientists are political theorists" (p. 2). The discussion then turns to what aspects of political theory the group ought to favor. On the one hand, Stewart paraphrases David Easton of Chicago, arguing, "There are two trends that can be observed in contemporary political and social science. There is, on the one hand, a return to the old tradition that demands intensive analysis of early writers. There is, on the other, a keen interest in showing the relationship of contemporary political theorizing and political behavior. Both are important, but the second is more important" (p. 3). Several other participants, however, vigorously oppose Easton's view. Norman Jacobson of UC Berkeley objects to it being "assumed that all the integration is to take place by political theorists going to behavioral science" (p. 3). Herbert Deane, the former consultant for LAPP and now at Columbia, chimes in, "Is there not already enough emphasis on the behavioral? Why should this program be made at least quasi-behavioral?" (p. 4).

At the end of Stewart's notes, he shows this disagreement has still not been resolved. Easton insists once more, "The important thing to remember is that our political theorists ought to get out in the field of behavior and test the validity of their theories" (p. 7). Stewart rejoins, "You [Easton] imply that the behavioral scientists are not already doing this work of formulating hypotheses, collecting relevant data, and checking the hypotheses against the data to discover whether the hypotheses can be considered as laws. If they are not doing this, then what are they doing?" (p. 7). Shortly after recording his exchange with Easton, Stewart notes the close of the meeting, underscoring that deep differences about which approaches to political theory the group ought to support had not been resolved.

Table 3.1 SSRC LAPP Awards by Category, 1955–1963

1. Legal theory and public law	12
2. Conceptual analyses	10
3. Studies of one thinker or philosophical movement (a. pre–twentieth century; b. twentieth century)	21a; 6b
4. Studies of American or European social scientists or schools of social science	8
5. Studies of American or world politics (a. pre–twentieth century; b. twentieth century)	2a; 10b
6. International relations theory	3
7. Application of mathematical techniques	2
Studies included in more than one category	18

Source: "Committee on Political Theory and Legal Philosophy Fellowships, Report on the Fellowship Program, 1954–55—1962–63," 14 pp., Folder 2472, Box 255, series 200E, R.G. 1.2, Rockefeller Foundation Archives, Rockefeller Archive Center.

The disagreements that marked this initial meeting of the SSRC's Advisory Committee for LAPP remained throughout the eight-year life of the program. For instance, a 1955 SSRC brochure announcing its fellowship programs presented the areas covered by the new LAPP fellowships in terms so broad that none of the approaches to political theory discussed at the 1954 conference were excluded.[57] More importantly, from 1955 through 1963, the program funded studies representing a wide variety of approaches to political and legal theory (Table 3.1). Despite some committee members' criticisms of historical studies of political thought, fellowships for such studies still made up at least one-third and close to one-half of all fellowships awarded. At the same time, fellowships were also awarded for studies of contemporary political issues, American or European social science, legal theory, theories of international relations, and application of mathematical techniques to political issues.

While there was lively disagreement about what ought to count as "political theory" and what varieties of it merited the most support, those who advocated narrower definitions never succeeded in making them the program's ruling standard. LAPP may have fulfilled its architects' aim to boost the academic "prestige" of political theory and philosophy.[58] In doing so, however, it did not dampen conflicts over what the substance and boundaries of the field should be. Given these conflicts, eclectic conceptions of the field sounded more like pleas for a temporary truce than coherent attempts to expand the boundaries of political theory. Yet in the program's final phase, Assistant Director Thompson came close to making such an attempt when he argued for substantial institutional grants to support building three departments' capacities in political theory.

LAPP Institutional Grants

In addition to the LAPP fellowship programs, Rockefeller made institutional LAPP grants to the political science or government departments at Harvard, Columbia, and UC Berkeley.[59] The grants to Berkeley and Columbia shared the same purpose: "research in political theory and the theoretical aspects of international relations." For Harvard, the purpose was "research on the inter-relations of political theory and institutions." Of the three, only UC Berkeley received a second grant in 1961. The focus of the 1961 grant, however, shifted markedly toward funding teaching and research at "selected universities of Africa, Asia and Latin America"; political theory was much less prominent in it.[60] Whatever ambitions Rockefeller officers may have had for the field of political theory in the 1950s, by the early 1960s they were assigning it considerably less importance. These grants, then, provided a brief but still significant opportunity to redefine and expand political theory's place in the discipline. In what follows, I analyze the grants made to Berkeley's political science department. I take up the consequences of these grants for the Berkeley department at greater length in chapter 5.

Before the first grant for political theory and "theoretical aspects of international relations" was formally made to the political science department at UC Berkeley, people at both the Rockefeller Foundation and the Berkeley department itself were skeptical that its aims could be realized. Rusk worried that political science at Berkeley, like the entire university itself, was so "sprawling and disjointed" that not even a substantial, long-term grant could give it direction. Robert Scalapino and Norman Jacobson, members of the Berkeley department serving on LAPP advisory committees, voiced similar concerns. Each warned that unless there were explicit standards for disbursing the grant, "its boundaries might be too liberally construed," or, worse, it might become "an invitation to people in the department to come up with boondoggles."[61]

Once the grant was approved, a small committee of Berkeley faculty tried to address these concerns by drafting a list of instructions for disbursing funds. Nevertheless, the instructions developed by this committee were far from restrictive. "International relations" was defined broadly enough to include comparative politics; the definition of "political theory" was spacious as well: "political theory means any study of a political philosopher or of a concept or idea which possesses political relevance and in which the emphasis is analytical and evaluative rather than biographical or descriptive."[62] These definitions ruled far more in than out; nevertheless, some of the projects funded by the first grant clearly fell outside these expansive bounds. Some were simply left unspecified, as in the case of one faculty member awarded a grant "to 'think through' the mass of social problems he has been compelled to deal with during the past 17 years." In other cases, there were only the most tenuous connections between projects and the substance of the grant.[63] Most of the projects that did fall within the wide bounds set by the committee did not cluster around any discernible foci. Instead, they sprawled, as Rusk had worried they would.

Throughout the five-year life of this first grant, most of the exchanges between the department and the Rockefeller Foundation focused on the department's annual progress reports. But in the early months of 1961, less than a year before the grant was scheduled to come to a close, Thompson made clear that it would be renewed only if directly connected to Rockefeller's new commitment to aiding universities in "underdeveloped areas," particularly in Africa.[64] The second grant (approved in October 1961) made this shift in priorities explicit; the amount of money awarded to the department was the same ($200,000 over five years). Further, the grant action specified that of the $40,000 allocated for each year, $30,000 be reserved "for scholars . . . toward research, teaching, and travel costs incurred in assignments to developing universities in Latin America, Africa, and Asia." The remaining $10,000 would be awarded for "research at Berkeley by scholars . . . participating in the proposed new faculty seminars."[65] Although a seminar in political theory was to be one of the two proposed faculty seminars, the center of gravity in this grant had clearly shifted away from political theory, broadly defined, to funding research and teaching in the developing world.

The new chair of the department, Robert Scalapino, struggled at first to find faculty who would commit to teaching abroad. Indeed, Scalapino reported that upon polling the faculty, "no permanent member of the staff is willing to go abroad" for the academic year 1962–1963. Ultimately, the department sent a recent PhD, James Sewell, to spend the year at University College of Rhodesia and Nyasaland. Still, some Rockefeller staff expressed frustration with what they saw as the department's "minimum effort" to live up to the spirit of the new grant; between themselves, they wondered whether Scalapino "is . . . supplying men of lesser experience *because* he believes that is what Africa needs or deserves?"[66]

By 1963, these difficulties dissipated quickly. Scalapino reported that three persons, two of them permanent faculty, were scheduled to take up positions in Africa and Malaya in the fall, adding grandly, "The sun never sets on the Political Science Department of the University of California!"[67] Scalapino's tone about the new grant remained upbeat in his progress report to the foundation for 1963, where he noted that the portion of the grant devoted to teaching abroad "has proven to be more successful than we dared to hope and it is now fully accepted by our Department, something which was not true at the outset."[68] Berkeley continued to send faculty and advanced graduate students abroad throughout the term covered by the second grant, although never in great numbers.

Of the faculty seminars funded by this grant, the one devoted to comparative politics met the most frequently and was highly praised; a seminar in political theory was also organized, but it met only a few times in the fall of 1963.[69] Overall, the department continued to adjust its activities to fit the broad outlines of the Rockefeller Foundation's new priorities—so much so that when the second grant was ending in 1966, the department submitted a proposal for the next five years for "a program to help develop and strengthen Political Science Departments in Rockefeller Foundation-supported universities abroad." This proposal made no specific mention of funding political theory; most of the funds requested were earmarked for research and travel abroad, the rest for "support of research by junior members of the Department." Though it was not funded, this grant proposal shows how far both the department and the foundation had traveled from the purpose affirmed in 1956 of strengthening Berkeley's contributions to political theory and the theoretical aspects of international relations.[70]

Rockefeller's program in Legal and Political Philosophy ran simultaneously on two tracks for most of its life. On the one hand, some of those responsible for the LAPP fellowship programs wanted to support humanistic modes of knowledge to counter the recent rise of behavioral social science. This proved a difficult position to maintain, given that the program was from start to finish part of Rockefeller's social sciences division and relied on the SSRC to administer one of its phases. Those who attempted to narrow or redirect the field onto this track never succeeded in entirely excluding what they saw as endangering it. Eclectic working definitions of political theory were the result, with many approaches allowed in but almost nothing ruled out. Still, LAPP funded hundreds of projects, some of which—like the early work of John Rawls leading up to *A Theory of Justice*, Hannah Arendt's *The Human Condition*, and Sheldon Wolin's *Politics and Vision*—undeniably reinvigorated political theory and philosophy in the late twentieth century.[71] Even for those who thought it misguided, LAPP's persistent eclecticism gave those who considered themselves political theorists one of their earliest forums in which to think about their place in the discipline and their relationship to social science. These issues became more urgent and more political in the mid-1960s.

The institutional grant to UC Berkeley's political science department, however, was the fullest expression of LAPP's second more overtly ideological track that attempted to press political theory and political science into Cold War service. A number of Rockefeller's most powerful officials laid out these more ideological aims in broad strokes. Thompson, however, did the most to realize them, especially in shaping and then redirecting the LAPP institutional grants to Berkeley's political science department. As I discuss in more detail in chapter 5, these grants were crucial to building up the theory field at Berkeley even though the parameters set for disbursing them were loose at the outset. They were therefore easily stretched to accommodate Rockefeller's 1960s commitment to sending US political scientists to universities in the developing world—a commitment Thompson wholeheartedly endorsed. For Thompson, investing foundation resources in political theory was one expression of a more fundamental commitment: to foster an ethical, philosophically educated intelligentsia who saw influencing foreign policy making at home and disseminating Western ideals abroad as an intellectual challenge and a moral duty.[72] Of all the programs discussed in this chapter, this overtly ideological track of LAPP made the most ambitious bid for government patronage for academic political science to pick up where Rockefeller support left off.

Conclusion

To maximize their long-term effects, Rockefeller officers tried to give all of the grants discussed in this chapter more staying power than short-term investments in narrowly circumscribed individual projects might have. Even the most project-oriented of them, the grant that supported the writing of V. O. Key's *Southern Politics*, still had an infrastructural dimension. Beginning as a grant to a state university's bureau of public administration, this grant ultimately also lent legitimacy to the new SSRC Committee on Political Behavior that Key chaired. Compared to Carnegie and Ford, the Rockefeller Foundation was a cautious and late supporter of the scientific study of political behavior. Still, the grants it made to Michigan's Survey Research Center in the late 1950s and early 1960s were substantial and long-lasting enough to fund further work on the SRC's burgeoning research infrastructure. The most sustained infrastructure building projects, however, happened under the aegis of the Legal and Political Philosophy program. LAPP fellowship programs relied on two separate advisory committees on which dozens of academics served. And LAPP institutional grants provided substantial sums to three departments to support research in political theory, broadly defined. Of all of these, the institutional grant to Berkeley's political science department lasted the longest and expressed Rockefeller officers' ambitions to connect academic political science to foreign policy making agencies the most clearly.

Compared to Carnegie and Ford's focused interest in the behavioral sciences, Rockefeller's Division of Social Sciences chose a diversified grant-making strategy, offering significant support for different, even incompatible modes of knowledge. A foundation's grant-making is, of course, in the first instance an expression of the commitments and beliefs of its trustees and officers. But foundations also craft their programs with an eye to what other foundations are doing—or not doing.[73] Carnegie and Rockefeller's strategies in the 1940s were therefore different by design. And in the 1950s, in a bid to counter the influence of the newly massive Ford Foundation, Rockefeller aided some approaches its officers believed Ford would not support. Rockefeller's commitment to a diversified social science program, seen in this context, expresses the constant push and pull for influence among the big mid-twentieth-century foundations.

In addition to these considerations, exploring Rockefeller's wide-ranging commitments in the social sciences also reveals the fluidity and openness of postwar political science. These qualities are evident even in Carnegie and Ford's more concentrated efforts. As we saw in the previous two chapters, Carnegie and Ford invested as much time and resources as they did in the behavioral sciences not because they seemed a sure bet but rather because they were far from securely established in academic institutions. Rockefeller's broad array of commitments in political science make the midcentury fluidity of the discipline even more evident. Public administration, survey research, international relations theory, political theory and philosophy—Rockefeller invested its postwar resources in them all. For a conservative, older foundation that chose in this instance not to "bunch its hits," there were many appealing targets to aim for.[74]

PART II

UNIVERSITIES

CHAPTER FOUR

The Transformation of Political Science at Michigan

Patronage and the Rise of Political Behavior Research

Introduction: Active Patronage and Its Reception at the University of Michigan

One assessment of the role of public and private patronage in recent US history stresses its initiatory qualities; it shows how patrons often become hands-on directors of what grant recipients do with their money. Along with the many social scientists who have offered versions of this view, the University of Michigan's Jack Walker was one of the first political scientists to do so. In the posthumously published book *Mobilizing Interest Groups in America*, Walker and his collaborators argued that the patronage of private foundations and government agencies is often an active force in the lives of the groups they support. Sometimes even "urging" groups into existence, patrons tend to continue to direct the activities of the groups they launch. Patronage, therefore, has profound effects on the character of political life: "The number of interest groups in operation, the mixture of group types, and the level and direction of political mobilization in the United States at any point in the country's history will be largely determined by the composition and accessibility of the system's major patrons of political action."[1]

Walker and his collaborators focused principally on patronage for interest groups with significant lobbying arms in Washington, DC. Despite his long career at the University of Michigan (1964–1990), Walker never applied his analysis to the substantial patronage that supported academic political and social science at the university. Recently, several political scientists have moved in this direction, building upon Walker's work to analyze foundation patronage for primary and secondary education and university programs as well.[2] In the chapters of part 1, I took a similar approach, emphasizing the fundamental changes the three major mid-twentieth-century foundations—Carnegie, Ford, and Rockefeller—initiated in academic social science. Both Carnegie and Ford were enthusiastic patrons of the new behavioral sciences: they publicized them, underwrote large research projects that made use of them, and, ultimately, funded a number of academic programs and institutions devoted to them. By contrast, Rockefeller's more eclectic social science program not only supported the behavioral sciences but also simultaneously cultivated very different visions of political knowledge, including initiatives in political philosophy and international relations theory. Walker's conclusions about the patrons of the interest groups he studied are applicable here: the social science divisions of each of these foundations were pointedly "urging" academic orientations into existence. Once successful, each remained involved for a time in trying to sustain them.

The energetic promotion of particular ways of doing social science by foundations, however, is just part of the story. How universities received, modified, and extended these initiatives is the other. These issues are central to this chapter and the next one on UC Berkeley. To be sure, foundations sometimes built new institutions from the ground up to further their vision for the social sciences—Ford's massive investment in building and endowing the Center for the Advanced Study of the Behavioral Sciences (CASBS) in Menlo Park, California, is the most notable example.[3] For the most part, however, postwar foundation patronage went to social scientists at established universities. Initiating new approaches in such contexts posed a different set of challenges than building a new institution from scratch. For a start, foundations as well as federal agencies had to forge alliances with people in universities who had their own reasons for challenging existing curricula and academic hierarchies. The academics who played these intermediary brokering roles had some discretion over where the patronage they received flowed and which established university structures it affected most. This allowed them to reshape the practice and reproduction of their disciplines.

By the late 1950s, several now well-known University of Michigan political scientists—Warren Miller, Samuel Eldersveld, Donald Stokes, and Philip Converse—had each participated in large funded projects that were coming to define the social science version of "big science" in the postwar research university. Such generous patronage and the prospect of its continuation put them in an unusually strong position to transform Michigan's political science department. They, especially Miller and Eldersveld, did so by leveraging the abundant resources available to them through the Institute for Social Research (ISR) and its affiliates to amend the department's PhD program and advocate for a more behavioralist-friendly leadership.

This chapter explores how these advocates of the would-be "Michigan model" went about transforming the department as well as the opposition they faced, relying principally on the archived personal papers of department members and an array of university records to do so. Though they are replete with conflicts and disagreements on many issues, I found no sustained opposition to the substance of the new behavioralist program in these archived records. Tensions between people tied to the department and those with strong links to ISR were real; but they were less about the merits of the new approaches to studying political behavior than the place and power of sponsored research in the university. Rather than being divided over the merits of the new survey-research based study of political behavior and the quantitative analytic methods that accompanied it, members of Michigan's political science department disagreed the most deeply about the academic and public purpose of political science. Most senior members of the department at midcentury who had taken their degrees in the 1920s and 1930s regarded educating students for careers in public service as the primary purpose of the discipline. By contrast, the younger advocates of the new program in political behavior saw encouraging research in the graduate curriculum and in faculty members' careers as the discipline's primary purpose.

Those who built the new program in political behavior began cautiously, first presenting the program as a modest addition to the existing PhD program. Thanks to the generous private and public patronage supporting political behavior research, infrastructure, and curricula *outside* the political science department in the 1950s, what may have initially appeared to be a modest new program was unusually well-developed and well-funded from the start. This not only helped it succeed but also allowed it to transform the department quickly. Just fourteen years after its adoption, political behavior had so "permeated" the PhD program that Miller and its other supporters felt a special program devoted to it "was no longer necessary." What began as a modest addition to the graduate program now defined the whole.[4]

Translating Patronage-Funded Resources
into Departmental Power

The substantial patronage that supported ISR and its subsidiary spin-offs like the Survey Research Center (SRC) and the Inter-university Consortium for Political Research (ICPR) looked especially formidable when compared to the paltry foundation and government patronage available to the mid-century political science department.[5] Miller, one of the most important early intermediaries between national patrons, the SRC, ICPR, and the department, drew on an array of patronage-funded resources to gain a curricular foothold in the department and transform it. Since grant-seeking by both individuals and academic units has long been so major a part of contemporary academic life, the significance of the grants Miller and his colleagues won can easily be underestimated today. For the time, however, the sums that Miller and his colleagues secured to support the study of political behavior were large for unclassified social science research projects.[6] Especially when compared to the meager grant income of the whole political science department during the 1950s and early 1960s, the grants secured by the SRC and ICPR were more significant still.

Moreover, outside sponsorship for university research of any kind was still a novelty during the early postwar period. The most generously sponsored research on university campuses was being done by large organized groups in laboratories and research institutes, many of which had begun outside universities during World War II. According to historian of higher education Roger Geiger, since many of these research facilities bore the distinct marks of corporations or governmental agencies that had created them, university administrators struggled to figure out how to connect them to existing university structures. For one, whether those affiliated with such research facilities should also belong to established departments and on what terms was unclear. Also, university officials were initially overwhelmed by trying to plan where the research money these facilities were bringing in should go; though the volume of the money was great, the timing of its arrival was highly unpredictable. Still, universities that jumped into this new research economy—as Michigan did—quickly became very different institutions as a result.[7]

When these labs and research centers worked out new affiliations with universities after the war ended, their legal status certainly changed. The kind of research they did, however, did not. Neither did who was paying for it. Two University of Michigan examples illustrate this point. First, some of the facilities at Willow Run, the site of Ford's massive production of bombers during World War II, were purchased by the university in 1946. Though Willow Run Laboratories was no longer in the business of manufacturing bombers, its contracts were still focused on many aspects of aerial warfare, doing "more classified research in the early 1950s than all the sponsored research on the rest of the Michigan campus." By the end of the 1950s, Willow Run was still bringing in a sizable chunk of the university's research income. In the 1959–1960 fiscal year, Willow Run brought in $7.4 million in sponsored research income from defense agencies and corporations, nearly a third of such income for the entire university.[8]

The history of the Institute for Social Research resembles Willow Run's in several ways. Founded at the University of Michigan in 1949, ISR became the institutional home for two older organizations, the SRC and the Research Center for Group Dynamics (RCGD). The SRC was a spin-off of a federal government research unit in the Department of Agriculture created during World War II. Shortly after the US Congress cut its federal funding in 1946, some of its staff affiliated with the University of Michigan.[9] Though ISR's early years at Michigan were financially precarious, by the end of the 1950s the institute was already bringing in a substantial $1.45 million in sponsored research in one year—small compared to Willow Run Laboratories' total, but still an impressive sum for a social-scientific research institute. Over the course of its first ten years, ISR's sponsored research income came in roughly equal thirds from federal government agencies, corporations, and philanthropic foundations. As Hunter Crowther-Heyck has noted, Michigan's ISR continued to be unusually successful at securing the patronage of both private foundations and federal agencies in the decades to come.[10]

Of course, Miller and others linked to both ISR/SRC and the political science department had access to only a portion of these funds. Nevertheless, access to the patronage of private philanthropies and federal agencies put them in a strong position relative to their political science colleagues. Unlike their colleagues, they were not primarily dependent on department or university resources to pursue their research or their plans for revising the PhD program. Their research agendas, the extensive infrastructure they required, and the array of programs for training new cohorts of survey researchers were all sustained by income from external grants. This gave them several specific advantages in realizing their ideas for transforming political science at Michigan.

First, substantial grants for election studies from the Carnegie Corporation in 1952 and the Rockefeller Foundation in 1956 and 1960 underwrote what would become a significant and ongoing research program at the SRC; *The American Voter* was their most widely recognized early result.[11] Securing a succession of sizeable grants must have raised hopes both at the SRC and among university administrators that SRC projects would be able to win similar levels of outside support in the future. Nationally, the publication of *The American Voter* and the numerous pieces that led up to and followed it increased Converse, Miller, and Stokes's visibility among political scientists. Bolstered by the recognition they were beginning to receive for their well-funded research program, Miller and others were in a strong position to reshape the department's graduate program and leadership to be more congenial to their views.

Second, in addition to enabling it to build an ongoing research program, these sizable grants also laid the foundations of the research infrastructure the SRC and its later spin-offs used to conduct and distribute survey research on future elections—the same research infrastructure that would later support the data-collection and distribution mission of ICPR from the 1960s onward. Among the largest at any US university, this substantial infrastructure for conducting, archiving, and distributing survey data put SRC and ICPR-affiliated faculty in an excellent position to offer graduate students numerous ongoing research positions. Also, beginning in the 1960s, the prospect of being affiliated with these formidable research institutions helped attract new faculty to the Michigan department.[12] What is more, once private philanthropies began to scale back their investments in the university research economy, ISR-linked institutions demonstrated they could continue to win support from the increasingly important federal agency patrons. For instance, ICPR was one of the first political science-connected entities to receive substantial National Science Foundation support.[13] This was especially significant since the NSF did not include political science among the social sciences it supported until the latter half of the 1960s. Therefore, only those political scientists connected to interdisciplinary entities like the SRC or ICPR could benefit from the first phase of its patronage. During the crucial post-Sputnik period up through the end of the 1960s, therefore, those political scientists who had access to NSF funds had a substantial head start in advancing their research agendas over their colleagues who did not.[14]

Third, the 1950s Ann Arbor summer workshops taught by ISR/SRC staff

for graduate students or faculty had also been funded by private foundations.[15] These workshops taught participants new statistical and programming techniques for analyzing survey data and allowed them to work with
SRC election data. The earliest of these ISR/SRC workshops significantly
predated any course offered in quantitative research methods by the political science department; some became the basis for the summer training programs ICPR began offering in the early 1960s. Endorsing the SRC's
work in response to a Rockefeller Foundation officer's query, the prominent
early behavioralist David Truman noted that by offering so many training
courses, SRC had nearly "become a specialized and important graduate
school."[16] Most crucially, these workshops gave those who ran them considerable experience in constructing courses and building research relationships that they would later draw on to construct the special PhD program
in political behavior they proposed.

Just a few years later, SRC-affiliated political scientists were able to secure
yet another stream of federal funds for workshops and training programs.
In addition to winning significant early NSF support for ICPR's ambitious
data collection projects, Miller and Eldersveld negotiated a cluster of fellowships from the National Defense Education Act (NDEA) and NSF to support graduate students focusing on political behavior. Though the NDEA
fellowship program was short-lived, it provided generous support for a
handful of political behavior PhD students each year from 1961 up through
1972.[17] After the NDEA program ended, NSF patronage continued: in addition to its underwriting early ICPR data collection and distribution efforts,
it supported fellowships and summer workshops throughout the 1960s and
well into the 1970s.[18] In sum, from the late 1950s throughout the 1960s, the
SRC and then ICPR were strong contenders in the new postwar research
economy. Generously supported by foundations with nationwide programs,
they had launched an ongoing research program, were adding to an already
substantial research infrastructure, and had early contacts at the NSF when
it was on the cusp of becoming a much more significant patron for the social
sciences.[19]

By contrast, Michigan's political science department reported almost no
sponsored research income for its full-time faculty in the 1959–1960 fiscal year.[20] This was in part a problem of access to the new NSF. But it was
also a sign that many political scientists' conceptions of worthwhile scholarly activity did not mesh with the emerging imperatives of the postwar
research university. Perhaps in an attempt to counter the growing influence

of the SRC, department chair James Kerr Pollock tried in the late 1950s to raise funds for several department-linked research centers—a Michigan affiliate of the Citizenship Clearing House and the Vandenberg Foreign Policy Center. In the Michigan affiliate of the Citizenship Clearing House proposal, Pollock argued for a redesigned graduate curriculum emphasizing "systematic observational" data-collection methods rather than survey research as well as "training for active citizenship" in summer seminars partially supported by Michigan's principal political parties. The proposal for the Vandenberg Foreign Policy Center that Pollock sent to Dean Roger Heyns around the same time focused on offering adult education programs or training for high school teachers as well as providing summer salaries for around six department faculty members to do research on foreign-policy issues. As Pollock represented them, both centers were to have public service missions; neither would rely principally on sponsored research.[21] Although Pollock was still pitching both centers in his last year as chair, neither proposal ever received more than nominal preliminary funding. Neither made it off the drawing board.[22]

The great imbalance between the external funds from major national patrons available to those linked to ISR versus those available to their other colleagues in political science set up the department's profound reorientation in the 1960s and 1970s. The effects of this imbalance on the department, however, were neither simple nor immediate. Even the most energetic intermediaries backed by the most directive foundation or federal program cannot dissolve existing academic structures overnight. Instead, what seems in retrospect to be a dramatic shift in the character of the Michigan department was an accretion of a number of smaller, incremental changes that piled up over a decade or more. In the remainder of this chapter, I present two extended examples of such incremental but cumulatively profound changes: the emergence of political behavior and quantitative methods as important departmental fields, and changes in department leadership that coincided with a shift in the relative prestige of public service versus research. Along the way, I attend to the department, college, and university-level norms and procedures that all involved observed, including those who saw them as obstacles to the changes they wished to effect. To represent both the incremental pace of these changes and the particular paths their advocates chose to take, I rely on departmental records, department members' archived personal papers, and records of correspondence between faculty members, Michigan administrators, and political scientists at other institutions. In this unpublished material, Miller, Eldersveld, Pollock, and others comment extensively on the kinds of political science the department ought to practice and its place within the university and the discipline.

Political Behavior, Research Methodology . . .
and Political Theory?

[ISR courses] all gave me a great introduction as to how to think scientifically, how to design research, and how to analyze and interpret data. Without these courses I would have been just another political philosopher!

—Sam Eldersveld[23]

Political behavior and quantitative methods began to define political science at the University of Michigan soon after the people and research missions of the SRC and what would become ICPR found a niche in the political science department's graduate program. Miller was a principal figure here: he was the first SRC researcher to join the department's faculty (in 1956) and the first to be tenured there (in 1958). He was also one of the lead architects of the department's special PhD program in political behavior; remarkably, the department approved it unanimously in May 1959 without requiring any major slow-downs or dilutions along the way.[24] Still, the program probably would not have come into being as soon as it did—or perhaps not even at all—in the absence of several important elements. Miller's talents as an academic entrepreneur and the patronage-funded resources he was able to draw upon certainly helped. But so did the choice to graft the new program in political behavior onto a seemingly unlikely area of the department's curriculum—political theory.

Miller also had the help of an important ally with deep roots in the Michigan department: Sam Eldersveld. A 1946 University of Michigan PhD who went on to spend his entire academic career on the Michigan faculty, Eldersveld was an early and vocal proponent of behavioralism.[25] Though Eldersveld never joined the SRC or its later spin-off, the Center for Political Studies, his support was nevertheless crucial to launching the political behavior program and the curricular changes it set in motion. Before Eldersveld accepted the position of department chair in 1964, he made his intention to hire faculty who would strengthen the department's behavioral research profile explicitly clear to the then dean of the College of Literature,

Science, and the Arts, William Haber, and insisted he be given the resources to do so.[26] Eldersveld realized these transformative aims on several fronts. Among the many notable figures who joined the department during Eldersveld's time as chair were J. David Singer, Philip Converse, A. F. K. Organski, Ronald Inglehart, Raymond Tanter, and Herb Weisberg. Despite their different fields and orientations, all employed quantitative analytic methods to study political behavior; all also had strong connections to at least one research center under the ISR umbrella. When Eldersveld's term as chair ended in 1970, the "Michigan model" was almost as predominant in the department as at ISR and SRC.[27]

Once adopted, the PhD program in political behavior set profound department-wide changes in motion; yet when they approved it in 1959, department members do not seem to have regarded it as a major reorientation of the whole PhD program. This, I suspect, was what its advocates intended. Instead of highlighting its challenge to the department's core fields of public administration, American and foreign government, and international politics, Miller and Eldersveld deftly opted for presenting the new program as a modest sideline rather than as a substantial revision of these core fields. For instance, when Miller and Eldersveld were still explaining the substance of this new program to their colleagues, they stressed that it was to be "wide ranging" and "catholic" rather than a restrictive approach intended to challenge older, existing fields.[28]

Eldersveld and Miller also emphasized the new program's connections to another field: political theory. Besides avoiding conflict with other fields, what explains this seemingly unlikely connection? Some clues turn up in the structure of the department's fields and program requirements. Well before Miller and Eldersveld proposed the political behavior program, the department had consistently defined political theory as a distinct field and made it prominent among the requirements of the graduate program. For example, from 1940 until 1964, political theory was the *only* specific examination field explicitly required of *all* PhD students. Although some faculty challenged this requirement, it stayed on the books for a long time. Lawrence Preuss, who specialized in international law but had frequently taught courses in political theory in the 1930s and 1940s, rebuffed one such challenge in 1949. Eliminating the requirement that all PhD students be examined in political theory, Preuss argued, would damage the department's reputation for academic rigor. In 1950 a provision allowing individual students to opt out of the examination requirement appears in the graduate catalog; it was only in 1964 that the requirement disappeared.[29] Though documents of this kind cannot convey how seriously or thoroughly faculty examined PhD students in political theory, the prominence and longevity of this formal requirement are still significant.

The twisting and turning classification of the methodology subfield also sheds some light on why Miller and Eldersveld initially chose to propose the program in political behavior as an addendum to the theory field. When it first appears in the department's graduate program in 1950, methodology is classified a subdivision of political theory in which MA (but not PhD) students could be examined.[30] In 1952 political theory and methodology became a broader category, with five subfields—three periods in the history of political thought, American political thought, and scope and methodology of political science. Over the next fifteen years, the subfield migrates and morphs: renamed "research methodology and techniques," it leaves political theory to become a subfield of parties, elections, and political behavior in 1963; by 1966 it becomes a field of its own. Finally, in 1967 the field is renamed "quantitative research methods," a change that almost completely erases its former connection to political theory.[31] By this time, the political behavior program was firmly rooted in the department's PhD program. There was no longer any need to portray its substantive focus or its emphasis on research methods as "wide-ranging" and "catholic."

These shifts in definition and classification happened within the graduate program as a whole. Within the special PhD program in political behavior, however, the connections between political theory, political behavior, and research methods stayed in place for a longer time. When representatives of other fields weakened the formerly robust political theory requirement for PhD students, the political behavior program initially moved in the opposite direction. During its first seven years (1960–1967), the political behavior program required all its PhD students to choose either American political thought or recent political theory as one of their five examination fields; research methodology and techniques were also specifically required. Only from 1968 on did the program weaken its theory requirement to coincide with what was now required of all other PhD students: six hours of graduate credit in political theory courses. The first department-wide statistics requirement for all PhD students began the same year.[32] New hires, new courses, and substantial cohorts of new graduate students grew the program in political behavior quickly. As the program developed, it steadily shed its former connections with the theory field. Many of its graduate students received fellowships from the NSF or the NDEA; some of its faculty and their courses, including Converse's "Formal Models of Political Sociology" course and Converse himself, were no longer classified under the theory field but under political behavior instead. By the end of the 1960s, the program had a substantial number of its own faculty, courses, and students. It no longer needed the temporary shelter of the theory umbrella.[33]

Short-lived though it was, how should this connection between political theory, political behavior, and research methodology be understood? One possibility is that those who identified with these fields had real intellectual affinities. Indeed, many people who studied political behavior not only affirmed an interest in political theory—they characterized their own work *as* political theory. And, at least for a time, many people who identified themselves primarily as political theorists reciprocated that interest. Also, interest in both the philosophy of the social sciences and in methodological issues was more common among incipient behavioralists and theorists than among those in other fields.[34] From this perspective, the connection between political theory and political behavior may have been an expression of a coincidence of intellectual interests. That this coincidence was short-lived (no more than ten to fifteen years) does not mean that it wasn't real.

This explanation, however, better captures intellectual developments within US academic political science as a whole than it does the affinities between intellectual communities at the University of Michigan. Though Miller had had some intellectual exchanges with theorists elsewhere, there is no evidence he sought to build strong relations with any of the theorists at Michigan—nor they with him.[35] Eldersveld's breezy comment cited at the beginning of this section—that taking courses sponsored by ISR saved him from the humdrum fate of being "just another political philosopher"—suggests that, at least in retrospect, he did not consider political theory or philosophy significant to his intellectual development either. In sum, there is little evidence to suggest that the connection Miller and Eldersveld asserted between political behavior and political theory was rooted in particular intellectual sympathies between representatives of these fields in the Michigan department.[36]

This specific absence suggests the other line of explanation I have presented here—one that highlights strategy over substance. I think it possible that Miller and Eldersveld emphasized the new program's connection with political theory because (curricular affirmations of its importance notwithstanding) political theory was at the time a relatively weak field at Michigan.

In the late 1950s, James Meisel and Frank Grace were the only full-time members in a department of twenty-four who were regularly teaching theory courses. And though the theory requirement for PhD students remained robust until the early 1960s, I suspect it was becoming increasingly vestigial.[37] As mentioned previously, the requirement that all PhD students be examined in political theory was first seriously challenged as early as 1949; by 1964 it was gone. For Miller and Eldersveld, then, asserting a connection between their proposed new program and the field of political theory did not encroach on any particularly well-defended curricular turf. Perhaps it was also prudent to emphasize to their potentially skeptical mid-twentieth-century colleagues how political behavior had affinities with a field many would have regarded as one the most venerable and foundational in the discipline. As a field, political theory was neither strong nor growing at Michigan in 1959. It was, however, familiar and still unimpeachably legitimate.

Purpose and Prestige: Public Service versus Research in Political Science

The political scientist who would understand political phenomena must be trained as a scientist and not as a super citizen.

—Warren Miller, 1962[38]

When they argued for the new special PhD program in political behavior, Miller and Eldersveld were careful to avoid conflict with large sectors of the department. In other contexts, however, they were not so deferential. In letters to those they assumed shared their views, Eldersveld and Miller vented their frustrations about the shortcomings of the political science practiced by many of their colleagues. As Eldersveld put it, it was "dated," "formalistic" and "outside the mainstream of scholarly intercourse in the profession."[39] In the same letter cited at the outset of this section, Miller complained, "A mandate for a department to emphasize public service and political participation is a mandate for the department to withdraw from serious interest in the intellectual problems of its profession." To that verdict, Miller added, "The political scientist who would understand political phenomena must be trained as a scientist and not as a super citizen." Both Miller and Eldersveld were clearly out of patience with older, more established political science. But to what about it were they objecting?

Miller pointedly identified his senior colleagues' commitment to public service—not their resistance to survey research methods or the basic tenets of behavioralism—as the most stubborn obstacle to the further development of the kind of political science he supported. Indeed, in an oral history interview recorded in 1988, Miller went so far as to say that Pollock had a plausible claim to being the "father of empirical political science," had Pollock chosen to make it.[40] This striking comment squares with broader patterns evident in departmental records and personal papers. These reveal close and complex relationships between department members of different generations—people one might expect to have disagreed sharply on the merits of behavioralism.

The relationship between Pollock and Eldersveld is particularly interesting in this regard. On the one hand, there is ample evidence that Eldersveld, Pollock's former student and eventual successor as chair, aimed to change how political science was done and taught at Michigan. Once he became chair in 1964, he often contrasted his ideas for the department's future with what he perceived as the shortcomings of Pollock's long tenure. On the other hand, there is also plenty of evidence of intellectual collaboration between Eldersveld and Pollock, lasting far beyond Pollock's supervision of Eldersveld's PhD or the eventual divergence in their research orientations. Early collaborations between them indicate that Pollock thought highly of Eldersveld's work and even took some unusual steps to promote it. For example, Pollock and Eldersveld coauthored *Michigan Politics in Transition*; both contributed pieces to *British Election Studies, 1950*.[41] While Eldersveld was serving in the Philippines during World War II, he wrote to Pollock, recounting what he was learning about local governments in various provinces. Without Eldersveld's knowledge, Pollock gathered these letters together and sent them in Eldersveld's name to the *National Municipal Review*.[42] Though Pollock did not adopt behavioralist analyses of voting behavior in his own research on elections in the United States or Germany, he clearly was interested in some aspects of them. For example, in the fall of 1949 Pollock taught a proseminar in political behavior for which he provided an extensive and up-to-date bibliography, including numerous works by researchers affiliated with the SRC. He also participated in the Carnegie Corporation–sponsored conference, organized by the SSRC Committee on Political Behavior in Ann Arbor in 1949.[43]

For his part, Eldersveld continued to express intellectual admiration for Pollock well after he received his PhD in 1946. For example, in 1960, when

Eldersveld had finished *Fulcrum of Party Power: The Urban Presidential Vote 1920–1956*, a manuscript that expanded upon his dissertation research on patterns in urban voting, he still went out of his way to thank Pollock in his acknowledgments. "Above all," Eldersveld wrote, "I am grateful to James K. Pollock who inspired me to work in the field of voting behavior while I was a graduate student, who encouraged me in this specific undertaking at its outset, and who has constantly advised and supported me in its execution."[44] Around the same time, in the summer of 1959, Eldersveld and Miller ran a complete draft of the proposed curriculum of the special PhD program in political behavior past Pollock. Though Eldersveld groused about some of the changes Pollock made to it, he also mentioned that Pollock had contacted Pendleton Herring, the head of the SSRC, about offering graduate student fellowships for the new program.[45]

Perhaps Eldersveld was merely being prudently deferential toward the still-chair Pollock in both these cases. Eldersveld did criticize Pollock in other ways, however, especially for his hiring and promotion decisions that Eldersveld complained bolstered Pollock's own power at the expense of the department and its students. That is, when Eldersveld made substantive criticisms of Pollock, he focused on his lukewarm commitment to building a research-centered department rather than his resistance to various tenets of behavioralism. Eldersveld and Miller made the criticisms cited at the beginning of this section at a time when they, as younger postwar PhDs, had unusual access to resources from outside the university. With the support of foundations and federal agencies behind them, they and their allies had little to fear when they challenged their still powerful but not so generously funded seniors.

The Older Public Service Imperative

Setting aside the aforementioned criticisms for the moment, grasping what political science was like in its first fifty years as an organized discipline is difficult for us today for several reasons. For one, behavioral science–inspired critiques of this earlier period have become part of the contemporary discipline's common sense; these make early twentieth-century political science seem old and stale, unworthy of any sustained investigation.[46] Second, the field of public administration, though central to political science in the first half of the twentieth century, has become unfamiliar territory to most contemporary political scientists. By the 1960s, many public administration faculty were either leaving the political science department to form a new professional program or recasting the field as public policy.[47] Keeping these difficulties in understanding early twentieth-century political science in mind, I turn now to recovering some central features of political science at the University of Michigan in its first fifty years—when being part of the disciplinary mainstream meant emphasizing public service.

Public service's declining prominence in the discipline occurred in the broader context of the new postwar research economy I sketched earlier. Public universities like Michigan that participated energetically in this new research economy learned quickly that they were no longer so tightly constrained by their states' budgets and therefore could set their sights on goals beyond serving constituencies in their states.[48] The new sources of patronage available in the postwar research economy and what these new patrons favored also affected what happened to political science at Michigan. The people connected to ISR and to the New York–based SSRC were in one of the best positions to notice and respond to new, increasingly nationalized opportunities for sponsored research in the social sciences.[49] Conversely, those who specialized in the administration of state and local governments no longer had institutionally provided front row seats on a patronage system increasingly dominated by philanthropies with national and international programs and agencies of the federal government. Belonging to the National Municipal League[50] or its state-based affiliates had been a professional asset in the first part of the twentieth century; beginning in the mid-1950s, however, being part of a grant- and contract-supported research institute and perhaps an SSRC committee became much more professionally desirable. Research—not public service or educating future public servants—was becoming the most desirable commodity in the postwar academic economy. Significant, strategic patronage aided and accelerated this fundamental change.

Several older conceptions of a public service-centered political science inevitably clashed with the newer emphasis on nationally focused and nationally funded research. For some Michigan faculty, teaching students to become public officials was their primary charge; though many were active researchers, their published work often focused on the very roles they were teaching students to assume. For others, the prominent positions they held in government and in the discipline exemplified public service and were more important than published research. When funded research began to overshadow and even undercut the perceived value and prestige of older career patterns based on these conceptions of public service, some scholars seemed resigned to the change. Others railed against it.

Public administration was undeniably central to the early life of the political science department at Michigan. According to several accounts, the university created the first professorship in political science shortly after the 1908 state constitution granted home rule to municipalities.[51] Michigan was but one of many states that began implementing municipal home rule during the Progressive Era; emerging classes of professionals claimed that the tasks involved, like drafting city government charters and then administering the utilities and services of those cities, required special training.[52] And universities, particularly those offering courses in political science, accounting, public health, and engineering, were increasingly where people were trained to perform them. At the University of Michigan, training local public administrators was a major practical justification for establishing a distinct curriculum and faculty in political science in the early twentieth century.

A number of important figures in the political science department's first fifty years at Michigan devoted a considerable portion of their professional lives to such training. Among the most important were Robert Crane and Arthur Bromage.[53] The career of Robert Crane, one of the "prominent figures in the city manager movement," exemplifies both the local and national prestige of public administration during the first half of the twentieth century as well as its subsequent decline.[54] Crane taught a wide array of courses in the 1920s and early 1930s, including world politics and the history of political thought. He also directed the university's Bureau of Government, an early twentieth-century ancestor of postwar research institutes. Progressives and their patrons first organized such research bureaus in large cities to investigate what they deemed the corrupt politics of elected officials and party bosses. When universities began their own versions of them, these bureaus primarily conducted research projects on local or statewide matters rather than national ones.[55]

Crane left his positions at the University of Michigan in 1932 to assume the nationally prominent role of executive director of the Social Science Research Council, a position he held until his retirement in 1945. As the head of the SSRC, Crane was one of the most important intermediaries between academics and their major philanthropic patrons, in frequent contact with prominent officers at both the Rockefeller Foundation and Carnegie Corporation regarding their programs for funding the social sciences. As discussed in chapter 1, prior to World War II, Crane's vision for the SSRC was already beginning to be criticized by some foundation officers committed to what would later be called the behavioral sciences. When he was appointed to lead the SSRC, Crane's close identification with public administration had seemed fitting. By the end of World War II, however, critiques of the field as outdated and incompatible with newer trends in social science had intensified; Crane retired from his post in 1945.[56] Those who succeeded him at the SSRC—the sociologist Donald Young and the political scientist Pendleton Herring—were both deeply committed to the new, research-oriented behavioral sciences.

After Crane left the Michigan faculty, the department's most prominent specialist in public administration was Arthur Bromage. Bromage, who was on the faculty from 1929 to 1974, regularly taught courses on state, county, and municipal administration. Though he chaired a substantial number of dissertations during his long career, the number of future city managers and professional public administrators whose training Bromage supervised was probably far greater.[57] Bromage had long-standing professional connections to the International City Managers' Association and the Michigan Municipal League; according to his colleague, Richard Park, the honors Bromage received from each of these organizations mattered the most to him. He also served two terms as alderman on Ann Arbor's city council from 1949 to 1953 and was appointed to numerous advisory boards by state officials.[58] Though Bromage's public positions were not especially prominent ones, he held a number of them for long stretches throughout his academic career. As a teacher of future public servants and a participant in public life, Bromage's public service focused on his city and his state.

In addition to his career-long commitment to public administration, Bromage served as chair from 1961 to 1964 during a crucial transitional period in the Michigan department's history. At the beginning of 1961, Pollock abruptly announced his decision to resign as chair; this caught many of his colleagues by surprise, even though some clearly welcomed it. Dean Roger Heyns then persuaded Bromage to serve as chair for what was intended to be an interim three-year term, during which the department would decide on its future course and choose a longer-term chair. Throughout this period, Dean Heyns—joined later by Dean William Haber—tried to persuade Eldersveld to become the department's next chair.

Though the question of the future direction of the department was unsettled during his term, Bromage does not appear to have used his position to reassert the primacy of public administration. Instead, his colleagues later praised his commitment to greater transparency in department decision-making as well as his quiet acceptance of new directions in the discipline that he did not personally welcome.[59] When Bromage's term as chair was about to end in 1964 and Eldersveld's to begin, many of his colleagues clearly saw that the department was on the cusp of a new phase. Those among them who felt some attachment to Bromage himself and to the practice of the discipline he represented took the opportunity to host an off-campus celebration to honor Bromage's service as chair. A remarkable mock Festschrift that includes many written contributions to this part celebration, part roast, provides an unusually detailed window onto some department members' anxieties on the verge of what all knew would be a major change.[60]

For instance, one piece, titled "Diary of a Chairman," portrays Bromage preparing for a meeting with the dean of his college by dutifully coding the qualifications of a short list of candidates for a position in Chinese politics so he can "process the whole shebang through our IBM computer." He performs this task not out of conviction, but for cover: "When our *Quantifex Maximus* takes over, he won't find *me* culpable of misbehaviorism!" The punch line to this satirical piece: the "IBM-determined rating" matches the alphabetical ordering of the five-person short list. The mock-Bromage greets this result with mock wonderment: "Well! If the two lists aren't identical! Here's a true miracle of scientific method."[61]

Another piece written for this informal celebration, titled "Agreed: One Man, One Vote. Yes, but—*Which* Man?," is a send-up of a department meeting held to discuss the voting rights of department members who were also affiliated with the SRC and the Institute for Public Policy Studies (IPPS). One unnamed department member warns his colleagues about the growing power of the SRC:

> Who knows what thirst for power lurks in the hearts of political scientists. Why, with the current wave of behaviorism sweeping over the country, who knows how long it will be before those power hungry computers over in the Survey Research Center will be running the Department. Besides, I'm not giving those one-twentieth or one-thirtieth time visiting members over there in that den of behaviorism equal voting rights with someone like me, whose [sic] been teaching full time for 70 years.

A faculty member affiliated with IPPS (referred to here as "Rackham," the building where it was housed) objects; he and his colleagues "pose just as big a threat as the Survey Research Center, in taking over the department. So there!" A number of different voting schemes are then considered and dismissed, each absurd or arbitrary in different ways—elaborately fractionalized voting, voting by body weight, by wealth, by formal or informal power, and by the distance of one's office to the washroom. The most elaborate and elaborately absurd proposal comes from someone "known as the 'brain' of the Department." Everyone listens attentively, prepared to be impressed by "the brain's" proposal, but it's even more absurd (and absurdly detailed) than the rest.[62]

Though one should not infer anything too substantial or specific from brief satirical pieces like these, they illustrate department members making fun of what worried or vexed them. At this informal off-campus send-off, those who organized the festivities joked about the new forces ascendant in the university in ways that revealed their anxieties about them. Finding themselves held to new expectations for research and grant seeking that postwar research centers and institutes like the SRC and IPPS had helped fuel, many political science faculty who had begun their careers before World War II tried on this occasion to make fun of the rapid changes to which they were expected to adapt. The sympathetic portrayal of their bemused out-going "old chairman" trying to navigate these new expectations, and the digs at Eldersveld, the in-coming "Quantifex Maximus," are the jokes of a group of political scientists who felt the professional ground shifting under their feet.

Bromage's career illustrates how those allied to the early twentieth-century field of public administration supported a particular conception of the public service offered by political science departments. Such a public administration–centered conception, however, was not the only way in which political scientists of this generation understood what it meant to serve the public. The career of James Pollock, a member of the department from 1925 until 1968 and its chair from 1947 to 1961, exemplifies another conception of public service in which taking on public duties outside the university was paramount. Pollock used his 1950 American Political Science Association (APSA) and 1958 International Political Science Association (IPSA) presidential addresses as well as his remarks at the department's fiftieth anniversary celebrations in 1960 to argue for the merits of this conception; I cite these speeches extensively below. To complement these widely publicized speeches, I also discuss portions of several unpublished pieces written by

Pollock's Michigan colleagues to mark his retirement in 1968. Though these poked some gentle fun at Pollock's highly public career, they skewered the emerging grant-funded research ethic more vigorously.

Not surprisingly, Bromage and Pollock's conceptions of the public-service political scientists overlapped. For one, both believed that political science departments' primary function should be educating future citizens and public officials rather than future political scientists. Several speeches given at the celebration of the department's fiftieth anniversary Pollock organized repeatedly underscored this point.[63] In his own address at this event, Pollock warned that "any tendency which pulls our discipline away from public affairs and public policy needs to be watched," especially given the "steady growth of graduate work in all fields." To underscore his commitment to these principles during his term as chair, Pollock proudly cited the number of University of Michigan graduates who made careers in the State Department (86) and CIA (182). Pollock closed this speech with a passage from Cicero's On the Republic that extols the fundamental obligation to serve one's country.[64]

Like Bromage, Pollock was also deeply involved in Michigan state politics for much of his professional life. Most notably, he chaired a 1930s commission tasked with professionalizing the civil service in the state. According to a lengthy profile that appeared in the Ann Arbor News shortly after Pollock's retirement, there was some speculation that Pollock might run for governor on the strength of his work on this well-publicized commission. Though his term as Washtenaw County's Republican delegate to the 1962 state constitutional convention was the only public elective office he ever held, Pollock intimated that he had declined many other invitations to run for public office.[65]

Pollock and Bromage both valued training future public officials as well as their own involvement in local and state politics. Still, there were some important differences in how they conceived of the public service political scientists ought to do. Unlike Bromage, Pollock did not spend most of his professional life studying public administration; instead, he studied elections in the United States and Europe from the 1930s until the end of his career. On the strength of his published work analyzing levels of support for the German National Socialist Party by region, Pollock became an advisor to US military and civilian governors of postwar Germany. To do this work, Pollock requested and received a number of substantial leaves from the university to participate in the US military government of postwar Germany and to serve on the first Hoover Commission from 1947 to 1949. Far from regarding these posts as interruptions of his scholarly career, Pollock saw them as fulfillments of his prior research. By contrast, though Bromage clearly thought it important for political scientists to assume public duties, his only leave of absence from the university was to serve as a commissioned officer during World War II—but not to serve as alderman in Ann Arbor or on various state-level commissions.[66]

Pollock used the platforms of his presidencies of both the APSA and the IPSA to urge other political scientists to follow his public service example. In his APSA presidential address, Pollock urged political scientists to respond to the immense growth of US international power after World War II not only by training "a new type of public servant" but also by becoming such public servants themselves. Referring frequently to his service on the Hoover Commission, Pollock also suggested that political scientists had a special responsibility to address the organizational problems faced by a rapidly growing federal government as well as to warn of the dangers it posed to popular control. They could do this more effectively, Pollock suggested, by serving in some public capacity rather than as full-time professors.[67]

At the time of his APSA speech, Pollock still seems to have believed that some postwar trends might bolster his vision for a public service–centered political science. In particular, he expressed the hope that the Ford Foundation's recently released overview of its new, ambitious programs in the social sciences might turn out to be "the greatest boon to fruitful and constructive research and action in the political field we have ever had." Though there are a few grumbles in this 1950 speech about the incursions of other social sciences into political scientists' rightful domain, Pollock still sounded confident when he insisted that "political science is the integrating and synthesizing discipline" whose practitioners should "use other social sciences and accept a definite leadership in our relationships to them."[68]

Over the course of the 1950s, however, Pollock's optimism on both these fronts faded quickly. For one, the Ford Foundation's 1950s programs in the social sciences contributed more to the development of the interdisciplinary behavioral sciences than to supporting the sort of "research and action in the political field" Pollock imagined. In particular, Ford's Behavioral Sciences Program's substantial support for some branches of sociology and psychology as research disciplines probably further undermined any potential political science might have had to "leadership" over the other social sciences. Also, though the NSF began to fund some social sciences more generously in the late 1950s, political science was not yet among them.

By the late 1950s, Pollock was still insisting that political science ought to have a leading role among the social sciences. In his 1958 IPSA presidential address, however, he presented this more as a missed opportunity rather than a goal on the not-so-distant horizon. Condemning the disparity between "natural and physical scientists [who] are now the darlings of governments" with "billions of dollars . . . lavished upon them" and the fortunes of political scientists, who are "impoverished and neglected," Pollock no longer held out hope of this changing. All he could do was wax indignant that the NSF was among those guilty of this neglect. Instead of calling upon his colleagues to lead the other social sciences and aid public officials, Pollock could only warn them to be vigilant and "not to be pushed aside or overwhelmed by the over-weening development of science and technology." He expected no help in this cause from his behavioral science colleagues, whom he chastised for turning away "from the practical world into a realm of self-sufficient abstractions."[69]

After resigning as chair in 1961, Pollock remained on the faculty for six more years. In the spring of 1967, Pollock's colleagues marked his retirement in an event similar to the off-campus dinner held for Bromage discussed previously.[70] Several short pieces composed for this occasion pay homage to Pollock's public and scholarly accomplishments while also remarking on the battles he lost and the disciplinary trends he could not resist. As with the pieces composed for the dinner held for Bromage, the affectionate mockery directed toward Pollock in these tributes is propelled by a steady undercurrent of anxiety about new trends in the department, university, and profession that even as powerful a man as Pollock could not resist.

One such tribute adapted Tennyson's long poem "Locksley Hall," a moody evocation of romantic nostalgia, disappointments, and destructive rage focused on a childhood home. In his fellow department member Henry Bretton's rewriting, the mock-Pollock reflects on his career from the political science department's home in Haven Hall while also trying to apprehend what the future holds. Most of what he discerns is bleak: he sees the university building a "splendid" new home for ISR rather than the Faculty Club for which Pollock had long advocated. The discipline too pursues the wrong course, moving away from political scientists like him in favor of "a pulsing hoard of data" run by contentious "counters." Straining to close on a less gloomy note, Bretton's poem concludes by imagining the victory of "common sense" over "clattering computers" and wishing not for the violent destruction of Haven Hall but for divine protection for it instead.[71]

Another tribute took the form of a mock scripture, making liberal use of biblical tropes and King James cadences. Most of this text remarks on the ascent of a caricatured survey researcher with anxious envy—he is "blessed," the "jet prof" who thinks his "lofty thoughts" on the go, on whom foundation funds fall like "manna." Compared to this fortunate person, he "who hath no model, who hypothesizeth not . . . shall be cast into outer darkness." Though this tribute ends with the "voice of the University" commending and thanking Pollock for his scholarly work and public service, it shares Pollock's sense that he had become yesterday's hero among his disciplinary and university colleagues.[72]

When Pollock died in the fall of 1968, Michigan's governor, George Romney, called him an "activist academician" whose career was a "happy blend of scholarship and public service."[73] This tribute squared with Pollock's own idea that for political scientists, public service meant taking on public roles outside the university—something Pollock himself had done for over three decades. By the end of the 1950s, however, Pollock grew increasingly vexed by a discipline that appeared to be turning away from what he saw as his exemplary practice of it. In 1961, shortly after announcing his intention to step down as department chair, Pollock complained to several newspapers that as chair he had been among the "forgotten men" at the university.[74] Though on its face this was a complaint about the paltry administrative support Pollock thought the university gave its department chairs, I read it as an upwelling of deep bitterness directed against the discipline Pollock had so recently thought he led. Despite having been decorated by both the US and German governments for his service, despite having being chosen as president of both APSA and IPSA, Pollock's career was no longer a model for the discipline or for the university. Eldersveld's and Miller's were.

The New Postwar Research Imperative

Our resources are always supplied by someone else and they are always in short supply. We try to limit our dependency but we seldom enjoy the luxury of freedom without sacrifice.

—Warren Miller, circa 1971[75]

By the 1960s, the department was moving steadily away from seeing the training of state and local administrators as its primary raison d'être. The moral language of the Progressive Era, however, lingered on. For instance, when Eldersveld criticized Pollock's long term as chair, he inveighed against the "cronyism" and "vicious patronage system" he claimed had marred Pollock's term. During this time, Eldersveld contended, department members seeking support for their research or teaching plans either strove to win Pollock's favor or risked his retribution if they looked for such support elsewhere. Given how long this patronage system had lasted, Eldersveld warned that putting the department back on a sound course would be difficult. What the department ideally needed was a new chair who would be "in favor of progress and intellectual rehabilitation," a change of course perhaps achievable only by means of "'shock treatment." Someone well beyond an ordinary, stay-the-course "manager" was called for.[76] Several years later, weighing in on the question of who should become chair after Bromage stepped down, J. David Singer acidly remarked that a large portion of the department resembled "a nice, happy club of good fellows virtually undifferentiable from the local Kiwanis," none of whom were "fully committed to" or even "understand social science."[77] Casting one's opponents as venal bosses or provincial local worthies was as old as the early twentieth-century emergence of professional political science itself. The images Eldersveld and Singer used to criticize their older colleagues were themselves old and familiar. What they advocated, however, was new.

Miller, Eldersveld, Singer, and others in the ascendant field of political behavior placed a premium on funded research and the research centers outside the department that supported it rather than on what Bromage or Pollock had understood as the department's public service mission. Affirmations of the value of funded research became increasingly common, even obligatory, from the 1960s on. But what about research or its value was being affirmed? Miller and others certainly did not present their research projects as "pure research."[78] Instead, they cited its "social utility" as well as its value to "those who want a . . . more democratic society." At the same time, they acknowledged that such research was fraught with social and political risks.[79]

Consider, for example, an extraordinary draft memo Miller addressed to his colleagues in political science, titled "Some Thoughts on Classified Research." In it, Miller not only conceded that had he done classified, "mission-related research" for the Department of Defense (DOD) but also that his research had been "sometimes fradulently [sic], sometimes manipulatively misused." These frauds and manipulations, Miller intimated, were not trifling; indeed, in some cases, he wrote, they "may have increased" the "power of those who would repress others." While such statements could have easily led into a declaration that he would accept no more DOD funds, Miller took a different turn. Yes, he admitted, the risks and costs of doing classified research for DOD were real; but its benefits—greater "understanding," "better description and explanation," as well as the "ability to serve those who want a more responsive, more democratic society"—outweighed them. Closing in a more combative tone, Miller called upon the university to adhere to the "basic values of the academic community" and allow him and others "the freedom to choose" to continue to do classified research.[80]

Significantly, the copy of this memo I have cited turns up not in Miller's personal papers but in those of his colleague, A. F. K. Organski. Organski, along with other members of the department, had also done significant classified research. As many items in Organski's papers make clear, a number of military and intelligence agencies funded his research.[81] Any changes in university policy on classified research done by its faculty, therefore, would likely have affected him. During the Reagan administration, after the most intense scrutiny of classified research on the Michigan campus had subsided, university officials enthusiastically backed Organski's plan to start a new research center that would advise the DOD on national security issues. By 1992, Organski and Bruce Bueno de Mesquita, an early graduate of the political behavior program, were pitching the predictive algorithms developed by their new consulting firm, Decision Insights Incorporated, back to the defense and intelligence agencies that had initially funded some of their research.[82] In this case, Organski and his associates were hoping the very patrons who had initially invested in their research would pay for its products too.

The earliest pitches researchers at the SRC made to government, financial, and corporate entities for which they did contract research foreshadowed these entanglements. Whether from the US Air Force, the Federal Reserve, or the auto industry, these contracts specified the focus, aim, and audience of the research the SRC was to do as well as stipulating with whom the results could be shared. Such contracts made up a larger portion of the SRC's income during its first decade at Michigan than did research grants from foundations.[83] Although foundation grants gave the intellectual aims of those who conducted this kind of research freer rein, here too the aims and parameters of research had to remain within the bounds set by the foundations that made them. In all these cases, the assessments of the patrons who sponsored or commissioned research projects carried great weight not only because they made judgments about the value of the projects they funded early but also because they decided which were worthy of further support. In these ways, these early judgments had an outsized influence on any downstream judgments that academics or the public might later make.

Similarly, ICPSR directs social scientists' attention to data on government agencies that are now among its most significant patrons. In its first decade, ICPR relied on substantial NSF grants to become a major repository of government data, acquiring over a century of county-level electoral results and making these machine-readable. In the 1970s, the accumulated election studies begun by the SRC were renamed the American National Election Studies (ANES), effectively nationalized and supported by the NSF as a "national resource."[84] Although today's ICPSR is no longer the members-only portal it once was to these election studies, it still has many strong ties to government entities. For one, ICPSR receives major funding from over a dozen US government agencies, including not only the NSF but also the Departments of Energy, Health and Human Services, and Justice, multiple arms of the National Institutes of Health, and the US Agency for International Development. Though ICPSR's latest available annual report (2017–2018) does not itemize the sources of the gifts and grants it receives, gifts and grants have surpassed membership fees as the largest source of its income every year since 1996. Along with the many government agencies that fund it, ICPSR also continues to archive and maintain enormous sets of government agency data. A little over ten years ago, it celebrated a grant of $7.45 million from the Substance Abuse and Mental Health Services Administration in what an article in its 2009–2010 annual report called "the largest award in ICPSR's history." In 2017, ICPSR announced that it would host a new searchable repository of US Census Bureau data while also citing its "long-standing partnership" with the Census Bureau that began in the 1960s.[85] No midcentury foundation officers could have foreseen how the research grants they made to Michigan's SRC in the 1950s would help it and its organizational heirs secure such significant, long-term government patronage in the future. Still, if their aims were as I presented them in the chapters in part 1, the endurance and relative prosperity of ISR, ANES, and ICPSR, along with the approaches to social science they reproduce, have fulfilled them.

Conclusion

The principal foundation and government patrons of ISR, the SRC, and ICPR supported specific projects these organizations undertook and the new directions in academic social science they represented. As the chapters in part 1 illustrate, the big mid-twentieth-century foundations were often hands-on patrons of the academic social sciences. Sometimes, as in the case of the Ford Foundation's Behavioral Sciences Program, they promoted new orientations still unfamiliar to most academics. Sometimes, as in the case of the Carnegie Corporation's grant for the SRC's 1952 election study, they imposed quite specific conditions on the recipients of their grants. And sometimes, as in the case of the Rockefeller Foundation's funding for an SSRC fellowship program in political philosophy, they pressed reluctant recipients into embarking on projects they did not endorse. My analysis of the effects of private philanthropic patronage on universities, therefore, pays close attention to the specific programmatic aims of each foundation's social science officers and staff.

Some important patronage-fueled developments in the social sciences, however, ultimately expressed the aims of their academic recipients more clearly than the aims of their patrons. The transformation of the University of Michigan political science department's graduate program, its leadership, and its faculty are all examples of changes driven more by the recipients of patronage rather than by the patrons themselves. Though there is no evidence that Carnegie, Rockefeller, or the National Science Foundation opposed these plans, they were not actively encouraging or directing them either. It was primarily Miller and Eldersveld, aided by university administrators, who made these changes happen.

Miller and Eldersveld could not have advanced their vision of a political science fully integrated into the postwar research university without substantial private and public patronage or the support of key administrators. These were essential preconditions to transforming political science at Michigan as they did. It remained up to them, however, to choose the routes by which they could begin to move the department in the direction they wished it to go. Their strategic choice to connect the new PhD program in political behavior to the field of political theory took advantage of a short-lived and now largely forgotten affinity some midcentury political scientists saw between political theory and the study of research methods.

Fifteen years later, with the game won, asserting this affinity no longer mattered. When he pressed a dean for more hires in political behavior, Miller claimed that it was he and his colleagues in the field who had vaulted the Michigan department "in the front ranks" of PhD programs nationwide. Instead of highlighting its "wide-ranging" breadth as he and Eldersveld had done in 1959, Miller now claimed that the "unique" and "pioneering" qualities of "behavioral science methodology" had "permeated the other subfields in the Department."[86] To hear Miller tell it, all of political science at the University of Michigan had now become behavioral.

From the 1960s onward, nearly any political scientist who knew of Miller or Eldersveld would have associated them centrally with the study of political behavior and, in Miller's case, the institutions at Michigan devoted to it. Also, neither Miller nor Eldersveld was shy about identifying opponents to their aims, both when they were trying to realize them and in retrospect. It therefore seems easy to infer that those who opposed Miller and Eldersveld opposed them because they opposed behavioralism. As I read the archival record, however, the fundamental conflict in the mid-twentieth-century Michigan department was not about the merits of behavioralism. Instead, it was about whether the purpose of political science ought to be educating future researchers or public servants. The transformation of political science at the university from the 1960s on did not just mean that the quantitative analysis of political behavior became central to its identity. More fundamentally, the changes Miller and Eldersveld set in motion made long-term research, generously funded by private and public patrons, rather than public service the coin of the departmental realm. This was the heart of the transformation they sought—and the heart of what their opponents tried to resist.

CHAPTER FIVE

Political Science at Berkeley

Growth, Conflict, and Dispersal

In the previous chapter on the University of Michigan, I focused on how individuals affiliated with well-funded research organizations outside the department transformed the teaching and reproduction of political science there in less than twenty years. At the University of California, Berkeley, by contrast, there were no organizations as formidable as Michigan's Institute for Social Research or the Survey Research Center during the immediate postwar period. When similar entities formed at UC Berkeley during the 1950s, those affiliated with them did not exert as much power over the department's curriculum as Warren Miller had at Michigan. Instead, the transformation of political science at Berkeley began when the whole university system quickly intensified its research mission at a time of rapid system-wide growth and reorganization. In this environment, political science was more eclectic and experimental in the 1950s at Berkeley than at Michigan. When conflicts began to erode that openness in the mid-1960s, they were not conflicts between representatives of different generations or disciplinary backgrounds as they had been at Michigan. Instead, they were conflicts between contemporaries, especially bitter when they divided people who had recently found some common intellectual ground. Powerful centrifugal forces were at work in the rapidly growing university, making it much easier for faculty to create new structures than to cultivate and maintain a departmental core. In addition to these broad factors, the increasingly bitter tenor of department life prompted a number of different subgroups within the department to try to leave it.

The postwar development of international and area studies also mattered far more at Berkeley than at Michigan. Though the emphasis on these fields was as old as the Berkeley department itself, it took on some new aspects in the 1950s and 1960s. A number of generously funded new international and area studies centers emerged during this period, offering some members of the department second academic homes to use as research redoubts during an increasingly turbulent period in the university's history. Centers like these were of course not the only extra-departmental research units with which Berkeley political scientists were affiliated.[1] Overall, however, the postwar emergence of international and area studies centers solidified the centrality of these fields to political science at Berkeley. By contrast, the political theorists' sharp critiques of the department, discipline, and university struck many of their colleagues in other fields as dangerous attempts to "politicize" political science that needed to be countered or quashed.

Imperial Beginnings: The Founding and Early Years of the Berkeley Political Science Department

The expansion of American colonial responsibility was reflected in the evolving curricula.

—from a brief history of Berkeley's political science department by Eleanor Van Horn and Eric Bellquist[2]

At the University of Michigan, a department of political science was established to meet the demand for credentialed local administrators during the Progressive Era. In California, however, the overseas imperial ventures of the United States were more salient. UC Berkeley's political science department came into being in 1903 when Bernard Moses, a professor of history, returned to the university after playing a leading role on the US Philippine Commission.[3] Moses, who became the new department's first chair, had written several books on Spanish rule in the Americas. These exemplified what the field of "international relations" meant in the early twentieth century: the study of hierarchical relations between "races," with an emphasis on colonial administration.[4] Beginning in the 1880s, Moses also taught courses on the history of political theory; in his view, the rise of the United States as an imperial power as well as Spain's decline were important periods in that history.[5] International or "race" relations and political theory fit together.

His onetime student and successor as chair, David Barrows, endorsed these views. In his 1930 eulogy for Moses, Barrows called Moses "an American 'imperialist,'" not to criticize but to celebrate him.[6] As chair, Barrows deepened Moses's commitment to pressing political science into the service of US power overseas. Like Moses, Barrows had also participated in the US rule of the Philippines, overseeing the development of the US-sponsored education system there for nearly ten years. A PhD in anthropology, Barrows wrote his dissertation on the Cahuilla indigenous people of what is now Southern California. His work on the history of the Philippines followed a similar "anthropological" approach, categorizing the peoples of the islands by culture and language but also by racialized physical characteristics.[7]

The new political science department's offerings reflected Moses and Barrows's experience and interests. For example, Moses offered "The Government of Dependencies" as one of the first eight courses taught in the department during the 1903–1904 academic year. Ten years later, Barrows assumed responsibility for that course after Moses retired, in addition to other courses on international relations with emphases on Spanish America and the Far East. At that time, a description of the areas in which department members would oversee graduate study highlighted Barrows's interests, including "the government of the Mexican republic, the government of American dependencies, [and] international relations in the Pacific." After Barrows retired, the department sought to hire someone with an expertise in "Dependent Areas," the field Barrows had so prominently shaped, to replace him. A version of the dependencies course Moses and Barrows had taught continued to be offered as late as 1961.[8] Though "Dependent Areas" as a name for a field of study disappeared in the 1960s, Barrows's own name did not. When it opened in 1964, the new building that housed the political science department and many other academic units was called Barrows Hall. Citing Barrows's publicly declared racist views, a July 2020 student-led petition called for removing his name from the building; a few months later, the Building Name Review Committee concurred. Barrows Hall became the Social Sciences Building.[9]

Barrows was not the only early twentieth-century faculty member to extend the life of Moses's ideas. Raymond Gettell, the first member of the Berkeley department who specialized in political theory, also affirmed the connection between political theory and international relations in his published works, albeit in less sanguine terms than Moses had done. Gettell argued that the dominant political theories of a historical period reflect not only the current "stage of intellectual development" but also "influence political development." Throughout his massive 1924 *History of Political Thought*, Gettell presented particular "objective political conditions" he saw as crucial to the political thinking of distinct periods in ancient, medieval, and modern history. Relations between nations were among the political conditions Gettell believed historians of political thought should consider. A number of his chapters included sections on the theories of international relations of particular periods; chapter 27 was devoted to nineteenth-century "theories of nationalism, imperialism and internationalism."[10] Among the "deficiencies" Gettell cited in what was considered the definitive multivolume history of political thought by William Dunning was Dunning's failure to address "the development of the theory of international relations." In Gettell's view, early twentieth-century imperialism and colonialism were having a profound influence on political thought by calling into question whether the nation-state ought still to be understood as a "geographic and ethnic unity."[11] Accounts of contemporary political theory therefore needed to include theories of international relations.

When Gettell died in 1949, Barrows and several other colleagues cited the international influence of his 1924 *History*, noting in particular that "its Portuguese and Spanish editions extended its use as a teaching text to several countries of the Americas."[12] Though Gettell had not personally served the US empire as Moses and Barrows had done, his colleagues suggested that his book had.

Echoes of this racialized, colonial rule–inflected conception of international relations are still audible in a brief history of the department written over sixty years after its founding. Celebrating the department's early leaders' "participation in public affairs," its authors suggest that Moses and Barrows's experience as colonial officials shaped the new department's course offerings: "The expansion of American colonial responsibility was reflected in the [department's] evolving curricula." They also cite several events that "stimulated even greater interest" in subjects they called "international studies and *interracial problems.*" One of these was the 1915 Panama Pacific International Exposition.[13] This vast exposition, which Barrows helped promote, took place just across the bay in San Francisco. The largest exhibit in the Palace of Education showcased the achievements of US "colonial education" in the Philippines, emphasizing the dramatic increase in the number of students enrolled in schools that taught them "agricultural and manufacturing skills," now in English rather than Spanish.[14] Some variations of the racialized ideas that infused US colonial policy in the Philippines were on display at another exhibit in the Palace of Education, the explicitly eugenicist "Race Betterment Booth."[15]

The authors of the 1960s department history offered no criticisms of these early twentieth-century conceptions of political science; instead, they celebrated Moses and Barrows's colonial positions as "public service" and continued to call the department's curricular focus "international studies and interracial problems." Echoes of this early twentieth-century colonial-inflected international relations are still audible in the mid-twentieth-century grants the Rockefeller and Ford Foundations made to the department and university as well. Rockefeller's insistence that the department participate in its program to shape universities in Africa, Asia, and Latin America according to US models exemplified the "cultural imperialism" that marked US foreign policy during the Cold War, as did the advent of multiple Ford-funded postwar area studies institutes.[16] In subsequent sections of this chapter, I consider each in detail.

Postwar Expansion

During its first forty years, the number of faculty in Berkeley's political science department grew steadily but slowly—from three members in the 1903–1904 academic year to fifteen in 1943–1944. Six years after that, however, the number of department faculty had more than doubled; nearly half were assistant professors, lecturers, or instructors.[17] The rapid pace at which Berkeley's political science department grew illustrates in microcosm the dramatic postwar expansion of the University of California system as a whole. Immediately after the end of the war, returning veterans swelled the number of enrolled students at Berkeley to nearly 26,000 in 1948–1949, exceeding prewar enrollments by over 8,000. And given the rapidly rising population of California, state and federal officials predicted that a "second wave" of new students would enroll in the university after most of the veterans had graduated. University officials responded to these postwar changes in a number of ways: acquiring new land for the Santa Barbara campus, expanding undergraduate offerings at the Davis and Riverside campuses, and hiring many new faculty. From 1941 to 1950, the number of faculty system-wide nearly doubled.[18]

At the same time, research was also becoming more important at Berkeley. This happened for two separate but mutually reinforcing reasons. First, as John Douglass has pointed out, mobilization during World War II meant a second "gold rush" for California—this time consisting largely of federal funds. The state's universities were among the beneficiaries, especially their federally sponsored laboratories like the Lawrence Radiation Laboratory and Los Alamos. Their work became an important model for the size and organization of university-based research in the immediate postwar era. Second, when higher education officials and state legislators formalized distinctions between California's public universities, regional colleges, and junior colleges in the 1960 California Master Plan, they strengthened the identity of the principal UC campuses as research institutions.[19]

On the smaller scale of the political science department, these broader factors helped to make the 1950s a decade of dramatic change. For one, there was the influx of a large number of new, younger faculty at the beginning of the decade along with the continuing prospect of adding more to their number. Also, for the first time in its history, the department was being led by an "outside chair" rather than a long-time member of its faculty. Peter Odegard, a prominent political scientist who had been president of APSA and part of the Study Commission for the Ford Foundation charged with designing Ford's massive postwar philanthropic program, chaired the department from 1948 until 1955.[20] Changes at the level of the upper administration mattered as well. Shortly after becoming Berkeley's first chancellor in 1952, Clark Kerr drew a number of younger department faculty into significant advisory roles, bringing them close to the hub of university administrative planning and decision-making. At a time when the social sciences had little access to federal patronage, Kerr also encouraged Berkeley's social scientists to forge connections with private philanthropies with programs in their fields.[21] The Ford and Rockefeller grants to the university and the department discussed below were made during this unusually fluid time.

All of these factors made it easier for faculty to develop and teach new courses, redesign the curriculum, and rethink their fields and discipline. There is ample evidence that they did all of these things. For example, in a report to the president of the university concerning the first three years of his tenure as chair (1948–1951), Odegard listed nearly fifty new courses that had recently been developed and mentioned that significant revisions of the department's undergraduate and graduate programs were underway. Indeed, a significantly larger number of courses were offered in the 1950–1951 academic year than just a few years earlier, indicating that most of the new courses Odegard listed had gotten off the drawing board.[22]

The foundation grants made to the university and especially to the department during the 1950s added even more ferment to this heady mix. The most substantial of these came from Ford's Behavioral Sciences Program and Rockefeller's Legal and Political Philosophy Program. In earlier chapters, I discussed the life of each of these programs in the broader context of Ford and Rockefeller's postwar agendas. Here, I consider the reception of these grants at Berkeley and the changes they accelerated in the political science department. These were the first important sources of external funding for faculty research; they also provided groups within the department the occasion to define—or redefine—their ideas about political science and their relation to it. For a time, this meant a lot of intellectual experimentation, including a lot of enthusiasm for both theory and behavioralism, especially among the younger faculty. Ultimately, however, the new initiatives encouraged by these grants intensified the centrifugal forces coursing through the department. Rather than seeking to redefine the department, a number of groups opted to leave it.

Reception of the 1950 Ford Grant

Foundation funding added fuel to Berkeley's already rapid growth by prompting many members of the political science department to try to align their intellectual interests with these new initiatives' apparent aims. The career of Eugene Burdick illustrates this dynamic particularly well. Principally remembered today for his popular novels, like *The Ugly American*, Burdick taught in the political science department at Berkeley from 1953 until his death in 1965. For a significant portion of his time on the faculty, he also served as an administrative consultant to Clark Kerr during Kerr's tenure both as chancellor and as UC's president. Burdick's scholarly work on topics ranging from the history of syndicalism to voting behavior reflected his eclectic intellectual interests. He also taught courses in several areas of concentration in the department's curriculum, including several courses in political theory, a course on politics and literature, and a "how-to" course called "Problems in the Analysis of Political Behavior" in the behavior concentration that included "instruction in the use of punched-card equipment."[23]

One of Burdick's early tasks as a consultant to Kerr involved helping the new chancellor plan how to spend the $300,000 Ford Foundation grant "for research 'in individual behavior and human relations.'"[24] As discussed in chapter 2, this large grant came as a surprise to its recipients—at Berkeley, no member of the social sciences faculty or any administrator had applied for it. Once Kerr became chancellor, it fell to him and his staff, including Burdick, to figure out how to spend this large grant in a way that would meet with Ford's approval.[25] Burdick worked on this issue mainly by vetting proposals for how to spend the money but also by reporting to Kerr on how he thought Ford's other ventures in behavioral social science were working out. Among the most significant of these was the newly established Center for Advanced Studies in the Behavioral Sciences (CASBS), which opened in 1954 and received $10.35 million from Ford between 1952 and 1957.

In an early proposal to President Gordon Sproul for how Berkeley ought to spend the Ford grant, Kerr suggested it be used to create two new centers: a Survey Research Center and a Center for the Integration of Social Science Theory. The goal of the latter, Kerr argued, should be achieving the "unity of the social sciences." Theoretical work was therefore central: "The overriding qualification [for a center for social science theory] is that each member of the group must believe in the importance of theory. This would be no place for an empiricist."[26] Burdick shared Kerr's enthusiasm for what the Center for the Integration of Social Science Theory would mean for the social sciences at Berkeley, but he was less thrilled about the prospect of a new Survey Research Center. In one of his earliest memos to Kerr concerning the Ford grant, Burdick argued that Berkeley ought to direct the Ford money toward theoretical approaches, in part because the "Ford people are not interested in finding specific answers to empirical problems." Further, he argued that establishing a Survey Research Center at Berkeley would be redundant because centers of this kind already existed at Michigan and Princeton.[27] These quibbles aside, Burdick and Kerr agreed that what was by now officially Ford's behavioral sciences program offered exciting new opportunities to pursue theoretical work.

Burdick's enthusiasm for theoretically rich behavioral social science was, if anything, strengthened by the year he spent as a fellow at CASBS (1954–1955). In response to Kerr's request that he list some Berkeley faculty that he might nominate as future CASBS fellows, Burdick emphasized that the center seemed a theory-friendly place and would therefore be poorly suited to "the empiricist who is deeply committed to exploration of some narrow area." Later, in a letter thanking CASBS's director, Ralph Tyler, for his time at the center, Burdick said that as a theorist he had felt very much at home there. This was, however, not what Burdick had expected. Indeed, he confessed that in the months leading up to his residency, he had crammed to improve his knowledge of mathematics under the mistaken impression that such knowledge would be "terribly important" to the intellectual life of the center. "It was an enormous relief," Burdick concluded, "to find that the so-called behavioral sciences were not as far different from political theory as I had imagined."[28]

As these extracts from his correspondence show, Burdick tacked back and forth between anxious confusion over Ford's aims and genuine excitement over what its Behavioral Sciences Program might help him and his colleagues in political theory do. He was by no means alone in this; Kerr and others expressed a similar ambivalence. On the one hand, they struggled to figure out how to pitch their plans in terms that might be acceptable to Ford. On the other, their excitement over the prospects they thought the grant offered for doing big new things was real.

For a time, a number of Burdick's departmental colleagues in political theory felt a similar kind of interest and even excitement about the behavioral sciences as well. This group included Norman Jacobson, Sheldon Wolin, John Schaar, and Michael Rogin, all of whom had joined the department between the early 1950s and the early 1960s. All professed an interest in both behavioral approaches and political theory in ways that went well beyond collegial politeness. And all except Wolin taught courses in what became the political behavior and public opinion concentration. For example, Jacobson taught courses on the politics of labor and the politics of business in the early 1950s. In correspondence with Rockefeller Foundation officers, he also expressed support for the survey research central to what became *The American Voter* project and especially for one of its authors, his former Berkeley colleague, Michigan's Warren Miller.[29] In an oral history interview many years later, Miller recalled that both Jacobson and Wolin had been part of his small intellectual circle during his brief time at UC Berkeley. Wolin too recalled that after Miller left Berkeley, he supported hiring another scholar of political behavior to maintain what he then saw as the valuable eclectic quality of the department.[30]

Both Schaar and Rogin came to the department already familiar with behavioral approaches; initially, both taught more courses in American politics than political theory. Schaar, who joined the faculty in the late 1950s, coauthored several articles with Herbert McClosky, the scholar of political psychology hired to replace Miller. Schaar also taught undergraduate courses in the public opinion, parties, and pressure groups concentration up through the early 1960s. And Rogin, whose early work relied on electoral data to debunk linking Midwestern Populism to support for Senator Joseph

McCarthy, taught the graduate course "Parties, Public Opinion and Interest Groups."[31] The deep opposition between behavioralism and political theory that became so central to disciplinary debates by the late 1960s was nowhere to be seen in the 1950s and early 1960s in Berkeley.

Such affinities between behavioralism and political theory were not nearly as strong in the University of Michigan department. What explains their presence at Berkeley? For one, as Berkeley's chancellor, Kerr drew a number of younger theorists in addition to Burdick into his administration or into grant-disbursing roles. He also encouraged them to cultivate relationships with the Social Science Research Council (SSRC) and major philanthropies. Practically, this meant that along with Burdick, Jacobson and Wolin also had some responsibility for working out the place and meaning of the behavioral sciences in their department, university, and discipline. That Kerr did not present their advent at the university as a fait accompli but rather as a process faculty, theorists included, could have a hand in shaping their greater interest and openness to it. Finally, these Berkeley theorists were of the same generation as many of the figures central to behavioralism; many had fought in World War II and completed their degrees shortly thereafter. The theorists at Michigan in the 1950s were older.

When the behavioral-theory alliance came apart in the late 1960s, the not-so-distant memory of it may have intensified feelings of betrayal on both sides. On the one hand, some theorists felt their colleagues had deliberately marginalized them. On the other, those who continued to affirm behavioralism were stung by the openly political critiques their theorist colleagues directed at them.

Later Ford Grants for International and Area Studies

The money UC Berkeley received to develop its capacities in the behavioral sciences was part of an early round of grants Ford made to academic institutions shortly after its debut as the largest foundation in the United States. Though this grant was hugely significant at the time, it would later pale in comparison to the much more considerable sums Ford directed to Berkeley's Institute for International Studies (IIS) and various affiliated area studies centers in the late 1950s and 1960s.[32] Like its earlier behavioral science–focused grants, these later Ford grants also brought new academic entities into being. At Berkeley and elsewhere, the sudden advent of such well-funded institutes and research centers shifted the balance of power in departments and disciplines. These newly created international and area studies centers at US universities offered those affiliated with them considerable prestige. Not only were those linked to these new institutions likely to have more generous research and travel funds than those who remained department-bound; they were also more likely to move into foreign policy making circles.

When Ford and other midcentury foundations established and funded international and area studies centers, they were not just investing in a particular academic orientation; as Edward Berman put it, they were acting as "intermediaries" between academics and the foreign-policy making world. Such institutes and centers were the hubs of networks foundations built to link universities and the state; fellowships for US and overseas students as well as programs directed toward universities outside the United States reinforced these networks as well. From the late 1950s through the mid-1960s, Ford committed $138 million to such programs, more than any other foundation.[33] These programs gave international and area studies considerable academic standing—a standing that, as Inderjeet Parmar argues, was inseparable from their political aims. Parmar shows how instrumental Ford, along with Rockefeller and Carnegie, were to constructing networks of academics and policy-makers focused on Asia, Africa, and Latin America. Doing so depended on a number of different programs: funding area studies centers in US universities, supporting universities overseas, and then linking the two. These ambitious network-building projects also sometimes included financing the creation of professional associations along with sponsoring their meetings and scholarly publications.[34] Such multifaceted programs had a fundamental purpose: to cultivate and direct academic expertise toward the many parts of the world US political and economic elites thought vital to what one prominent consultant for Ford called "our new national interest."[35]

The initial grants Ford made to develop academic capacities in the behavioral sciences had been bold attempts to redirect the social sciences. Ford's international and area studies program was even more ambitious and "hands-on." The foundation's decision to end its Behavioral Sciences Program in 1957, therefore, did not mean the end of Ford's support for the social sciences. Instead, Ford's priorities shifted from the behavioral sciences to international and area studies.[36] Ford was not alone here; Carnegie and Rockefeller devoted considerable resources to building the capacities of

US universities in international and area studies as well. In the subsequent two sections of this chapter, I analyze the effects of a ten-year Rockefeller Foundation grant on Berkeley's political science department that, particularly in its later phase, exemplified this broad commitment.

Reception of the 1956 Rockefeller Grant

Ford opted to make its initial round of grants to develop the behavioral sciences to the presidents of universities rather than to specific departments or institutes within them. As Bernard Berelson, the head of Ford's Behavioral Sciences Program, understood it, this approach was meant to encourage grantees to create new things rather than to channel the funds into ongoing ventures. Which academic units and faculty might benefit from such grants was an open question each recipient institution had to answer.

By contrast, the grants Rockefeller made to support political theory, theoretical approaches to international relations, and comparative politics went directly to the political science department.[37] This approach, of course, did not settle exactly how and to whom these funds would be disbursed; but it did make clear that the foundation wished this to be primarily a departmental matter—albeit it with some nominal oversight from Chancellor Kerr. After one member of the department expressed the concern that Odegard, the outgoing chair, had suggested that nearly every member of the department could tap into this grant, a committee of department faculty drew up more field-specific instructions for how to allot these funds.[38] Members of this committee were therefore tasked with spelling out what ought to count as work in political theory and international relations to be able to justify their spending to Rockefeller. The instructions they drew up were nevertheless exceedingly flexible. They defined "international relations" broadly enough to include comparative politics; their definition of "political theory" was spacious as well: "political theory means any study of a political philosopher or of a concept or idea which possesses political relevance and in which the emphasis is analytical and evaluative rather than biographical or descriptive."[39] These definitions ruled more in than out; still, in a few instances, the department opted to fund a few projects that clearly fell outside even these expansive bounds. Given the loosely defined parameters of this program and the even looser way in which they were interpreted, an average of ten faculty received awards from this grant each year from 1957 to 1960. During the 1959–1960 academic year, more than half the department (fifteen people) received awards.[40]

The individual research projects supported by these awards did not coalesce around any distinctive approaches to political theory or international relations. Many, however, did at least gesture toward a field-crossing eclecticism. A number of grantees who taught international relations or comparative politics highlighted the theoretical ambitions of their projects: for example, Ernst Haas wanted to "advance a general theory of international community formation"; Richard Park planned a study of the political thought of modern India.[41] In a complementary way, several of those who taught political theory also emphasized how their proposed projects might bridge fields—as did Burdick in proposing a project on revolutionary organizations and Jacobson in focusing on political scientists' conception of science. Along similar lines, the public administration scholar Dwight Waldo proposed a project that would "emphasize the theoretical connections between the two enterprises of 'political theory' and 'public administration.'"[42] Projects with such broad ambitions gradually gave way to more field-specific ones over the ten-year life of these grants. They were numerous enough in the late 1950s, however, to suggest that many members of the department saw the first Rockefeller grant as an invitation to rethink field boundaries and cross them.

Even more clearly, the grant gave faculty a strong incentive to make published research their highest priority. Most of those who received awards used them to reduce their teaching responsibilities to do research and write, as the committee of faculty who drew up instructions for disbursing this grant clearly intended.[43] The new department chair, Charles Aikin, particularly encouraged younger faculty to apply for and use awards in this way. In a more extensive report submitted to the foundation when the first five-year grant was about to end, Aikin suggested that the availability of these funds had made it easier for the department to attract new faculty.[44] Though the first Rockefeller grant in 1956 was not the primary impetus for the rapid growth of the department, it both accelerated that growth and steered its increasingly younger faculty toward research-focused careers.

Imperial Zenith: "The Sun Never Sets on the Political Science Department of the University of California!"

The second grant Rockefeller made to the department in 1961 retained a commitment to research but changed the fields it supported. Comparative politics became its primary focus, replacing theoretical approaches to international relations; political theory was still supported, but to a lesser degree. Several new stipulations reinforced these changes. From his new position as the head of the Social Sciences Division at Rockefeller, Kenneth Thompson made clear that any new grant to Berkeley would be designed to support Rockefeller's new University Development Program (UDP), focused on universities in Africa, Latin America, and Asia. This program aimed to build curricula on US models in universities in Africa, Asia, and Latin America and construct international networks of academic elites in the process.[45]

Though these were new foundation priorities, they were also continuous with Rockefeller's 1956 grant to the department. In addition to an unusually expansive conception of political theory that Thompson built into the first grant, he hoped it would make academic political theory more interesting and useful to policy makers. A PhD in international relations with a strong affinity for political theory, Thompson had been advocating for connecting theorists to policy-makers for years.[46] In his conversations with his contacts at Berkeley, Thompson pitched Rockefeller's new emphasis on building connections between US universities and those in Africa, Asia, and Latin America as consistent with the broad, practical, policy-oriented conception of political theory central to the first grant.

Over the next few years, Rockefeller officials repeatedly pressed department leaders to meet the new UDP requirements of the grant and commit some of its faculty to teaching abroad. The carefully negotiated replies from the department express both a strong endorsement of the new priority given to comparative politics coupled with an unwillingness to take time away from their own research or their graduate students to teach in developing countries.[47] Ultimately, after Rockefeller softened its initial insistence that only tenured or tenure-track faculty teach abroad, Robert Scalapino (who had become chair in 1962) quickly filled the required slots with recent PhDs on short-term appointments. This arrangement allowed the department to meet its obligations to the grant's new UDP requirements without committing many full-time faculty to going abroad.

This round of give-and-take between the foundation and the department also specified that those who remained at Berkeley participate in one or more research-oriented faculty seminars. Once the foundation's new priority for teaching abroad became clear, a group of department faculty suggested the inclusion of these seminars as a way to allow those remaining on campus to continue to receive some research support from the grant.[48] Initially, the department made a strained attempt to argue that those participating in the seminars in Berkeley would interact frequently with those teaching overseas—something that did not happen regularly.[49] Instead, the seminar in comparative politics and the research funds tied to it intensified the department's already considerable emphasis on this field. Just one year after it began, Scalapino judged this seminar an "outstanding success," saying that it offered its dozen members a rare and "meaningful intellectual association."[50] A grant initially designed to support political theory and theoretical approaches to international relations now supported theoretical work in comparative politics and area studies. As the 1956 grant had done for the field of political theory, the subsequent 1961 grant gave scholars in area studies and comparative politics opportunities to define themselves as an intellectual group.

Thompson hoped that the Berkeley faculty's planned comparative politics research seminar would explore the applicability of concepts central to US political science to "non-western areas and cultures." A less sanguine Rockefeller Foundation official, however, warned that the Berkeley area studies and international relations faculty still had to "reconcile" their research interests with the foundation's university development priorities.[51] His skepticism seemed warranted; both in the department's formal grant proposal and in a report on the first year of the grant, the comparative politics seminar focused on issues that were not central to UDP.[52] Only in one year, when the Africanist David Apter led it, was the seminar's focus as Thompson had hoped: its participants, which included many Africanists and Asianists, presented work on the themes of "Tradition and Innovation" and "The Uses of Ideology in Development."[53] That year, though, was an anomaly. Overall, participants in the comparative politics seminar were more interested in discussing new theoretical works in comparative politics and getting a handle on the rapidly changing field than they were in advancing Rockefeller's university development initiative.[54]

Rockefeller officials, however, cared much more about faculty participating in its university development initiative than they did about the faculty seminars. The UDP was one among many anti-Communist Cold War foundation programs; in microcosm, it illustrates what Berman called the foundations' role as "silent partners" in US foreign policy making.[55] Developing cadres of US-friendly academic and governmental elites in Africa, Asia, and Latin America—in some cases at universities the foundation had itself launched—was the UDP's core mission. Such programs also paid broader political dividends. As several studies have shown, the networks constructed by foundation programs like the UDP linking US academics with students and colleagues overseas were also used by diplomatic and intelligence officials.[56] A great deal of political work happened under the innocuous banners of "education" and "development."

Given these aspects of the UDP and programs like it, it is unsurprising that the Berkeley political scientists who went abroad under its auspices did much more than teach classes. One of their missions was to advise their hosts on their political science curricula, using current US political science as a model. One participant who spent a year at the Gokhale Institute in Poona, India, likened this task to "a missionary type activity" that required considerable energy, since political science was still being taught there according to outdated British models. Still, he clearly understood that a primary objective of his visit was "'legitimating' contemporary political science."[57] Another mission focused on exporting US approaches to governance and administration, especially in conducting research and writing reports. Several Berkeley faculty ran workshops or set up research projects on everything from budgeting and taxation to running elections and prisons.[58]

Finally, most faculty who participated in this program worked on research projects on topics of potential interest to foreign policy and intelligence officials and filed reports with the foundation about their activities. Carl Rosberg worked with a "former British administrator" at the Royal College in Nairobi to do a study of the 1952 Mau Mau rebellion. Clement Moore conducted "a sample survey of student attitudes in Morocco and Tunisia" and established "good unofficial contacts" with students in "revolutionary socialist Algeria"; and Philippe Schmitter interviewed hundreds of public officials and interest-group leaders in Brazil in 1965, just a year after the US-backed military coup.[59] Not surprisingly, a few reported that who they were and what they were doing aroused suspicions. For instance, Schmitter, who began his time in Brazil just a year after the Project Camelot debacle, acknowledged, "It was almost inevitable that I would be denounced, covertly, if not overtly, as a spy. This happened and the fact that I was actively teaching served immeasurably to protect me from the consequences of such denunciations."[60] In some settings, however, the potential consequences of being suspected of spying were too dire to risk. This seems to have been the case when Scalapino declined a State Department request, endorsed by Rockefeller, to send someone to the University of Teheran in 1963. Though he complimented the "Shah's reforms," Scalapino warned that "the Iranian intelligencia [sic] was still largely dissident, creating a continuing problem."[61] Under such circumstances, he implied, teaching would be no protection.

Announcing the first group of UDP assignments overseas he had arranged, Scalapino declared grandly, "The sun never sets on the Political Science Department of the University of California!"[62] From one perspective, these far-flung, foundation-funded assignments bolstered the department's already considerable prestige. But there were other less complimentary ways to read them. For one, such overseas assignments were but one of the host of tasks department members took on that drew them away from teaching students in Berkeley. Their frequent absences reinforced the idea that the department itself was becoming as anonymous as the "multiversity" to which it belonged.[63] Also, by choosing the particular image he did, Scalapino made the department's ambitions sound unapologetically imperial. In the next few years, a range of groups criticized the department harshly on both these fronts.

Leaving the Department of Political Science: The Flight from the Disciplinary Center

The eclectic field-crossing projects pursued under the aegis of the 1956 Rockefeller grant soon gave way to groups defined by subfield. The faculty seminars supported by the second grant reinforced this: in addition to the comparative politics seminar discussed previously, other seminars in American government and politics and political theory began somewhat later. Though the vast majority of department faculty participated in these seminars, only a few took part in more than one.[64] In the late 1950s, the department committee's first definition of what ought to count as "political theory" welcomed nearly any project that might be undertaken by a political scientist. By 1964, however, when Wolin characterized the theory seminar he chaired as "somewhat unorthodox and flexible," it was not for its stance toward other fields within political science. Instead, the Berkeley theory seminar invited people outside the political science department to join it—faculty from other departments and political theorists at UCLA. This turning away from political science foreshadowed the 1967 attempt by some theorists to leave the department altogether.[65]

Theorists were not alone in seeking to build an intellectual community beyond the confines of the department. By the end of the 1960s, a number of scholars of international and area studies had already done so; and a graduate school of public administration separate from the political science department was about to open. When older structures like established departments with their majors, required courses, and disciplinary affiliations began to seem too rigid in this time of rapid growth, designing new academic structures especially suited to particular intellectual communities seemed appealing to many. Those affiliated with foundation-funded international and area studies centers had the easiest time of it, as they did not have to build these new academic homes themselves. Most who joined such centers, however, did not sever their ties with the political science department. For some, the center was their primary residence; for others, it was more of a pied-a-terre.

Around the same time, public administration faculty were on the cusp of achieving their long-standing aim to leave political science to form their own Graduate School of Public Affairs (GSPA) despite the objections of many faculty both inside and outside the department.[66] The archived papers of the university's upper administration suggest that plans to form this school had been in the works for nearly a decade. As early as 1960, some department faculty circulated a proposal to establish a Master's in Public Administration program; over the next seven years, with the support of Berkeley's vice chancellor, the proposal expanded into a plan for a stand-alone professional school.[67] Several faculty committees rejected that proposal in 1967, citing concerns about the proposed school's curriculum, the large number of faculty required to staff it, and its contributing to the perception that Berkeley was growing too quickly.[68] But the vice chancellor overrode these objections and the school was formally approved by the regents of the university at the end of 1967. It opened in 1969.

One of the leaders of the public administration initiative, Aaron Wildavsky, also played a central part in quashing the formation of a separate department of political theory in 1967 during his term as chair of the political science department from 1966 to 1969. Wildavsky then left the department in 1969 for the new Graduate School of Public Affairs, along with a number of his colleagues in public administration. He served as the GSPA's first dean, a position he held until 1977.[69]

The proposed secession of the political theorists faced long odds for a host of reasons on top of Wildavsky's opposition. For one, it never seems to have had any significant support among the upper administration or even among department faculty. Peter Dale Scott, a political theorist and professor of English literature at Berkeley who supported the proposal, remarked that planning to call the new department "political theory" rankled other faculty in political science. "Department of Weird Alternatives," Scott said ironically, might have been an acceptable name; a name that included "political" or "politics," however, was not. Jack Citrin, who had been a graduate student at Berkeley in the 1960s and later joined the faculty, remarked that some members of the department may have disliked the idea of the proposed department calling itself "political theory," since the name insultingly implied that everyone else in political science was atheoretical.[70]

Additionally, those who wanted to form new academic units in public administration or international and area studies could expect markedly greater support beyond Berkeley than could those who supported the political theory proposal. There were numerous examples across the United States of public administration faculty leaving political science departments to form separate schools as well as a burgeoning number of centers and institutes devoted to international and area studies. By contrast, there were no freestanding schools, departments, or institutes of political theory in the late 1960s; nor are there any today.[71] There was also no professional association specifically devoted to political theory in the 1960s comparable in stature to the then nearly thirty-year old American Society for Public Administration or the more recent International Studies Association (founded in 1959).[72]

It is far more difficult to understand failed academic initiatives than successful ones, given that the former often leave only fragmentary trails in universities' archives. On the one hand, there is plenty of material concerning proposals to establish the GSPA in the archived records of Berkeley's Office of the President, chancellor, and the Academic Senate. None of these offices, however, preserved any record of the proposal to establish a department of political theory. As a result, what little evidence I have been able to piece together concerning this proposed department has some notable gaps. It comes from oral histories and personal communications with some of the faculty and students involved, a lone draft of a fourteen-page "Proposal for a Department of Political Theory," dating from the summer of 1967, and retrospective references to the failed proposal in several documents from the next few years.[73] It is therefore impossible to give a full account of why the proposal failed or of who supported or opposed it and why. In what follows, I analyze the attempt to form a separate department of political theory mindful of these limitations.

Wolin, one of the leaders of this initiative, recalled that plans to secede from the political science department began in 1966 when Aaron Wildavsky became its chair. The atmosphere in the already fractious department had become "poisonous" by then, Wolin said, prompting the political theorists to propose forming their own academic unit. Other political theorists joined Wolin's effort, most notably John Schaar, with whom Wolin coauthored a number of pieces for the *New York Review of Books* about the student protests at Berkeley.[74] Faculty members from other departments were also involved in fleshing out the interdisciplinary conception of political and social theory that informed this proposal. Among them were the sociologist Philip Selznick and the professor of English literature and political writer, Peter Dale Scott.[75] Shortly after the failure of this attempted secession, Schaar and Wolin each resigned their positions at Berkeley. They also tried to establish similar programs elsewhere, first at Stanford and then at UC Santa Cruz, though neither of these efforts succeeded. In 1972 Wolin became the head of Princeton's interdisciplinary program in political philosophy.[76]

The proposal to form a department of political theory dovetailed with a number of better-known experiments and reports that unfolded from 1964 to 1970. Of all of these, the student-led Free Speech Movement (FSM) that began in 1964 is probably the most important and most widely known. For the students who made this movement, criticizing the "multiversity's" ever-increasing bureaucratic sprawl was a natural extension of their demand that the university treat them as adults with the right to political speech.[77] Private and public funders, they argued, had "imposed a pattern of growth and development" on the university, reducing the student to a "student-cog" working in a "factory" designed to meet "the purely technical needs of society"; such a system deprived them of "meaning" and "the freedom to learn."[78] Physically resisting such malign forces in the growing multiversity—"to put your bodies upon the gears and upon the wheels, upon the levers, upon all the apparatus . . . to make it stop"—was an intellectual and a moral imperative.[79] In a piece initially published several months after the FSM's dramatic fall 1964 sit-ins, Wolin and Schaar commented on the salutary effect the movement had had on the faculty: "For a time, the faculty forgot its lust for

research; its shameful neglect of teaching, its acquiescence in the bureau-
cratization of the University. Setting aside the ethos of power and growth,
the faculty stirred to ancestral memories of the ideal of a community of
scholars bound together in the spirit of friendly persuasion and pledged to
truth rather than abundance."[80] This vision of a university as a "community
of scholars" animated Wolin and Schaar's plans for a department of political theory.

Before Wolin and Schaar developed their plans, other experiments and
proposals for educational reform were proliferating on the Berkeley campus
in response to the FSM's critique of the bureaucratized, impersonal multiversity. The small Experimental College that began in 1965 was one of
the earliest.[81] Its organizer, the philosopher Joseph Tussman, constructed
a "great books" curriculum around the theme of "cultures in crisis." Such
a curriculum, Tussman argued, could best equip students to take up their
"political vocation" as democratic citizens.[82] Though Tussman discouraged
students from discussing their political activities in class, the deliberately
small size of the college as well as its self-conscious refusal to assign grades
set it apart from the bureaucratized "multiversity" the Free Speech Movement had so pointedly criticized. Not only was Jacobson briefly among its
faculty; Schaar and Wolin were beginning to articulate commitments similar to Tussman's "great books" curriculum as well as to his aim that students
be educated for their "political vocation."[83]

In addition to small-scale experiments like Tussman's, faculty and students made several detailed campus-wide proposals for educational reform.
Prompted by the FSM to examine how the university's rapid growth was
undermining its educational ideals, the Berkeley division of the Academic
Senate commissioned several special committees to recommend remedies.
In 1966 the first such committee recommended the creation of a new body
charged with preserving "the traditions of humane learning" in a rapidly
growing university. Under the aegis of what became the Board of Educational Development (BED), faculty and students could propose new classes
on topics of interest to them that were smaller and less hierarchical than the
increasingly common large lectures. Some of the courses developed, like
"The Nature of the University" and "Critical Analysis of Ideas of the University," explicitly extended the committee's charge into the classroom. Scott,
the English professor who would later sign onto to the proposed department of political theory, sent this committee an undated proposal titled, "A
Liberal Education Program at Berkeley," which he explicitly distinguished

from Tussman's Experimental College. Jacobson designed one of the two political science courses taught under the aegis of this board. Entitled "Film: Towards the Expression of an Idea of Freedom," it was offered in the fall of 1968.[84]

The BED also commissioned interviews with faculty and staff of individual departments to identify where the greatest obstacles to its ideals lay in each. A November 1966 interview with a small number of faculty and staff in political science, including Wildavsky and Wolin, depicted a department in which "educational innovation is made difficult" in part because it was so "overwhelmed" by student demand that "relationships with undergraduates are almost non-existent." The situation did not improve in the next few years; a 1968 pamphlet written by department students and faculty commented it was still "more difficult to initiate these [BED] courses in the political science department than in most others."[85]

In response to intensifying criticisms of the university's hierarchical structure, in 1967 the Academic Senate along with the senate of the Associated Students of UC (ASUC) created a Study Commission composed of an equal number of students and faculty to propose reforms to university governance. This body issued its nearly 100-page report calling for a "radical redirection" of the university in early 1968. It advocated a decentralized approach to governance paired with meaningful faculty and student participation as the best hope for restoring educational community at Berkeley.[86] Wolin, one of the four professors who contributed to and signed the final report, was working on it at the same time that he was involved in planning a new department of political and social theory.

The university's existing system of governance, the Study Commission argued, was geared primarily toward managing growth rather than to cultivating educational community.[87] "Size and scale are important conditions in promoting a lively sense of membership," the report's authors wrote. "What student or faculty member is likely to feel part of an intellectual community when his department may contain faculties of nearly 100 members, 700 undergraduate majors, and over 300 graduate students?" (p. 24). Worse, instead of giving students and faculty a primary role in defining the educational culture of the university, the report's authors warned, "External interests . . . have increasingly . . . shaped the direction of its educational activities" (p. 9). Why should one expect students and faculty to be loyal and committed to such a university? The report's case for decentralization, then, meant more than colleges ceding some decision-making to overgrown departments; it meant creating "new and smaller programs" and removing the formidable administrative obstacles to doing so (pp. 26–28, 30). Only in such smaller, more authentically participatory settings might it be possible to recover the values the report's authors claimed ought to guide "a true university": "individual dignity, freedom, and intellectual creativity"—a vision they acknowledged might strike many as "utopian and perhaps arcadian" (p. 80).

The tight link the Study Commission drew between educational values and university governance animated the proposal to establish a department of political theory as well, especially its emphases on decentralization, small educational settings, and intellectual community. To the proposal's unnamed authors, decentralization meant breaking up an overly large department both to reduce its size and to allow for greater intellectual pluralism. The "concerted effort . . . to unify Political Science" around "a common methodology" and the shrinking departmental space for divergent approaches was making real pluralism within it impossible.[88] Several curricular changes reinforced this trend toward epistemological centralization, including the new policy that the "only required upper-division course for undergraduate majors will be a three-quarter course treating scientific methods in political inquiry, together with an examination of current research techniques." This new requirement coincided with the plant "to abolish the Theory requirement [for graduate students] altogether" (p. 6). The authors of the proposal also note that students interested in political theory "find themselves disadvantaged by the current system of rewards" and cite the majority of the department's resistance to hiring additional theory faculty (p. 7). In the face of these strong trends, leaving the department seemed more feasible than trying to reform it. At least one well-established aspect of epistemological decentralization supported doing so: "The study of politics . . . is not currently the recognized monopoly of the Political Science Department. It is being studied in numerous courses and from different points of view in the Departments of History, Sociology, and Anthropology" (p. 8). Why not in a department of political theory as well?

The undergraduate and graduate programs in the proposed department began with a common core of classes, followed by individualized programs of study. Most classes were to be small—introduction to political theory taught in a seminar format for undergraduates, and small seminars for graduate students, ideally with a student-faculty ratio of "6 to 1."[89] Specific course requirements were few for both programs, though both were emphatically interdisciplinary in scope. As outlined, each academic program began with strictly defined points of academic focus that set the stage for individualized programs of study. For instance, first-year graduate students were to be examined on a small number of books decided upon by faculty ("Proposal," G2); undergraduate majors were to take an introductory seminar to political theory focused on "one significant work of political theory" ("Proposal," U1). Along with such narrowly specified points of focus, however, the draft programs also stress students' responsibility for crafting their own individualized programs of study and for graduate students and teachers to engage with each other as colleagues.[90]

These aspects of the proposed undergraduate and graduate programs in the proposed department of political theory expressed some of the broader educational goals endorsed by the Study Commission. The commission's report included detailed proposals for establishing small lower-division colleges emphasizing interdisciplinary learning as well as decentralizing departmental advising (appendices C and D). Each lower-division college was to be limited to five hundred undergraduates and devoted to a set of disciplines or a broad, interdisciplinary topic. By offering "a form of community appropriate to an educational institution," the report's authors hoped these small colleges would "help students and faculty to realize the goal of learning as shared experience and mutual participation" while also encouraging students' "individual self-determination" (p. 29).[91] The proposed decentralized advising system, which paired groups of twenty to thirty upper-division majors with a particular faculty member, had similar goals. The communities formed by these small advising "sections" promised to prevent the "intellectual atomization" many undergraduates were experiencing, in part because they would be given a meaningful responsibility for recommending changes to their current programs as well as proposing new courses (p. 89). "Such community settings," the Study Commission concluded, "provide the minimum conditions through which a large university can enlist the greater involvement of its members in its educational venture" (p. 9).

Both the Study Commission Report and the Proposal for a Department of Political Theory aspired to radical departures from existing university and departmental structures. Yet for as radical as the visions that animated them were, their authors were still arguing for space to realize their visions within or alongside existing structures rather than for remaking those structures entirely. Radical restructuring, however, was the express aim of the Reconstitution Movement.[92] This immense movement, in which Wolin was a prominent participant, grew out of campus-wide protests against the US invasion of Cambodia in the spring of 1970. It was a fundamental if brief attempt to reconceive the structure and workings of the university.

On May 6, 1970, Wolin read a seven-point proposal to a crowd of 17,000 people in the university's Greek Theater. It began: "This campus is on strike to reconstitute the University as a center for organizing against the war in Southeast Asia. . . . We will organize not only against the war, but against the structures in society that facilitate that war. And we will organize to end our University's complicity with that war."[93] A later statement by the Strike Coordinating Committee made clear that the "reconstituted university is dedicated to the reversal of the university's normal function." Rather than "train students to manipulate objects, persons, and ideas in ways which support, justify, and implement the American world system," the newly remade university would be "dedicated to the enrichment of human life and the enhancement of the scope of human freedom."[94] For the remainder of the spring quarter, a good deal of university life was reoriented toward these goals. Acknowledging the strong support for pursuing reconstitution, UC Berkeley's chancellor directed schools and departments to be "flexible" about rules concerning grades, course loads, and course content. Most notably, this policy also made it possible for students to receive academic credit for "reconstituted" courses in which they did "antiwar related academic work." While some faculty welcomed all of these changes, others balked at the idea of reconstituting course curricula, especially if that meant allowing students to participate in making these changes. They also opposed students picketing some unreconstituted classes that continued to meet.[95]

In retrospect, many of those who took part in this movement said that they learned not only in such classes but outside them as well. The chance to interact with people with whom they usually had little contact, whether in small planning groups including a mix of students, faculty, and staff or while canvassing local East Bay area residents, seemed especially important. It was these aspects of the movement that Wolin cited in a June 4 speech at the end of the spring quarter at a rally organized as a "reaffirmation" its intertwined goals: reforming the university and opposing the war. Wolin's speech ended with a call for a "campus constitutional convention" at the end of the winter quarter in 1971.[96]

The Reconstitution Movement did not survive that long, however; its energy dissipated as many students left campus for the summer. Early in the fall quarter, the university regents imposed new restrictions "designed to reduce the likelihood of another 'reconstitution.'" Wolin also did not return, resigning his position at Berkeley to begin teaching at UC Santa Cruz. Over twenty years later in a long oral history interview, however, Wolin underscored the importance of the movement. Reconstitution, he said, had had a great influence on his thinking about democracy as a "movement, concept and practice" and, more generally, on building a "Berkeley tradition" of student participation in education.[97]

As these examples illustrate, the proposal to establish a department of political theory drew on some broader educational experiments at Berkeley that began in the mid-1960s. After the proposal ran aground, graduate students and some faculty continued to pursue the ambitions that had animated it in other ways. The radical, even militant, ways in which they did so deepened the already sizable rifts within the department over what role, if any, students ought to have in decisions about course content, curriculum, and personnel. As one graduate student commented, the "real split" in the department was not over the merits of different methods of studying politics; it was "over student participation" instead. What was happening at UC Berkeley was happening in the discipline nationwide as well. In 1967 the Caucus for a New Political Science formed to organize dissenters within the American Political Science Association, sharpening debate among political scientists about the place of politics in their discipline and its relations with the state.[98]

Politicizing Political Science: From SLATE to GASP

Throughout the 1960s, both undergraduate and graduate students who took political science courses at UC Berkeley tried to make sense of the wide range of approaches they encountered in them. Increasingly, a number of students' critical reviews of the department began to understand the divergences in "methods" they encountered as expressions of political disagreements. In response, they began to make their own political commitments clear as well. That students should publish any such reviews seemed impertinent and annoying to some. When these reviews grew into full-throated political critiques, some faculty pushed back, calling their authors "unprofessional" and warning that a "community of scholars" could not survive such coercive tactics that politicized political science.[99]

One of the best sources for gauging some undergraduate students' sense of the department during this time are the SLATE Supplements to Berkeley course catalogs that began to appear in late 1963. SLATE, one of the principal student-run organizations that sparked the Free Speech Movement, ran alternative slates of candidates for student government positions, mainly to challenge the fraternities, sororities, and athletes that had dominated them.[100] The SLATE Supplements offered practical and often irreverent student-to-student advice about life in the university in general as well as particular departments, courses, and professors. Early supplements mocked the absurdities of the multiversity while advising readers how to make their way through its byzantine structures. For example, an early edition began by listing "ways to get an education in spite of the system."[101] By 1967, however, the tone of the supplements as a whole—and the reviews of the political science department in particular—had begun to shift from canny amusement to warning and denunciation.

Those who wrote the political science course reviews for the SLATE Supplements were clearly aware of the starkly different approaches on offer in the department. For example, a spring 1965 review of a course in political behavior taught by Peter Sperlich, an early graduate of the University of Michigan program in political behavior, advised: "an excellent introductory course in the empirical side of political science . . . but stay away if methodology and statistics bore you." And in spring 1967, Chalmers Johnson's "Government and Politics of Northeast Asia" course earned this wry compliment: "[Mr. Johnson] is articulate, clever, witty, enthusiastic, and opinionated. In fact he is a living example of the futility of any attempt to make political science value-free."[102]

One of the first attempts to grapple with the deep political divides in the department appeared in the spring 1967 supplement's section on political science, which began with a pair of dueling quotations:

"A fact is a fact and what the Hell can you do about it?" (Herbert McClosky)

"I have just come from watching the T.V. reports of the events in Selma. It takes something like this to make one fully realize the total inadequacy of the language of social science for the description of political reality." (Michael Rogin).

The authors then offered some practical advice to potential majors: "Students who have become attracted by one language found within the department should understand that as majors, and even more so as graduate students, they will have to at least learn the contents of the standard phrase book in several others: you might get stuck with a taxi-driver who speaks only structural-functionalese or a tour guide who speaks a dialect of Fortran." At first, students might think such a disagreements to be principally about "method(s) or . . . language." They would soon learn, however, that this was not the half of it; members of the department also disagreed about "its purpose, its style, its educational philosophy [and] its subject matter."[103] How should students negotiate such a divided department that "attempts to instruct students about the features of political order, yet it is itself a model of chaos"? The SLATE Supplement authors opted for analyzing the apparent "chaos" as a contest between "two factions":

> The dominant faction, made up of a mixed bag of survey researchers, systems analysts, and pluralist theorists, is determined to make political science into a "true" science. Their dream is a neat set of scientific statements about politics, purged of as much human bias and passion as is possible, and empirically validated. . . . The other faction is marked by a belief that any set of scientific statements can, at best, only provide the beginnings of an understanding of politics. Its adherents, primarily in political theory, emphasize that the exclusion of values and passion from the study of politics is basically a sham, obscuring an implicit justification of "pluralist democracy" (U.S.-style politics) and ruling out any consideration of political alternatives.[104]

This analysis inched toward linking specific approaches to the study of politics with particular political commitments. That link became explicit in a SLATE Supplement published a year later. Prevailing standards for "professionalism" in political science that stress the merits of being "detached, 'scientific,' and scholarly," its authors argued, aid and preserve the current political system. "The good student finds that he must not be troubled about the fact that Stanford political scientists designed the strategic hamlet program for Vietnam . . . that Cal professors contribute to the ideology of the managerial society by equating political apathy with political health." By contrast, studying political theory became political resistance; it was "studying with the dissidents, learning about things that matter, and also . . . picking up pointers on political action as well as theory."[105]

Around the same time, graduate students in the department were beginning to articulate their own politically informed critique. In spring 1968, a sizable group of graduate students along with some faculty wrote and distributed a pamphlet titled, "Political Science at Berkeley: Invitation to a Discussion."[106] The proposal to establish a department of political theory had recently failed; in light of that, the authors of the pamphlet called on the department to "look at itself critically and . . . locate the sources of discontent" (p. 1). Some of their diagnoses of what was wrong in the department were similar to the justifications for forming a separate department of political theory: a lack of "genuine pluralism" in the department and its neglect of undergraduate and graduate education (pp. 2, 12–17). While the authors of the secession proposal had held their critical fire, the authors of this pamphlet no longer did so. Instead, they offered a sustained critique of the political failings of the department and discipline to criticize what they called the "profoundly conservative" character of political science as well as to indict many of its members' invocation of "objectivity, detached scholarship and methodological rigor in order to escape the commitments of action and responsibility" (pp. 5, 21).

These criticisms intensified over the next few years. From the mid-1960s on, students and some faculty took part in numerous strikes and sit-ins on campus. Some of these protested against the war; others explicitly demanded more power for students over university programs and conditions of their employment.[107] These protests took several specific forms in the political science department. Some political science graduate students working as teaching assistants were fired for having joined broad, university-wide strikes in 1966 and 1969.[108] In 1970 the Graduate Association of Students of Politics (GASP) joined groups of Blacks, women, undergraduates, and junior faculty in the department to demand student representation on policy committees for curricula, hiring, and tenure. At the same time, some graduate students were organizing a panel on "The Situation at Berkeley" at the Western Political Science Association (WPSA) meeting under the auspices of the Caucus for a New Political Science. The panel allowed them not only to present their views to an audience outside UC but also to appeal to the WPSA as a professional organization to investigate their grievances against the department.[109] Around the same time, GASP wrote a letter intended for all new graduate students accepted for the fall of 1970. They informed prospective students that the "invitation to a discussion" they had extended two years earlier had not led to any positive change; instead, they cited the "suppression" of debate about the character of the department and discipline as well as some professors' effort to "end" it. Despite such formidable resistance, the students announced their intention to "struggle against attempts to divorce our lives as students of politics from our lives as political actors." They welcomed those students who were ready to join a "common struggle and . . . fight to do the kind of work you feel matters" to UC Berkeley but advised those "looking for a quiet spot" to pursue graduate study elsewhere.[110]

The Berkeley campus was anything but a quiet spot during the next several months. To show their support during earlier strikes, students briefly interrupted a few political science classes that continued to meet.[111] In spring 1970, students adopted more militant tactics, organizing so-called Red Star Tours of the offices of faculty they believed to be complicit with the US war in Southeast Asia. Carl Rosberg, the current chair of the department, wrote to UC's chancellor, Roger Heyns, to decry this "innovation in coerciveness," warning that it threatened the university's "survival as a community of scholars."[112] Other faculty in the department also complained of the intimidation, coercion, and violence directed at themselves or at students who were not supporting the strikes.[113]

The chief criticism, however, that some department faculty directed against the increasingly militant students and their faculty supporters was that they were politicizing the department and the university.[114] In one of many letters to Berkeley's chancellor in the midst of Reconstitution Movement, department chair Rosberg acknowledged that since the subject matter of courses in the department was necessarily political, "controversial matters" would inevitably come up in them. This was especially true, Rosberg conceded, since many department faculty also consulted for a host of state agencies. These features of the department notwithstanding, Rosberg and others still insisted that politicizing the department was unwarranted. The implicit claim at the heart of the injunction, "don't politicize our department of politics," seemed to be "our authority as teachers and experts about politics is legitimate; don't challenge it." As Rosberg put it, the members of his department could teach politics "without subverting the educational process" thanks to their "objectivity and high analytic skill and insight based on years of scholarship." A politicized department, he implied, would challenge rather than respect the authority of these faculty.[115]

These concerns about a politicized department and university were even more explicit in a brief essay written by department member and State Department consultant Paul Seabury. Among his many criticisms of the Reconstitution Movement, Seabury pointedly warned against its anti-authoritarian aspirations to eliminate "rank and tenure"—aspirations that threatened to reduce the university to an "egalitarian compost heap." The events at Berkeley, Seabury argued, were disturbingly similar to the more militant leftist movements he claimed had overturned traditional authority structures in universities in Western Europe, where "coalitions of students . . . typists, janitors, etc. actually can outvote faculty members even in doctoral examinations." Contemptuous of Wolin for his support of reconstitution, Seabury portrayed him as a naïf whose "idyllic dream of a campus of humane self-gratification" would inevitably be overwhelmed by leftist ideologues bent on using the university as "a political weapon." During the Reconstitution Movement, UC Berkeley had come perilously close to becoming a "whole-politicized university," utterly intolerant of "free rational inquiry."[116]

Conclusion

Members of the political science department at UC Berkeley responded in a wide variety of ways to the dramatic growth of the university during the immediate postwar period. Initially, many expressed genuine excitement about the intellectual opportunities offered by the bountiful new foundation funds that accelerated that growth. Release time for research and writing, a vibrant graduate program, and intellectual exchanges with colleagues quickly became important to many faculty. Soon, however, sustaining broader, experimental intellectual ventures became difficult—especially after funders themselves lost interest. Specialization seemed more sustainable in the frenetic pace of life in a growing research university. Then, largely because of the powerful interventions of the student-led movements of the 1960s, some groups within the university and department began to consider what they had sacrificed during this period of unremitting growth and what they could do differently. By the end of the period, several different groups had pulled away from the political science department—some to pursue the varied missions of the multiversity in new research centers or professional schools, others to try to create smaller, more communal spaces for learning elsewhere.

Across the university, faculty and administrators had to scramble to figure out how best to advance their projects in this time of rapid growth. When administrators and political science department faculty thought about the future of political theory, international relations, and comparative politics—the fields favored by the Ford and Rockefeller grants—they did so with an eye to adapting each field to emerging features of the multiversity. The Ford Foundation's preference for creating new structures outside existing departments reinforced the proliferation of extra-departmental research organizations at UC Berkeley. These research organizations' independence from departmental control, however, came at a price: most could not expect support from university funds after their initial foundation funding ran out. Hence, those who received Ford funding had to consider how—or whether—they could continue to win the external grants or secure the contracts they would need to keep a research center going. Moreover, the organized research unit form, so important to postwar Berkeley, was far from equally hospitable to all fields. The prospects of a theory-focused research center that had initially seemed so exciting to Eugene Burdick in the early 1950s were never bright. What became the Center for Social Science Theory was never large; once its three years of Ford funding ran out in the early 1960s, it closed.[117] By contrast, Berkeley's Survey Research Center had a much longer run; it closed in 2010, after just over fifty years. The Institute for International Studies (IIS), which will mark its seventieth year in 2025, and a number of the area studies centers affiliated with it, have proven more viable still.

Unlike Ford's grants, the grants the Rockefeller Foundation made to the department did not encourage the creation of new research centers. Instead, by investing in strengthening the department's capacity in "political theory and theoretical approaches to international relations," Rockefeller hoped to cultivate a new generation of theoretically inclined academics who would help the foreign policy making elite fight the Cold War. Initially, the first Rockefeller grant encouraged many people in the department to think of the whole discipline as fundamentally theoretical and to highlight the theoretical aspects of their work. However genuine these expressions of interest might have been, they were too diffuse to give any discernible form to what political theory would mean at Berkeley. The short-lived Rockefeller investment made political theory a vibrant, eclectic, but also an inchoate field.

When Rockefeller's priorities shifted toward enlisting members of the department to export US political science to universities in Africa, Asia, and Latin America, its focus shifted away from political theory. Though the Rockefeller funds had undoubtedly strengthened the field of political theory at Berkeley, it never developed the international orientation Rockefeller's Kenneth Thompson hoped it would. Instead, the critical, oppositional identity of the field was just beginning to gel once the second Rockefeller grant began. A conception of political theory as an alternative pedagogy was emerging, strengthened by student critiques of the mechanized, heartless multiversity and by theorists' own awareness of political science's part in it. Already in 1963, Norman Jacobson argued that political scientists pressed into the service of projecting US power overseas were doing far more than just teaching others about how to study politics; they were creating and reinforcing US-friendly political orders as well. Political science education was becoming legislation.[118] Jacobson's critique of the educational missions at the heart of initiatives like Rockefeller's University Development Program raised a fundamental question: how could those who taught about politics avoid such complicity?

Along with other educational experiments at Berkeley, the proposed department of political theory offered an extended answer to that question. Its authors criticized the dominant pedagogy of political science for using quantitative research methods and understanding politics ahistorically; there was no room, they said, in such a political science for the kind of teaching and research theorists did. Worse, this dominant approach to political science was not meeting the "manifest educational needs" of many students.[119] As the advocates of the proposed department understood them, students not only needed smaller classes; they also wanted to be treated as "valued members of a genuine intellectual and moral community."[120] In their most idealistic moments, teachers of political theory at Berkeley hoped they might be able to undo the alienation pervading the multiversity. The intensive study of a "canon" of political thought in the right setting could, they hoped, deepen students' understanding of their current political situation and thereby empower them in ways the dominant pedagogy of political science could not.

Many scholars have since roundly criticized these ideas as oblique, grandiose, and historically questionable.[121] Placed in the context of the rapid growth of UC Berkeley during the postwar period, however, these simultaneously oblique and grandiose claims about the political relevance of "epic theory" sound more like last-ditch, long-shot attempts to claim a small space to do things differently in an inhospitable environment. Even when it was getting the most attention from foundations and administrators, political theory was in a strange, insecure position in the Berkeley department. What great contributions could it make to the research university? How could it justify its existence there? In this light, the defensive aspect of the appeal to an older, "arcadian" ideal of intellectual life and community stands out.[122] Only with the catalyst of the student-led movements did these ideas at times veer toward a more radical critique. Ultimately, many elements of that critique ran into dead ends at Berkeley. Despite all of its defeats, however, versions of this conception of theory still survive. Perhaps one reason why is that they continue to resonate with those of us struggling to define our stance toward educational institutions we find deeply wanting but also do not want to leave.

CONCLUSION

*The foundations seem to like the name behavioral science, and we shall raise
no objection to it lest Cinderella miss her chance to ride in a golden coach
provided by the Foundation. Up to now [the social] sciences have been riding
in a Ford model T.*

—Gordon Allport, address at Wellesley College

In 1955 the psychologist Gordon Allport heralded the biggest, wealthi-
est philanthropic foundations' patronage for the social sciences. He then
remarked wryly that if the foundations wanted to call what they were so
munificently supporting "behavioral science," so be it; he was not about to
risk losing their support by objecting to the phrase. Would Cinderella have
complained if some of the accoutrements of so magnificent and unexpected
a golden coach were not entirely to her taste? Still, like Allport, many social scientists could not help but note that these postwar patrons were as
"hands-on" as they were generous. In this time of rapid growth in US higher
education in which social scientists were gaining access to unprecedented
levels of external funding, however, it was easy to joke about the strings attached to it.[1]

This light-hearted attitude did not last long. By the 1960s social scientists in a number of disciplines including political science were beginning to
see how the new availability of external funding was altering their departments, their universities, and their disciplines. Those in fields that attracted
little or no foundation interest struggled—often in vain—to maintain some
standing in relation to their grant-rich colleagues. By the 1980s even those
political scientists most favored by the discipline's new major patron, the
National Science Foundation (NSF), were struggling too. After a harrowing
round of budget cuts in the early 1980s, political science program associate
director William Mishler took to the pages of *PS*'s "News in the Profession" section, trying his best to counter the widespread perception among
his colleagues that "NSF" now meant "Non-Sufficient Funds."[2] In just a few

168

decades, the golden coach had become a Ford Fiesta with little fuel in its tank.

Few histories of political science have grappled with the influence of philanthropic foundations on the discipline. As a result, most overlook how important foundation priorities were to directing political scientists toward particular problems as well as particular ways of studying them. I have argued throughout this book that the mid-twentieth-century programs of the Carnegie, Ford, and Rockefeller philanthropies influenced academic political science in powerful, lasting ways. In what follows, I review the major features of my analysis and note its most significant historiographical contributions. I then discuss how what happened to the discipline during the postwar period offers some insight into several prominent features of contemporary political science. Finally, I comment on how the postwar research ethic these foundations shaped in a time of growth has become ever poorer as a guide for academic life in a time of austerity.

When US universities first became major centers of research during the postwar period, overt government funding for work by political scientists was still negligible. Philanthropic foundations were therefore in an unusually powerful position to shape the future of the discipline. All three of the foundations discussed throughout this book capitalized on this opportunity—sometimes by working together, sometimes by striking out on their own. All three supported the study of political behavior at a time that it was still marginal in academic political science. Ford's overwhelming support for the behavioral sciences is well known; but, as I showed in chapters 1 and 3 respectively, Carnegie supported them even earlier than Ford did; so too did Rockefeller, although with some ambivalence. All three—especially Carnegie and Ford—also saw underwriting new research centers rather than older university departments as the best way to change the social sciences quickly. And, as discussed in chapter 5, Rockefeller and Ford built extensive international networks that drew many US political scientists into teaching, research, and consulting with students and scholars from overseas.

In addition to the priorities they shared, Carnegie, Ford, and Rockefeller were all powerful enough on their own to pursue programs to which each was uniquely committed. As we saw in chapter 1, Carnegie staff realized their ambition to make the Social Science Research Council (SSRC) friendlier to the behavioral sciences in spite of Rockefeller's initial opposition and before Ford was big enough to be a meaningful ally. Although Ford and Carnegie did not share Rockefeller's commitment to cultivating an internationally oriented political theory, Rockefeller pursued this program long enough in a variety of venues to boost the status of political theory relative to other fields in the discipline—at least temporarily. And Ford's massive assets allowed its staff to develop plans for building new research infrastructure in the behavioral sciences without the help of any of the other foundations.

The chapters in the first part of this book on each foundation's grant programs for the social sciences highlighted how "hands on" these were. Internal foundation documents are replete with staff members' ambitious, sweeping visions for transforming the academic social sciences as well as their vigorous debates over which visions to pursue and how. Once a program took shape and began making grants, staff members often closely monitored what grantees were doing, sometimes even stepping in to redirect or edit their work. Foundations wanted what they built to last. To that end, they elicited long-term funding commitments from recipient institutions, endowed them themselves, or sought to hand off responsibility for their long-term support to federal government agencies. Overall, my studies of these three major foundations show that the staff members responsible for the social sciences in each of them were well informed, active, and sometimes interventionist managers of the grants they supervised.

Just on its own, this part of the story already reveals some things about how foundations influenced the development of academic political science that are not widely known. For example, these major foundations gave significant, early support to the postwar turns toward survey research, quantitative analysis, and international and area studies. Without this support, these fundamental reorientations in postwar political science might not have happened at all; if they had, they probably would have been considerably weaker. Foundation programs that favored behavioral science and interdisciplinary research also eroded some boundaries between social science disciplines. This made it possible, for instance, for people with backgrounds in social psychology not only to join political science departments but also to reorient the discipline in fundamental ways.

Beyond the programs they designed and oversaw themselves, foundations forged multiple links between political science and the powerful postwar state. Many prominent foundation officers and staff members sought to secure long-term state patronage for all the social sciences. They publicized the part social scientists had played in government agencies during World War II and pitched their expertise as a new "national resource" the postwar

United States should not forego.[3] They also advocated that plans for a new National Science Foundation include significant commitments to the social and behavioral sciences. Far from regarding state patronage as an unwelcome competitor, the big foundations at the heart of this book sought not only to increase public funding for the social sciences but also to make it a long-term, stable source of support for social scientific research.

Throughout this book, I have argued that the profound influence of foundation programs on the practice and reproduction of political science comes to light most clearly in particular institutional environments. In part 1, those environments are the offices of the foundations that made the grants; in part 2, the universities that received them. Each of the chapters in part 2 traced several long-term foundation grants made to the University of Michigan and the University of California, Berkeley, from pre-award negotiations to later assessments of their significance. The success of these foundation initiatives depended on close professional ties between foundation staff, university administrators, traditional faculty, and those affiliated with research organizations. Even the most well-informed, active, and interventionist foundation staff had to cultivate these relationships and make allowances for the established and sometimes intransigent features of universities' institutional culture. The alliances and compromises many formed with university administrators and faculty, therefore, proved crucial not only to the longevity of these initiatives but to their very substance as well. Ultimately, what university administrators and faculty did with foundation funds mattered just as much as the foundations' initial motivation for disbursing them.

Political science changed dramatically at Michigan and Berkeley from the late 1940s to around 1970. Though foundation funding set some of these changes in motion, what happened at each of these institutions directed their eventual course. At Michigan, 1950s grants first from Carnegie and then from Ford and Rockefeller supported the still new research program in the political behavior of voters in US national elections. By the 1960s this research program also won significant support from the still new NSF. On the strength of this support, some of the recipients of these grants were able to build a new PhD program in political behavior in the University of Michigan's political science department. This program, designed by faculty rather than any foundation, grew some of the deepest institutional roots of any effort related to political behavior. At Michigan, foundations' academic allies successfully used foundation support to design lasting structures—and did so largely without specific foundation direction. The new PhD program in political behavior began to shift the center of gravity of political science at Michigan away from educating students for public service and toward training them for careers in research. Though some faculty criticized this change, they could not stop it. By the 1960s the university as a whole was deeply committed to large externally funded research projects and had left its early twentieth-century conception of its ties to the state of Michigan and its localities behind.

Foundation funds began pouring into UC Berkeley at a time when the whole University of California system was rapidly expanding. During its initial postwar growth spurt, the political science department added so many members so quickly that its central emphases were up for grabs. Additionally, Ford's support for the behavioral sciences and Rockefeller's for political theory and theories of international relations in the 1950s encouraged an experimental attitude toward defining disciplinary fields, especially among young faculty. For a brief period, it seemed possible for nearly anyone in the department to present themselves as behavioral scientists or as theorists—and sometimes as both. This experimental attitude toward disciplinary fields proved hard to sustain, however, once the foundations themselves lost interest. By the 1960s both Ford and Rockefeller made clear that their primary commitment had shifted toward building international knowledge networks led by US-trained scholars. The early political science department at Berkeley emphasized the study of "foreign governments," "race relations," and international relations, all expressions of its first two chairs' service to the US occupation of the Philippines. Later, the bulk of Cold War–inspired investments gave new heft to the fields of international relations and comparative politics, making them the postwar department's de facto centers of gravity. The role of the department as an academic division, however, had changed; bloated and amorphous, it no longer seemed viable as a center of intellectual life in the research university. The rapid, foundation-fueled growth of the department in the 1950s built the pressure that led to its eventual splintering into distinct and increasingly hostile fields. In the following decade, sharp political and pedagogical disagreements intensified the centrifugal forces that had already begun to pull smaller groups within the department away from it.

The story I have told in this book is a distinctively mid-twentieth-century story. It also works, however, as a powerful lens for examining the origins of the subdisciplinary divisions that mark contemporary political science. Nearly everyone working in the discipline today has experienced political science as a methodologically fractured discipline; most also know that sociology, anthropology, and psychology are similarly fractured. Yet most political scientists have neither a sense of the history of these fractures nor an understanding of their political dimensions. To be sure, some political scientists have gamely tried to celebrate the presence of these divisions as "methodological pluralism" or an opportunity to fashion "mixed methods." Disagreements about methods, however, are often more fraught than technical disagreements over which tools to choose from the methodological bazaar. Instead, as the stories of the mid-century political science departments at both Michigan and Berkeley illustrate, such disagreements are also often disagreements about the greatest obstacles to political knowledge or the merits of the political aims such knowledge serves.

How, when, and why did it happen that people belonging to the same discipline came to differ so fundamentally on how to understand and explain political life, to the point that one subfield's local methodological knowledge is either unintelligible or rejected outside of it? And how does this fragmentation express or amplify political disagreements? Several good recent answers to these questions, like those offered by Clyde Barrow, Paulo Ravecca, and Robert Vitalis, emphasize that while such disagreements provoked small-scale battles fought in professional academic spaces, much broader political conflicts intensified them.[4] My different but complementary answer draws on the material at the heart of this book: the grants that foundations made to universities and academic intermediaries like the SSRC. In quite specific and lasting ways, these grants set in motion some of the deep methodological divisions that characterize the social sciences today. As we saw in the chapters in part 1, Carnegie and Ford enthusiastically backed a behavioral sciences–focused vision of the future of the social sciences. By contrast, internal debates at Rockefeller's Division of Social Science ultimately led its staff to support several markedly different visions of social-scientific inquiry at the same time. Just on their own, these foundations' programs began to reshape the social sciences, building incipient fractures into them in the process. Then, when allied academics drew on foundation support to design graduate education programs and form professional institutions to help reproduce them, they began to plant particular ideas about the nature and purpose of social-scientific knowledge in discrete plots of subdisciplinary terrain.

Some of these ideas have now grown deep institutional roots. Consider the following examples.

Methods Training and Access to Data

As discussed in chapter 4, the behavioral sciences–inspired grants of the 1950s helped make the University of Michigan's Institute for Social Research (ISR) a hub for new research programs in political and organizational behavior and also for the teaching of statistical analysis and programming skills on which this research depended. Drawing on their prestige as researchers who had won a number of external grants, some members of ISR were able not only to make political behavior part of graduate education in Michigan's political science department but also to create a broader institution that continues to loom large in contemporary political science: the Interuniversity Consortium for Political and Social Research (ICPSR). ICPSR today does many things, including offering a summer methods training program for graduate students that in 2020 consisted of more than eighty methods courses. Some pluralism is almost inevitable in such an extensive menu; still, nearly all of the longer four-week ICPSR summer courses focus on approaches that take the analytic value of mathematics and computer models as given.[5] Students who take courses in simultaneous equation models, Bayesian models for the social sciences, or applying concepts in machine learning to social research will learn complex techniques; perhaps some come to appreciate the analytic power of the techniques they learn. By its very nature as a workshop or boot camp for quantitative methods, however, ICPSR's summer program promises its students technical depth rather than epistemological breadth. For many, learning, applying, and mastering such techniques is so demanding that it crowds out learning—or caring—about what people in different fields do.

In addition to its summer training program, ICPSR has become one of the world's most important portals to troves of social-scientific data. Over the course of sixty years of collecting and curating thousands of data sets accessible to its approximately eight hundred fee-paying members, the consortium's power as a discipline-defining entity waxed as the disciplinary ideals from the early twentieth century centered on public service in both teaching and research waned.[6] By the 1970s ICPSR overshadowed most state- and city-based bureaus of public administration, the predominant form of the social-scientific research organization in the first half of the twentieth century. In their place, the consortium provided its members a re-search infrastructure that was far larger and more expensive than what even the largest research universities could sustain on their own. Those affiliated with its fees-paying institutional members pass through ICPSR's portal to learn to analyze the large, cumulative data sets it curates; many then embark on research careers that depend on maintaining access to them. In effect, ICPSR standardizes at the same time that it narrows what people in several fields of political science analyze, how they learn to analyze it, and the ex-pensive computing tools they use to do so. As both a training institute and a toll-charging node in the social-scientific research infrastructure, ICPSR exercises considerable reproductive power in training successive genera-tions of students in quantitative analytic methods so specialized that most political scientists do not use or even understand them. Nevertheless, the consortium sets at least subdisciplinary standards for what counts as profes-sionally recognized research.

Professional Associations

Other subdisciplinary institutions exercise some power analogous to ICPSR's—though none has nearly so extensive a teaching and training ca-pacity. Like the area and international studies centers discussed in chap-ter 5, some professional associations for area studies specialists with strong foundation ties serve as nodes for access to state and private funds for their members. For example, as Inderjeet Parmar thoroughly documents, the Ford Foundation and Carnegie Corporation played central roles in estab-lishing and supporting the African Studies Association and the Associa-tion for Asian Studies.[7] These professional associations functioned openly as intermediaries between their founding patrons and the state, prompting some of their dissident members to challenge their role in the US state-centric knowledge they help reproduce. Many methodological disputes among their members about the best way to study the politics of Africa or Asia were therefore also political disputes about the exercise of US power abroad. A more recent iteration of such disputes broke out in the 1990s, when in response to foundations pivoting away from their earlier commit-ment to area studies, the SSRC dissolved its area studies committees in favor of a new emphasis on global studies.[8] Here again, a methodological debate over how to study politics outside the United States dovetailed with political differences and rival assessments of the relationship between globalism and the US exercise of economic and political power around the world. Once this shift happened, it was clear that those who questioned the merits of focusing on problems with putatively "global" dimensions would have little access to the resources allocated by the SSRC.

Professional associations for political theorists and philosophers are less directly the products of foundation funding than those discussed above; instead, they formed more often as professional self-defense strategies against the dominance of other fields in the discipline. This general pattern notwithstanding, the Rockefeller Foundation grants made to UC Berkeley's political science department discussed in chapters 3 and 5 provided an important impetus for political theorists there to begin to define their approaches to studying politics and contrast them with those of other fields. What began as a self-conscious attempt to give shape to an amorphous field later informed the 1967 attempt on the part of some theorists at Berkeley to leave the discipline of political science altogether. As discussed in chapter 5, this effort at Berkeley asserted the epistemological distinctiveness of political theory and justified it on political and pedagogical grounds. Similarly, the first professional association focused on political theory, the Conference for the Study of Political Thought (CSPT), formed in 1967 to assert and defend the greater value of a "humanistic style of thinking" for the study of politics as opposed to "a science of behavior." As the leaders of the initiative to form a department of political theory at Berkeley had done, the authors of the CSPT's founding statement sought to justify the value of a humanistic approach to the study of political thought both pedagogically and politically. "Those trained without knowledge of this [humanist] tradition," they warned, "are incomplete as men, citizens, and political analysts. . . . The study of politics, if reduced to a science of behavior, leaves to the demagogues and ideologues that all-important area where ethics and politics converge in the discussion of purposes and goals."[9] Such aspirations notwithstanding, later efforts to articulate a political outlook informed by a commitment to a "humanist style of thinking" or what Sheldon Wolin termed "epic theory" did not win wide support within the theory subfield.[10] Marked differences in "style" and pedagogy between theorists and those in other subfields endured—but without connection to any discernible political differences.

With the benefit of several decades of hindsight, I now see how the

Association for Political Theory (APT), which I helped found in 2000, fits this pattern. Those of us who formed APT did so for practical, professional reasons: to build intellectual community among political theorists and philosophers and alleviate the intellectual isolation many of us experienced in political science departments. Though we were hardly apolitical people, we were not inspired to found APT by any explicitly political critique of other fields or of the discipline as a whole. Nor were the larger disciplines to which APT members belong our focus. Instead, we wanted APT to affirm the plurality of approaches within the theory/philosophy field and build an association that supported those in the field. For the most part, we were the students of people who had come to accept political theory's place in a methodologically and epistemologically fractured political science. Without really knowing what we were doing, we were reproducing those fractures.

I do not mean to suggest that the methodological fractures of the kind discussed here did nothing but damage to the discipline. Nor do my comments stem from nostalgia for some mythic time of methodological or epistemological wholeness. Rather, I mean to underscore that these fractures are not "givens" in the contemporary study of politics; they are of recent origin and have discernible and specific histories. Knowing their origins is central to doing a critical history of the discipline.

A specific example Barrow presents in his discussion of the history of the Caucus for a New Political Science helps illustrate these points. In what is by no means a celebration of all things caucus, Barrow emphatically highlights some important, good consequences of the disciplinary fractures formalized by the now familiar organized sections within the American Political Science Association (APSA). These subdisciplinary groups came into being in the late 1960s after several years of caucus pressure to make more space for the diversity of views among APSA members. Initially, organized sections' members won the ability to put together a portion of the panels at the association's annual meeting; some later started journals or created other outlets principally for their own members. Barrow concludes, I think rightly, that these subdisciplinary organized sections offered many APSA members a greater measure of intellectual autonomy and diluted the power of the discipline's elite core.[11]

The Caucus for a New Political Science won this significant organizational concession only because its explicitly political critique posed so serious a challenge to the APSA's establishment. Yet as Barrow also notes, some of those responsible for advancing this critique saw the organizational reforms it sparked as insufficient or diversionary responses and resigned from the caucus to pursue other strategies. The fragmentation of the caucus in the early 1970s was one manifestation of this. More broadly, the story of the Caucus for a New Political Science illustrates that methodological critiques do not suggest the same political remedies to all who endorse them.[12] Another, longer-term manifestation of methodological critique also matters. Subfield specific professional groups that form around shared methodological commitments can become intellectual cul-de-sacs that constrain any move toward critical perspectives on other subfields, the discipline, and their connection to broader social and political problems. Methodological fragmentation may offer some intellectual autonomy. Few, however, have used that autonomy to offer critical analyses of the discipline.

The Mid-Twentieth-Century Research Ethic in a Time of Austerity

In practice, many current professional institutions beyond the few discussed here continue to weave the mid-twentieth-century reorientations that the foundations initiated into the fabric of academic political science. Yet the conditions under which those foundation-sponsored reorientations began no longer exist. The resulting conception of an active research career that emerged in 1960s and 1970s political science rested on the assumption that growing or at least stable spending on higher education would be the norm, and that periods of contraction would be anomalous and brief. Things have not turned out that way. In the past forty years, periods of growth (like the brief boom of the 1990s) have been anomalous, while contraction and austerity have become the norm. Born in boom times, the midcentury foundation-initiated research ethic works poorly, even perversely, in times of austerity.

For starters, PhD programs in political science tend to overproduce hyper-specialists in research who are either unsuited for or uninterested in academic jobs not focused on research. What these programs inadvertently but inevitably produce, therefore, is a large pool of overqualified, underemployed academics whose cheap teaching labor cost-cutting universities readily exploit. The ideal of the research career is unattainable and therefore essentially meaningless for those who go from PhD programs into part-time or adjunct teaching, since those in such positions have no time and little

immediate incentive to do the research they were taught to see as the fulfill-
ment of their academic lives.[13] Even under the best of circumstances—some
employer-granted time and incentives—much of what counts as research
in political science depends on access to library databases, research nodes,
and data portals that are behind paywalls so high that they are practically
inaccessible to those not affiliated with institutions that pay their substantial
membership fees.

Additionally, public universities are finding active researchers who expect ample release time from teaching increasingly cost-prohibitive, given
declining revenues from states and the saturated, competitive higher education market. In this environment, social scientists, whose prospects for
bringing in significant funds from external grants have diminished significantly over the past few decades, look more and more like liabilities on
university balance sheets. To be sure, external funds for political science
research have not dried up completely; but they are less plentiful and more
focused on particular topics tied to particular political agendas. For example, when funding for work in area studies had all but ebbed away, the lesser
sums funders began offering in the 1990s for work on "globalization" proved
irresistible to many scholars and universities, prompting them to reformu-
late their research programs accordingly.[14] Also, national security–focused
programs designed to prosecute the "war on terror," like the Minerva Initiative, a collaboration between the NSF and the Department of Defense, were
comparatively well funded in a grant-poor time. Such programs have given
academics incentives to commercialize their work and move into what Joy
Rohde calls "the gray area" between academic and classified military and
intelligence research to bid on national security contracts.[15] Finally, beginning in the last three decades of the twentieth century, newer foundations
with explicitly proclaimed libertarian or conservative agendas emerged as
important funders of academic research, a trend that has continued up to
the present.[16]

The vulnerabilities of NSF funding for political science offer a particularly vivid illustration of the narrowing of options available to researchers
in the discipline. Though the NSF gradually overcame its founders' aversion
to funding many of the "other sciences" (as the social sciences were initially
termed), it resisted forming a political science program until the late 1960s.
The inauguration of that program gave some sectors of political science scientific legitimacy even though the support it offered was never bountiful.
As historians and former NSF program officers have meticulously shown,

overall NSF commitments to the social sciences have remained consistently low, hovering between 3 percent and 6 percent of its total spending.[17] Political scientists got a small slice of this already meager pie, with support for political science research lagging well behind NSF commitments to economics and anthropology. Nevertheless, by the early 1980s the NSF had become what it remains today—a primary source for external funding for research in political science. Such support went principally to what social-science program officers explicitly dubbed the "hard-core" scientific sectors of the discipline. This orientation placed many fields that remained incorrigibly humanistic or political well beyond the NSF's pale.[18]

Its narrowly defined scientific bounds notwithstanding, the NSF program for political science remained highly vulnerable to internal NSF reorganizations as well as to public challenge by members of Congress throughout its life. For example, many members of Congress supported the Reagan administration's 1981 proposal to deeply cut NSF spending for all social and behavioral sciences. Though the cuts were ultimately less drastic than the whopping 70 percent initially proposed, this episode served to warn many social scientists that they would have to fight to claim shrinking NSF resources. Congressional challenges to the larger directorate to which the political science program belonged continued in the 1990s and into the first decade of the twenty-first century. Then, in 2009, Senator Tom Coburn (R-OK) launched a targeted challenge to the political science program itself. Coburn proposed eliminating all NSF funding for political science, including NSF support for the American National Election Studies (ANES), the bedrock of the discipline's claim to scientific legitimacy.[19] Though these efforts did not immediately succeed, they underscored the vulnerability of the never-large NSF program in political science. In early 2020 the National Science Foundation began to phase out its program in political science altogether, directing prospective grant seekers from the discipline to its new Accountable Institutions and Behavior and Security and Preparedness programs.[20] Given the troubled history of political science funding at the NSF, it is hard to imagine that funding for political science research will either increase or be protected from challenge when channeled through these new multidisciplinary programs.

For all of these reasons, academic careers built around research are becoming luxury goods in political science, with fewer funders and fewer universities willing or able to support them. Yet most political science PhD programs continue to reproduce the research ethic assiduously, teaching cohort after cohort of students the importance of highly specialized research above all else. This ethic has proven tenacious, even in such inhospitable times. The powerful, well-institutionalized legacy of mid-twentieth-century foundation funding for the academic social sciences so woven into the fabric of our discipline is undoubtedly one reason why.

NOTES

PREFACE AND ACKNOWLEDGMENTS

1. Some of the best-known identifications of the behavioral adversaries responsible for marginalizing political theory are Leo Strauss, "An Epilogue," in *Essays on the Scientific Study of Politics*, ed. Herbert J. Storing (New York: Holt, Rinehart & Winston, 1962); and Sheldon Wolin, "Political Theory as a Vocation," *American Political Science Review* 63, no. 4 (1969): 1062–1082. Richard Ashcraft, "One Step Backward, Two Steps Forward: Reflections upon Contemporary Political Theory," in *What Should Political Theory Be Now?*, ed. John S. Nelson (Albany, NY: SUNY Press, 1983), offers a sustained critique of the latter. Terence Ball, "Whither Political Theory?," in *Reappraising Political Theory: Revisionist Studies in the History of Political Thought* (Oxford: Clarendon, 1995); John Gunnell, *Between Philosophy and Politics: The Alienation of Political Theory* (Amherst: University of Massachusetts Press, 1986); and Jeffrey C. Isaac, "The Strange Silence of Political Theory," *Political Theory* 23, no. 4 (1995): 636–652, all identify internal weaknesses in the field. I read Wendy Brown, "At the Edge," *Political Theory* 30, no. 4 (2002): 556–576, as a cautious celebration of its autonomy.

2. John Gunnell, *The Descent of Political Theory: The Genealogy of an American Vocation* (Chicago: Chicago University Press, 1993); all cited material on p. 1. Chapters 8–9 discuss the émigrés' critiques; chapter 10, the response of the would-be behavioralists to those critiques.

INTRODUCTION

1. According to Federal Election Commission records, from October 2019 through the end of March 2020, Bloomberg contributed $1.047.6 billion to his own campaign; Steyer contributed $315.7 million. For Bloomberg, see https://www.fec.gov/data/candidate/P00014530/; for Steyer, see https://www.fec.gov/data/candidate/P00012716/.

2. https://www.realclearpolitics.com/epolls/2020/president/democratic_delegate_count.html.

3. Each of the phrases cited in the text appeared prominently on these foundations' 2020 homepages. See Jeffrey A. Winters, *Oligarchy* (Cambridge: Cambridge University Press, 2011), and Chuck Collins, *The Wealth Hoarders: How Billionaires Pay Millions to Hide Trillions* (Bedford, MA: Polity, 2021) for discussions of what Winters initially termed "the wealth defense industry."

4. Ben Whitaker, *The Foundations: An Anatomy of Philanthropy and Society* (London: Eyre Methuen, 1974), provides an excellent discussion of this aspect of philanthropy. See in particular his chapter 3, "Some Paradoxes of Philanthropy: The Founders and Their Motives."

5. David C. Hammack and Helmut K. Anheier, *A Versatile American Institution: The Changing Ideals and Realities of Philanthropic Foundations* (Washington, DC: Brookings Institution Press, 2013), 9–12, offer a comprehensive summary of these rules in the section "What Can Foundations Do? Law and Practice."

6. In recent decades, several quasi-philanthropic variations on the corporate form—low-profit L3Cs or B corporations—have developed as alternatives to the older private philanthropic foundation. Shannon K. Vaughn and Shelly Arsenault, "The Public Benefit of Benefit Corporations," *PS: Political Science & Politics* 51, no. 1 (2018): 54–60, provide a concise overview of these new forms.

7. On attention to "megadonors," see Drew Linsay, "Beware the Bearer of Big Gifts," *Chronicle of Philanthropy,* February 7, 2017. Some recent studies of organized philanthropy are Nancy MacLean, *Democracy in Chains: The Deep History of the Radical Right's Stealth Plan for America* (New York: Penguin, 2017); Rob Reich, *Just Giving: Why Philanthropy Is Failing Democracy and How It Can Do Better* (Princeton, NJ: Princeton University Press, 2018); Anand Giridharadas, *Winners Take All: The Elite Charade of Changing the World* (New York: Knopf, 2018); David Callahan, *The Givers: Wealth, Power and Philanthropy in a New Gilded Age* (New York: Knopf, 2017); Hammack and Anheier, *Versatile American Institution;* Linsey McGoey, *No Such Thing as a Free Gift: The Gates Foundation and the Price of Philanthropy* (London: Verso, 2015); Steven M. Teles, *The Rise of the Conservative Legal Movement: The Battle for Control of the Law* (Princeton, NJ: Princeton University Press, 2008); Alice O'Connor, "The Politics of Rich and Rich: Postwar Investigations of Foundations and the Rise of the Philanthropic Right," in *American Capitalism: Social Thought and Political Economy in the Twentieth Century,* ed. Nelson Lichtenstein (Philadelphia: University of Pennsylvania Press, 2006); Inderjeet Parmar, *Foundations of the American Century: The Ford, Carnegie and Rockefeller Foundations in the Rise of American Power* (New York: Columbia University Press, 2012); and Joan Roelofs, *Foundations and Public Policy: The Mask of Pluralism* (Albany, NY: SUNY Press, 2003).

8. These symposia appeared in *PS* in 2016 and 2018 respectively.

9. The major role philanthropic foundations have played in higher education in the early to mid-twentieth century has been well documented. See, for instance, Robert S. Morison, "Foundations and Universities," *Daedalus* 93, no. 4 (1964): 1109–1141; Merle Curti and Roderick Nash, *Philanthropy and the Shaping of American Higher Education* (New Brunswick, NJ: Rutgers University Press, 1965); Carol S. Gruber, *Mars and Minerva: World War I and the Uses of Higher Learning in America* (Baton Rouge: Louisiana State University Press, 1975); Robert F. Arnove, ed., *Philanthropy and Cultural Imperialism: Foundations at Home and Abroad* (Bloomington: Indiana University Press, 1980); Ellen Condliffe Lagemann, *The Politics of Knowledge: The Carnegie Corporation, Philanthropy and Public Policy* (Middletown, CT: Wesleyan University Press, 1989); Roger L. Geiger, *Research and Relevant Knowledge: American Research Universities since World War II* (Oxford: Oxford University Press, 1993); Donald Fisher, *Fundamental Develop-*

ment of the Social Sciences: Rockefeller Philanthropy and the United States Social Science Research Council (Ann Arbor: University of Michigan Press, 1993); Roelofs, Foundations and Public Policy; Parmar, Foundations of the American Century; and Mark Solovey, Shaky Foundations: The Politics-Patronage-Social Science Nexus in Cold War America (New Brunswick, NJ: Rutgers University Press, 2013).

10. For example, Larry Bartels, Unequal Democracy: The Political Economy of the New Gilded Age, 2nd ed. (Princeton, NJ: Princeton University Press, 2016), devotes one chapter to analyzing the breadth of public support for repealing the estate tax rather than the attitudes of the wealthy elites who had the most to gain from this policy.

11. See Martin Gilens, Affluence and Influence: Economic Inequality and Political Power in America (Princeton, NJ: Princeton University Press, 2012), 2, for "lack sufficient data." Jeffrey A. Winters and Benjamin I. Page, "Oligarchy in the United States?," Perspectives on Politics 7, no. 4 (2009): 731–751, discuss how "wealth defense" works in the United States. See Winters, Oligarchy, 20–26, for a broader overview.

12. Both Parmar, Foundations of the American Century, 3–6; and Roelofs, Foundations and Public Policy, 32–33, comment critically on the term the "third sector." Hammack and Anheier, Versatile American Institution, find the term useful; "incomplete institutions" and "they do not act" on p. 9.

13. For an examination of these conflicts in the late nineteenth century, see Mary O. Furner, Advocacy & Objectivity: A Crisis in the Professionalization of American Social Science, 1865–1905 (Lexington: University Press of Kentucky, 1975). Timothy Kaufman-Osborn, "Disenchanted Professionals: The Politics of Faculty Governance in the Neoliberal Academy," Perspectives on Politics 15, no. 1 (2017): 100–115, comments not only on the early twentieth-century origins of ideas of academic freedom but also on the endurance of the tight constraints built into these ideas. Among the most vivid accounts of academics' vulnerability to political pressures during the Cold War are Sigmund Diamond, Compromised Campus: The Collaboration of the Universities with the Intelligence Community, 1945–55 (New York: Oxford University Press, 1992), and Ellen W. Schrecker, No Ivory Tower: McCarthyism and the Universities (New York: Oxford University Press, 1986).

14. Insightful, critical discussions of professions may be found in Furner, Advocacy & Objectivity; Thomas Frank, Listen, Liberal: Or, What Ever Happened to the Party of the People? (New York: Henry Holt, 2016); and Jeff Schmidt, Disciplined Minds: A Critical Look at Salaried Professionals and the Soul-Battering System that Shapes Their Lives (Lanham, MD: Rowman & Littlefield, 2000).

15. On conservative philanthropists and their opposition to some types of government patronage, see MacLean, Democracy in Chains, and O'Connor, "Politics of Rich and Rich." Solovey, Shaky Foundations, 71, provides a concise synopsis of federal government funding for the social sciences from the 1930s to 1960s. A more detailed discussion of the rise of government funding in the late 1950s appears in chapter 3 of Solovey's more recent Social Science for What? Battles over Public Funding for the "Other Sciences" at the National Science Foundation (Cambridge: MIT Press, 2020). Geiger, Research and Relevant Knowledge, 105, 115–116, pinpoints when federal government support exceeded that of foundations. Crowther-Heyck, "Patrons of the Revolution," 422, discusses "successive patronage systems for the postwar social science."

16. Solovey, *Shaky Foundations*, 71–88, discusses the importance of the Office of Naval Research, the army's Special Operations Research Office, the air force's RAND, and the Central Intelligence Agency as examples of new postwar federal agencies that provided some support for the social sciences. "Social science weapons of war" on p. 74. See also Allan A. Needell, "Project Troy and the Cold War Annexation of the Social Sciences," in *Universities and Empire*, ed. Christopher Simpson (New York: New Press, 1998) on Project Troy, an important ONR-funded psychological warfare project that included a number of social scientists.

17. See Solovey, *Shaky Foundations*, 59–71, on the decline of federal patronage right after World War II, and *Social Science for What?*, chapters 1 and 2, on the social sciences at the new NSF, and 90–100, on the late advent of the political science program. Otto Larsen, *Milestones and Millstones: Social Science at the National Science Foundation, 1945–1991* (New Brunswick, NJ: Transaction Publishers, 1992); and Henry Riecken, "Underdogging: The Early Career of the Social Sciences in the NSF," in *The Nationalization of the Social Sciences*, ed. Samuel Z. Klausner and Victor M. Lidz (Philadelphia: University of Pennsylvania Press, 1986), offer insiders' account of the fortunes of the social sciences at the NSF in the first few decades of its existence.

18. The cited phrase is the title of part 3 of Jean Converse, *Survey Research in the United States: Roots and Emergence, 1890–1960* (Berkeley: University of California Press, 1987).

19. My thinking on this issue is indebted to Parmar's analysis of the "state-private network" in *Foundations of the American Century*, 15–25, as well as Crowther-Heyck's argument that foundation and government agency-centered patronage systems "overlapped between 1958 and 1970" in "Patrons of the Revolution," 429–430.

20. See Christopher Simpson, *Science of Coercion: Communication Research and Psychological Warfare, 1945–1960* (New York: Oxford University Press, 1994); and Solovey, *Shaky Foundations*, 75–79, on the role of patrons in creating the discipline of communications. See Nicolas Guilhot, *The Invention of International Relations Theory: Realism, the Rockefeller Foundation, and the 1954 Conference on Theory* (New York: Columbia University Press, 2011); and Robert Vitalis, *White World Order, Black Power Politics: The Birth of American International Relations* (Ithaca, NY: Cornell University Press, 2015), on the importance of patrons to the field of international relations. Fisher, *Fundamental Development*, discusses the central part philanthropic patrons played in creating and supporting the Social Science Research Council.

21. How patrons build networks that bind their academic clients to themselves and each other is thoroughly discussed by Parmar, *Foundations of the American Century*; Solovey, *Shaky Foundations*; and Sarah Reckhow, "More than Patrons: How Foundations Fuel Policy Change and Backlash," *PS: Political Science & Politics* 49, no. 3 (2016): 449–454. For a recent discussion of the significance of patronage for the study of the history of science, see Casper Andersen, Jakob Bek-Thomsen, and Peter C. Kjærgaard, "Money Trail: A New Historiography for Networks, Patronage, and Scientific Careers," *Isis* 103, no. 2 (2012): 310–315. The unforgettable image of a "ratking" in the epigraph to Simpson, *Universities and Empire*, vividly depicts tangled density. Simpson, *Science of Coercion*, 94–106, emphasizes how government patronage not only gave those who received it financial support but also "insulated" them from what their patrons did with

their research and protected them from political suspicion. Joy Rohde's conception of "the gray area" in *Armed with Expertise: The Militarization of American Social Research during the Cold War* (Ithaca, NY: Cornell University Press, 2013), introduced on pp. 6–7, captures the institutional indeterminacy of Cold War social-scientific research done in venues that were neither wholly military nor academic.

22. Some notable early works, like Anna Haddow, *Political Science in American Colleges and Universities, 1636–1900*, ed. William Anderson (New York: D. Appleton-Century, 1939); and Albert Somit and Joseph Tanenhaus, *The Development of American Political Science: From Burgess to Behavioralism* (New York: Irvington, 1982), focus on documenting the emergence and evolution of political science as a distinct academic discipline. By contrast, Bernard Crick, *The American Science of Politics: Its Origins and Conditions* (Berkeley: University of California Press, 1959); Raymond Seidelman and Edward J. Harpham, *Disenchanted Realists: Political Science and the American Crisis, 1884–1984* (Albany: SUNY Press, 1985); and Dorothy Ross, *The Origins of American Social Science* (Cambridge: Cambridge University Press, 1991) attend to the broader intellectual and socioeconomic patterns to which political scientists contributed. The more recent works discussed above hew more closely to the latter approach.

23. Robert Adcock, *Liberalism and the Emergence of American Political Science: A Transatlantic Tale* (Oxford: Oxford University Press, 2014); John G. Gunnell, *The Descent of Political Theory: The Genealogy of an American Vocation* (Chicago: Chicago University Press, 1993); Ido Oren, *Our Enemies and US: America's Rivalries and the Making of Political Science* (Ithaca, NY: Cornell University Press, 2003); Nicolas Guilhot, *The Democracy Makers: Human Rights and the Politics of Global Order* (New York: Columbia University Press, 2005), "double agents," 10–14; Vitalis, *White World Order*; Jessica Blatt, *Race and the Making of American Political Science* (Philadelphia: University of Pennsylvania Press, 2018).

24. For discussions of the beginning of political science's life as an academic discipline in the United States, see Adcock, *Emergence of American Political Science*; Furner, *Advocacy & Objectivity*; Haddow, *Political Science*; Ross, *Origins of American Social Science*; Somit and Tanenhaus, *Development of American Political Science*.

25. Among such studies are Clyde W. Barrow, *Universities and the Capitalist State: Corporate Liberalism and the Reconstruction of American Higher Education, 1894–1928* (Madison: University of Wisconsin Press, 1990); Gruber, *Mars and Minerva*; and Mark C. Smith, *Social Science in the Crucible: The American Debate over Objectivity and Purpose, 1918–1941* (Durham, NC: Duke University Press, 1994).

26. Some studies of political science departments at specific universities include Rebecca S. Lowen, *Creating the Cold War University: The Transformation of Stanford* (Berkeley: University of California Press, 1997); and Richard Merelman, *Pluralism at Yale: The Culture of Political Science in America* (Madison: University of Wisconsin Press, 2003). Related studies include part 3 of Converse, *Survey Research*, which focuses on the life of survey research centers at several universities; Joel Isaac, *Working Knowledge: Making the Human Sciences from Parsons to Kuhn* (Cambridge, MA.: Harvard University Press, 2012), on the Department of Social Relations at Harvard; Rohde, *Armed with Expertise*, on the US Army's Special Operations Research Office's relation to American

University; and Parmar, *Foundations of the American Century*, on, among others, relations between Berkeley's department of economics and universities in Indonesia.

27. See Geiger, *Research and Relevant Knowledge*, 19–29, for an extended discussion of his conception of the "postwar federal research economy." The postwar redesign of the concept of the "research university" became concrete in the early 1970s when the Carnegie Commission on Higher Education began slotting colleges and universities into rank-ordered categories based on research activity. http://carnegieclassifications.iu.edu /methodology/basic.php.

28. Geiger, *Research and Relevant Knowledge*, 196–197. Even Sheila Slaughter and Gary Rhoades, who argue in *Academic Capitalism and the New Economy: Markets, State and Higher Education* (Baltimore: Johns Hopkins University Press, 2004), 28–30, that commercialization and patents superseded the federal research economy in the last two decades of the twentieth century, concede that in large sectors of higher education, the federal research economy still endures.

29. See Geiger, *Research and Relevant Knowledge*, 75–79, for Berkeley's Radiation Lab; for the discussion of Michigan's Willow Run Laboratories, along with "more classified research," see p. 57. For in-depth studies of the effects of war research on MIT and Stanford, see Stuart W. Leslie, *The Cold War and American Science: The Military-Industrial-Academic Complex at MIT and Stanford* (New York: Columbia University Press, 1993); Lowen, *Cold War University*; and Dorothy Nelkin, *The University and Military Research: Moral Politics at M.I.T.* (Ithaca, NY: Cornell University Press, 1972).

30. On the overwhelming importance of Department of Defense funding during the 1950s, see Leslie, *Cold War and American Science*, 1–2, 6–8.

31. See Simpson, *Science of Coercion*, 52–62, for a discussion of government funding for communications research from 1945 to 1955. Rohde, *Armed with Expertise*, discusses Project Camelot in detail in chapter 3; "Fundamental causes," "antidotes," and "Manhattan project," p. 63; and "public scrutiny," p. 88.

32. See, for example, Sonja M. Amadae, *Rationalizing Capitalist Democracy: The Cold War Origins of Rational Choice Liberalism* (Chicago: University of Chicago Press, 2003); Sonja M. Amadae, *Prisoners of Reason: Game Theory and Neoliberal Political Economy* (Cambridge: Cambridge University Press, 2016); Daniel Bessner, *Democracy in Exile: Hans Speier and the Rise of the Defense Intellectual* (Ithaca, NY: Cornell University Press, 2018); Joy Rohde, "Pax Technologica: Computers, International Affairs, and Human Reason in the Cold War," *Isis* 108, no. 4 (2017): 792–813; and Simpson, *Science of Coercion*.

33. The phrase "the nationalization of the social sciences" comes from the title of Samuel Z. Klausner and Victor M. Lidz, eds., *The Nationalization of the Social Sciences* (Philadephia: University of Pennsylvania Press, 1986). The volume pays homage to Talcott Parsons for his efforts to win federal government patronage for the social sciences.

34. Dwight Waldo, "Political Science: Tradition, Discipline, Profession, Science, Enterprise," in *Political Science: Scope and Theory. Volume 1, Handbook of Political Science*, eds. Fred I. Greenstein and Nelson Polsby (Reading, MA.: Addison-Wesley, 1975), 61–66, discusses the incompatibility between public administration and universities' postwar research mission.

35. Erik Austin, "ICPSR: The Founding and Early Years," 2011, https://www.icpsr

.umich.edu/web/pages/about/history/early-years.html, discusses the first large NSF grant won by the ICPR (the forerunner of the ICPSR) for a project to collect and make machine-readable all county-level US electoral data from the early nineteenth century to the present.

36. Lowen, in *Cold War University*, argues that administrators drove such reorientation even more aggressively at Stanford. See, for example, her preliminary discussion of this point on p. 11 as well as her substantial account of what this meant for the political science department there on pp. 212–223.

37. For a discussion of Rockefeller making unrestricted research funds available to departments in the early twentieth century, see Earlene Craver, "Patronage and the Directions of Research in Economics: The Rockefeller Foundation in Europe, 1924–1938," *Minerva* 24, nos. 2–3 (1986): 220. On the importance of ORUs as sites for university research in the postwar period, see Geiger, *Research and Relevant Knowledge*, 47–57; as well as Geiger, "Organized Research Units—Their Role in the Development of University Research," *Journal of Higher Education* 61, no. 1 (1990): 1–19.

38. Converse, *Survey Research*, 346.

39. On Berkeley as "the country's most fertile breeding ground of organized research units," see Geiger, *Research and Relevant Knowledge*, 75. The resemblance to the structure of Michigan's ISR is not coincidental. Warren Miller had briefly been a faculty member at Berkeley from 1954 to 1956; Angus Campbell also spent some time in Berkeley to advise the administration on creating a survey research center. See Charles Y. Glock, *Recollections of Charles Y. Glock, First SRC Director*, reprinted from Charles Y. Glock, *A Life Fully Lived: An Autobiography*, "Chapter 12: Directing the Survey Research Center," 2001, 2007, http://srcweb.berkeley.edu/backup_2010_10_05/50anniv.html, 3.

40. On Kerr's role in the founding of Berkeley's Survey Research Center, see Geiger, *Research and Relevant Knowledge*, 81. On political scientists associated with that center, see Glock, *Recollections*, 8–9, 11. A list of the directors of the center appears at http://srcweb.berkeley.edu/backup_2010_10_05/50anniv.html. The university closed the center in 2010.

41. On NSF support for Berkeley's SRC, see Glock, *Recollections*, 23–24. Bruce Cumings, "Boundary Displacement: Area Studies and International Studies during and after the Cold War," in *Universities and Empire: Money and Politics in the Social Sciences during the Cold War*, ed. Christopher Simpson (New York: New Press, 1998), 163–173, discusses the Cold War origins of many area and international studies centers as well as their reliance on foundation and government patronage.

42. See Christopher Loss, *Between Citizens and the State: The Politics of American Higher Education in the 20th Century* (Princeton, NJ: Princeton University Press, 2012), 158–160, for a discussion of the changes in graduate education, and pp. 2, 13–15 for an overview of the federal programs most responsible for increasing access to higher education.

43. Eldersveld to Miller, June 23, 1959, comments specifically on how Eldersveld and some Michigan administrators were trying to secure NDEA fellowships for the new political behavior program. In Folder: "Correspondence—January—June 1959," Box 4, Miller Papers, Bentley Historical Library. National Defense Graduate Fellowships enabled Miller and others to recruit potential graduate students with multiyear federal support to join the political science department's new political behavior program. Re-

garding the educational component of the ICPR, Miller recalled that this was also made possible by funds from the NDEA: "With a little fudging of what we were doing, the mathematics group funded by NDEA decided to improve the quantitative skills of political science." Miller, "Oral History Interview," July 20, 1997, p. 4 [7], BHL. Misspellings and omissions mar the typed transcript of this interview. I therefore provide both the page number of the notes I took on the VHS tape of this interview (available upon request) and the page number of the typed transcript in square brackets.

44. For specific discussions of NDEA support of students in the political behavior program, see Miller-Stokes correspondence, Box 4, Miller Papers. Department graduate program brochures list NDEA fellowships among the available sources of financial support through 1972.

45. The Board of Educational Development, an entity created by the Academic Senate, conducted this evaluation in response to the student-led Free Speech Movement's demand that students have more control over curricula, administration, and hiring. The report concluded that ample resources were available to graduate students affiliated with either the Institute for International Studies (IIS) or the Institute for Governmental Studies (IGS). Students in political theory, however, were in a much weaker position, since "financing of graduate political theory is dependent on the university." Department chair Aaron Wildavsky responded to this disparity by suggesting that political theory faculty start their own ORU to make seeking external funds to support graduate students in the field easier. See Emily Hauptmann, "The Evolution of Political Theory in a Climate of Experiment and Secession," *PS: Political Science & Politics* 50, no. 3 (2017): 793.

46. *Reminiscences of Charles Dollard*, 1967, 25–26, Carnegie Corporation project, Columbia Center for Oral History Archives, Rare Book and Manuscript Library, Columbia University, New York.

47. The cited phrase comes from Thorstein Veblen, *The Higher Learning in America.* It appears in a longer passage that serves as the epigraph to Leslie, *Cold War and American Science.*

48. Readers will note that I rely heavily on archival, unpublished sources throughout the book rather than on the published works of the political scientists who play major parts in it. What I have gleaned from my principal sources regarding, say, V. O. Key, Warren Miller, Robert Scalapino, or Sheldon Wolin, should therefore be read alongside others' treatments of their published work.

CHAPTER 1. "PROPAGANDISTS FOR THE BEHAVIORAL SCIENCES"

1. For a discussion of when the term "behavioral sciences" began to be widely used, see Jefferson D. Pooley, "A 'Not Particularly Felicitous Phrase': A History of the 'Behavioral Sciences' Label," *Serendipities: Journal of the Sociology and History of the Social Sciences* 1 (2016): 61–62.

2. Both committees investigated whether foundations were violating the terms of their tax exemption, including the bar against political advocacy. The Cox Committee was the Select Committee to Investigate Tax-Exempt Foundations and Comparable Organizations of the 82nd Congress, 2nd session, House of Representatives, chaired by

E. E. Cox (D-GA). The Reece Committee was the Special Committee to Investigate Tax-Exempt Foundations and Comparable Organizations of the 83rd Congress, 2nd session, House of Representatives, chaired by B. Carroll Reece (R-TN). The second epigraph to this chapter comes from the statement Dollard drafted as his testimony to the Reece Committee, later published as "In Defense of the Social Sciences," *American Journal of Economics and Sociology* 14, no. 1 (1954): 31–37.

3. For example, Converse, *Survey Research in the United States*, 217, says *The American Soldier* relied on "funding from SSRC" but does not mention Carnegie. Anne Frantilla, *Social Science in the Public Interest: A Fiftieth-Year History of the Institute for Social Research* (Ann Arbor: Bentley Historical Library, University of Michigan, 1998), 33, mentions Rockefeller funding for the 1956 and 1960 election studies, but not Carnegie's for the 1952 study. Solovey, *Shaky Foundations*, 64, acknowledges that Carnegie and the SSRC "asked Chase to write a book" about social scientific accomplishments but discusses neither their partnership nor Carnegie's strongly directive role in it. The exception is Lagemann, *The Politics of Knowledge*, 147–184, which emphasizes Carnegie's role in all of the projects discussed in this chapter.

4. Frederick Osborn, "To What Extent Is a Science of Man Possible?" *Scientific Monthly* 49, no. 5 (1939): 452–459.

5. On Osborn, see M. S. Watson, *Chief of Staff: Prewar Plans and Preparations*, United States Army in World War II series (Washington, DC: Center for Military History, United States Army, 1950), 232. For Dollard and Young's wartime service, see Charles Dollard, Reminiscences of Charles Dollard, 1967, Carnegie Corporation project, Columbia Center for Oral History Archives, Rare Book and Manuscript Library, Columbia University, 77, 86, 105–106; Lagemann, *Politics of Knowledge*, 162; W. E. Moore, "Donald Ramsey Young, 1898–1977," *ASA Footnotes* 5, no. 6 (1977): 12. On Herring's consulting for the Bureau of the Budget as well as advising Eberstadt, see Herring, "APSA Oral History Interview," 22, 28–29. On the National Security Act, see the obituaries by Fred I. Greenstein and Austin Ranney, "Pendleton Herring," *PS: Political Science & Politics* 38, no. 1 (2005): 120; and Matt Schudel, "Political Intellectual Pendleton Herring, 100," *Washington Post*, August 20, 2004, national edition, B06.

6. Charles Dollard, "A Middleman Looks at Social Science," *American Sociological Review* 15, no. 1 (1950): 17, where Dollard comments that as a foundation executive, he stood between academics and the foundation's Board of Trustees. I use the image of the "middleman" more broadly to mean anyone who worked primarily as an intermediary between academics and a range of other groups.

7. In addition to Dollard's "Middleman," other pertinent publications include Pendleton Herring, "Political Science in the Next Decade," *American Political Science Review* 39, no. 4 (1945): 757–766; and Donald Young, "Techniques of Race Relations," *Proceedings of the American Philosophical Society* 91, no. 2 (1947): 150–161.

8. Fisher, *Fundamental Development of the Social Sciences*, provides a detailed account of relations between the Rockefeller Foundation and the SSRC from 1923 to 1945.

9. Fisher, *Fundamental Development*, 203–208.

10. George W. Gray, "Advancing the Science of Social Relations," *Confidential Monthly Report for the Information of the Trustees*, no. 131, June 1951, 2. Copy in Area V Files, FFA, RAC. When Gray refers to "these councils," he meant not only the SSRC but also

the National Research Council, the American Council on Education, and the American Council of Learned Societies. Gray's long-time service as editor of the *Confidential Monthly Report* is discussed in his obituary on pp. 27–30 of the January 1961 *Report*.

11. The Foundation Center, created in 1956 by an officer of the Russell Sage Foundation with the support of Carnegie, Ford, and Rockefeller, formalized the already well-established practice of consultation among foundation officers. See David C. Hammack, "American Debates on the Legitimacy of Foundations," in *The Legitimacy of Philanthropic Foundations: United States and European Perspectives*, ed. Kenneth Prewitt, Mattei Dogan, Steven Heydemann, and Stefan Toepler (New York: Russell Sage Foundation, 2006), 74–75. The Foundation Center recently merged with GuideStar; the new organization is now called Candid. See https://candid.org/about.

12. Hunter Crowther-Heyck, "Patrons of the Revolution: Ideals and Institutions in Postwar Behavioral Science," *Isis* 97, no. 3 (2006): 434–437.

13. Solovey, *Shaky Foundations*, 1–13.

14. Lagemann, *Politics of Knowledge*, 149–151; "thickening matrix" on p. 149; "strategic philanthropy" is the title of the book's part 3; "venture capital" on p. 150.

15. The partnership between Carnegie and the SSRC included more than the five projects I discuss in this chapter. For another such project, Carnegie selected the psychologist Donald Marquis to write one of several social-scientific responses to Vannevar Bush's *Science, the Endless Frontier* at the same time that Talcott Parsons was writing another. Though Marquis never completed this project, Carnegie staff were planning for the SSRC to publicize it. See the items in Folder 12, "SSRC: Overall Survey of the Nature and Needs of the Social Sciences (Don Marquis), 1946," Box 329, series IIIA.8, Carnegie Corporation Records (hereafter abbreviated CC).

16. For "useful," see Schudel, "Political Intellectual Pendleton Herring," B06; for "accessible," see Greenstein and Ranney, "Pendleton Herring," 120.

17. In addition to promoting the behavioral sciences through the SSRC, Carnegie made substantial grants to Harvard. These supported the formation of several institutions—the Department of Social Relations, the Laboratory of Social Relations, and the Russian Research Center—and the work of prominent social scientists associated with them, like Talcott Parsons, Samuel Stouffer, and Clyde Kluckhohn. See Lagemann, *Politics of Knowledge*, 166–175, for a discussion of these grants as well as Isaac, *Working Knowledge*, for a comprehensive account of these institutions.

18. Dollard, Reminiscences, 10, for "game . . . pretty well won." Lagemann, *Politics of Knowledge*, 178–179, briefly discusses how Ford's H. Rowan Gaither and his staff relied upon some aspects of Dollard and Gardner's work with the behavioral sciences in crafting Ford's own programs.

19. On Charles Dollard's graduate work in sociology, see Lagemann, *Politics of Knowledge*, 158–159. Charles Dollard is sometimes confused with his older brother, John, a PhD in sociology who spent most of his career at Yale's Institute for Human Relations. On John Dollard and his influence on Charles, see Lagemann, 154–159.

20. Dollard, Reminiscences, 15–16, 188. "Belligerent" on p. 16.

21. For Dollard's comments on unproductive debates, see "Notes on Annual Meeting of the SSRC," September 9–12, 1940, 2, 3. For comments on arid squabbling, see "General Notes on the Annual Meeting of the SSRC," September 11–14, 1939, 1. Both

in Folder 12, Box 327, series III A, CC. All subsequent Carnegie documents cited in this section and the next appear in Box 327, series III A.8, unless otherwise noted. Fisher, *Fundamental Development*, 171–172, 195, offers a similar portrait of Crane as an embattled leader of the SSRC.

22. Dollard, "Interview Notes on Annual SSRC Meeting," September 13–15, 1938, 2, Folder 12. Keppel served as president of the Carnegie Corporation from 1923 to 1941.

23. Osborn to Keppel, September 16, 1938, 2; Keppel to Osborn, October 4, 1938. Both in Folder 12.

24. EG (Carnegie staff), "SSRC: Memo prepared by reading the annual reports of the Council, and the documents in Carncor files," September 5, 1944, Folder 11. The documents from 1935 to which EG refers appear in Folder 10. "Carncor" was staff shorthand for "Carnegie Corporation."

25. Dollard, Reminiscences, 77, 105–106; Moore, "Donald Ramsey Young," 12.

26. Dollard, "General Notes on the Annual Meeting of the SSRC," September 11–14, 1939, 2, Folder 12, remarked that Young intended to leave the SSRC by July 1940 and worried that his departure would make things move even more slowly at the already understaffed and conservatively led SSRC. Young appears to have stayed on at the SSRC somewhat longer but resigned to join the War Department in 1941 or 1942.

27. Crane to Joseph Willits, Director of Rockefeller's Division of Social Sciences, n.d., p. 5, attached to Dollard to Willits, September 15, 1947, Folder 14. Although Crane's letter is undated, internal references suggest it was written sometime in 1947.

28. Young to Josephs, April 13, 1946; discussions of research planning appear on pp. 4 and 6–7; social scientists' "outstanding contributions" to the war effort, p. 8. In an earlier note marked "personal," Dollard urges Young to "try your hand at drafting a statement of the function and operation of the SSRC as of 1946 and thereafter." He also advises Young to discuss how he envisions "relations with the foundations." Dollard to Young, March 29, 1946. Both letters in Folder 14.

29. I infer that Willits solicited Crane's memo from Dollard to Willits, September 15, 1947, Folder 14.

30. Dollard, "Interview notes on meeting with Willits," September 8, 1947, Folder 14. "JW obviously had the wind up about the SSRC meetings," Dollard suggests, because Willits perceived the "rumored criticisms" of the foundations to be directed mostly at Rockefeller.

31. Dollard, interview notes with Joseph H. Willits, Rockefeller, February 22 and 23, 1947, Folder 14. Dollard notes that he tried to ease Willits's concern that Young was leaving the SSRC because of his conflicts with Willits.

32. Dollard, Reminiscences, 119, recalls how Carl Hovland (a Yale psychologist and one of the coauthors of *The American Soldier*) presented the committee's choice to him: "He [Hovland] came to us—we had been most critical—and said, 'All right. Here's the solution: Herring.'"

33. For "liaison," see Dollard, Reminiscences, 118–119; Herring, "APSA Oral History Interview," 28–30. For Herring's work with Osborn, see Dollard, Reminiscences, 119–120, 150; and Frederick Osborn, Reminiscences of Frederick Osborn, 1967, Carnegie Corporation project, Columbia Center for Oral History Archives, Rare Book and Manuscript Library, Columbia University, 66.

34. Mark Solovey, "Riding Natural Scientists' Coattails onto the Endless Frontier: The SSRC and the Quest for Scientific Legitimacy," *Journal of the History of the Behavioral Sciences* 40, no. 4 (2004): 402–410; Solovey, *Shaky Foundations*, 29–55. Already in 1945, Dollard expressed concerns about how the social sciences were being sidelined in plans for the NSF. See Dollard to Josephs, December 18, 1945, attached to letter drafted by Young, December 10, 1945. Both in Folder 11.

35. Converse, *Survey Research*, 180–181.

36. Herring, "Political Science," 762.

37. Herring to David E. Lilienthal (Chair, Atomic Energy Commission), July 9, 1948, Folder 13. For fellowship programs, see Earl D. Johnson (Assistant Secretary of Army) to Bryce Wood (SSRC), February 14, 1951, as well as Wood to Johnson, February 15, 1951, in which Wood says SSRC fellowship proposal is also being considered by the Department of State and CIA. Both in Folder 15. For contract research for federal government agencies, see Dollard, "Notes on SSRC Meetings," April 1 and 2, 1950, Folder 16.

38. Herring, "The Social Science Research Council and Foundation Operations," December 28, 1950, Folder 15. "Intermediary" appears on p. 2; "official consultant relationships" on p. 5. Herring notes that he is a consultant for "five [unnamed] governmental agencies" on p. 5 as well.

39. For the $10,000 per year comment, see Dollard, notes on interview with Herring, October 17, 1949. For Herring's query regarding Carnegie's interest in supporting work on political behavior, see James Perkins (Carnegie staff), notes on interview with Herring, October 4, 1950. For Herring on the CPB's possible "research planning," see Gardner, notes on interview with Herring, November 2, 1950. All documents in Folder 16.

40. In "Notes on interview with Herring," June 23, 1950, Dollard writes that he "confessed his own misgivings about [Ford's] program and his feeling that a very large amount of money would be wasted unless SSRC took considerable responsibility for planning and guidance." Several months later, Dollard was still voicing similar concerns. See Dollard to Herring, October 9, 1950. Both in Folder 16.

41. Jessup, in "Interview Notes on Meeting with Willits," May 28, 1943, Folder 11, notes that Willits expressed the hope that Carnegie would continue to support the SSRC, as Rockefeller intended to do.

42. In his Reminiscences, Dollard commented, "Most of Ford's blunders have been made because it had too much money and it had to spend it in a hurry," 313. A 1951 report prepared for Rockefeller trustees noted the dramatic decline of Rockefeller's postwar contributions to the SSRC relative to those of other foundations. In 1946 Rockefeller grants made up 80 percent of the funds received by the SSRC; five years later, they were below 40 percent. See Gray, "Advancing the Science of Social Relations," 17. Copy in Area V files, FFA, RAC.

43. Francis X. Sutton to Files, "Notes on a meeting to discuss relations with SSRC," January 25, 1956, Folder 236 (Behavioral Sciences, Miscellaneous, 1953–1957), Box 9, Series III, Vice President William McPeak Office Files (FA704), FFA, RAC.

44. For example, Talcott Parsons's attempt to draft a response to the exclusion of the social sciences from the NSF was officially sponsored by the SSRC's Committee on Federal Government and Research; the funds for it appear to have come from the American

Psychological Association and perhaps other professional associations as well. See "Excerpt from Minutes of Committee on Federal Government and Research," November 15, 1946, Folder 12, Box 329. Dollard, however, clearly knew about the project in its early stages and sought reassurance from Young that it wouldn't conflict with the Marquis project Carnegie was funding (see note 15). See Dollard, "Interview Notes with Young," December 2, 1946, Folder 14. On Parsons's project, see Klausner and Lidz, *Nationalization of the Social Sciences*, and Solovey, "Coattails," 412–415.

45. EG (Carnegie officer) to Jessup, March 12, 1942, Folder 11. In his Reminiscences, Dollard underscored the importance of Carnegie and Rockefeller support for the SSRC: "Until the Ford Foundation came along, by which time the game was pretty well won, the only two foundations that would listen to the social sciences were the Rockefeller and the Carnegie. In good season and bad, we fought our trustees, who didn't understand what the social sciences were about, and got money for the Social Science Research Council, and got it in increasing amounts," p. 10.

46. "Confidential Memorandum for personal use of Dr. Keppel from Robert T. Crane," August 12, 1935, Folder 10. In this memo, Crane, executive director of the SSRC, asks Carnegie's President Keppel for more funds to counterbalance the support it received from Rockefeller, noting that the SSRC's overwhelming dependence on Rockefeller made it unable to use "its own discretion" to launch programs. "It would seem time," Crane concluded, "to give the Council a little more rein."

47. Fisher, *Fundamental Development*, 46–50, 207–211, provides numerous examples of how "hands on" Rockefeller support for the SSRC was during the interwar period. Expressing Carnegie's almost proprietary relationship to the SSRC, a Carnegie official wrote, "In addition to coordinating research in the social sciences, the [SSRC] advises the Corporation on proposals in its field and offers valuable assistance in framing studies undertaken on Corporation initiative." See "SSRC Administrative Expenses," n.d. [1940?], p. 1, Folder 12.

48. The title of the entire four-volume work was *Studies in Social Psychology during World War II*. The Carnegie grants that supported this project were the biggest of the five projects I consider; they totaled well over $100,000 and lasted the longest—from 1941 through 1949.

49. See Dollard, Reminiscences, 104, for a retrospective discussion of President Keppel's use of the term "buffer state." The term "buffer state" also occurs in Dollard, "Interview notes with Frank Keppel and Samuel Crocker, Associate Executive Director, Joint Army and Navy Committee on Welfare and Recreation," October 31, 1941, Folder 1, Box 192, series IIIA.8, CC. Frank Keppel, an aide to General Osborn, was Carnegie president Frederick Keppel's son. All Carnegie documents cited in this section, Box 192, series IIIA.8, unless otherwise noted.

50. In Harper to Jessup, November 25, 1941, p. 1, Fowler Harper, the first chair of the Committee of Trustees, spelled out its nominally nongovernmental status to Carnegie president Jessup: "This is to make the record clear that the gift [Carnegie's $100,000 grant] is not made to an agency or a sub-agency of the government but is made to a voluntary association of individuals [the Committee of Trustees]." The "Osborn fund" reference occurs in President Keppel, "Interview notes with Colonel Stedman Hanks," November 3, 1941. Carnegie granted the Committee of Trustees $100,000 in 1941. See

Secretary, Carnegie Corp., to S. Crocker, Joint Army and Navy Committee on Welfare and Recreation, October 16, 1941. All documents in Folder 1, CC.

51. Osborn, Reminiscences, 75.

52. For $23,000 spent on research, see John M. Russell to Devereux C. Josephs, June 1, 1945. For "greasing the wheels," see Robert M. Lester, secretary, Carnegie Corp., "Interview notes on meeting with Josephs and Russell," June 6, 1945. On the final grant of $76,000, see "Report to Carnegie Corporation of New York for the Year 1945–46," 2–3, John M. Russell, Chair, Committee of Trustees, n.d. Internal references in this document suggest it was written shortly after early July 1946, when Russell reported "the books [of the Committee of Trustees] were closed," p. 1. All in Folder 1, CC.

53. Russell to Josephs, October 11, 1945, Folder 4, CC.

54. Young to Osborn, October 1, 1945, Folder 4852, Box 398, subseries 74, series 1, Accession 2, SSRC, RAC. Although Osborn does not mention the SSRC's involvement, he recalled later that both he and Stouffer had proposed the idea of funding this project to Carnegie after the war. See Osborn, Reminiscences, 118–119.

55. Russell to Josephs, October 11, 1945, Folder 4; sentence cited on p. 2.

56. Russell to Young, November 9, 1945; Young to Russell, November 15, 1945; Russell to Young, November 19, 1945. All in Folder 4852, Box 398, subseries 74, series 1, Accession 2, SSRC, RAC. Young's November 15 letter to Russell lists the following members of the proposed SSRC committee: Osborn (chair), Leonard Cottrell, Leland DeVinney, Carl Hovland, Russell, and Stouffer.

57. Among those I consider most important are Osborn, Russell (chair of the Committee of Trustees, former officer and aide to Carnegie's President Keppel, member of the SSRC special committee), DeVinney (officer of the Research Branch, member of the SSRC special committee, coauthor of Vol. I, Social Science Division officer at the Rockefeller Foundation), Dollard, and Young.

58. Peter Buck, "Adjusting to Military Life: The Social Sciences Go to War, 1941–1950," in *Military Enterprise and Technological Change: Perspectives on the American Experience*, ed. Merritt Roe Smith (Cambridge, MA: MIT Press, 1985), 219. For a discussion of the considerable size of Stouffer's research team, see Buck, 216.

59. Converse, *Survey Research*, 218, 223.

60. Datus C. Smith, Director, Princeton University Press, to Herring, SSRC, March 19, 1949, p. 1, Folder 4852, Box 398, subseries 74, series 1, Accession 2, SSRC, RAC.

61. See Buck, "Adjusting to Military Life," 217–218, for a discussion of the military leadership's resistance to the Research Branch's survey-based demobilization plan, which was later cited as one of the Research Branch's greatest wartime contributions.

62. All quotations in this paragraph are from General Brehon Somervell to Frederick Osborn, April 14, 1949, pp. 1–2, Folder 2, Box 328, series IIIA.8, CC. Somervell also complimented the book, saying he thought it would be "of great value in the formulation of policy and decisions on the problems covered." Still, most of the letter is critical. All subsequent references to Carnegie records for this project appear in series IIIA.8.

63. See Osborn to Dollard, n.d., appended to Somervell to Osborn, April 14, 1949, Folder 2, Box 328, CC. Osborn's note to Dollard comments in part on "the gap between the scholar and the man of active affairs" and adds slyly, "Not for Sam—yet!" Dollard replies, "Somervell's letter is a jewel" but agrees that Stouffer might not find it so amusing.

64. Dollard, "The social sciences," excerpt from a report to Carnegie Board of Trustees, p. 33, May 16, 1946, Folder 14, Box 327, CC.

65. Dollard to Samuel Stouffer, April 22, 1949; Stouffer to Dollard, May 4, 1949. Both in Folder 2, Box 328, CC.

66. Dollard's secretary to Leroy Wilson (AT & T) and Sir Alexander Carl-Saunders (London School of Economics and Political Science), June 21, 1949 (cover letter for portions of Stouffer et al.'s book); Paul Lazarsfeld to Dollard, September 7, 1949 (letter accompanies draft of review of first volumes of Stouffer et al. that Lazarsfeld was writing for *Public Opinion Quarterly*). Both in Folder 2, Box 328, CC.

67. "We [the Research Branch] had published absolutely nothing, and we made a solemn promise to the young people, all of whom were making their careers in the social sciences, that when the War was over that data would be published." Dollard, Reminiscences, 139.

68. Buck, "Adjusting to Military Life," 247–252; Converse, *Survey Research*, 222–224; Ron Robin, *The Making of the Cold War Enemy: Culture and Politics in the Military-Intellectual Complex* (Princeton, NJ: Princeton University Press, 2001), 19–24.

69. Stuart Chase, *The Proper Study of Mankind* (New York: Harper & Bros., 1948), 302–303.

70. In a formal letter notifying Young of the Carnegie grant to support Chase's project, Dollard stipulates that the SSRC "act as fiscal agent . . . without assuming any collateral editorial responsibility." Dollard to Young, January 23, 1946. Young explained this arrangement to Chase several days later, writing that "for organizational reasons" Carnegie wanted the SSRC to be "fiscal agent" for the project. Young to Stuart Chase, January 25, 1946. All Carnegie documents cited in this section are in Folder 6, Box 328, series IIIA.8, unless otherwise noted. For another discussion of Chase's book, see Solovey, *Shaky Foundations*, 64–66.

71. For Dollard's pitch, see his "Notes on Lunch Meeting with Stuart Chase, Frederick Dewhurst (20th Century Fund), Donald Young," December 28, 1945; Dollard, "Interview Notes on Dinner for Stuart Chase," March 13, 1946; Dollard to Louis Wirth, January 6, 1947. Dollard's interview notes list over ten social scientists with current or former government positions who participated in the dinner. Dollard's letter to Wirth was a model for multiple letters; it informed its academic recipients (of whom Wirth was one) of Chase's project and asked them to send their responses to a list of questions to Chase.

72. Dollard reports in his notes on a meeting with Young and Chase, October 23, 1947, that he and Young criticized Chase's manuscript extensively and requested that he rewrite one of the first five chapters. Dollard later reports that he and Young agreed on a short list of people who would read Chase's manuscript for a small honorarium. Dollard, "Notes on Meeting with Young," May 3, 1948.

73. Stuart Chase, Memorandum re. *The Two Billion Dollar Question: Can the Social Sciences Catch Up with Atomic Energy?*, November 6, 1946, p. 5. *The Two Billion Dollar Question* was an early working title of *The Proper Study of Mankind*.

74. Chase, *Study of Mankind*, 178. On technical sophistication of polls, see 161–163.

75. Dollard, "The Social Sciences," excerpt from report to Carnegie Board of Trustees, p. 29, May 16, 1946, Folder 14, Box 327, series IIIA.8, CC.

76. "Appalling ignorance" in Dollard to Louis Wirth, January 6, 1947; Louis Wirth

to Dollard, January 31, 1947. "Mine run" in Dollard to Louis Wirth, February 5, 1947. All in Folder 6, Box 328. In the last letter cited, Dollard explicitly contrasts the aims and intended audiences of Chase's book with those directed toward Congress or academics, such as the projects on which Talcott Parsons, Donald Marquis, and Elbridge Sibley were currently working. For the Marquis and Parsons projects, see note 15 above.

77. "Dissertation" in Dollard to Young, June 17, 1948. Two years prior to the book's publication, Dollard laid out the terms of Carnegie's financial support for the project, including what would happen in the "quite possible" event of the book doing poorly. Dollard to Young, January 23, 1946. Both in Folder 6, Box 328, CC. Regarding the SSRC's use of part of the book's royalties, see Pendleton Herring to Dollard, December 14, 1949, in which Herring requests that the SSRC be allowed to use the royalties from Chase's book to support the new Committee on Political Behavior. Herring to Dollard in Folder 1428, Box 129, Subseries 16, Series 1, Accession 2, SSRC, RAC.

78. SSRC Committee on Analysis of Pre-Election Polls and Forecasts, "Report on the Analysis of Pre-Election Polls and Forecasts," *Public Opinion Quarterly* 12 (winter 1948–1949): 605.

79. Dollard, "Notes on Interview with Leland C. DeVinney, Rockefeller Foundation," November 8, 1948, Folder 1, Box 328, series IIIA.8, CC. All Carnegie documents cited in this section appear in Box 328, series IIIA.8, unless otherwise noted. For another discussion of this committee, see Sarah E. Igo, *The Averaged American: Surveys, Citizens, and the Making of a Mass Public* (Cambridge, MA.: Harvard University Press, 2007), 153–156, 186–189. Igo, 103–149, sees the work of this SSRC committee as one moment in polling firms' broader, ongoing public relations effort to win public trust.

80. Dollard, "Notes on meeting with Pendleton Herring, Paul Webbink (SSRC), John W. Gardner (Carnegie)," November 8, 1948; and Dollard, "Notes on interview with Pendleton Herring," November 10, 1948; both in Folder 1. This SSRC committee was just one of a number of efforts on the part of social scientists to explain the failure of the commercial firms' forecasts. See Converse, *Survey Research*, 374–376.

81. Herring to Robert M. Lester, Secretary, Carnegie, May 24, 1949, p. 2, Folder 1. For Herring's association with *Public Opinion Quarterly*, see Herring, "APSA Oral History Interview," 30–31.

82. The only person who contributed to this report who was employed by a quasi-commercial polling firm was Herbert Hyman of the National Opinion Research Center. See SSRC Committee, "Report," 600.

83. For each of these three points, see SSRC Committee, "Report," 600, 608–609, and 618.

84. SSRC Committee, "Report," 601–603, 622.

85. Robert K. Merton and Paul K. Hatt concluded that the failure of the commercial polls' forecasts had not damaged the legitimacy of the social sciences among newspaper editors and publishers, since most of those they interviewed drew no connection between commercial polling and social science. Merton and Hatt, "Election Polling Forecasts and Public Images of Social Science: A Case Study in the Shaping of Opinion among a Strategic Public," *Public Opinion Quarterly* 13, no. 2 (1949): 220–221. On p. 185 support from a Carnegie grant is acknowledged.

86. Truman, introduction to "A Report on Activities of the Committees," p. xv. The

committees referred to are the Committee on Political Behavior and its successor, the Committee on Governmental and Legal Processes. The full report appears in Folder 1119, Box 189, subseries 19, series 1, Accession 1, SSRC Records, RAC.

87. See note 39 for citations regarding Herring's request that Carnegie support the CPB at the rate of $10,000 per annum. Though founded in 1945, the Committee on Political Behavior did not become active until Herring prompted the appointment of new members in the fall of 1949. I discuss the early life of this committee in more detail in Hauptmann, "The Development of Philanthropic Interest in the Scientific Study of Political Behavior," report on research conducted at the Rockefeller Archive Center, 2011, available at https://rockarch/issuelab.org.

88. Truman, introduction to "A Report on Activities of the Committees," ix, Folder 1119, SSRC.

89. Leiserson to Herring, September 6, 1949, Folder 5831, Box 470, subseries 76 (CPB), series 1, Accession 2, SSRC, RAC.

90. In Campbell to Herring, January 25, 1952, Angus Campbell explained that he planned to pitch the Michigan Survey Research Center's 1952 election study to Carnegie's John Gardner as one pay-off of Carnegie's investment in 1949. Campbell added, "I feel the study we have in mind could act as a powerful stimulus to the general field of quantitative research in political behavior." In Folder 5858, Box 473, subseries 76 (CPB), series 1, Accession 2, SSRC Records, RAC.

91. Truman, introduction to "Activities of the Committees," pp. xi–xiv, discusses the SSRC's Committee on Comparative Politics as "spinning-off" of the CPB and mentions how initiatives for research on state politics as well as American governmental and legal processes grew out of the CPB's work. All of the foundation-funded conferences and research projects were carried out under the aegis of the CPB on pp. 44–59 and 72–88 of "A Report on Activities of the Committees." A full citation for this report appears in note 86.

92. Campbell to Gardner, August 4, 1960, Folder 13, Box 329, series IIIA.8, CC. Campbell was the lead author of *The American Voter*. All subsequent Carnegie documents cited appear in Folder 13, Box 329, series IIIA.8, CC. To distinguish Carnegie documents from those in other collections, I include the CC abbreviation in subsequent references.

93. For several recent assessments of the legacy of *The American Voter*, see Philip E. Converse and Donald R. Kinder, "Voting and Electoral Behavior," in *A Telescope on Society: Survey Research and Social Science at the University of Michigan and Beyond*, eds. James S. House, F. Thomas Juster, Robert L. Kahn, Howard Schuman, and Eleanor Singer (Ann Arbor: University of Michigan Press, 2004); and Michael Lewis-Beck, Michael S., Helmut Norpoth, William G. Jacoby, and Herbert F. Weisberg, with a Foreword by Philip E. Converse, *The American Voter Revisited* (Ann Arbor: University of Michigan Press, 2008). In comparison, Robin, *Cold War Enemy*, 22–23, argues that Stouffer et al.'s *American Soldier* has had a less enduring influence.

94. For a synopsis of the origins of the ANES, see http://electionstudies.org/overview/origins.htm.

95. Gardner makes this clear in "Interview Notes on Meeting with Campbell," January 27, 1955, CC. Campbell and his team then received Rockefeller Foundation grants for their studies of the 1956 ($110,000) and 1960 ($206,800) elections. Rockefeller made

both directly to the Survey Research Center. See Rockefeller Foundation grant action 55143, October 31, 1955, and RF grant action 60002, January 22, 1960. Both in Folder 4993, Box 583, series 200S, R.G. 1.2, RFA, RAC.

96. Some Carnegie and SSRC documents suggest, albeit indirectly, that Campbell and Gardner may have conferred about making the grant to the CPB—and that this may have been Campbell's preference as well. See excerpt from Campbell to Gardner, February 19, 1952, CC; and Campbell to Key, February 28, 1952, CC. Campbell to Herring, January 25, 1952, asks Herring to have two prominent members of the CPB, David Truman and V. O. Key, contact Carnegie to endorse the planned 1952 election study. In V. O. Key (chair of CPB) to Campbell, February 22, 1952, Key says it was Gardner's idea that the CPB apply for the grant and called this suggestion "wholly unanticipated," adding he did not understand Gardner's reasoning. These last two documents appear in Folder 5858, Box 473, subseries 76, series 1, Acc. 2, SSRC, RAC. All subsequent references to SSRC documents related to this project appear in the folder cited in the preceding sentence.

97. Gardner to Herring, March 7, 1952, SSRC.

98. Herring to Executive Committee of SSRC, March 12, 1952, SSRC.

99. Warren Miller, one of the researchers involved with the 1952 study, recalled that the SSRC's CPB proposed the study to Carnegie and that Michigan's Survey Research Center "was really the committee's 'chosen instrument.'" See Warren E. Miller, "APSA Oral History Interview," in *Political Science in America: Oral Histories of a Discipline*, eds. Michael A. Baer, Malcolm E. Jewell, and Lee Sigelman (Lexington: University Press of Kentucky, 1991), 237. The documentary evidence cited above contradicts Miller's recollection of the CPB's involvement in this project.

100. Rene A. Wormser, *Foundations: Their Power and Influence* (San Pedro, CA: Covenant House, 1993), 328–330.

101. Gardner to Herring, April 8, 1952, SSRC.

102. Florence Anderson, Associate Secretary, Carnegie, to Herring, March 21, 1952, SSRC.

103. For a discussion of the Survey Research Center's 1946 move to Michigan from its earlier life as the Division of Program Surveys under the Department of Agriculture and the tenuous relationship between it and the University of Michigan, see Converse, *Survey Research*, 244–248, 340–349.

104. See Pollock to Campbell, April 30, 1952, attached to Pollock to Herring, April 30, 1952, SSRC.

105. The cited passage appears on p. 8 of "Social Science Research Council, Grant of $90,000 for Research on Political Behavior," no author, n.d., attached to Florence Anderson, Associate Secretary, Carnegie, to Herring, March 21, 1952, CC. The cited text was probably prepared for a meeting of Carnegie's Board of Trustees in the spring of 1952.

106. Campbell intimated to Herring: "Jim [Pollock] is unhappy at the prospect of an important project of obvious political science content being done on the Michigan campus without his Department being integrally associated with it," adding, "I do not, of course, want Jim to see himself as having executive control over" the project. Campbell to Herring, March 7, 1952, 1, 2, SSRC. Converse, *Survey Research*, 348, presents a similar analysis, noting that the SRC's "relationship with political science was prickly."

107. Campbell, "Report to SSRC," July 16, 1954, 2, SSRC.

108. See Converse, *Survey Research*, 244–266, on academics' reception of survey researchers. Campbell, "Report to SSRC," July 16, 1954, 1, SSRC. I believe Campbell's comments about treating these data as a public good are meant to imply that he did not plan to sell them. Some researchers who worked under the auspices of Michigan's Survey Research Center, however, did sell the data they collected. See Converse, *Survey Research*, 355. I discuss the history of mid-twentieth-century data-sharing practices at greater length in Emily Hauptmann, "Why They Shared: Recovering Early Arguments for Sharing Social Scientific Data," *Science in Context* 33, no. 2 (2020): 101–119.

CHAPTER 2. THE FORD FOUNDATION'S "GOLDEN EGGS" AND THE CONSTITUTION OF BEHAVIORALISM

1. Roger L. Geiger, *Research and Relevant Knowledge: American Research Universities since World War II* (Oxford: Oxford University Press, 1993), 93; Albert Somit and Joseph Tanenhaus, *Development of Political Science: From Burgess to Behavioralism* (New York: Irvington, 1982), 168–169. Geiger's figures are not discipline specific; Somit and Tanenhaus focus on political science.

2. Ford Foundation, *1957 Annual Report* (New York: Ford Foundation), 22–23. For a wide-ranging assessment of Ford's international and area studies programs, see Robert A. McCaughey, *International Studies and Academic Enterprise: A Chapter in the Enclosure of American Learning* (New York: Columbia University Press, 1984), chapters 6–8. Parmar, *Foundations of the American Century*, 124–148, presents a case study of Ford's international and area studies programs focused on Indonesia. For an overview of Ford's behavioral sciences program implications for all the social sciences, see Solovey, *Shaky Foundations*, 103–147.

3. For an analysis of the behavioral revolution as part of political scientists' common sense of the discipline, see Joshua R. Berkenpas, "The Behavioral Revolution in Contemporary Political Science: Narrative, Identity, and Practice," PhD diss, Western Michigan University, 2016. Variations on the theme that behavioralism advanced political science appear in David Easton, "APSA Oral History," in *Political Science in America: Oral Histories of a Discipline*, ed. Michael A. Baer, Malcolm E. Jewell, and Lee Sigelman (Lexington: University Press of Kentucky); Heinz Eulau, *Micro-Macro Dilemmas in Political Science* (Norman: University of Oklahoma Press, 1996); and Somit and Tanenhaus, *Development of Political Science*. By contrast, those who question the revolutionary qualities of behavioralism include Robert Adcock, "Interpreting Behavioralism," in *Modern Political Science: Anglo-American Exchanges since 1880*, ed. Robert Adcock, Mark Bevir, and Shannon C. Stimson (Princeton, NJ: Princeton University Press, 2007); John Dryzek, "Revolutions without Enemies: Key Transformations in Political Science," *American Political Science Review* 100, no. 4 (2006): 487–492; James Farr, "Remembering the Revolution: Behavioralism in American Political Science," in *Political Science in History: Research Programs and Political Traditions*, ed. James Farr, John S. Dryzek, and Stephen T. Leonard (Cambridge: Cambridge University Press, 1995); and Gunnell, *The Descent of Political Theory*.

4. Analyses of universities' ties to powerful political and economic entities during the

late nineteenth and early twentieth centuries include Barrow, *Universities and the Capitalist State*; Gruber, *Mars and Minerva*; and Larry Owens, "MIT and the Federal 'Angel': Academic R & D and Federal-Private Cooperation before World War II," *Isis* 81, no. 2 (1990): 189–213. Studies of how this relationship changed after World War II include Crowther-Heyck, "Patrons of the Revolution," 420–446; Geiger, *Research and Relevant Knowledge*; Klausner and Lidz, *Nationalization of the Social Sciences*; and Slaughter and Rhoades, *Academic Capitalism and the New Economy*.

5. Peter Seybold, "The Ford Foundation and the Triumph of Behavioralism in American Political Science," in *Philanthropy and Cultural Imperialism: The Foundations at Home and Abroad*, ed. Robert F. Arnove (Boston: G. K. Hall, 1980), 274.

6. Some early defenders of behavioralism who called it revolutionary include Gabriel Almond, "Political Theory and Political Science," *American Political Science Review* 60, no. 4 (1966): 869–879; Robert Dahl, "The Behavioral Approach in Political Science: Epitaph for a Monument to a Successful Protest," *American Political Science Review* 55, no. 4 (1961): 763–772; and David Truman, "Disillusion and Regeneration: The Quest for a Discipline," *American Political Science Review* 59, no. 4 (1965): 865–873. Austin Ranney, "Committee on Political Behavior: 1949–64, and the Committee on Governmental and Legal Processes, 1964–72," *Items* 28, no. 3 (1974): 39, argues behavioralism changed political science irreversibly. David Easton, "The New Revolution in Political Science," *American Political Science Review* 63, no. 4 (1969): 1051–1061, declared the behavioral period over. See Adcock, "Interpreting Behavioralism," for an assessment of the impact of behavioralism on the fields of American and comparative politics in the United States. For a specific illustration of how behavioralism has remained central to graduate courses on research methods into the twenty-first century, see Peregrine Schwartz-Shea and Dvora Yanow, "'Reading' 'Methods' 'Texts': How Research Methods Texts Construct Political Science," *Political Research Quarterly* 55, no. 2 (2002): 476.

7. See Adcock, "Interpreting Behavioralism," 190–191, 195, 197–198, for detailed arguments on these points. Stephen Wertheim, "Reading the International Mind: International Public Opinion in Early Twentieth Century Anglo-American Thought," in *The Decisionist Imagination: Sovereignty, Social Science, and Democracy in the 20th Century*, ed. Daniel Bessner and Nicolas Guilhot (New York: Berghahn, 2019), underscores the differences between early and mid-twentieth-century conceptions of public opinion. Gunnell, *Descent*, 222–227, discusses some behavioralists' appeal to neopositivist ideas; see also John G. Gunnell, "The Reconstitution of Political Theory: David Easton, Behavioralism, and the Long Road to System," *Journal of the History of the Behavioral Sciences* 49, no. 2 (2013): 190–210, for a discussion of Easton's general theories of systems. Among the most well-known critiques of behavioralism are Charles McCoy and John Playford, eds., *Apolitical Politics: A Critique of Behavioralism* (New York: Thomas Y. Crowell, 1967); Strauss, "An Epilogue"; and Wolin, "Political Theory as a Vocation," 1062–1082.

8. Kurt Danziger, *Naming the Mind: How Psychology Found Its Language* (London: Sage, 1997), 97–98, 101–102; "practical science of social control," on 98. Gabriel Almond, "APSA Oral History," in *Political Science in America: Oral Histories of a Discipline*, ed. Michael A. Baer, Malcolm E. Jewell, and Lee Sigelman (Lexington: University Press of Kentucky, 1991), 123; Dahl, "Behavioral Approach," 764–765; and Easton, "APSA Oral

History," 201–205, all acknowledge their debt to social scientists outside political science. For discussions of the differences between Skinnerian behaviorism and the behavioral sciences, see Ellen Herman, *The Romance of American Psychology: Political Culture in the Age of Experts* (Berkeley: University of California Press, 1995), 8; and Pooley, "A 'Not Particularly Felicitous Phrase.'"

9. Crowther-Heyck, "Patrons of the Revolution," 430.

10. See Seybold, "Triumph of Behavioralism," 288–292; and Adcock, "Interpreting Behavioralism, 194–207, for excellent discussions of the importance of SSRC Committees to the rise of behavioralism. Key and Truman each served as chairs of the Committee on Political Behavior. I discuss Herring's role at length in chapter 1; Miller's role in chapter 4. I follow Crowther-Heyck's use of the term "broker"; see Crowther-Heyck, "Patrons of the Revolution," 431.

11. The $24 million figure excludes grants made primarily in the mental health area. With these included, the program made grants totaling $38.5 million. Ford Foundation, *1957 Annual Report*, 13.

12. Seybold, "Triumph of Behavioralism," 273–274, suggests otherwise, arguing that this Ford program was squarely directed at political science. I do not believe its grant-making record supports that view. Pooley, "'Behavioral Sciences' Label," 57–58, concludes, as I do, that political science was relatively marginal to this program.

13. For examples of Area I grants to political scientists specializing in area studies and public administration projects overseas, see Ford Foundation, *1954 Annual Report*, 31, and *1956 Annual Report*, 108. Organizations receiving substantial Area II grants appear in Ford Foundation, *1952 Annual Report*, 31.

14. See "Behavioral Sciences Program, Final Report, 1951–1957," 3; appended to Berelson, "Oral History Transcript," July 7, 1972, as well as Report #002072, December 1951, 11. All in Ford Foundation Archives (hereafter abbreviated FFA). The Total List of Grants appended to the BSP's Final Report itemizes persons as well as universities or other institutions to whom grants were made; their disciplines or departments do not appear. When well-known political scientists appear here, they are either part of an interdisciplinary group (i.e., David Truman, A-1) or receive relatively small sums ($20,100 to Leo Strauss, A-7). For a synopsis of Berelson's career in academic, government, and foundation circles, see Solovey, *Shaky Foundations*, 117–118.

15. On the close ties between foundations and the federal government during this period, see Klausner and Lidz, *Nationalization of the Social Sciences*; George T. Mazuzan, *The NSF: A Brief History* (General Publication, NSF8816, 1994), http://www.nsf.gov/about/history-publications.jsp; Needell, "Project Troy and the Cold War Annexation of the Social Sciences"; and Solovey, *Shaky Foundations*. How much the federal government spent on social-science research during the immediate postwar period is hard to pin down. See the estimates offered by Crowther-Heyck, "Patrons of the Revolution," 428–430; Geiger, *Research and Relevant Knowledge*, 157–197; and Simpson, *Science of Coercion*, 52.

16. Lowen, *Creating the Cold War University*.

17. "BSP Final Report," 7, appended to Berelson, "Oral History," FFA. Solovey, *Shaky Foundations*, 119–120, emphasizes Ford Trustees' skepticism of Area V programs, the animus of Trustee Donald David in particular.

18. Pooley, "'Behavioral Sciences' Label," 51–58, provides a detailed account of the internal discussions at Ford that culminated in the adoption of the behavioral sciences label.

19. Donald G. Marquis, "Report of the Social Science Division of the Study Committee," 1950, FFA. "Social reform," "socialism" on pp. 20–21; "diagnoses . . . " on pp. 21–22. On Marquis's postwar position on the Committee on Human Resources, see Simpson, *Science of Coercion*, 57–58. On Marquis's wartime work for the National Research Council, see Robert R. Sears, "Donald George Marquis," *American Journal of Psychology* 86, no. 3 (1973): 662. Regarding the Office of Scientific Resource Development, see Lowen, *Cold War University*, 199–200. Marquis also considered "human resources" as another possible replacement for "social sciences." See Donald Marquis, "Oral History Transcript," October 27, 1972, 8, FFA. See Nelkin, *The University and Military Research*, 36–45, for a discussion of an analogous postwar figure, C. S. Draper. As director of MIT's Instrumentation Lab, Draper also held positions on several government bodies devoted to military research. Nelkin argues that Draper actively shaped the direction of that research, pitching projects he and his colleagues at the I-Lab had begun to the military to fund.

20. Marquis, "Oral History," 7, FFA, for "a different label." On p. 8 Marquis takes some credit for having come up with the term "behavioral sciences," although he says James [Grier] Miller could claim credit for doing so as well. On this point, see James G. Miller, "Toward a General Theory for the Behavioral Sciences," *American Psychologist* 10, no. 9 (1955): 513. Pooley, "'Behavioral Sciences' Label," 42–47, discusses one of Marquis's teachers at Yale, Clark Hull, using of the term the "behavioral sciences" in the interwar period. According to Pooley, however, the term did not become widely used until after Marquis prompted Ford to adopt it.

21. Donald K. Price, "Oral History Transcript," June 22, 1972, 102, FFA.

22. On Herring's role on a three-person "advisory panel" to Marquis, see Marquis, "Report of the Social Science Division," 1; Herring, "The 5.1 Program," Report # 010834, September 25, 1951, p. 2, FFA.

23. Bernard Berelson, "Behavioralism," in *International Encyclopedia of the Social Sciences*, ed. David Sills (New York: MacMillan, 1968), 43.

24. Report #003025, "A Program in Behavioral Science Research," Instituted by the Ford Foundation in the Summer of 1950, FFA. A list of the universities that received this initial set of grants appears on p. 1. The Universities of California, Chicago, Columbia, Cornell, Harvard, Michigan, and Yale and the SSRC received grants of $300,000 each; Illinois, Minnesota, North Carolina, Pennsylvania, Princeton, and Stanford received $100,000 each. On the issue of new programs, UC's President Sproul recalled that Ford officials had made clear to him in 1950 that the grant money was to be used "for new enterprises rather than for 'going concerns.'" See President Gordon Sproul to Rowan Gaither, January 3, 1955, p. 1. In Grant #50–005, "Research in Individual Behavior and Human Relations, UC Berkeley," FFA.

25. B. J. Craig, Secretary and Treasurer, Ford Foundation, to Sproul, July 28, 1950, and September 29, 1950, in Grant # 50–005, FFA. Lowen, *Cold War University*, 204, recounts that, like Berkeley, Stanford received a sizable grant under this program without ever having submitted a formal application to Ford.

26. Berelson, "BSP Final Report," 14; Report #003025, p. 3, FFA; Ford Foundation, *1955 Annual Report*, 36. The universities criticized in Report #003025 that still received substantial support in 1955 were Harvard, Stanford, Columbia, and Chicago.

27. Chancellor Clark Kerr to Sproul, October 8, 1954, as well as "Memo from Social Science Department Chairs to Kerr," November 15, 1954, both expressed the worry that Ford might withdraw its still unspent grant. Both in Folder 26, "$300,000 Ford Grant to University, Uses of," Box 54, Office of the Chancellor Records, University of California Archives (abbreviated OCR, UCA in subsequent references).

28. James D. Hart to Sproul, January 3, 1958, Folder 6, "Institute for Social Science," Box 54, OCR, UCA.

29. In addition to the initial grant of $300,000, Berkeley received a $75,000 terminal grant from the Behavioral Sciences Division when it made its final round of grants in 1957. That terminal grant came with the condition that Berkeley match Ford's funds by devoting an additional $50,000 to behavioral science research. See Berelson to Kerr, July 12, 1957, Folder 15, Box 54, OCR, UCA.

30. Eugene C. Lee to Blumer, June 3, 1958; Blumer to Robert W. Chandler, Ford, March 21, 1961, pp. 3–5; Blumer to Chandler, January 9, 1961, p. 2. Survey Research Center projects during the 1960–1961 academic year were largely devoted to the analysis of public opinion or to the development of statistical techniques. Center for Social Science Theory projects were often interdisciplinary in conception and ambition. All in Folder 6, Box 54, OCR, UCA.

31. According to the report ISS submitted to the Ford Foundation, it made eighty-three grants in 1958 and forty-two in 1959. By the 1960s the number of grants diminished to around a dozen, with the total disbursed averaging just under $16,000 per annum. ISS list of Ford Grantees in Grant #50–005, UC Berkeley, FFA.

32. For instance, in 1958 Hans Kelsen received a Ford grant via the ISS for a study of the "Social Philosophy of Plato," and Dwight Waldo received one for an "Annotated Bibliography of the Administrative Novel"; 1958–1959 ISS list of Ford Grantees in Grant #50–005, UC Berkeley, FFA.

33. Advisory Committee Minutes, ISS, April 3, 1961; Blumer, "Memo to directors of eight U.C. Berkeley research centers," October 3, 1960, p. 2. Both in Folder 6, Box 54, OCR, UCA.

34. Herbert Goldhamer, RAND, to Berelson, 2 May 1952, pp. 1–2. Excerpt of letter in PA 53–01, FFA. Records marked with PA numbers are part of the Grants and Reports for Area V in the Ford Foundation's Archives cited in the bibliography.

35. These three were the only political scientists out of a group of forty-one to be admitted. Ultimately, only Wahlke attended. A list of those admitted to the 1953 Summer Institute, "Mathematics for Social Scientists," is included in "Support for a program on the mathematical training of behavioral scientists, SSRC." See also "Report of the Committee on the Mathematical Training of Social Scientists," December 1952 to June 15, 1953. Both in PA 53–01, FFA.

36. "Report of the Committee on the Mathematical Training of Social Scientists to the SSRC," December 14, 1954, pp. 2–3; Flier for SSRC 1953 Summer Institute, "Mathematics for Social Scientists." Both in PA 53–01.

37. For summer workshops organized by the Committee on Political Behavior, see SSRC, *Annual Reports*, 1953–1954, 1954–1955.

38. For Ford's announcement of the endowment of CASBS, see the foundation's *1957 Annual Report*, 33. Berelson recalled that when the idea of the center was nearly dead due to a lack of support from foundation officers and academics, the sociologist Samuel Stouffer rescued it by enthusiastically endorsing the idea at a crucial meeting. Stouffer had led the large, interdisciplinary team of social scientists who produced the multi-volume *American Soldier* study after World War II, discussed in chapter 1. See Bernard Berelson, "Oral History," 51–52, FFA.

39. For several examples of CASBS fellows' enthusiasm about their interactions with fellows from other disciplines, see Kenneth Boulding to Kerr, January 27, 1955, Folder 9, "Center for the Integration of Social Science Theory"; and Eugene Burdick to Ralph Tyler, November 30, 1955, Folder 11, "Junior Fellows—CASBS." Both in Box 54, OCR, UCA. The quotations cited appear in Berelson, "Oral History," 57, FFA.

40. Seybold, "Triumph of Behavioralism," 274, 285–292; "set the agenda" on p. 274.

41. See Geiger, "Organized Research Units—Their Role in the Development of University Research," *Journal of Higher Education* 61, no. 1 (1990): 1–19; and Geiger, *Research and Relevant Knowledge*, 47–57, 73–82 (regarding UC Berkeley), for analyses of the relationship between foundations and university research institutes and centers.

42. Ford Foundation, *1955 Annual Report*, 36–37.

43. Marquis, "Oral History," 16–17; "List of fifty names" on p. 17. According to the Total List of Grants appended to Berelson's final report for the Behavioral Sciences Program, Marquis received $50,000 in 1953 for "Self-study in the behavioral sciences," and $220,250 in 1955 for "Development and improvement of work in the behavioral sciences," A-2, A-6, FFA. See note 14 for full citation for List of Grants.

44. Marquis, "Oral History," 16, for the passage regarding Eldersveld.

45. Eldersveld Memoirs, 30, 32–33, Biographical Folder 2 of 2, Box 5, Samuel J. Eldersveld Papers, Bentley Historical Library (BHL). In a later work, Eldersveld thanks Ford for a "grant for political behavior research" as well as for a year's residence at the CASBS (1959), where he completed the manuscript. See the unpaginated acknowledgments to *Fulcrum of Party Power: The Urban Presidential Vote 1920–1956*, c. 1960, reproduced 2001, in Folder 10 of 15, Academic Career series, Miscellaneous Writings, Speeches and Reports, 1955–2000, Box 5, Eldersveld Papers, BHL. As I discuss at some length in chapter 4, Eldersveld played a crucial role in reorienting Michigan's political science department toward behavioral research.

46. For 1952 figures, see Berelson, "Appendix to Final report, BSP," p. A-1. For 1955, see Ford Foundation, *1955 Annual Report*, 37. I converted 1952 dollars to 2021 dollars using the Bureau of Labor Statistics' Consumer Price Index Inflation Calculator (https://www.bls.gov/data/inflation_calculator.htm).

47. Retrieved from https://casbs.stanford.edu/people/past-fellows-research-affiliates-and-visiting-scholars. Not all political scientists who were fellows during this period were associated with behavioralism—Leo Strauss (1960–1961), for instance.

48. See Robert Dahl, *Who Governs? Democracy and Power in an American City* (New Haven, CT: Yale University Press, 1961), v; and Heinz Eulau, "APSA Oral History," in

Political Science in America: Oral Histories of a Discipline, ed. Michael A. Baer, Malcolm E. Jewell, and Lee Sigelman (Lexington: University Press of Kentucky), 179. For a discussion of Miller's role in founding ICPR in the early 1960s, see chapter 4, as well as Hauptmann, "Why They·Shared: Recovering Early Arguments for Sharing Social Scientific Data." For a list of APSA presidents, see https://www.apsanet.org/ABOUT/Leadership-Governance/APSA-Presidents-1903-to-Present. For Solovey's discussion of Berelson's aims, see *Shaky Foundations*, 128–134.

49. Lowen, *Cold War University*, 202, 203–204, 209–212, 222–223.

50. Lowen, 212–213, 215–217. The passage cited appears on p. 213.

51. Lowen, 221–222, 210, 219. The passage cited appears on p. 221. Paff does not come up in Lowen's account. Joe Paff, conversation with the author, July 22, 2005.

52. Gunnell, *Descent*, 238–239.

53. See Ford Foundation, *1953 Annual Reports*, for an announcement of this program; "improving . . . relationship" appears on p. 67. In Berelson to Martin Diamond, 22 November 1955, Section IV, PA #56–279, FFA, Berelson wrote: "You can't scare me! Let's see what the Professor has to propose." The postscript reads, "This is a much more encouraging reply that [*sic*] I usually make. I hope you understand it as such!"

54. These and other commentaries were published in Herbert J. Storing, ed., *Essays in the Scientific Study of Politics* (New York: Holt, Rinehart & Winston, 1962). In his evaluation of the proposal, Harold Lasswell wrote to Berelson on April 11, 1956, "There are so few examples of large scale empirical work in the field that an appraisal at this time would probably be more rhetorical than helpful." Dahl and Simon commented favorably on Strauss's scholarly reputation but were less enthusiastic about his proposed project. For instance, on April 9, 1956, Simon wrote to Berelson, "The relation between theory and empirical work is not going to be settled by political philosophers or methodologists." Dahl also had reservations but concluded in a letter to Berelson on April 10, 1956, that a Straussian critique might still be worthwhile: "Strauss isn't really going to stop empirical political science from moving on with its tasks. But he may help direct it toward relevance, significance, clarity in its assumptions, and some continuity with the political traditions of our civilization," p. 2. All references in this paragraph are to documents included in PA #56–279, FFA.

55. Strauss to Berelson, December 14, 1955. Hardin left the University of Chicago to become a program officer at the Rockefeller Foundation in 1961. He later returned to academia, spending the rest of his career teaching political science at the University of California, Davis. See *In Memoriam* 1998, University of California History Digital Archive. Berelson to Strauss, December 28, 1955. Both in #PA56–279, FFA. Berelson coauthored *Voting: A Study of Opinion Formation in a Presidential Campaign* (Chicago: University of Chicago Press, 1954) with Lazarsfeld and William McPhee.

56. Strauss, "Research Project Proposal," March 17, 1956, 3. Sheldon, Memo to Files, May 2, 1956, 1–2. All in #PA56–279, FFA.

57. Strauss to Ford Foundation, March 14, 1960. All in PA#56–279, FFA.

58. A longer excerpt from Dahl's April 10, 1956, letter to Berelson appears in note 54 above.

59. My argument on this point is indebted to Christopher Simpson's excellent *Science of Coercion*, in which he argues that the academic discipline of communications was

constituted by wartime communications and psychological warfare research funded by the federal government and foundations.

60. Gunnell, *Descent*, 222, comments on the "considerable difficulty" many midcentury political scientists had "describing the core meaning of behavioralism."

61. See primarily pp. 2–6 of Garceau's "Memorandum for the SSRC Committee on Political Behavior Research," March 8, 1950, Folder 5833, Box 470, subseries 76, series 1, accession 2, SSRC Records, RAC. For a less detailed version of this report published somewhat later, see Oliver Garceau, "Research in the Political Process," *American Political Science Review* 45, no. 1 (1951): 69–85.

62. The index of the December issue of each volume of the *American Political Science Review* (*APSR*) lists all articles in the volume under subject headings. In the 1950s and 1960s, announcements of upcoming American Political Science Association meetings appeared in the "News and Notes" section of the June issue of the previous year's *APSR*. Political behavior first appears as a distinct area in the conference program for 1963. See "News and Notes," *APSR* 56 (June 1962): 520. Comparative political behavior appears among the program areas for the 1967 conference. See "News and Notes," *APSR* 60 (June 1966): 476. Finally, the now familiar categorization of political scientists' fields and concerns by "organized sections" did not begin until the early 1980s. See Joseph Losco, "Whither Intellectual Diversity in American Political Science? The Case of APSA and Organized Sections," *PS: Political Science & Politics* 31, no. 4 (1998): 836–846. Seybold, "Triumph of Behavioralism," 299, note 6 and 301–302, note 38, provides several benchmarks for the increasing disciplinary power of behavioralism: the APSA presidencies of self-proclaimed behavioralists and the publication dates of important books expressing the approach. Most occur in the 1960s.

63. Pooley, "'Behavioral Sciences' Label," 39.

64. Heinz Eulau, "Social Science at the Crossroads," *Antioch Review* 11, no. 1 (1951): 117. In a 1955 speech Allport expressed some reservations about the term "behavioral science," adding: "But the foundations seem to like the name *behavioral science*, and we shall raise no objection to it lest Cinderella miss her chance to ride in a golden coach provided by the Foundation. Up to now these sciences have been riding in a Ford model T." Cited in Herman, *Romance of American Psychology*, 133.

65. See Eulau, *Micro-Macro Dilemmas*, 45–56, for his time at Berkeley; 57–68, notes 2 and 3, 396–397 for his wartime work on Lasswell's Rockefeller funded project; note 5, 382–383 mentions the overlap between his wartime work and his pseudonymous publication in the *New Republic*. Prior to the mid-1950s, traditional theoretical concerns were prominent in Eulau's scholarly work. Among Eulau's pre-behavioral work, see "Theories of Federalism under the Holy Roman Empire," *American Political Science Review* 35, no. 4 (1941): 643–664; and "Wayside Challenger: Some Remarks on the Politics of Henry David Thoreau," *Antioch Review* 9, no. 4 (1949): 509–522. Long ago, Norman Jacobson drew my attention to this pattern in Eulau and other first-generation behavioralists' scholarly careers.

66. Eulau, *The Behavioral Persuasion in Politics* (New York: Random House, 1963), v, 115–119. "New skills" on p. 115; allusion to Socrates on p. v. The book's dedication reads: "To Harold D. Lasswell, Persuader." See Eulau, "APSA Oral History," 188–189, as well as *Micro-Macro Dilemmas*, chapter 10, for his account of the Michigan summer seminar.

67. Dahl, "Behavioral Approach," 763, 765, 766. "Rough sledding" on p. 765; "powerful stimuli " on p. 763; "revolutionary sectarians" on p. 766.

68. Heinz Eulau, "Understanding Political Life in America: The Contribution of Political Science," *Social Science Quarterly* 57, no. 1 (1976): 123.

69. For a contemporaneous example of Dahl's pluralist commitments, see *Who Governs?*. Dahl acknowledges on p. x the generous Ford and SSRC financial support he received while working on this book. In "Behavioral Approach," 765, Dahl acknowledges how important contacts between academics and foundations were—but does not make clear how many influential academics also held foundation positions or consulted for them.

70. The phrase "defense intellectual" is central to Bessner, *Democracy in Exile*. For a brief discussion of Speier's career in the mid-twentieth century, see Lowen, *Cold War University*, 199–202.

71. Other figures discussed in later chapters whose multiple affiliations fueled their ability to influence political science—though not always in a behavioral direction—include Kenneth Thompson (chapter 3); James Pollock and Warren Miller (chapter 4); and Robert Scalapino (chapter 5). For an analogous point, see Lowen, *Cold War University*, pp. 277–278, note 13, for the many ties scholars affiliated with Harvard's Russian Research Center had to foundations and the military. Simpson, *Science of Coercion*, provides numerous examples of social scientists with close foundation and military connections. For an overview of the many figures he discusses, see Simpson, "Biographical Data on Key Personalities," 129–131.

72. As Simpson, *Science of Coercion*, 57–62, 82; Needell, "Project Troy"; and Frances Stonor Saunders, *The Cultural Cold War: The CIA and the World of Arts and Letters* (New York: New Press, 1999) have all shown, military and intelligence funds were often funneled through private foundations. This is another reason why making any precise breakdown of private versus public funding is, at best, difficult.

73. On Gaither's multiple strong ties to government, see Amadae, *Rationalizing Capitalist Democracy*, 34–39; Lowen, *Cold War University*, 198–199; and Needell, "Project Troy," 23–24. "Outposts of Government" is the title of chapter 5 of Simpson, *Science of Coercion*. The phrase comes from Jean Converse, *Survey Research in the United States*, 340–341, who applies it to Michigan's Survey Research Center, one of several centers under the ISR umbrella.

74. Farr, "Remembering the Revolution," 209–210. "Chicago School" on pp. 209–210; Merriam's role in the SSRC, on p. 210. On Ruml and the Rockefeller Foundation's role in creating the SSRC, see Fisher, *Fundamental Development of the Social Sciences*, 27–66; "sophisticated conservatives" on pp. 32–33.

75. Farr, "Remembering the Revolution," 212–213; "crucial decade" on p. 213.

76. Dryzek, "Revolutions without Enemies," 490. For a discussion of early scientistic arguments for NSF support for the social sciences, see Solovey, *Social Science for What?*, 32–35, 51–77.

77. Somit and Tanenhaus, *The Development of American Political Science*, 167, 183–185; "widespread dissatisfaction," on p. 184; "less than human," on p. 167; "lip service" on p. 185.

78. Terence Ball, "American Political Science in Its Postwar Political Context," in *Dis-*

cipline and History: Political Science in the United States, ed. James Farr and Raymond Seidelman (Ann Arbor: University of Michigan Press, 1993), 208–214.

79. Ball, "Postwar Political Context," 216; Adcock, "Interpreting Behavioralism," 193–197, 200–206, discusses the crucial roles of the SSRC's Committees on Political Behavior and Comparative Politics as well as the University of Michigan's Survey Research Center; each was heavily dependent on foundation funding. See my extended discussion of the funding for Michigan's Survey Research Center in chapter 4.

80. Ball, "Postwar Political Context," 216–218; "shape the kinds of questions," on pp. 216–217; "uses of power," p. 218; "unconsciously," on p. 216. Simpson, *Science of Coercion*, 94, 115–116, also speaks to these points.

81. BSP Final Report, 20, for "major intellectual invention"; Berelson, "Oral History," 18, for "here to stay."

82. Dahl, "Behavioral Approach," 770; Eulau, "Crossroads," 118.

83. Dahl, "Behavioral Approach, 768.

CHAPTER 3. A "CATHOLIC" APPROACH

1. On Carnegie's support for a range of institutions, see Lagemann, *The Politics of Knowledge*. For its support of Harvard's Department of Social Relations, see Isaac, *Working Knowledge*.

2. See my discussion of the conflict between Carnegie and Rockefeller over the direction of the SSRC in chapter 1, pp. 30–31, 33.

3. Rockefeller's support for the emerging field of international relations has been well documented and analyzed by Nicolas Guilhot and the contributors to his edited volume, *Invention of International Relations Theory*. I touch on Rockefeller's interest in this field in my discussion of the LAPP institutional grant to UC Berkeley below.

4. Geiger, *Research and Relevant Knowledge*, 99, estimates that Rockefeller's Division of Social Sciences spent around $30 million from 1939 to 1954. See Geiger, 94–110, for a broader overview of private foundation support for the social sciences from 1945 to 1960. The term "scatteration" was used in 1949 by Edwin Embree to criticize foundations for distributing their resources so widely that they made no impact. Cited in Curti and Nash, *Philanthropy and the Shaping of American Higher Education*, 228.

5. "Joseph H. Willits," Rockefeller Foundation Biographical File, Rockefeller Foundation Archives, Rockefeller Archive Center (abbreviated hereafter as RFA, RAC).

6. Fosdick pressed Willits to justify continued foundation spending on the social sciences, asking Willits to explain "what have [institutions funded by the RF, like the SSRC] *accomplished?*" Fosdick, October 20, 1943, p. 9, Folder 17, Box 3, series 910, RG 3, RFA, RAC; emphasis in original. For all subsequent citations to documents in series 910 (Program and Policy), I provide only document, folder, and box numbers, followed by P&P. See Craver, "Patronage and the Directions of Research in Economics," for a discussion of Fosdick's skepticism toward the social sciences.

7. Norman S. Buchanan argued that a "public philosophy" to counter communism be the division's postwar "unifying theme," whereas Leland C. DeVinney argued that the division should support the sciences of social relations and human behavior. See Buchanan

to Willits, July 7, 1949, and DeVinney to Willits, "Opportunities in the Social Sciences," no day, no month, 1948. Both in Folder 18, Box 3, P&P.

8. The passages cited appear in Willits, "Social Sciences Program Brief Review, 1939–1949, and Future Targets," Oral Report by Willits at Trustees' Meeting, December 7, 1949, Folder 18; "catholic" first appears in Willits, October 20, 1943, "The Social Sciences in 1944," Folder 17; Willits, "Social Science and Social Studies," April 25, 1952, p. 3, Folder 19. All folders in Box 3, P&P.

9. See Buchanan, "Notes on the Rockefeller Foundation Program in the Social Sciences," August 1, 1955, Folder 19, Box 3, P&P. Buchanan published numerous articles in economics journals in the 1930s and 1940s on the structure and decision-making of corporations. See, for example, Norman S. Buchanan, "Toward a Theory of Fluctuations in Business Profits," *American Economic Review* 31, no. 4 (1941): 731–53; and Buchanan, "The Economics of Corporate Reorganization," *Quarterly Journal of Economics* 54, no. 1 (1939): 28–50. See also "Norman Sharp Buchanan," RF Biographical Files.

10. See Guilhot, *Invention of International Relations Theory*, 145–149; and Farhang Rajaee, *Kenneth W. Thompson, the Prophet of Norms: Thought and Practice* (New York: Palgrave Macmillan, 2013), 25–28, for discussions of Thompson's intellectual connection to Morgenthau.

11. Craver, "Directions of Research in Economics"; Rockefeller Foundation, *Annual Report 1952*, 213.

12. DeVinney, "Opportunities in the Social Sciences," p. 3, 1948 [no day, no month], Folder 18, Box 3, P&P. In the same folder, also see DeVinney, "Guideposts to RF's Research Program in the Social Sciences," June 4, 1948, for similar arguments.

13. DeVinney received his PhD in Sociology from the University of Chicago in 1941. He worked under Stouffer in the Research Branch of the War Department 1943–1946 and then served as associate director of the Stouffer-led Laboratory of Social Relations at Harvard (1946–1948). He joined the Rockefeller social sciences staff in 1948, serving principally as an associate director of the division for around eighteen years. He retired in 1971. Leland C. DeVinney, RF Officer Biography.

14. DeVinney's diaries from 1951 through 1953 (R.G. 12.2) indicate that he had far less contact with political scientists than with sociologists, psychologists, and anthropologists.

15. V. O. Key's earliest published work was *The Administration of Federal Grants to States* (Chicago: Public Administration Service for the SSRC Committee on Public Administration, 1937). For a discussion of Key's graduate training in working with quantitative data at Chicago and his early work in the area of public administration, see Andrew M. Lucker, *V.O. Key, Jr.: The Quintessential Political Scientist* (New York: Peter Lang, 2001). Adcock, "Interpreting Behavioralism," 193–199, discusses the tensions between those, like Key, who relied on aggregate data, and behavioralists, who relied on surveys of the attitudes individuals to make sense of US politics.

16. V. O. Key, Jr., *Southern Politics in State and Nation*. (New York: Alfred Knopf, 1949).

17. See R. C. Martin to J. H. Willits, undated note attached to R. C. Martin to Virginius Dabney, December 15, 1944, Folder 4797, Box 560, series 200S, R.G. 1.2, RFA, RAC. Unless otherwise noted, all subsequent references in this section are to folders in the box, series, and record group noted in the previous sentence. The annual reports of the

Alabama Bureau of Public Administration (1945–1946; 1947–1948), included in Folder 4798, focus on projects specifically about Alabama; some appear to have been requested by Alabamans.

18. J. H. Willits to R. C. Martin, July 6, 1949, Folder 4799. For a discussion of Rockefeller's long-standing support for public administration, see Fisher, *Fundamental Development of the Social Sciences*, 137–144.

19. After refusing several times, Key finally agreed to direct the project sometime in the summer of 1946. See R. C. Martin to J. H. Willits, September 10, 1946, Folder 4798. Around a year later, Key described his aims to Martin this way: "Our objective has been to come out ultimately with a report that would constitute something of a contribution to the literature of political science as well as a study of interest to a fairly large body of citizenry." Key to Martin, "One Year of the Electoral Process Survey," p. 1, September 20, 1947, Folder 4798. The reviews mentioned are included in "Comments on *Southern Politics*," attached to York Willbern, Acting Director of Alabama's Bureau of Public Administration, to Roger F. Evans, December 21, 1949, Folder 4799. For a discussion of Carnegie Corporation funding for the 1949 Ann Arbor conference on political behavior devoted in part to Key's book, see chapter 1, pp. 43–44.

20. Key chaired the SSRC Committee on Political Behavior from 1949 to 1953. SSRC *Annual Reports*, 1950–1954. I analyze archived SSRC records regarding the formation and early life of this committee in Hauptmann, "The Development of Philanthropic Interest in the Scientific Study of Political Behavior," report on research conducted at the Rockefeller Archive Center, 2011, https://rockarch/issuelab.org.

21. RF Grant action 51082, May 31, 1951, Folder 4431, Box 519, series 200S, R.G. 1.2, RFA, RAC. Unless otherwise noted, all subsequent references to RF documents in this section are to material in the same folder, box, series, and record group.

22. See V. O. Key, "A Project for the Collection of State Election Statistics," pp. 5–7, n.d. [attached to J. H. Willits's interview notes, February 20, 1951]; and V. O. Key, "Report on Project, 'Studies in State Election Statistics,'" August 20, 1952, p. 3. In the latter report, Key also expressed his "grave doubts about many of the conclusions widely propagated as a result of some of the opinion survey analyses. Some tedious but fairly simple studies of the larger range of data available in the returns ought to contribute a better understanding of the ways in which the voter acts and, perhaps, in the long run, contribute to the more rational conduct of public affairs," p. 3.

23. V. O. Key to E. S. Mason, Dean, Harvard Graduate School of Public Administration, April 18, 1951. Key also submitted a "Supplementary Statement on Plan for Collection of State Election Statistics," April 18, 1951, to Rockefeller to address the concern about the overemphasis on quantification in his earlier project proposal.

24. Deane, interview notes with Key, p. 1, March 26, 1953. Later that year, Thompson praised an essay of Key's and asked to meet with him, "with or without obbligato from the Committee on Political Behavior." Thompson to Key, December 31, 1953. Key joined the committee shortly thereafter in 1954, as indicated by Joseph Willits to members of the LAPP advisory committee (which included V. O. Key), February 18, 1954, Folder 78, Box 9, P&P.

25. Campbell, Converse, Miller, and Stokes, *The American Voter*.

26. Unless otherwise noted, all documents cited in this section may be found in Folder 4993, Box 583, series 200S, R.G. 1.2, RFA, RAC.

27. For a discussion of the sources of SRC funding in the early postwar period, see Frantilla, *Social Science in the Public Interest*, 21.

28. Rockefeller Foundation, *Annual Report 1950*, 218; *Annual Report 1952*, 219, 232–234.

29. In his interview notes, June 2, 1955, DeVinney mentions that Campbell requested his comments on a draft proposal. In his July 1, 1955, cover letter to his final fourteen-page proposal (dated June 29, 1955), Campbell addresses DeVinney as "Lee" and says he believes he and his SRC team have fulfilled the CPB's objective to "stimulate the interest and if possible the involvement of political scientists," p. 1; "seen fit . . . " on p. 3. DeVinney's term as acting director of the DSS ended in July 1955.

30. See Buchanan to DeVinney, interoffice correspondence, August 3, 1955. In an earlier report to the DSS, Buchanan had argued that Rockefeller should not make funding voter and consumer behavior studies a high priority, since this work was already well funded by other sources. See Buchanan to Willits, July 7, 1949, p. 4, Folder 18, Box 3, P&P.

31. Buchanan, interview notes on visit to Institute for Social Research, University of Michigan, July 1 and 2, 1957.

32. James M. Burns to Thompson, September 3, 1957, offers the best paraphrase of the questions Thompson posed. David Truman offered the strongest endorsement; E. E. Schattschneider and Robert Dahl were the most critical. Among the lukewarm or mixed responses were Gabriel Almond's and Norman Jacobson's.

33. DeVinney and Thompson, interview with Angus Campbell, September 3, 1957. All quotations from p. 1 of document.

34. Dulles chaired Rockefeller's Board of Trustees from 1950 to 1952; Rusk became the foundation's president in 1952. The cited passage appears in Stewart to David Kettler, p. 1, October 28, 2005—a personal communication Kettler shared with the author.

35. Deane was a PhD candidate at Columbia University during the time of his service; Stewart received his PhD from Columbia in 1953. Herbert A. Deane officer's diary, 1952–1953, R.G. 12.1; John B. Stewart officer's diary, 2 vols., 1953–1955, R.G. 12.1, RFA, RAC. Deane ceded responsibility for LAPP to Stewart in the fall of 1953.

36. Kenneth Winifred Thompson, curriculum vitae, Rockefeller Foundation Biographical File, RFA, RAC.

37. Unless otherwise noted, all documents cited in this section may be found in Box 8, P&P. "Pedestrian . . . " appears in Deane to Willits, November 18, 1952, p. 1, Folder 75; Franz Neumann to Willits, November 24 , 1952, p. 1, Folder 75, argued for addressing contemporary problems; Robert MacIver to Willits, "Suggested Program for Conference," p. 2, July 31, 1952, Folder 73, for closer relations to government officials. For the complementarity between theory and empirical research, see Franz Neumann to Willits, November 12, 1952, and Willard Hurst to Dean Rusk, November 10, 1952. Both in Folder 75.

38. George Sabine summarized the comments of conference participants in a conference on LAPP in "The Conference on Political and Legal Philosophy," n.d., pp. 1–6, Folder 75. Louis Hartz to Willits, April 28, 1952, p. 1, Folder 73; Hartz reiterates the

point about meager "research funds" for political theory in Hartz to Willits, November 6, 1952, Folder 75.

39. DeVinney to Willits, February 11, 1953, p. 1, Folder 76.

40. Deane to Willits, January 12, 1953, pp. 1, 2, Folder 76.

41. Deane to Willits, February 6, 1953, pp. 1–3, Folder 76.

42. Deane to Willits, February 6, 1953, pp. 1–2, Folder 76.

43. Willits to Rusk, March 3, 1953, pp. 1, 2, Folder 76.

44. Deane to Rusk, "Agenda for the First Meeting of the Advisory Committee on Legal and Political Philosophy," June 18, 1953, p. 1, Folder 77.

45. Minutes of the LAPP Advisory Committee Meeting on March 21, 1955, p. 5, Folder 78, Box 9.

46. Minutes of the LAPP Advisory Committee Meeting, p. 6, Folder 78, Box 9.

47. Stewart to DeVinney, April 13 and 15, 1955, Folder 78, Box 9.

48. Rusk, Comments at Meeting of the Advisory Committee for LAPP, March 12, 1956, pp. 1–2, Folder 79, Box 9, P&P.

49. The total number of LAPP grants-in-aid made directly by the foundation was around 190. A list of all LAPP grants-in-aid from 1953 to 1962, n.d., Folder 80, Box 9, P&P. The specific LAPP grant actions for the individual fellowship recipients mentioned Hannah Arendt, Grant Action (GA) SS 6019, approved February 23, 1960, Folder 4170, Box 487; Allan Bloom, GA SS 5740, approved May 24, 1957, Folder 4885, Box 570; Henry Kissinger, GA SS 5458, approved May 24, 1954, Folder 4092, Box 344, R.G. 1.1; Herbert McClosky, GA SS 5831, approved March 24, 1958, Folder 5015, Box 586; Herbert Storing, GA SS 5937, approved March 24, 1959, Folder 4922, Box 575; Leo Strauss, GA SS 5734, approved May 15, 1957, Folder 4923, Box 575; and Gordon Tullock, GA SS 6007, approved May 4, 1961, Folder 5083, Box 594. Unless otherwise noted, all in series 200S, R.G. 1.2, RFA, RAC.

50. On ambitions to expand the bounds of political theory, see Adcock, "Interpreting Behavioralism," 189–190; and Gunnell, "The Behavioral Reformation," in *The Descent of Political Theory*, 221–250.

51. Herbert McClosky, "Statement Concerning Proposal," n.d., p. 1; Dahl to Thompson, October 22, 1957, pp. 1–2. Both in Folder 5015, Box 586, series 200S, R.G. 1.2, RFA, RAC.

52. Minutes of Division of Social Sciences Staff Meeting, Legal and Political Philosophy, October 9, 1953, pp. 4–5, Folder 77, Box 8, P&P.

53. "Social Science Research Council—Fellowships in Legal and Political Philosophy," Grant Action RF 53181, December 1–2, 1953, p. 53633, Folder 2470. Later grant actions renewing appropriations to the SSRC for this program (RF 57102, May 23, 1957, and RF 60122, June 24, 1960, both in Folder 2470) no longer highlighted the conflict between political philosophy and social science. Unless otherwise noted, all documents cited in this section appear in Box 255, series 200E, R.G. 1.2, RFA, RAC.

54. JBS (Stewart) interview notes from a meeting with Board of Directors, SSRC, September 13 and 14, 1954, p. 1, Folder 2470.

55. Minutes of the SSRC Conference on Legal Philosophy and Political Theory, no author given, November 20, 1954, pp. 2, 5, Folder 2470.

56. JBS (Stewart) interview notes on Conference on Legal Philosophy and Political

Theory, SSRC, November 20, 1954, Folder 2470. The page references in the subsequent paragraphs all refer to this document.

57. "The Council recognizes the desirability of encouraging young scholars, who are pursuing theoretical and philosophic studies, to secure further training through research into legal and political thought and institutions. In some cases the study conducted under the fellowship may be in a related field. For example, a fellow previously trained in law might study social philosophy, while one already versed in political theory might wish to broaden his preparation for further research by work in history and economics." SSRC brochure, 1955, pp. 11–12, Folder 2470.

58. Willits cited increasing the prestige of the field as one of the main aims of LAPP in "Legal, Social and Political Philosophy," March 3, 1953, p. 3, Folder 76, Box 8, P&P.

59. Rockefeller's records of the initial awards ("grant actions") are specifically numbered. For the 1956 grants to Harvard, see RF 56129; for Columbia, RF 56128; for UC Berkeley, RF 56127.

60. RF Grant Action 61135 to the University of California–Department of Political Science, approved October 20, 1961, pp. 61815–61816, Folder 4855, Box 567, series 200S, R.G. 1.2, RFA, RAC.

61. Unless otherwise specified, all the documents cited in this section appear in folders found in Box 567, series 200S, R.G. 1.2, RFA, RAC. Interview notes from a meeting between Rusk, Thompson, and DeVinney, January 17, 1955; Kenneth W. Thompson interview notes from a meeting with Robert Scalapino, June 8, 1956; Norman Jacobson to Kenneth Thompson, May 31, 1956. Thompson advocated adding Scalapino to the RF's advisory committee for LAPP in a memo to DeVinney, November 25, 1959, Folder 80, Box 9, P&P.

62. Leslie Lipson, Chair; Eugene Burdick, Ernst Haas, Sheldon Wolin, "Proposed Instructions from the Chancellor to the Committee that will Disburse the Rockefeller Grant," n.d., pp. 1–2, Folder 4855.

63. The first cited passage refers to the grant made to Albert Lepawsky, p. 3, "Report on the Rockefeller Grant to Political Science," June 1957. A 1958 award made to George Belknap for a project on Bay Area urban politics was tortuously justified: "The study will be relevant to political theory because a theory of politics in a society such as ours must take into account the 'realities of fluid decision-making populations.'" In "Report on the Rockefeller Grant to Political Science," February 20, 1958, p. 5. Both reports in Folder 4856.

64. Kenneth W. Thompson interview notes, "University of California–Department of Political Science: re. renewal of grant in political theory," conversations with Robert A. Scalapino, January 24 and March 9, 1961, pp. 1–2, Folder 4857.

65. RF Grant Action 61135 to the University of California–Department of Political Science, approved October 20, 1961, p. 61817, Folder 4855.

66. "No permanent member of the staff," in Gerald Freund interview notes on meeting with Scalapino, April 4, 1962, p. 1. Regarding Sewell, see Scalapino to Freund, April 24, 1962. Expressions of staff frustration appear in Charles M. Hardin interview notes with Scalapino, February 14, 1962, and in Robert L. West to Freund, May 7, 1962. "Minimum effort" and "men of lesser experience" in the latter; emphasis in original. All in Folder 4857.

67. Scalapino to Thompson, July 10, 1963, Folder 4858.

68. Scalapino to Freund, February 17, 1964, p. 5, Folder 4859, Box 568.

69. Scalapino to Freund, February 17, 1964, pp. 8–11; Le Roy Graymer, Departmental Administrator, to Joseph E. Black, November 4, 1966, p. 5, Folder 4860, Box 568.

70. See for instance Ralph K. Davidson interview notes on conversation with Ralph Retzlaff, September 10, 1965, Folder 4859, Box 568. The department's final, unfunded grant proposal was called, "A Proposal to the Rockefeller Foundation from the Department of Political Science, University of California at Berkeley, for a Program of Assistance to Political Science Departments of Asia, Africa and Latin America," November 1966, Folder 4860, Box 568. The two passages cited appear in its title and on p. 7.

71. See note 49 full citation of the grant to Arendt. For the LAPP grant to Rawls, see Grant Action 5618, approved April 2, 1956, Folder 4281, Box 501. Wolin's first grant from LAPP was approved August 10, 1954, Folder 4873, Box 569. Both in series 200S, R.G. 1.2, RFA, RAC.

72. Rajaee, *Prophet of Norms*, 102–105. I discuss Thompson's own intellectual biography and commitments at greater length in Hauptmann, "The Theorists' Gambit: Kenneth Thompson's Cultivation of Theoretical Knowledge about Politics during the Early Cold War," *International History Review* 42, no. 3 (2020): 625–638.

73. Teresa Odendahl, *Charity Begins at Home: Generosity and Self-Interest among the Philanthropic Elite* (New York: Basic, 1990), 33–42, discusses the dense "philanthropic networks" that tie philanthropists and their staffs to one another.

74. The phrase "bunch their hits" was Abraham Flexner's image for what he believed was sound foundation strategy—investing in already established institutions and encouraging other foundations to do the same. Cited in Curti and Nash, *Philanthropy and the Shaping of American Higher Education*, 219.

CHAPTER 4. THE TRANSFORMATION OF POLITICAL SCIENCE AT MICHIGAN

1. Jack L. Walker, Jr., *Mobilizing Interest Groups in America. Patrons, Professions, and Social Movements*, prepared for publication by Joel Aberbach et al. (Ann Arbor: University of Michigan Press, 1991); "urging" groups into existence on pp. 78, 89–92; the longer cited passage on p. 102. Other notable works that advance versions of this view are Arnove, *Philanthropy and Cultural Imperialism*; Edward H. Berman, *The Influence of the Carnegie, Ford, and Rockefeller Foundations on American Foreign Policy: The Ideology of Philanthropy* (Albany: SUNY Press, 1983); Fisher, *Fundamental Development of the Social Sciences*; and Roelofs, *Foundations and Public Policy*.

2. Sarah Reckhow, *Follow the Money: How Foundation Dollars Change Public School Politics* (Oxford: Oxford University Press, 2013), focuses on primary and secondary schools. Teles, *The Rise of the Conservative Legal Movement*; and Nabih Haddad and Sarah Reckhow, "The Shifting Role of Higher Education Philanthropy: A Network Analysis of Philanthropic Policy Strategies," *Philanthropy and Education* 2, no. 1 (2018): 25–52, focus on universities.

3. See chapter 2 for an extended discussion of Ford's role in creating and sustaining CASBS.

4. According to Miller, the place of methods in the department's graduate curriculum also changed: "At the same time that Political Behavior was eliminated as a subfield ... the field of methods was elevated to a coordinate place along with the other major subfields." Memo from Miller to Dean Frank Rhodes, March 18, 1974; Subject: Department of Political Science Methods Field. In folder "UM Admin Files—Dept. of Political Science—Subfield Structure," Box 2, Warren E. Miller Papers, Bentley Historical Library (hereafter abbreviated BHL). Folders in most Bentley Library collections are not numbered. I therefore provide folder titles instead. Most archival documents cited in this chapter are housed at the Bentley Historical Library, unless otherwise noted.

5. ICPR was renamed the Inter-university Consortium for Political and Social Research in 1975. I call it ICPR when I refer to its pre-1975 history and ICPSR for 1975 and later.

6. See the discussion of the Carnegie and Rockefeller grants to the SRC in chapters 1 and 3. The NSF also supported the ICPR early; its first grant to the consortium was $95,000 for eighteen months. ICPR, *Annual Report* 1962–1963, pp. 6, 10. ICPR *Annual Reports* for each year from 1962 to 1969 are available at https://www.icpsr.umich.edu /icpsrweb/content/about/history/histdocs.html.

7. Geiger, *Research and Relevant Knowledge*, 60–61. Some institutions, however, were more wary of what the new emphasis on funded research would mean for their traditional commitment to undergraduate education. For example, see Geiger's discussion, pp. 82–90, of how Yale's "reluctance" during the 1950s to embrace sponsored research made it increasingly difficult for it to attract and keep faculty. "Reluctance" on p. 90.

8. "More classified research" in Geiger, 57; Report #8, "Research Projects Supported by Gifts, Grants or Contracts" (for period 7.1.59—6.30.60); date: September 1960— Robert L. Williams, Administrative Dean. In folder "Research—Sponsored, 1960–61," Box 132, College of Literature, Science and the Arts; University of Michigan Records, 1846–2014, BHL.

9. Both Frantilla, *Social Science in the Public Interest*, 16–21, and Converse, *Survey Research in the United States*, 340–349, spell out how an office within the wartime federal government became Michigan's Survey Research Center. The Research Center for Group Dynamics was founded in 1945 at MIT. It moved to the University of Michigan in 1948. See Frantilla, 22.

10. Converse, *Survey Research*, 343–347, discusses the sources of ISR's sponsored research income; Crowther-Heyck, "Patrons of the Revolution," 421, 428, 436, provides several examples of ISR's success in securing patronage from various sources over time.

11. The Carnegie Corporation's 1952 grant was for $90,000; the Rockefeller Foundation made similar grants in 1956 ($110,000) and 1960 ($206,800). See my discussions of these grants in chapters 1 (Carnegie) and 3 (Rockefeller). Campbell, Converse, Miller and Stokes, *The American Voter*.

12. Among those whose affiliations with ISR began around the same time they joined the political science department were M. Kent Jennings, Donald Kinder, and Kenneth Organski. See John E. Jackson and Arlene W. Saxonhouse, "Not Your Great-Grandfa-

ther's Department," unpublished manuscript prepared for Bicentennial of University of Michigan (2014), 18–19, on Jennings and Donald Kinder. For Organski's association with ISR, see the description of his Michigan career in the regents' memorial for him in 1998. Accessed through the Faculty History project, http://faculty-history.dc.umich .edu/faculty/abramo-fimo-kenneth-organski/memorial-0.

13. According to. Miller, "APSA Oral History Interview," 241, a start-up grant from a private foundation, the Stern Family Fund, helped launch ICPR. It received substantial support from the NSF in the early 1960s, receiving over $1.4 million in grants for repository development, the summer training program, computing equipment, and other projects from the NSF from 1962 through 1969. Though ICPR also received grants from the Ford Foundation, private corporations, and the University of Michigan, the NSF was by far its biggest, most consistent grantor during this period. ICPR, *Annual Reports*, 1962–1969.

14. Solovey, *Social Science for What?*, 90–100, discusses the political pressure campaign that ultimately won political science a program at the NSF in the late 1960s.

15. For example, the Ford Foundation supported the SSRC's 1953 Summer Institute program "Mathematics for Social Scientists." The Carnegie Corporation made several grants in the mid-1950s to the SSRC's Committee on Political Behavior to support summer workshops focused on survey research, presidential elections, and state politics. See my discussions of both in chapter 2. See Miller, "APSA Oral History," 240–241, for a discussion of how ICPR grew out of these summer workshops, and Eulau, "APSA Oral History," 188–189, for an account of the importance of these summer sessions to his own intellectual development.

16. David Truman to Kenneth W. Thompson, September 9, 1957, Folder 4993, Box 583, Record Group 1.2, Series 200S, Rockefeller Foundation Archives (RFA), Rockefeller Archive Center (RAC).

17. Eldersveld to Miller, June 23, 1959, comments specifically on how Eldersveld and some Michigan administrators were trying to secure NDEA fellowships for the new political behavior program. In folder "Correspondence—January—June 1959." For specific discussions of NDEA support of students in the political behavior program, see multiple items in the folder titled "Correspondence—Topical—Donald Stokes, 1963–1966." Both in Box 4, Miller Papers. Department graduate program brochures list NDEA fellowships among the available sources of financial support through 1972. These brochures appear in the folder "Topical Files: General Department Information," Box 9, Department of Political Science/UM Records, 1910–2009, 1970–2000. The NDEA supported graduate study at many institutions across the United States. For overviews of the program, see Geiger, *Research and Relevant Knowledge*, 220–222; and Loss, *Between Citizens and the State*, 156–160.

18. For an overview of NSF support in the 1960s, see the discussion of ICPR *Annual Reports* in note 6 above.

19. Geiger, *Research and Relevant Knowledge*, 174–179; Solovey, *Shaky Foundations*, 148–187.

20. The political science department reported just under $4,000 in sponsored research for the 1959–1960 fiscal year. For the same year, ISR reported $1.45 million. See Report #8, "Research Projects Supported by Gifts, Grants or Contracts," (for period

7.1.59—6.30.60); date: September 1960—Robert L. Williams, Administrative Dean. In folder "Research—Sponsored, 1960–61." Box 132, College of Literature, Science and the Arts, University of Michigan Records, 1846–2014, BHL.

21. See pp. 2–6 of "Proposal for a Field Training Program in the Political Process," attached to Pollock to Roger Heyns, Dean, LS &A, June 24, 1959; Proposal for Vandenberg Center attached to Pollock to Heyns, June 9, 1959. Both in folder "Department of Political Science, 1959–60," Box 123, College of Literature, Science and the Arts, University of Michigan Records, 1846–2014, BHL.

22. A University of Michigan press release issued April 9, 1960, for the department's celebration of its fiftieth anniversary in 1960, the year Pollock resigned as chair, mentions both proposed research centers. "Pollock, James Kerr," Folder 2, Box 104, Michigan News and Information Service, University of Michigan Faculty and Staff Files, 1944–2005, 1960–1995, BHL.

23. "The Memoirs of Sam Eldersveld: His Family History and His Career in Political Science at the University of Michigan," January 29, 2008, Biographical Folder 2 of 2, Personal/Biographical series, Box 5, Eldersveld Papers, BHL. "Memoirs" is a self-published autobiography.

24. The department's unanimous approval of the new program in May 1959 is mentioned in "The Objectives and Needs of the Graduate Degree Program in Political Behavior," p. 1, June 1959, attached to Eldersveld to Miller, June 23, 1959, folder "Correspondence—January–June 1959," Box 4, Miller Papers.

25. In his self-published memoirs, Eldersveld recalls sitting in on numerous courses offered through ISR in the late 1940s. He also says that an SSRC-sponsored 1951 summer seminar at the University of Chicago intensified his enthusiasm for doing research in political behavior. "The Memoirs of Sam Eldersveld: His Family History and His Career in Political Science at the University of Michigan," January 29, 2008, p. 32. Biographical Folder 2 of 2, Personal/Biographical series, Box 5, Eldersveld Papers, BHL.

26. In "Memoirs of Sam Eldersveld," p. 65, Eldersveld says he began his time as chair with the intention of making the department "more 'behavioral'"; on pp. 65–67 he discusses how the hires he made contributed to this. There are two drafts of Eldersveld's letter to Dean William Haber in Eldersveld's Papers. One is dated January 1, 1964; the other, January 3, 1964. Both stress the resources Eldersveld believes he will need to improve the department's national standing. Both in folder "University of Michigan, Department of Political Science, ca. 1960s, 1980s–1990s," Academic Career Series, Box 6, Eldersveld Papers, BHL.

27. Eldersveld served as chair 1964–1968 and 1969–1970. The phrase the "Michigan model" refers to the distinctive features of the study of public opinion and elections that grew out of *The American Voter*. See Converse and Kinder, "Voting and Electoral Behavior," 74, 76, 83–84, for more extensive explanations of the phrase. For a list of people hired during Eldersveld's time as chair, see Richard L. Park to Department Faculty, October 15, 1975, "The University of Michigan, Department of Political Science: Faculty," in folder "Topical Files—Political Science Department—Faculty List, 1910–1976," in Box 5, J. David Singer Papers, BHL.

28. "The Objectives and Needs of the Graduate Degree Program in Political Behav-

ior," pp. 1–2, June 1959, attached to Eldersveld to Miller, June 23, 1959, in folder "Correspondence—January–June 1959," Box 4, Miller Papers.

29. Lawrence Preuss to Department Executive Committee, April 25, 1949, in folder "Course and Degree, Ph.D. Program Guidelines, 1940–1960 (Folder 1 of 3)," Box 6, Department of Political Science Records. Beginning in 1950, students who opted out of taking theory as an examination field were still required to take six hours of graduate credit in political theory classes. Graduate Catalog, 1950–1951, p. 291. Theory is no longer specifically mentioned as a required examination field in the 1964–1965 Graduate Catalog, pp. 269–270. All department requirements for the PhD discussed appear in the Graduate Catalogs, 1940–1964, in the General Register of the University of Michigan. For a recent overview of the status of political theory in political science curricula, see Matthew J. Moore, "Political Theory Today: Results of a National Survey," PS: Political Science & Politics 43, no. 2 (2010): 265–272.

30. Report of the Departmental Committee on Requirements for the MA and Ph.D. Degrees, September 18, 1950, in folder "Course and Degree, Ph.D. Program Guidelines, 1940–1960 (Folder 1 of 3)," Box 6, Department of Political Science Records.

31. For the field called "political theory and methodology," see "General Examination for M.A. Candidates in Political Science," attached to Joseph Kallenbach to Edward H. Litchfield, Executive Director, APSA, March 18, 1952, Folder 1 of 3: "Course and Degree, Ph.D. Program Guidelines, 1940–1960." The next changes discussed appear in the respective Department of Political Science, The Graduate Program in Political Science, Procedures and Rules: Fall, 1963, 1966 and 1967. All in Folder 2 of 3: "Course and Degree, Ph.D. Program Guidelines, 1960–1970." Both folders in Box 6, Department of Political Science Records.

32. The Graduate Program Procedures and Rules for 1963 mention the more specific theory requirement in the PhD program for political behavior on pp. 10–11. A weakened requirement first appears in the 1967 version of these procedures on pp. 11–12. Department of Political Science, The Graduate Program in Political Science, Procedures and Rules, Revised, Fall, 1968, p. 9. Both in Folder 2 of 3: "Course and Degree, Ph.D. Program Guidelines, 1960–1970," Box 6, Department of Political Science Records.

33. John Kingdon, Associate Chair of Political Science, to Donald Stokes, Dean of Graduate College, September 16, 1971, expresses concern that the NDEA and NSF fellowships for graduate students the department had relied upon to build its graduate program may be drying up. In folder "Political Science, 1964–1982," Box 92, Horace H. Rackham School of Graduate Studies Records (University of Michigan). For the changing classification of Converse's course, compare the informational brochures titled "Political Science at Michigan" for 1970–1971 and 1972–1973, p. 31. Both brochures in folder "Topical Files: General Department Information," Box 9, Department of Political Science/UM Records, 1910–2009, 1970–2000. A March 1971 list, titled "Political Behavior Program Students (excluding Fall 1970)," identifies over ninety names. In folder "UM Admin Files—Department of Political Science—Political Behavior Program Students, 1971–1972," Box 2, Miller Papers.

34. I discuss behavioralists who characterized their work as political theory in Emily Hauptmann, "From Opposition to Accommodation: How Rockefeller Foundation Grants Redefined Relations between Political Theory and Social Science in the 1950s,"

American Political Science Review 100, no. 4 (2006): 646–648. Gunnell, *The Descent of Political Theory*, 220–224, discusses the interest in logical positivism in the 1950s among American political scientists in a variety of fields.

35. In the tape recording of his full APSA oral history interview, Miller speaks positively of two political theorists on the UC Berkeley faculty (Norman Jacobson and Sheldon Wolin); he identifies them as belonging to his intellectual community during the time he was on the UC Berkeley faculty from 1954 to 1956 (at 34:30). I thank Herb Weisberg for alerting me to this portion of Miller's oral history—and for providing me with his 2015 notes on this recording. Full recordings of APSA oral history interviews, usually much longer than the transcripts that appear in Michael A. Baer, Malcolm E. Jewell, and Lee Sigelman, eds., *Political Science in America: Oral Histories of a Discipline* (Lexington: University Press of Kentucky, 1991), are available online through the University of Kentucky Library's Louie B. Nunn Center for Oral History.

36. A 1961 letter from Eldersveld to Dean Roger Heyns, however, suggests that Eldersveld believed the theorist James Meisel shared his concerns about the state of the department. See Eldersveld to Heyns, January 23, 1961, p. 5, folder "University of Michigan, Department of Political Science, ca. 1960s, 1980s–1990s," Academic Career Series, Box 6, Eldersveld Papers.

37. For courses taught in political theory by Meisel and Grace, see General Register, 1959–1960, vol. 2, p. 176. Jackson and Saxonhouse, "Not Your Great-Grandfather's Department," 47, offer a similar assessment of the political theory field during this period, writing that "Political Theory lived quietly on the side" of major changes in the postwar department.

38. Miller to Robert Clark (University of Oregon), March 20, 1962, p. 9. In folder "Correspondence—Chronological 1962," Box 4, Miller Papers.

39. Eldersveld to Roger Heyns, January 23, 1961; "dated" and "formalistic," p. 5; "outside the mainstream," p. 3. In folder "University of Michigan, Department of Political Science, ca. 1960s, 1980s–1990s," Academic Career Series, Box 6, Eldersveld Papers.

40. In the complete recorded version of his APSA oral history interview, Miller makes this comment a little after two hours; see note 35 for full citation to this recording. Thanks to Herb Weisberg who provided me his exhaustive 2015 notes on the recording of Miller's oral history.

41. James K. Pollock and Samuel J. Eldersveld, *Michigan Politics in Transition: An Areal Study of Voting Trends in the Last Decade* (Ann Arbor: University of Michigan Press, 1942); and James K. Pollock, et al., *British Election Studies, 1950* (Ann Arbor, MI: G. Wahr, 1951).

42. Samuel J. Eldersveld, "Jap Influence Fades Quickly," *National Municipal Review* 34, no. 9 (1945): 445–449. The "about the author" section, p. 445, explains that Eldersveld was on the verge of defending his dissertation when he received his commission as a lieutenant. Eldersveld later recalled that Pollock's initiative caused him some temporary difficulty: naval intelligence chastised him for failing to request prior permission to publish these letters. "The Memoirs of Sam Eldersveld: His Family History and His Career in Political Science at the University of Michigan," p. 25, January 2008. In "Biographical Folder 2 of 2, Personal/Biographical Series," Box 5, Eldersveld Papers.

43. See syllabus and bibliography in folder "Political Science 216 (Proseminar in Po-

litical Behavior)," U-M Course Materials series, Box 75, Pollock Papers. Pollock also participated in the Carnegie Corporation–sponsored conference, organized by the SSRC Committee on Political Behavior in Ann Arbor in 1949. See my discussion of that conference in chapter 1.

44. The passage cited appears in the acknowledgments section, which is not paginated. A full copy of *Fulcrum* (c. 1960, reprinted 2001) appears in Folder 10 of 15, "Miscellaneous Writings, Speeches and Reports, 1955–2000," Academic Career Series, Box 5, Eldersveld Papers.

45. Eldersveld to Miller, June 23, 1959. In folder "Correspondence—January–June 1959," Box 4, Miller Papers.

46. Some effective counters to this common sense include Gunnell, *Descent*, chapters 3–5; Oren, *Our Enemies and US*, chapters 1–2; and Seidelman with the assistance of Harpham, *Disenchanted Realists*, chapters 3–4.

47. Waldo, "Political Science: Tradition, Discipline, Profession, Science, Enterprise," discusses the secession of public administration from political science at length. A draft of an obituary for Eldersveld by John Jackson, M. Kent Jennings, Lawrence Mohr, and Hanes Walton credits Eldersveld for helping to transform public administration into public policy. Undated draft of obituary for *PS, In Memoriam*, pp. 5–6, folder "Personal, 1942–2007," Personal/Biographical Series, Box 5, Eldersveld Papers.

48. Geiger, *Research and Relevant Knowledge*, 74, notes that compared to other public universities, the Universities of Michigan and Wisconsin were hit especially hard by the contraction of state budgets during the 1930s Depression.

49. The SSRC frequently served as a clearinghouse for foundation programs and a conduit for their funds. I discuss the various ways in which the SSRC played these roles in each of the chapters in part 1. See Fisher, *Fundamental Development*, for a detailed analysis of what the pre–World War II SSRC did along these lines.

50. This organization, founded at the end of the nineteenth century, still exists. It is now called the National Civic League. https://www.nationalcivicleague.org/.

51. Several accounts of the Michigan department's history make this point: Gerald Eitig Faye, "Political Science at the University of Michigan 1910–1960," not paginated, in folder "Committee/departmental materials," Political Science Department Miscellaneous 1963–1967, Box 74, Pollock Papers. Faye's essay was printed as a pamphlet distributed at the department's fiftieth-anniversary celebration. Joseph Kallenbach, "The Department of Political Science," n.d., found in folder "University of Michigan, Department of Political Science, ca. 1960s, 1980s–1990s," p. 5, Academic Career Series, Box 6, Eldersveld Papers. Internal references suggest Kallenbach's essay was written in the late 1970s or early 1980s. See also Jackson and Saxonhouse, "Not Your Great-Grandfather's Department," 10–12, a departmental history written to mark the university's bicentennial in 2017.

52. On the advent of municipal home rule in Michigan, see Arthur W. Bromage, "Constitutional Aspects of State-Local Relationships: Municipal and County Home Rule for Michigan," Constitutional Convention Research Paper No. 3 (Detroit: Citizen Research Council of Michigan, 1961). On the importance of municipal home rule to the emergence of professional public administration, see Melvin G. Holli, "Urban Reform in the Progressive Era," in *The Progressive Era*, ed. Lewis L. Gould (Syracuse, NY:

Syracuse University Press, 1974); Martin J. Schiesl, *The Politics of Efficiency: Municipal Administration and Reform in America, 1800–1920* (Berkeley: University of California Press, 1977); and Camilla Stivers, *Bureau Men, Settlement Women: Constructing Public Administration in the Progressive Era* (Lawrence: University Press of Kansas, 2000).

53. Two other long-serving department faculty members also specialized in public administration: Harold Dorr and Joseph Kallenbach. Both received their PhDs from the Michigan department during the 1930s; their dissertations focused on state politics or federal-state intergovernmental relations. See "Ph.Ds. 1910–2009," in folder "Course and Degree, Ph.D. Recipients, 1910–2009," Box 7, Department of Political Science/UM Records.

54. Harold A. Stone, Don K. Price, and Kathryn H. Stone, *City Manager Government in the United States: A Review after Twenty-Five Years* (Chicago: Public Administration Service, 1940), 25.

55. Stivers, *Bureau Men*, 18–46; Schiesl, *Politics of Efficiency*, 111–132.

56. In *Fundamental Development*, 117, 171, Fisher discusses Crane's appointment as head of the SSRC as well as criticisms of his tenure.

57. Over the course of his career, Bromage chaired twelve dissertations—compared to Pollock's fourteen, Miller's fifteen, Converse's nineteen, and Eldersveld's twenty-one. For a comprehensive record of PhDs awarded by the department during its first 100 years, see the table titled "Ph.Ds. 1910–2009," in the folder "Course and Degree, Ph.D. Recipients, 1910–2009," Department of Political Science Records, Box 7, Department of Political Science/UM Records.

58. Remarks by Richard Park, Recognition Luncheon, February 15, 1979, p. 2, in folder "Topical—Biography," Box 1, Bromage Papers. For an overview of Bromage's public service, see the biographical note included in the Bentley Historical Library's finding aid for the Bromage Papers.

59. Eldersveld, "Building Political Science at Michigan (1964–1970): A Brief Memoir," p. 6, credits Bromage with beginning to democratize department decision-making, including making criteria for promotion decisions more transparent. In Folder 3 of 15, "Miscellaneous Writings, Speeches and Reports, 1955–2000," Academic Career Series, Box 5, Eldersveld Papers. Jackson and Saxonhouse, "Not Your Great-Grandfather's Department," 19, recount Bromage quietly persuading some of his colleagues to approve the appointment of M. Kent Jennings.

60. "Diary of a Chairman" and "Agreed: One Man, One Vote" are parts of this mock Festschrift, dated May 7, 1964, and found in the folder "Topical—Biography," Box 1, Bromage Papers. The authors of each of the pieces I cite below are pseudonymous.

61. "Quantifex Maximus" on p. 8; "scientific method," p. 9, in "Diary of a Chairman." Eldersveld had been offered and had accepted the position of chair by this time. It's clear, then, that it is Eldersveld who's been dubbed the "Quantifex Maximus." Emphasis in original.

62. "Agreed: One Man, One Vote" is subtitled, "Excerpts from the Minutes of a Department Meeting held on April 2, 1964." It appears on pp. 26–28 of the mock Festschrift. "Thirst for power" on p. 26, the retort by the person from IPPS on p. 27, and the proposed voting systems on pp. 27–28. The "brain's" proposal is a system of multiple voting granting extra votes for a grab-bag of "accomplishments." These include displays of wealth ("the purchase of a Saks Fifth Avenue suit," "Christmas gifts to fellow colleagues

... of pearl handled bone marrow picks"), extraordinary devotion to university and department ("membership in the Harlan Hatcher for President club"; "perfect attendance at Political Science Roundtables"), and highly specific intellectual pursuits ("a sabbatical leave studying Bantu dynamics in Tanganyika," "an article published in Izvestia"), as well as getting "a job offer at a higher salary" and "offering to at least 50 women, a Tiparillo cigar," p. 28.

63. The titles of two of the speeches, given by Lord Bridges (a high-ranking British civil servant) and John A. Perkins (president of the University of Delaware and a Michigan PhD), were "The University and the Public Service" and "Political Science Instruction as Training for Participation in Public Affairs and the Public Service." In "The Status and Prospects of Political Science as a Discipline," Papers Presented at the Fiftieth Anniversary Celebration of the Department of Political Science at the University of Michigan, April 8–9, 1960 (booklet). Folder: "Department of Political Science 1960–61," Box 129, College of Literature, Science and the Arts, University of Michigan Records, 1846–2014.

64. Pollock's speech, "Political Science at Michigan: Past, Present and Future," appears in the same booklet cited in the previous note. "Any tendency" appears on pp. 45–46; the numbers of Michigan graduates who went on to State Department or CIA careers on 46; "steady growth of graduate work" on p. 48.

65. Roy Reynolds, "Pollock's Notable Career Has Noticeable Windup," July 7, 1968, *Ann Arbor News*, Folder 1, "Pollock," Box 104, News and Information Services, University of Michigan Faculty and Staff Files 1944–2005, 1960–1995. For a fuller discussion of Pollock's biography, see the biographical note by Dennis Anderson, included in the Bentley Historical Library's finding aid to Pollock's Papers.

66. A University of Michigan News Service release, May 11, 1948, announced Pollock's six- to seven-week leave to travel to Germany to advise Gen. Lucius Clay. This release also mentions Pollock's previous leaves for the same purpose, including a ten-month leave from late 1945 to mid-1946 and a two-month leave in early 1947. Folder 1, "Pollock," Box 104, News and Information Services, University of Michigan Faculty and Staff Files 1944–2005, 1960–1995. The first Hoover Commission was charged with reorganizing the executive branch of the federal government.

67. James K. Pollock, "The Primacy of Politics," 1950 APSA Presidential Address, *American Political Science Review* 45, no. 1 (1951): 6, 13–14, 16; "new type of public servant" appears on p. 6. A note on what appear to be discrepant dates: Pollock gave his APSA presidential address at the end of December 1950. The text of the speech appeared in the *APSR* the following year.

68. Pollock, "Primacy of Politics"; "greatest boon" on p. 16; "integrating and synthesizing" on p. 15.

69. "Political Science in the Nuclear Age," IPSA Presidential address, September 16, 1958, in "Pollock—Folder 2," Box 104, News and Information Services, University of Michigan Faculty and Staff Files 1944–2005, 1960–1995. "Darlings of governments" on pp. 4–5; "overweening development" on p. 7; "self-sufficient abstractions" on p. 4. At the celebration of the department's fiftieth anniversary, Pollock remarked, "This policy [of not offering fellowships in political science] of the [National Science] Foundation is particularly galling to me for I worked so hard for the creation of the Foundation when I was a member of the First Hoover Commission." Pollock, "Political Science at

Michigan: Past, Present and Future," p. 45, in folder "Department of Political Science, 1960–61," Box 129, College of Literature, Science and the Arts, University of Michigan Records, 1846–2014.

70. Pollock took a retirement furlough for the 1967–1968 academic year. He stopped teaching and taking part in department meetings after the spring of 1967—a full year before his official retirement.

71. The stanza describing the view from Haven Hall reads: "Many a day I gazed out westward, across State Street/and all the hub,/ Saw a splendid edifice rising . . . it was not/ the Faculty Club," p. 2. The new ISR building, completed in 1965, was built several blocks west of Haven Hall across State Street. "Pulsing hoard of data," "clattering computers," and divine protection for Haven Hall on pp. 5–6. "James K. Pollock Reading 'Locksley Hall' And Reflecting Upon His Career As He Reads," As Written by Tennyson/Bretton, April 1, 1967, Folder 29–16, Box 29, Correspondence Series, James Kerr Pollock Papers.

72. The longer passages in which the cited words and phrases appear read: "Blessed is he that surveyeth and computeth, for unto him shall be granted." "And manna from Carnegie will flow unto him." "Consider the jet prof., how he goes. . . . Yea, he sippeth and suppeth in the heavens above the earth, and thinketh lofty thoughts." "And in the fullness of time, the voice of the University spake unto James K. Pollock, saying . . . To University, state, and nation has thou given advice and consultation. And scholarship profound has made thy name renowned. Praise and honor is thy due." "A Dead C+ Scroll," pp. 2–3, Folder 29–16, Box 29, Correspondence Series, James Kerr Pollock Papers.

73. "Romney Praises Pollock," *Lansing State Journal*, October 7, 1968. "Pollock— Folder 1," Box 104, News and Information Services, University of Michigan Faculty and Staff Files 1944–2005, 1960–1995.

74. "Prof. Pollock to Quit Department Chairmanship, Resume Teaching Career," March 3, 1961; "Pollock Discusses Resignation Reasons," by John Roberts, March 3, 1961. These articles were clipped for this folder in a way that removed the names of the newspapers in which they appeared. Both clippings may be found in "Pollock—Folder 1," Box 104, News and Information Services, University of Michigan Faculty and Staff Files 1944–2005, 1960–1995.

75. Miller to Department of Political Science, n.d., p. 3. Attached to ISR Policy & Plans Committee Agenda, February 22, 1971, in folder "Topical: Population Foundation, 1970–72," Box 3, A. F. K. Organski Papers, BHL.

76. Eldersveld to Heyns, January 23, 1961, pp. 6–7. In folder "University of Michigan, Department of Political Science, ca. 1960s, 1980s–1990s," Academic Career Series, Box 6, Eldersveld Papers.

77. J. David Singer to Theodore Newcomb (Psychology, U of M), August 26, 1963. In folder "University of Michigan, Department of Political Science, ca. 1960s, 1980s–1990s," Academic Career Series, Box 6, Eldersveld Papers. For a synopsis of Singer's affiliation with the political science department, see Jackson and Saxonhouse, "Not Your Great-Grandfather's Department," 41. For a broader overview of Singer's career at Michigan and his role in developing the Correlates of War database, see the biography in the online finding aid to Singer's papers at the Bentley Historical Library. Finding aids at https://bentley.umich.edu/research/catalogs-databases/finding-aids/.

78. An enduringly relevant critical assessment of labelling intellectual endeavors

"pure" is Daniel S. Greenberg, *The Politics of Pure Science: An Inquiry into the Relationship between Science & Government in the United States.* New York: New American Library, 1971.

79. Miller to Department of Political Science, n.d.; "social utility," p. 1; "more democratic society," p. 3. Attached to ISR Policy & Plans Committee Agenda, February 22, 1971, in folder "Topical: Population Foundation, 1970–72," Box 3, Organski Papers.

80. Miller to Department of Political Science, "Mission-related research," p. 1; all other cited passages, p. 3.

81. For instance, Organski received support from DARPA (Defense Advanced Research Projects Agency) and the ONR (the Office of Naval Research). See folders "ARPA/ DARPA Correspondence, 1976–1978" and "AFK Organski—Topical—List of Grants of 1990." Both in Box 3, Organski Papers.

82. Albert Sussman, Interim VP for Graduate Studies and Research, to UM Executive Officers; Subject: "A strategy by the D.O.D. to make new connections with certain universities," [marked "Confidential"], February 13, 1985, in folder "Topical: Defense— Collaboration between University of Michigan and Department of Defense (2 of 2), 1985." The Decision Insights material appears in the one unlabeled folder in the box. Bueno de Mesquita is cc'd on a June 15, 1992, letter Organski wrote on Decision Insights letterhead. He, along with Organski, was also on the board of Policon, a similar firm active in the 1980s. Both folders in Box 3, Organski Papers.

83. I discuss the financial importance but also the constraints of contract research at the early SRC in Hauptmann, "Why They Shared," 105–106.

84. For discussions of the SRC's sources of income as well as early electoral data acquisitions and funding for ICPR, see Hauptmann, "Why They Shared," 104–106, 112–115. ANES is overseen by a board of social scientists from institutions across the country and has received support from the NSF since 1977. See https://electionstudies.org/about-us /history/.

85. For the $7.45 million award, see ICPSR, *Annual Report*, 2009–2010, 11. For the announcement of the new Census data repository, see the *Annual Report*, 2017–2018, 12. "Long-standing partnership" appears in the ICPSR press release hyperlinked on p. 12. Annual reports up through 2017–2018 are accessible as pdfs under the "History" tab at https://www.icpsr.umich.edu/web/pages/.

86. Miller to Dean Frank Rhodes, March 18, 1974, p. 1, in folder "UM Administrative Files—Dept. of Political Science, Subfield Structure," Box 2, Miller Papers.

CHAPTER 5. POLITICAL SCIENCE AT BERKELEY

1. The Institute for Governmental Studies (IGS) was probably the most significant research center not geared toward international or area studies. Founded in the early twentieth century, it still exists today. For the history of the IGS, see the account available at the University of California History Digital Archive (https://www.lib.berkeley .edu/uchistory/index.html).

2. This history appears on the University of California History Digital Archive (https:// www.lib.berkeley.edu/uchistory/general_history/campuses/ucb/departments_a.html).

Up through the summer of 2020, this history also appeared on the department's website. It has since been removed.

3. For Moses's role on this commission, see "Addresses Delivered at the Memorial Service for Bernard Moses," April 13, 1930, available at the Online Archive of California (http://www.oac.cdlib.org/). Kristin L. Hoganson, *American Empire at the Turn of the Twentieth Century: A Brief History with Documents*, (Boston: Bedford/St. Martin's, 2017), 17–23, provides a concise, comprehensive summary of the US intervention in the Philippines. Hoganson also reprints an excerpt of Moses's wife, Edith's *Unofficial Letters of an Official's Wife*, about their time in the Philippines, pp. 121–123.

4. Moses's relevant works include *Spanish Dependencies in South America: An Introduction to the History of Their Civilization*, 2 vols. (New York: Harper, 1914), and *Spain's Declining Power in South America, 1730–1806* (Berkeley: University of California Press, 1919). See Robert Vitalis, *White World Order, Black Power Politics: The Birth of American International Relations* (Ithaca, NY: Cornell University Press, 2015), 43, for a discussion of Moses's connection to early twentieth-century international relations.

5. Moses taught history of political theory as a member of the department of history and political science and continued to do so once he became chair of the new political science department. For listings of his courses, see the *Register of the University of California*, 1889–1900, 33; 1903–1904, 149 (hereafter abbreviated as *Cal Register*). This annual catalog listed department faculty and courses offered at all UC campuses and was discontinued in the fall of 1959. At Berkeley, the *U.C. Berkeley General Catalogue* replaced it. Digitized copies of both are accessible in the UC Berkeley Library Digital Collections.

6. Barrows recalled the historicist sweep of Moses's views at a university memorial: "Moses taught us that . . . the Revolutionary movement, in which we still lived, began in North America, crossed back to Europe, and in France was given the expression which communicated itself to the Continent. . . . He further pointed out that the [French] Revolution, having shaken Europe, came back across the Atlantic to the Caribbean and South America, and produced the downfall of the Spanish American Empire." David P. Barrows, "Teacher and Public Servant" and "American 'imperialist,'" both on p. 19, the Online Archive of California, https://oac.cdlib.org.

7. For Barrows's educational history, including his PhD research in anthropology, see Kenton J. Clymer, "Humanitarian Imperialist: David Prescott Barrows and the White Man's Burden in the Philippines," *Pacific Historical Review* 45, no. 4 (1976): 495–517; as well as his obituary in *In Memoriam*, April 1958, 6. Elisabeth M. Eittreim, *Teaching Empire: Native Americans, Filipinos, and US Imperial Education, 1879–1918* (Lawrence: University Press of Kansas, 2019), 134–136, discusses the imperial, racialized assumptions central to Barrows's educational projects in the Philippines. These included Barrows's *A History of the Philippines* (Yonkers-on-Hudson, NY: World Book Co., 1914), written for use in Filipino schools. Hoganson, *American Empire*, 133–135, presents an excerpt from Barrows's 1901 instructions for investigators working under his direction as the head of the Bureau of Non-Christian Tribes in the Philippines. They include detailed instructions for how to measure people's heads, noses, and so on, as well as how to describe their hair, teeth, etc.

8. For Moses's "Government of Dependencies" course, see *Cal Register*, 1903–1904, 150; for Barrows's teaching that course and others as well as his teaching at the graduate

level, see *Cal Register*, 1913–1914, 217–218, 219. According to the *U.C. Berkeley General Catalogue*, 1961–1962, 499, "Dependent Peoples and Trusteeships" was still being taught nearly fifty years later. See Department Chair Peter Odegard, "Report of the Chairman, Department of Political Science to the President for the Academic Years 1948–49, 1949–50, 1950–51," n.d., 8, on replacing Barrows with another specialist in "Dependent Areas." In Department of Political Science Records.

9. For the initial petition, public comments, and the committee's recommendation, see https://chancellor.berkeley.edu/task-forces/building-name-review-committee/build ing-name-review-barrows-hall. My thanks to Robert Adcock for bringing the initial petition to my attention.

10. Raymond Gettell, *The History of Political Thought* (New York: Century, 1924). "Influence political development" on p. 5; chapter 27, 423–442. The chapters on Greek, Roman, and Medieval political thought include subsections devoted to the theory of international relations of each period.

11. Gettell, *History of Political Thought*, criticism of Dunning, including "theory of international relations," on p. v; Gettell, "The Nature of Political Thought," *American Political Science Review* 17, no. 2 (1923): 205, for "geographic and ethnic unity."

12. Barrows et al., *In Memoriam*, pp. 8–9. Digitized copies of *In Memoriam*, obituaries for UC faculty, are available at the UC History Digital Archive, fully cited in note 1 above.

13. Van Horn and Bellquist, paragraphs 1–3 (not paginated), emphasis added; for full reference, see note 2. Internal references suggest that this undated document was probably written in 1965 or 1966.

14. For Barrows's involvement in promoting this exposition, see "Faculty Committee for promotion of PPIE. Letters from faculty to colleagues, mailing lists, etc.," Carton 15 in the personal papers of David P. Barrows. Finding aid at https://oac.cdlib.org/findaid /ark:/13030/tf2f59n67s/entire_text/. A pamphlet published for this exhibit, *The Philippine Public Schools at the Panama-Pacific International Exposition* (San Francisco: Marnell and Co., 1915), highlights the Philippines' many natural resources (timber, hemp, and other materials for cloth-making) and handicrafts available to the world market. One portion of the "facts and figures" section focuses on the "races" of the islands; there, the "Negritos" or "dwarf negroes" are described as "among the lowest of mankind" on "the social scale," p. 55. The chart on p. 59 breaks down what Filipinos educated at different levels "are good for."

15. The site of this exposition is now a national park. For an overview of the many exhibits it included, see https://www.nps.gov/goga/learn/historyculture/ppie-palaces.htm. This page describes some of the exhibits in the Palace of Education, including the two I mentioned.

16. "Cultural imperialism" from the title of the critical collection of essays edited by Arnove, *Philanthropy and Cultural Imperialism*. Vitalis, *White World Order*, 133–142, draws a compelling connection between early twentieth-century social scientists' study of colonial dependencies and the mid-twentieth-century advent of "area studies."

17. See *Cal Register* for 1903–1904, 1913–1914, 1922–1923, 1932–33, 1943–1944 for numbers of department faculty from its founding up through the mid-1940s. See *Cal Register*, 1950–1951, 430–431, for a list of department faculty by rank.

18. Verne A. Stadtman, *The University of California, 1868–1968: A Centennial Publication of the University of California* (New York: McGraw-Hill, 1970), 349–350, for expansion of UC system and the "second wave" of new students; 359, for doubling of faculty system-wide. John Aubrey Douglass, *The California Idea and American Higher Education: 1850 to the 1960 Master Plan* (Stanford, CA: Stanford University Press, 2000), 11, provides an overview of the dramatic rise in the overall population of California.

19. Douglass, *California Idea*, "gold rush" on p. 170; research institutions according to Master Plan on pp. 14–15.

20. "Peter Odegard," *In Memoriam*, May 1968, 88. Celebrating Odegard's contributions to the department, his colleagues Leslie Lipson, Robert Scalapino, and Paul Seabury wrote: "In the course of a few years, with tremendous dynamism, he doubled the faculty, expanded and revolutionized the curriculum, secured a generous endowment of research funds, attracted many outstanding students, and brought the Department to a level where it has since been rated among the top three of the country. His greatness as a Chairman was due to his dedication to high quality and to the tolerance of diversity," 89.

21. Stadtman, *University of California*, 379, and Geiger, *Research and Relevant Knowledge*, 79–82, both discuss some of Kerr's 1950s initiatives as Berkeley's first chancellor.

22. Odegard, "Report to President," n.d., 18–19, Political Science Department Records. For a full citation for this report, see note 8. For course offerings in the 1950–1951 academic year, see *Cal Register*, vol. 1, 430–434.

23. See Eugene Burdick, "Syndicalism and Industrial Unionism in England until 1918," PhD diss., (Oxford University, 1950); as well as Burdick and Arthur J. Brodbeck, eds., *American Voting Behavior* (Glencoe, IL: Free Press, 1959). For the course description of "Problems in the Analysis of Political Behavior," see *UC Berkeley Course Catalogue*, 1961–1962, 495. For "Politics and Literature," see *UC Berkeley Course Catalogue*, 1963–1964, 511.

24. President Gordon S. Sproul announced Ford's gift at the end of 1950. See Sproul to Berkeley faculty in the social sciences, December 21, 1950, Folder 9, Box 54, Office of the Chancellor Records, University of California Archives, Bancroft Library. Hereafter, I abbreviate these records OCR and the archives, UCA. Unless otherwise noted, all UC archival sources are housed at Berkeley's Bancroft Library.

25. The Ford Foundation made a number of large grants in this area before it formally began its Behavioral Sciences Program. When the Foundation's Study Committee published its initial plans for its new national program in 1950, "individual behavior and human relations" was to be one of its five program areas. See Ford Foundation, *Report of the Study for the Ford Foundation on Policy and Program: November 1949* (Detroit, MI: Ford Foundation, 1950), as well as my discussion in chapter 2 of the other universities and academic institutions that also received such grants.

26. Kerr to President Sproul, April 11, 1951, Folder 9, Box 54, OCR, UCA.

27. Burdick to Chancellor Kerr, January 11, 1953, Folder 26, Box 54, OCR, UCA.

28. Burdick to Chancellor Kerr, January 19, 1954; Burdick to Ralph Tyler, CASBS, November 30, 1955. Both in Folder 11, Box 54, OCR, UCA.

29. For Jacobson's early 1950s courses, see *Cal Register*, 1950–1951, vol. 1, 436–437. Miller taught at Berkeley from 1954 to 1956. For Jacobson's support for Warren Miller specifically and survey research more generally, see Jacobson to Kenneth W. Thompson,

Rockefeller Foundation, September 27, 1957, Folder 4993, Box 583, series 200S, R.G. 1.2, Rockefeller Foundation Archives (RFA), Rockefeller Archive Center (RAC).

30. My thanks to Herb Weisberg for directing me to Miller's comment about his time in Berkeley at 34:30 in the full recording of Miller's 1988 APSA oral history interview. In this case as well as many others, the taped interview is much longer than the versions published in Baer, Jewell, and Sigelman, *Political Science in America*. Full recordings of APSA oral history interviews are available online through the University of Kentucky Library's Louie B. Nunn Center for Oral History. Wolin, conversation with the author, August 4, 2005.

31. See Herbert McClosky and John H. Schaar, "Psychological Dimensions of Anomy," *American Sociological Review* 30, no. 1 (1965):14–40; and Michael Paul Rogin, *The Intellectuals and McCarthy: The Radical Specter* (Cambridge, MA.: MIT Press, 1967). For Schaar's course offerings, see *U.C. Berkeley General Catalogue*, 1961–1962, 495; for Rogin's, *U.C. Berkeley General Catalogue*, 1966–1967, 410.

32. In lieu of a detailed tally of Ford's support for international and area studies centers at Berkeley, a few benchmark figures are suggestive. According to the Ford Foundation 1960 *Annual Report*, 68, the foundation made a $4 million grant to area and international studies centers at Berkeley and UCLA. According to the 1965 *Annual Report*, 34, 132, Ford granted $5 million to Berkeley alone for international studies.

33. Berman, *The Influence of the Carnegie, Ford, and Rockefeller Foundations on American Foreign Policy*, 101–104; "intermediaries" on p. 101.

34. For Parmar's discussion of Ford's financial support for professional associations, see *Foundations of the American Century*, 127–130. Parmar's chapter on Ford's support for Asian studies includes a substantial section on the program Ford sponsored to connect Berkeley's economics department with the University of Indonesia's Faculty of Economics. The goals of this program, Parmar argues, were to support "a pro-American counterhegemony within the Indonesian educational system . . . networked with several political parties, student organizations, Islamic groups, the national police, and the army," 142. Parmar specifically mentions Guy Pauker, a member of Berkeley's political science department and RAND affiliate, as one of the US academics involved in this network, on p. 144.

35. Donald K. Price, quoted in Berman, *The Influence*, 100.

36. McCaughey, *International Studies and Academic Enterprise*, 141–166, offers an extended analysis of this shift in Ford's program priorities.

37. Rockefeller made two such grants of $200,000 each; one in 1956 and another in 1961. Equal portions of the funds were disbursed each year over the five-year lives of these grants. For complete references to each of these grants, see chapter 3.

38. Norman Jacobson wrote to Kenneth Thompson, "Peter [Odegard], thus far, has played it in the usual way: intimations that everyone in the Dept. will be eligible to participate, etc." Jacobson to Thompson, May 31, 1956, p. 1, Folder 4855, Box 567. Unless otherwise noted, all Rockefeller documents cited in this and the following sections may be found in series 200S, R.G. 1.2, RFA, RAC.

39. Leslie Lipson, Chair; Eugene Burdick, Ernst Haas, Sheldon Wolin, "Proposed Instructions from the Chancellor to the Committee that will Disburse the Rockefeller Grant," n.d., pp. 1–2, Folder 4855, Box 567. A university press release announcing the grant also presented its aims broadly. Noting that the grant was made to "an entire de-

partment" rather than "separate individuals," the press release itemized the topics grant recipients might study this way: "international organization and state or regional groupings; the diplomatic, military, economic or cultural aspects of relations between nations; and the comparative politics of nations." Draft press release, University of California, November 9, 1956, Folder 4855, Box 567.

40. See the *U.C. Berkeley General Catalogue*, 1959–1960, 330–331, for a list of department faculty. Numbers of individual grants disbursed compiled by the author from progress reports to Rockefeller for 1957, 1958, 1959, 1960.

41. For Haas, see "Report on the Rockefeller Grant to Political Science," February 20, 1958, p. 6; for Park, see "Report on the Rockefeller Grant to Political Science," attached to Charles Aikin to Flora Rhind, Rockefeller Foundation, June 5, 1957, p. 5. Both in Folder 4856, Box 567.

42. For Burdick, see "Supplement to the Progress Report of February 20, 1958," p. 2; for Jacobson, p. 4 of "Report" attached to June 5 , 1957; for Waldo, p. 9 of "Report," February 20, 1958. Full citations for the two latter reports in the preceding note.

43. "Proposed Instructions," 2–3. Full citation in note 39 above.

44. Charles Aikin to Kenneth Thompson, pp. 1, 5, 8, March 1, 1961, Folder 4857, Box 567.

45. Thompson, interview notes re. renewal of grant in political theory with Scalapino, January 24 and March 9 , 1961, Folder 4857, Box 567. For an overview of the University Development Program, see Rockefeller's 1961 *Annual Report*, 19–20. Rajaee, *Kenneth W. Thompson, the Prophet of Norms*, 69–71, 101–115, discusses Thompson's deep commitment to this program.

46. See Kenneth W. Thompson, "Toward a Theory of International Politics," *American Political Science Review* 49, no. 3 (1955): 733–746, as well as my own discussion in Hauptmann, "The Theorists' Gambit," 625–638.

47. Gerald Freund, the Rockefeller officer responsible for overseeing this second grant, summarized such reservations in his interview notes with members of the department. May 11, 1961, p. 3, Folder 4857, Box 567.

48. Thompson interview notes with Scalapino, April 28, 1961. See also pp. 2–3 of the formal application to Rockefeller from Chairman Aikin, October 17, 1961. Scalapino also appealed to Rockefeller to allow him to use grant funds to induce senior faculty who were getting offers from other universities to stay at Berkeley. Freund interview with Scalapino, April 5, 1962, pp. 3–4. All in Folder 4857, Box 567.

49. See the formal application to Rockefeller from Chairman Aikin, p. 3, cited in the previous note.

50. Scalapino to Freund, February 5, 1963, p. 6, Folder 4858, Box 567. This seminar also seems to have been an important recruiting tool for the still rapidly growing department. Scalapino reported that as department chair, he pitched the "research and overseas training opportunities" the grant provided to prospective new hires.

51. Thompson interview notes with Scalapino, April 28, 1961, p. 1; Gerald Freund interview notes, May 11, 1961, p. 1. Both in Folder 4857, Box 567.

52. October 1961 grant proposal in Folder 4857; Scalapino to Freund, February 5, 1963, in Folder 4858, Box 567.

53. Scalapino to Freund, February 17, 1964, pp. 10–11, Folder 4859, Box 568.

54. LeRoy Graymer, Department Administrator to Freund, March 11, 1966, pp. 5–6, Folder 4860, Box 568.

55. Berman, *The Influence*, 4.

56. For example, Parmar, *Foundations of the American Century*, 135–148, argues that the network linking the economics department at Berkeley and the University of Indonesia was deeply implicated in the military coup against Sukarno and the brutal waves of anticommunist violence that followed. Berman, *The Influence*, 61, comments on the CIA practice of debriefing foundation-funded scholars.

57. Report by Ralph Retzlaff, attached to Graymer to Freund, November 3, 1966, Folder 4860, Box 568.

58. In the progress report sent to Rockefeller in February 1964, Scalapino reported that public administration scholar Eugene Lee had used his position at the University of Dar Es Salaam to advise local officials on running prisons, drafting constitutions, and budgeting. At the University of Singapore, Frances Starner completed a study of the Singaporean electoral system. Scalapino to Freund, February 17, 1964, pp. 2–3, 4–5, Folder 4859, Box 568. See also Lee's report, attached to Graymer to Freund, Folder 4860, Box 568.

59. Rosberg, Moore, and Schmitter's reports attached to Graymer to Freund, November 3, 1966, Folder 4860, Box 568.

60. The passages cited here appear on the pages cited in the following reports: Rosberg, p. 2; Moore, pp. 1–2; Schmitter, pp. 2–3, all attached to Graymer to Freund, November 3, 1966, Folder 4860, Box 568. See Rohde, *Armed with Expertise*, 63–75, for a thorough overview of Project Camelot's ambitions and very public fall.

61. Scalapino to Freund, September 26, 1963, Folder 4858, Box 567.

62. Scalapino to Thompson, July 10, 1963, Folder 4858, Box 567.

63. I discuss Kerr's use of the term "multiversity" as well as the criticisms of it below.

64. Of the forty-nine department members and visiting faculty listed as participants in these three seminars, only four are listed in more than one. Scalapino to Freund, February 17, 1964, pp. 9–10, Folder 4859, Box 568.

65. Wolin quoted in Scalapino to Freund, February 17, 1964, p. 10, Folder 4859, Box 568.

66. The school still exists, though it is now called the Graduate School of Public Policy.

67. "Proposal for a new program in Public Administration leading to the degree of Master of Public Administration," Political Science Faculty, May 9, 1960, and Professors of Political Science to Vice Chancellor Connick, November 2, 1966. Both in Folder 12, "Departments of Instruction: Political Science: Berkeley," Box 85, Office of the President Records, UCA.

68. See Academic Senate Committee on Educational Policy Report, February 22, 1967, and Graduate Council to Vice Chancellor Connick, April 21, 1967. Both in Folder 12, "Departments of Instruction: Political Science: Berkeley," Box 85, Office of the President Records, UCA.

69. References to these events occur in an interview with Brian Murphy, Graduate Student in Political Science, April 1970, Folder 29, Box 1, *Journal of Educational Change* Records, UCA; Wolin, August 4, 2005, personal communication; and Aaron Wildavsky, "On Being a Department Chair," *PS: Political Science & Politics* 25, no. 1 (1992): 83–89.

Wildavsky commented: "What proved to be impossible, at least for me, was keeping departmental conflicts wholly apart from campus-wide disputes. . . . The cost was the departure of two distinguished political theorists [Schaar and Wolin], a great loss, which I counted then and count now as a failure," 88. I thank Jim Wiley for directing me to this article. For Wildavsky's tenure as dean of GSPA, see his obituary in *In Memoriam*, UC History Digital Archive.

70. Scott, August 19, 2005, and July 5, 2006, personal communications; Citrin, July 28, 2005, personal communication. The name for the proposed department varies from source to source. Sometimes it is called "political and social theory"; other times, simply "political theory" or "social theory."

71. Some of the closest contenders might be the University of Chicago's Committee on Social Thought, UC Santa Cruz's History of Consciousness program, and Princeton's interdisciplinary program in political philosophy.

72. The Conference for the Study of Political Thought (CSPT) was founded in 1967, the same year that the proposal to form a department of political theory was made. See my discussion of this organization in this book's conclusion.

73. My thanks to Robert Adcock for sending me a copy of this "Proposal for a Department of Political Theory" (hereafter cited as "Proposal") that he found in Reinhard Bendix's papers, Folder 129, Box 10, Reinhard Bendix Papers, German Intellectual Émigré Collection, M. E. Grenander Department of Special Collections and Archives, University at Albany, New York. The proposal is divided into three parts. The first eight pages make the case for why political theory and political science should be academically separate units, followed by overviews of the proposed undergraduate and graduate programs. Retrospective references to this proposal appear in the 1968 SLATE Supplement to the General Catalogue, p. 43; in a 1968 pamphlet, "Political Science at Berkeley: An Invitation to a Discussion" (personal papers of Jeff Lustig; hereafter cited as "Invitation"); in an April 1970 interview with Brian Murphy, graduate student in political science; and in "Dear Prospective Student," an undated letter from the Graduate Association of Students of Politics (GASP). The first item appears in the SLATE Supplements stored in the UC Archives; the latter two items appear in Folder 29, Box 1, JEC, UCA. See also the brief discussion in Hal Sarf, *Masters and Disciples* (Berkeley, CA: Center for Humanities and Contemporary Culture and Regent Press, 2002), 157–160.

74. "Poisonous" from Wolin, conversation with the author, August 4, 2005. Sheldon Wolin and John H. Schaar, *The Berkeley Rebellion and Beyond: Essays on Politics and Education in the Technological* Society (New York: Random House, 1970), includes five essays that originally appeared in the *New York Review of Books* from 1964 through 1970. Some members of the theory faculty recalled that they did not fully support the effort to form this new department. For instance, Norman Jacobson, APSA Oral History, recalls thinking the proposed department a bad idea—others, including Wolin, APSA Oral History, confirm that Jacobson did not support the effort at the time. Hanna Pitkin, a recent Berkeley PhD, became an assistant professor at Berkeley the year before the attempted secession. When asked about her recollections of the proposal, Pitkin said she supported it mainly because she did not want Schaar and Wolin to leave Berkeley, rather than because she thought it a good idea; Hanna Pitkin, letter to the author, August 2002. Jeff Lustig and Gene Poschman, who had been graduate students in political theory in the

1960s, also recalled being skeptical about the proposal or not thinking it a serious effort. Jeff Lustig, conversation with the author, June 30, 2005; Gene Poschman, conversation with the author, July 14, 2005.

75. Wolin, conversation with the author, August 4, 2005; Scott, conversation with the author, August 19, 2005. Though Scott taught first in the speech department and then in the English department at Berkeley, he had a PhD in political theory from McGill and had been a Canadian diplomat. He was politically active throughout his time at Berkeley and has long written extensively about political matters. See especially Peter Dale Scott, *Coming to Jakarta: A Poem about Terror* (New York: New Directions, 1989), 55–59, on the involvement of Berkeley's political science department in the overthrow of Sukarno.

76. According to Joe Paff, a graduate student of Wolin's and a faculty member at Stanford in the late 1960s, Wolin and Schaar were in negotiations with people at Stanford to set up a program or department of political theory there toward the end of the 1960s. Conversation with the author, July 22, 2005. Wolin confirmed this in a conversation with the author, August 4, 2005. Wolin discusses his move to Princeton in "APSA Oral History."

77. In the 1960s, the "multiversity" was most closely associated with policies of UC chancellor Clark Kerr. The first of Kerr's early 1960s Godkin Lectures was titled, "The Idea of a Multiversity." The lecture appears as the first chapter in Clark Kerr, *The Uses of the University*, 3rd ed. (Cambridge, MA: Harvard University Press, 1982). In *Uses*, 135–142, Kerr notes how the "multiversity" was taken up more by critics than supporters. I rely on David Lance Goines, *The Free Speech Movement: Coming of Age in the 1960s* (Berkeley, CA: Ten Speed Press, 1993), an exceptionally thorough retrospective account by a student participant; and on Seymour Martin Lipset and Sheldon Wolin, eds., *The Berkeley Student Revolt: Facts and Interpretation*, (Garden City, NY: Doubleday, 1965), an edited collection of documents and analyses assembled when both were on the Berkeley faculty.

78. Unsigned Free Speech Movement leaflet, reprinted in Lipset and Wolin, *Berkeley Student Revolt*, 211, 213–215. One of the iconic images distributed by FSM at rallies was an IBM punch card, often "accompanied by signs saying, 'I am a student at the University of California. Please do not fold, spindle or mutilate me." Goines, *Free Speech Movement*, 395.

79. Mario Savio, December 2, 1964, speech, quoted in Goines, *Free Speech Movement*, 361. Around the same time, Savio wrote, "The 'futures' and 'careers' for which American students now prepare are for the most part intellectual and moral wastelands. This chrome-plated consumers' paradise would have us grow up to be well-behaved children. But an important minority of men and women coming to the front today have shown that they will die rather than be standardized, replaceable and irrelevant." Cited in Lipset and Wolin, *Berkeley Student Revolt*, 219.

80. Wolin and Schaar, *Berkeley Rebellion*, 31.

81. The Experimental College admitted its first class of 150 undergraduates in 1965; it remained open through 1969. Students who took part in the college remembered being discouraged from discussing the Free Speech Movement in their classes and were warned not to miss class to take part in on-campus protests. See Katherine Bernhardi

Trow, *Habits of Mind: The Experimental College Program at Berkeley* (Berkeley, CA: Institute of Governmental Studies Press, 1998), 48, 68, 331, 348.

82. Trow, 2, 9; see also Joseph Tussman, *Experiment at Berkeley* (New York: Oxford University Press, 1969).

83. For Jacobson's association with the Experimental College, see Trow, *Habits of Mind*, 83–129, 427 (appendix A). For commitments similar to some of Tussman's, see Wolin and Schaar, "The University Revolution," 43–72, in *Berkeley Rebellion*; and Wolin, "Political Theory as a Vocation."

84. Letter to department chairs, April 26, 1965; Correspondence folder, Box 1, Select Committee on Education Records (the Muscatine Report), 1965–1966. The Board of Educational Development (BED) was the mechanism created by this committee. For the courses mentioned as well as Scott's proposal, see Department and Individual Proposals—U.C. Berkeley, Box 1, Select Committee on Education Records. For the two BED courses taught in political science, including Jacobson's, see Folders 4 and 5, Box 2, Board of Educational Development (BED) Records.

85. Elizabeth Schorske, [Evaluation of] Political Science, November 1966. The cited passages appear on pp. 1 and 3, Folder 65, Box 3, BED Records. See also "Invitation," 15.

86. "The Culture of the University: Governance and Education," Report of the Study Commission on University Governance, University of California, Berkeley, January 15, 1968, 10. "Radical redirection" is part of the title of chapter 2 of the report—"The Need for Radical Redirection." From the personal papers of Jeff Lustig. The majority report of the Study Commission was published in San Francisco by Jossey-Bass in 1968. My in-text page references are to the former.

87. The Study Commission Report makes this case repeatedly, including on pp. 5, 14, 16, and 21.

88. "Proposal," 1. For a full citation for this unpublished proposal, see note 73.

89. The proposal is divided into three parts. The first eight pages make the case for why political theory and political science should be academically separate units. These are followed by two- and four-page overviews of the proposed undergraduate and graduate programs in a department of political theory. I preface text citations from these with "U" and "G." For discussion of small class sizes, see "Proposal," U1 and G1.

90. Most notably, the requirement that third-year graduate students give "two public lectures" in the course of the academic year—lectures that "faculty will consider it a duty to attend." "Proposal," G 3–4.

91. The 1968 pamphlet "An Invitation to a Discussion," discussed in the next section, voiced similar concerns. The political science graduate students and faculty who wrote it lament the lack of intellectual community in the department: "Students have little chance to learn from most professors. . . . Rarely can they share their common concerns or participate in a common enterprise with their teachers," p. 14. Instead, "graduate education even beyond the master's level is founded upon a basic mistrust," p. 16.

92. For an excellent discussion of this movement, see John A. Bilorusky, "Reconstitution at Berkeley: The Quest for Self-Determination," PhD diss. (University of California, Berkeley, 1972).

93. Wolin, cited in Bilorusky, "Reconstitution," 60–61. Bilorusky states that the movement took its name from the opening of what became known as the Wolin Proposal.

94. Strike Coordinating Committee, cited in Bilorusky, 69.

95. Bilorusky, 70–71, for chancellor's enjoining faculty to be "flexible"; academic credit for "antiwar related work," p. 72; faculty opposition to these proposals, pp. 74–75.

96. Bilorusky, 84–87, 64–65; "reaffirmation" and "campus constitutional convention," p. 78.

97. Regents' restrictions in Bilorusky, 80; Wolin on influence of Reconstitution on his thinking, the "Berkeley tradition" in "APSA Oral History," Tape #3.

98. "Real split" in Interview with Lonnie Hicks, April 1970, p. 2, Folder 29, Carton 1, *Journal of Educational Change* Records, UCA. For a thorough discussion of the formation of the Caucus for a New Political Science, see Clyde W. Barrow, "The Political and Intellectual Origins of New Political Science," *New Political Science* 39, no. 4 (2017): 437–472.

99. Goines, *Free Speech Movement*, 78–80, discusses the annoyance and even outrage some faculty and administrators expressed at the advent of the SLATE Supplements. For "unprofessional," see Interview with Lonnie Hicks, April 1970, p. 12, Folder 29, Carton 1, *Journal of Educational Change* Records, UCA. For "community of scholars," see Rosberg to Chancellor Roger Heyns, May 13, 1970, Folder 31, 893, "(ROTC Supplement) Special Folder: Reconstitution of Classes UCB, Vol. 2," Box 59, Office of the Chancellor Records, UCA. I discuss Rosberg's May 1970 letter to Heyns more thoroughly toward the end of this section.

100. Goines, *Free Speech Movement*, 65–82. Goines notes that SLATE was a "pseudo-acronym," p. 65. SLATE Supplements to the *General Catalogue* have been bound into several volumes and are stored in the UC Archives.

101. SLATE Supplement 1, no. 2 (1964): 3–10.

102. For comment on Sperlich, see SLATE Supplement 2, no. 3 (1965): 59; for that on Johnson, see SLATE Supplement, ASUC Synopsis of Courses (Joint Edition), Spring 1967, no volume number, A61. Volume numbers appear only up through early 1967.

103. McClosky and Rogin quoted in SLATE Supplement, ASUC Synopsis of Courses (Joint Edition), Spring 1967, no volume number, A58. Subsequent material cited in the text appears on A59 of the same edition.

104. SLATE Supplement Fall 1967, no volume number. "Model of chaos," p. 81; "two factions," p. 82.

105. SLATE Supplement Fall 1968, no volume number. All material cited appears on p. 43.

106. There is some disagreement among retrospective accounts about when this undated pamphlet was written. Jeff Lustig in an April 29, 1970, interview with the *Journal of Educational Change*, 10, says it was *written* in between the winter and spring quarters of 1968; Hicks, in an April 1970 interview with the same journal, pp. 6–7, says it was *published* in 1969. Perhaps both are correct. (Typed transcripts of both interviews in Folder 29, Carton 1, *Journal of Educational Change* Records, UCA.) What is most important for my purposes, however, is that the pamphlet was written after the proposal to form a department of political theory had been quashed. Internal references in the pamphlet make this clear. My copy of this pamphlet comes from the personal papers of Jeff Lustig.

107. University documents as well as local news reports mention significant strikes and sit-ins of this kind each year from 1965 through 1970. Some were directed against

ROTC programs, the presence of recruiters from the military, CIA, and corporations like Dow Chemical on campus. Others demanded greater student participation in university policy making and use of university property (People's Park) as well as new academic programs, like the 1969 strike in support of establishing a Third World College. On the former, see Chancellor Roger Heyns to the University Community, October 31, 1967, in folder "Policies on Student Discipline," Department of Political Science Records; on the latter, see Wolin and Schaar, "The Battle of People's Park," 73–95, in *Berkeley Rebellion*.

108. For example, the firing of one teaching assistant, Frank Bardacke, is mentioned in "Invitation," p. 2.

109. For the demand for student representation on such committees, see GASP's "The Situation at Berkeley," 2 April 1970, 2. The WPSA panel GASP organized is also mentioned there and in Hicks, April 1970 interview with the *Journal of Educational Change*, 11. Both in Folder 29, Carton 1, *Journal of Educational Change* Records, UCA.

110. GASP, "Dear prospective student," n.d., Folder 29, Carton 1, *Journal of Educational Change* Records, CU-311, UCA. "*Suppression*" and "*end*," pp. 1–2 (emphasis in original); "quiet spot" and "common struggle," p. 4.

111. In a letter to Dean Walter Knight, Wildavsky reported that two political science classes held in late January 1969 were briefly interrupted by students supporting the Third World Liberation Front strike. The interruptions were silent and peaceful; one involved students entering a classroom and writing "Lesson for Today: Observe the Strike" on the blackboard and then leaving. Wildavsky to Knight, February 4, 1969. Shortly thereafter, Wildavsky sent a memo to his department colleagues endorsing a proposal from another faculty member to constitute a "Barrows Hall Peace Patrol" to deter future disruptions. Wildavsky to Political Science Faculty Members, Re: Barrows Hall Peace Patrol, February 26, 1969. Both in folder "1969 Strike and Aftermath," Political Science Department Records.

112. Rosberg recounted that one such tour stopped in front of the office of a member of the political science department, where "the tour guides read out to the 'tourists' the indictment of him." Rosberg notes that this particular faculty member "fortunately was out of town," but does not name him. All material cited on p. 1. Rosberg to Chancellor Roger Heyns, May 13, 1970, Folder 31, 893, "(ROTC Supplement) Special Folder: Reconstitution of Classes UCB, Vol. 2," Box 59, Office of the Chancellor Records, UCA. Because these records contain several folders numbered 31, 893, I have given the full title of this particular folder here.

113. See Jack H. Schuster, Assistant to Chancellor, to Chancellor Heyns, Re.: Conversation with Professor Scalapino, June 2, 1970, Folder 31, 893, "(ROTC Supplement) Special Folder: Reconstitution of Classes UCB," Box 59, OCR, UCA.

114. For deep insights into these issues, see Paulo Ravecca, *The Politics of Political Science: Re-writing Latin American Experiences* (New York: Routledge, 2019).

115. Rosberg to Chancellor Heyns, May 14, 1970, Folder 31, 893, "(ROTC Supplement) Special Folder: Reconstitution of Classes UCB," Box 59, OCR, UCA. All material cited appears on p. 1.

116. Paul Seabury, "'Reconstitute' Universities?" *Freedom at Issue*, September-October, no. 3 (1970): 1–2, 13–15. "Compost heap," "idyllic dream," and "political weapon" all on p. 2; "outvote faculty members," p. 14; "whole-politicized university" and "free

rational inquiry," pp. 13–14. Seabury does not criticize Wolin by name, calling his target "Professor Sol Ipsism" instead. Given Seabury's specific reference to this professor's "mass-meeting speech proclaiming 'reconstitution,'" p. 2, and Wolin's prominent role in the movement, I think it's safe to assume that Seabury had Wolin in mind. The pseudonym is yet another barb, suggesting that like a solipsist, Wolin was incapable of perceiving anything about the world that did not conform to his ideas about it.

117. In 1961 Berkeley's chancellor reported that Herbert Blumer, director of the Institute of Social Sciences, supported closing the center to address the overall financial cutbacks ISS faced, in part because faculty associated with the center had been less successful at securing external grants compared to those associated with Berkeley's Survey Research Center. Chancellor Strong to President Kerr, November 7, 1961, Folder 6, "Institute of Social Sciences," Box 54, OCR.

118. Norman Jacobson, "Political Science and Political Education," *American Political Science Review* 57, no. 3 (1963): 569.

119. *Proposal for a Department of Political Theory.* No room for political theory in dominant political science pedagogy, pp. 6–7; "manifest educational needs," 1. A full citation to this unpublished proposal appears in note 73.

120. Wolin and Schaar, "Berkeley and the Fate of the Multiversity," 37, in *Berkeley Rebellion.*

121. See in particular the critiques throughout Ashcraft, "One Step Backward, Two Steps Forward"; and Gunnell, *The Descent of Political Theory,* 268–278. Gunnell, *Between Philosophy and Politics,* presents this critique at length; see the introduction, pp. 1–9, for an overview.

122. As I discuss above, the authors of the Study Commission on University Governance's report acknowledged others might find their recommendations "utopian and perhaps arcadian."

CONCLUSION

1. Gordon Allport, cited in Herman, *The Romance of American Psychology,* 133.

2. William Mishler, "Trends in Political Science Funding at the National Science Foundation." *PS* 17 no. 4 (1984): 848–849. Solovey, *Social Science for What?,* 239–244, discusses declines in NSF funding in the 1980s for many disciplines, including political science. For Solovey's mention of Mishler, 240.

3. I allude here to the title of Talcott Parsons's "Social Science: A Basic National Resource." Parsons' work was but one iteration of this common postwar pitch. Klausner and Lidz, *Nationalization of the Social Sciences,* summarize the fate of Parsons' report on pp. xi–xii and publish the full text on pp. 41–112.

4. Barrow, "The Political and Intellectual Origins of New Political Science,"; Paulo Ravecca, *The Politics of Political Science*; and Vitalis, *White World Order, Black Power Politics.* The larger political conflicts each discusses are the Vietnam War and urban crises in the United States (Barrow), the authoritarian regimes and their aftermath in Chile and Uruguay (Ravecca), and US imperialism from the beginning to the middle of the twentieth century (Vitalis).

5. https://www.icpsr.umich.edu/icpsrweb/content/sumprog/schedule.html#!firstSession. According to ICPSR website, over 1,200 students participated in its virtual summer program in 2021.

6. See chapter 4 for a discussion of ICPSR's current sources of funding. According to its website, ICPSR's fee-paying members include "universities, foundations, government institutions, nonprofits and more." For a current list of all members, see https://www.icpsr.umich.edu/web/membership/administration/institutions.

7. Parmar, *Foundations of the American Century*, 130, 160–164.

8. Isaac Kamola, *Making the World Global: U.S. Universities and the Production of the Global Imaginary* (Durham, N.C.: Duke University Press, 2019), 156–167.

9. A brief account of the CSPT's founding may be found at https://www.icspt.org/about-cspt. According to this portion of the website, John Pocock, Melvin Richter, and Neal Wood founded the CSPT in 1967 in Toronto. The website also reproduces the statement from which I cite.

10. For Wolin's conception of "epic theory," see his "Political Theory as a Vocation." In addition to his academic work, Wolin wrote for the *New York Review of Books* and the journal *democracy*, which he also edited. For some essays that appeared in the former, see Wolin and Schaar, *The Berkeley Rebellion and Beyond*. All issues of *democracy*, published from 1981 through 1983, are available at https://dja8183.org/.

11. Barrow, "Origins of New Political Science," 468–469.

12. Barrow, 462–467, 471.

13. See Herb Childress, *The Adjunct Underclass: How America's Colleges Betrayed Their Faculty, Their Students, and Their Mission* (Chicago: University of Chicago Press, 2019), for a deep, thoughtful critique of these trends.

14. Kamola, *Making the World Global*, 158–167.

15. Rohde, *Armed with Expertise*, 153, discusses the Minerva Initiative. She also discusses Barry Silverman, an academic engineer who designed a computer game simulating Afghan villages and used in training US military personnel, and Montgomery McFate, an anthropologist, who designed the Human Terrain System that placed social scientists in the US military units in Iraq as part of a counterinsurgency strategy, 150–155. See my discussion in chapter 4 of the political scientists A. F. K. Organski and Bruce Bueno de Mesquita marketing their game-theory–based predictive algorithms to defense and intelligence agencies.

16. MacLean, *Democracy in Chains*; O'Connor, "The Politics of Rich and Rich."

17. Solovey, *Social Science for What?*, 90–100, recounts the multiyear public pressure put on the NSF by Evron Kirkpatrick, long-time executive director of the American Political Science Association, to increase its funding for political science and start a political science program. The 3–6 percent figure, covering 1969–1989, appears on p. 242. Riecken, "Underdogging: The Early Career of the Social Sciences in the NSF" and Larsen, *Milestones and Millstones*, offer insiders' accounts of social science programs at NSF.

18. See Solovey, *Social Science for What?*, 212, 308, for the NSF as a primary source of funding for political science; pp. 98–100, 294–295 for those fields not supported by the NSF; "hard core," p. 7.

19. For accounts of challenges to NSF funding for political science in the 1980s and early 2000s, see Solovey, 210–229 and 307–309.

20. https://nsf.gov/funding/pgm_summ.jsp?pims_id=5418&org=SBE&from=home. This page is now archived. Last accessed May 12, 2022.

BIBLIOGRAPHY

ARCHIVAL COLLECTIONS AND DIGITAL SOURCES

Bentley Historical Library, Ann Arbor, Michigan (BHL)

Oral Histories
    Philip Converse, ISR Oral History Project
    Warren Miller, ISR Oral History Project
Personal Papers
    Arthur Watson Bromage Papers
    Samuel J. Eldersveld Papers
    Warren E. Miller Papers
    A. F. K. Organski Papers
    James Kerr Pollock Papers
    J. David Singer Papers
University of Michigan Records
    College of Literature, Science, and the Arts, 1846–2014
    Department of Political Science, 1910–2009, 1970–2000
    Graduate Catalog, 1910–1960. General Register. Available through HathiTrust Digital Library.
    Institute for Social Research
    Inter-university Consortium for Political and Social Research
    Michigan News and Information Service, University of Michigan Faculty and Staff Files, 1944–2005, 1960–1995

M. E. Grenander Department of Special Collections and Archives, University Libraries, University of Albany, New York

German Intellectual Émigré Collection (GIEC)
    Reinhard Bendix Papers

Online Archive of California, https://oac.cdlib.org/

Barrows, David P. "Teacher and Public Servant." Address Delivered at the Memorial Service for Bernard Moses, April 13, 1930.

Rare Book and Manuscript Library, Columbia University, New York

Carnegie Corporation (CC) Records
  Series IIIA.8 (Grant Files)
Columbia Center for Oral History Archives
    Reminiscences of Charles Dollard, 1967. Carnegie Corporation project.
    Reminiscences of Frederick Osborn, 1967. Carnegie Corporation project.

Rockefeller Archive Center (RAC), Sleepy Hollow, New York

Ford Foundation Archives (FFA)
  Oral Histories
      Bernard Berelson, Oral History Transcript, July 7, 1972
      Donald G. Marquis, Oral History Transcript, October 27, 1972
      Donald K. Price, Oral History Transcript, June 22, 1972
  Other Records
      Grants and Reports in Area V (Behavioral Sciences)
      Marquis, Donald G. "Report of the Social Science Division of the Study
        Committee," 1950.
Rockefeller Foundation Archives (RFA)
  Officer Biographical Files
      Norman S. Buchanan
      Leland C. DeVinney
      Kenneth W. Thompson
      Joseph H. Willits
  Officer Diaries, Record Group 12.2
      Herbert Deane, 1952–1953
      Leland C. DeVinney, 1951–1953
      John B. Stewart, 1953–1955
  Record Group 1.2 (Projects)
      Series 200E (Fellowships)
      Series 200S (Grants—United States)
  Record Group 3 (Administration, Program, and Policy)
      Series 910 (Social Sciences)
Social Science Research Council (SSRC) Papers
  Accession 1, Series 1 (Committee Projects)
      Subseries 19 (Miscellaneous Projects)
  Accession 2, Series 1 (Committee Projects)
      Subseries 1 (Ad hoc Committee and Associates)
      Subseries 16 (Completed Projects, 1950–1969)
      Subseries 74 (Miscellaneous Files)
      Subseries 76 (Committee on Political Behavior)

University of California Archives (UCA), Bancroft Library, University of California, Berkeley

Board of Educational Development (BED) Records
Journal of Educational Change (JEC) Records
Office of the Chancellor (OCR) Records
Office of the President Records
Personal Papers of David Barrows
Select Committee on Education Records (the Muscatine Report)
SLATE Supplements

*University of California Berkeley Library Digital Collections, https://digicoll.lib.berkeley
.edu*

Registers of the University of California, 1889–1959
U.C. Berkeley General Catalogue, 1959–1967

*University of California History Digital Archive (UCDHA), https://www.lib.berkeley.edu/
uchistory/index.html*

Histories of Department of Political Science, Institute for Governmental Studies *In Memoriam*

OTHER UNPUBLISHED SOURCES

Citrin, Jack. Conversation with the author, July 27, 2005. Berkeley, CA.
Department of Political Science Records. University of California, Berkeley. Copies made available to the author.
Graduate Students and Faculty, U.C. Berkeley Political Science Department. Invitation to a Discussion, 1968. Unpublished pamphlet from the personal papers of Jeff Lustig.
Jacobson, Norman. APSA Oral History. Full tape-recorded interview by the author. Reno, NV, January 4, 2000. American Political Science Association Oral History Archive. Lexington: University of Kentucky Library.
Lustig, Jeff. Conversations with the author, June 30 and July 14, 2005. Berkeley, CA.
Miller, Warren E. APSA Oral History. Full tape-recorded interview by Heinz Eulau. Scottsdale, AZ, February 11, 1988. American Political Science Association Oral History Archive. Lexington: University of Kentucky Library.
Paff, Joe and Karen. Conversation with the author, July 22, 2005. Berkeley, CA.
Pitkin, Hanna. Letter to the author, August 2002.
Poschman, Gene. Conversations with the author, July 14 and 27, 2005. Berkeley, CA.
Price, Robert. Conversation with the author, July 15, 2005. Berkeley, CA.
Scalapino, Robert. Conversation with the author, July 11, 2005. Berkeley, CA.
Scott, Peter Dale. Telephone conversation with the author, August 19, 2005.
———. Conversation with the author, July 5, 2006. Berkeley, CA.

Study Commission on University Governance. "The Culture of the University: Governance and Education." Report of the Study Commission, University of California, Berkeley, January 15, 1968. From the personal papers of Jeff Lustig.

Wolin, Sheldon. APSA Oral History. Full tape-recorded interview by Nicholas Xenos. Whitethorn, CA, July 10–11, 1992. American Political Science Association Oral History Archive. Lexington: University of Kentucky Library.

———. Telephone conversation with the author, August 4, 2005.

PUBLISHED WORKS

Adcock, Robert. "Interpreting Behavioralism." In *Modern Political Science: Anglo-American Exchanges Since 1880,* edited by Robert Adcock, Mark Bevir, and Shannon C. Stimson, 180–208. Princeton, NJ: Princeton University Press, 2007.

_____. *Liberalism and the Emergence of American Political Science: A Transatlantic Tale.* Oxford: Oxford University Press, 2014.

Almond, Gabriel A. "APSA Oral History." In *Political Science in America: Oral Histories of a Discipline,* edited by Michael A. Baer, Malcolm E. Jewell, and Lee Sigelman, 121–134. Lexington: University Press of Kentucky, 1991.

———. "Political Theory and Political Science." *American Political Science Review* 60, no. 4 (1966): 869–879.

Amadae, Sonja M. *Prisoners of Reason: Game Theory and Neoliberal Political Economy.* Cambridge: Cambridge University Press, 2016.

———. *Rationalizing Capitalist Democracy: The Cold War Origins of Rational Choice Liberalism.* Chicago: University of Chicago Press, 2003.

Andersen, Casper, Jakob Bek-Thomsen, and Peter C. Kjærgaard. "The Money Trail: A New Historiography for Networks, Patronage, and Scientific Careers." *Isis* 103, no. 2 (2012): 310–315.

Arendt, Hanna. *The Human Condition.* Chicago: University of Chicago Press, 1958.

Arnove, Robert F., ed. *Philanthropy and Cultural Imperialism: The Foundations at Home and Abroad.* Bloomington: Indiana University Press, 1982. First published 1980 by G. K. Hall (Boston).

Ashcraft, Richard. "One Step Backward, Two Steps Forward: Reflections upon Contemporary Political Theory." In *What Should Political Theory Be Now?,* edited by John S. Nelson, 515–548. Albany, NY: SUNY Press, 1983.

Austin, Erik. "ICPSR: The Founding and Early Years," 2011. https://www.icpsr.umich.edu/web/pages/about/history/early-years.html.

Baer, Michael A., Malcolm E. Jewell, and Lee Sigelman, eds. *Political Science in America: Oral Histories of a Discipline.* Lexington: University Press of Kentucky, 1991.

Ball, Terence. "American Political Science in Its Postwar Political Context." In *Discipline and History: Political Science in the United States,* edited by James Farr and Raymond Seidelman, 207–221. Ann Arbor: University of Michigan Press, 1993.

———. "Whither Political Theory?" Chap. 2 in *Reappraising Political Theory: Revisionist Studies in the History of Political Thought.* Oxford: Clarendon, 1995.

Barrow, Clyde W. "The Political and Intellectual Origins of New Political Science." *New Political Science* 39, no. 4 (2017): 437–472.

———. *Universities and the Capitalist State: Corporate Liberalism and the Reconstruction of American Higher Education, 1894–1928.* Madison: University of Wisconsin Press, 1990.

Barrows, David P. *A History of the Philippines.* Yonkers-on-Hudson, NY: World Book Co., 1914.

Bartels, Larry. *Unequal Democracy: The Political Economy of the New Gilded Age,* 2nd ed. Princeton, NJ: Princeton University Press, 2016.

Bennett, Eric. *Workshops of Empire: Stegner, Engle, and American Creative Writing during the Cold War.* Iowa City: University of Iowa Press, 2015.

Berelson, Bernard. "Behavioralism." In *International Encyclopedia of the Social Sciences,* edited by David Sills, 41–45. New York: Macmillan, 1968.

Berkenpas, Joshua R. "The Behavioral Revolution in Contemporary Political Science: Narrative, Identity, and Practice." PhD diss., Western Michigan University, 2016.

Berman, Edward H. *The Influence of the Carnegie, Ford, and Rockefeller Foundations on American Foreign Policy: The Ideology of Philanthropy.* Albany, NY: SUNY Press, 1983.

Bessner, Daniel. *Democracy in Exile: Hans Speier and the Rise of the Defense Intellectual.* Ithaca, NY: Cornell University Press, 2018.

Bilorusky, John A. "Reconstitution at Berkeley: The Quest for Self-Determination." PhD diss., University of California, Berkeley, 1972.

Blatt, Jessica. *Race and the Making of American Political Science.* Philadelphia: University of Pennsylvania Press, 2018.

Bromage, Arthur W. "Constitutional Aspects of State-Local Relationships: Municipal and County Home Rule for Michigan." Constitutional Convention Research Paper No. 3. Detroit: Citizen Research Council of Michigan, 1961.

Brown, Wendy. "At the Edge." *Political Theory* 30, no. 4 (2002): 556–576.

Buchanan, Norman S. "The Economics of Corporate Reorganization." *Quarterly Journal of Economics* 54, no. 1 (1939): 28–50.

———. "Toward a Theory of Fluctuations in Business Profits." *American Economic Review* 31, no. 4 (1941): 731–753.

Buck, Peter. "Adjusting to Military Life: The Social Sciences Go to War, 1941–1950." In *Military Enterprise and Technological Change: Perspectives on the American Experience,* edited by Merritt Roe Smith, 203–252. Cambridge, MA: MIT Press, 1985.

Burdick, Eugene. "Syndicalism and Industrial Unionism in England until 1918." PhD diss., Oxford University, 1950.

Burdick, Eugene, and Arthur J. Brodbeck, eds. *American Voting Behavior.* Glencoe, IL: Free Press, 1959.

Burdick, Eugene, and William J. Lederer. *The Ugly American.* New York: Norton, 1958.

Callahan, David. *The Givers: Wealth, Power and Philanthropy in a New Gilded Age.* New York: Knopf, 2017.

Campbell, Angus, Philip Converse, Warren Miller, and Donald Stokes. *The American Voter.* New York: Wiley, 1960.

Carnegie Corporation. *Annual Reports.* New York: Carnegie Corporation, 1923, 1934, 1944.

Chase, Stuart. *The Proper Study of Mankind.* New York: Harper & Bros., 1948.

Childress, Herb. *The Adjunct Underclass: How America's Colleges Betrayed Their Faculty, Their Students, and Their Mission.* Chicago: University of Chicago Press, 2019.

Clymer, Kenton J. "Humanitarian Imperialism: David Prescott Barrows and the White Man's Burden in the Philippines." *Pacific Historical Review* 45, no. 4 (1976): 495–517.

Collins, Chuck. *The Wealth Hoarders. How Billionaires Pay Millions to Hide Trillions.* Bedford, MA: Polity, 2021.

Converse, Jean. *Survey Research in the United States: Roots and Emergence, 1890–1960.* Berkeley: University of California Press, 1987.

Converse, Philip E., and Donald R. Kinder. "Voting and Electoral Behavior." In *A Telescope on Society: Survey Research and Social Science at the University of Michigan and Beyond,* edited by James S. House, F. Thomas Juster, Robert L. Kahn, Howard Schuman, and Eleanor Singer, 70–97. Ann Arbor: University of Michigan Press, 2004.

Craver, Earlene. "Patronage and the Directions of Research in Economics: The Rockefeller Foundation in Europe, 1924–1938." *Minerva* 24, nos. 2–3 (1986): 205–222.

Crick, Bernard. *The American Science of Politics: Its Origins and Conditions.* Berkeley: University of California Press, 1959.

Crowther-Heyck, Hunter. "Patrons of the Revolution: Ideals and Institutions in Postwar Behavioral Science." *Isis* 97, no. 3 (2006): 420–446.

Cumings, Bruce. "Boundary Displacement: Area Studies and International Studies during and after the Cold War." In *Universities and Empire: Money and Politics in the Social Sciences during the Cold War,* edited by Christopher Simpson, 159–188. New York: New Press, 1998.

Curti, Merle, and Roderick Nash. *Philanthropy and the Shaping of American Higher Education.* New Brunswick, NJ: Rutgers University Press, 1965.

Dahl, Robert A. "The Behavioral Approach in Political Science: Epitaph for a Monument to a Successful Protest." *American Political Science Review* 55, no. 4 (1961): 763–772.

———. *Who Governs? Democracy and Power in an American City.* New Haven, CT: Yale University Press, 1961.

Danziger, Kurt. *Naming the Mind: How Psychology Found Its Language.* London: Sage, 1997.

Diamond, Sigmund. *Compromised Campus: The Collaboration of the Universities with the Intelligence Community, 1945–55.* New York: Oxford University Press, 1992.

Dollard, Charles. "In Defense of the Social Sciences." *American Journal of Economics and Sociology* 14, no. 1 (1954): 31–37.

———. "A Middleman Looks at Social Science." *American Sociological Review* 15, no. 1 (1950): 16–20.

Douglass, John Aubrey. *The California Idea and American Higher Education: 1850 to the 1960 Master Plan.* Stanford, CA: Stanford University Press, 2000.

Dryzek, John S. "Revolutions without Enemies: Key Transformations in Political Science." *American Political Science Review* 100, no. 4 (2006): 487–492.

Easton, David. "APSA Oral History." In *Political Science in America: Oral Histories of a Discipline,* edited by Michael A. Baer, Malcolm E. Jewell, and Lee Sigelman, 195–214. Lexington: University Press of Kentucky.

———. "The New Revolution in Political Science." *American Political Science Review* 63, no. 4 (1969): 1051–1061.

———. *The Political System: An Inquiry into the State of Political Science.* New York: Knopf, 1953.

Eittreim, Elisabeth M. *Teaching Empire. Native Americans, Filipinos, and US Imperial Education, 1879–1918.* Lawrence: University Press of Kansas, 2019.

Eldersveld, Samuel J. "Jap Influence Fades Quickly." *National Municipal Review* 34, no. 9 (1945): 445–449.

Eulau, Heinz. "APSA Oral History." In *Political Science in America: Oral Histories of a Discipline,* edited by Michael A. Baer, Malcolm E. Jewell, and Lee Sigelman, 179–194. Lexington: University Press of Kentucky, 1991.

———. *The Behavioral Persuasion in Politics.* New York: Random House, 1963.

———. *Micro-Macro Dilemmas in Political Science.* Norman: University of Oklahoma Press, 1996.

———. "Perceptions of Class and Party in Voting Behavior." *American Political Science Review* 49, no. 2 (1955): 364–384.

———. "Social Science at the Crossroads." *Antioch Review* 11, no. 1 (1951): 117–128.

———. "Theories of Federalism under the Holy Roman Empire." *American Political Science Review* 35, no. 4 (1941): 643–664.

———. "Understanding Political Life in America: The Contribution of Political Science." *Social Science Quarterly* 57, no. 1 (1976): 112–153.

———. "Wayside Challenger: Some Remarks on the Politics of Henry David Thoreau." *Antioch Review* 9, no. 4 (1949): 509–522.

Farr, James. "Remembering the Revolution: Behavioralism in American Political Science." In *Political Science in History: Research Programs and Political Traditions,* edited by James Farr, John S. Dryzek, and Stephen T. Leonard, 198–224. Cambridge: Cambridge University Press, 1995.

Fisher, Donald. *Fundamental Development of the Social Sciences: Rockefeller Philanthropy and the United States Social Science Research Council.* Ann Arbor: University of Michigan Press, 1993.

Ford Foundation. *Annual Reports.* New York: Ford Foundation, 1957, 1960, 1965.

———. *Report of the Study for the Ford Foundation on Policy and Program: November 1949.* Detroit, MI: Ford Foundation, 1950.

Frank, Thomas. *Listen, Liberal: Or, What Ever Happened to the Party of the People?* New York: Henry Holt, 2016.

Frantilla, Anne. *Social Science in the Public Interest: A Fiftieth-Year History of the Institute for Social Research.* Ann Arbor: Bentley Historical Library, University of Michigan, 1998.

Furner, Mary O. *Advocacy & Objectivity. A Crisis in the Professionalization of American Social Science, 1865–1905.* Lexington: University Press of Kentucky, 1975.

Garceau, Oliver. "Research in the Political Process." *American Political Science Review* 45, no. 1 (1951): 69–85.

Geiger, Roger L. "Academic Foundations and Academic Social Science, 1945–1960." *Minerva* 26, no. 3 (1988): 315–341.

———. "Organized Research Units—Their Role in the Development of University Research." *Journal of Higher Education* 61, no. 1 (1990): 1–19.

———. *Research and Relevant Knowledge: American Research Universities since World War II.* Oxford: Oxford University Press, 1993.

Gettell, Raymond. *The History of Political Thought.* New York: Century, 1924.

———. "The Nature of Political Thought." *American Political Science Review* 17, no. 2 (1923): 204–215.

Gilens, Martin. *Affluence and Influence: Economic Inequality and Political Power in America.* Princeton, NJ: Princeton University Press, 2012.

Giridharadas, Anand. *Winners Take All: The Elite Charade of Changing the World.* New York: Knopf, 2018.

Glock, Charles Y. *Recollections of Charles Y. Glock, First SRC Director.* Reprinted from Charles Y. Glock, *A Life Fully Lived: An Autobiography,* "Chapter 12: Directing the Survey Research Center," 162–187. 2001, 2007. Accessed at http://srcweb.berkeley.edu/backup_2010_10_05/50anniv.html.

Goines, David Lance. *The Free Speech Movement: Coming of Age in the 1960s.* Berkeley, CA: Ten Speed Press, 1993.

Greenberg, Daniel S. *The Politics of Pure Science: An Inquiry into the Relationship between Science and Government in the United States.* New York: New American Library, 1971.

Greenstein, Fred, and Austin Ranney. "Pendleton Herring." *PS: Political Science & Politics* 38, no. 1 (2005): 120–121.

Gruber, Carol S. *Mars and Minerva: World War I and the Uses of Higher Learning in America.* Baton Rouge: Louisiana State University Press, 1975.

Guilhot, Nicolas. *The Democracy Makers. Human Rights and the Politics of Global Order.* New York: Columbia University Press, 2005.

———, ed. *The Invention of International Relations Theory: Realism, the Rockefeller Foundation, and the 1954 Conference on Theory.* New York: Columbia University Press, 2011.

Gunnell, John G. *Between Philosophy and Politics: The Alienation of Political Theory.* Amherst: University of Massachusetts Press, 1986.

———. *The Descent of Political Theory: The Genealogy of an American Vocation.* Chicago: Chicago University Press, 1993.

———. "The Reconstitution of Political Theory: David Easton, Behavioralism, and the Long Road to System." *Journal of the History of the Behavioral Sciences* 49, no. 2 (2013): 190–210.

Haddad, Nabih, and Sarah Reckhow. "The Shifting Role of Higher Education Philanthropy: A Network Analysis of Philanthropic Policy Strategies. *Philanthropy and Education* 2, no. 1 (2018): 25–52.

Haddow, Anna. *Political Science in American Colleges and Universities, 1636–1900.* Edited and with an introduction and concluding chapter by William Anderson. New York: D. Appleton-Century, 1939.

Hammack, David C. "American Debates on the Legitimacy of Foundations." In *The Legitimacy of Philanthropic Foundations: United States and European Perspectives,* edited by Kenneth Prewitt, Mattei Dogan, Steven Heydemann, and Stefan Toepler, 49–98. New York: Russell Sage Foundation, 2006.

Hammack, David C., and Helmut K. Anheier. *A Versatile American Institution. The*

Changing Ideals and Realities of Philanthropic Foundations. Washington, DC: Brookings Institution Press, 2013.

Hauptmann, Emily. "The Development of Philanthropic Interest in the Scientific Study of Political Behavior." Report on research conducted at the Rockefeller Archive Center, 2011. https://rockarch/issuelab.org.

———. "The Evolution of Political Theory in a Climate of Experiment and Secession." *PS: Political Science & Politics* 50, no. 3 (2017): 792–796.

———. "From Opposition to Accommodation: How Rockefeller Foundation Grants Redefined Relations between Political Theory and Social Science in the 1950s." *American Political Science Review* 100, no. 4 (2006): 643–649.

———. "The Theorists' Gambit: Kenneth Thompson's Cultivation of Theoretical Knowledge about Politics during the Early Cold War." *International History Review* 42, no. 3 (2020): 625–638.

———. "Why They Shared: Recovering Early Arguments for Sharing Social Scientific Data." *Science in Context* 33, no. 2 (2020): 101–119.

Herman, Ellen. *The Romance of American Psychology: Political Culture in the Age of Experts.* Berkeley: University of California Press, 1995.

Herring, Pendleton. "Political Science in the Next Decade." *American Political Science Review* 39, no. 4 (1945): 757–766.

Herring, E. Pendleton. "APSA Oral History Interview." In *Political Science in America: Oral Histories of a Discipline,* edited by Michael A. Baer, Malcolm E. Jewell, and Lee Sigelman, 22–39. Lexington: University Press of Kentucky, 1991.

Hoganson, Kristin L. *American Empire at the Turn of the Twentieth Century: A Brief History with Documents.* Boston: Bedford/St. Martin's, 2017.

Holli, Melvin G. "Urban Reform in the Progressive Era." In *The Progressive Era,* edited by Lewis L. Gould, 133–151. Syracuse, NY: Syracuse University Press, 1974.

Igo, Sarah E. *The Averaged American: Surveys, Citizens, and the Making of a Mass Public.* Cambridge, MA.: Harvard University Press, 2007.

Inter-university Consortium for Political Research. *Annual Reports.* Ann Arbor: ICPSR, 1962–1969, 1996–2018. https://www.icpsr.umich.edu/icpsrweb/content/about/history/histdocs.html.

Isaac, Jeffrey C. "The Strange Silence of Political Theory." *Political Theory* 23, no. 4 (1995): 636–652.

Isaac, Joel. *Working Knowledge: Making the Human Sciences from Parsons to Kuhn.* Cambridge, MA: Harvard University Press, 2012.

Jackson, John E., and Arlene W. Saxonhouse. 2014. "Not Your Great-Grandfather's Department." Unpublished manuscript prepared for Bicentennial of University of Michigan. Available from the authors by request.

Jacobson, Norman. "Political Science and Political Education." *American Political Science Review* 57, no. 3 (1963): 561–569.

Kamola, Isaac. *Making the World Global: U.S. Universities and the Production of the Global Imaginary.* Durham, NC: Duke University Press, 2019.

Kaufman-Osborn, Timothy. "Disenchanted Professionals: The Politics of Faculty Governance in the Neoliberal Academy." *Perspectives on Politics* 15, no. 1 (2017): 100–115.

Kerr, Clark. *The Uses of the University*, 3rd ed. Cambridge, MA: Harvard University Press, 1982.

Key, V. O., Jr. *The Administration of Federal Grants to States*. Chicago: Public Administration Service for the SSRC Committee on Public Administration, 1937.

———. *Southern Politics in State and Nation*. New York: Alfred Knopf, 1949.

Klausner, Samuel Z., and Victor M. Lidz, eds. *The Nationalization of the Social Sciences*. Philadelphia: University of Pennsylvania Press, 1986.

Lagemann, Ellen Condliffe. *The Politics of Knowledge: The Carnegie Corporation, Philanthropy, and Public Policy*. Middletown, CT: Wesleyan University Press, 1989.

Larsen, Otto. *Milestones and Millstones: Social Science at the National Science Foundation, 1945–1991*. New Brunswick, NJ: Transaction, 1992.

Leslie, Stuart W. *The Cold War and American Science: The Military-Industrial-Academic Complex at MIT and Stanford*. New York: Columbia University Press, 1993.

Lewis-Beck, Michael S., Helmut Norpoth, William G. Jacoby, and Herbert F. Weisberg. Foreword by Philip E. Converse. *The American Voter Revisited*. Ann Arbor: University of Michigan Press, 2008.

Linsay, Drew. "Beware the Bearer of Big Gifts: Philanthropists Are Facing Scrutiny, Suspicion, and Criticism Not Seen since the Gilded Age." *Chronicle of Philanthropy*, February 7, 2017.

Lipset, Seymour Martin, and Sheldon Wolin, eds. *The Berkeley Student Revolt: Facts and Interpretations*. Garden City, NY: Doubleday, 1965.

Losco, Joseph. "Whither Intellectual Diversity in American Political Science? The Case of APSA and Organized Sections." *PS: Political Science & Politics* 31, no. 4 (1998): 836–846.

Loss, Christopher. *Between Citizens and the State: The Politics of American Higher Education in the 20th Century*. Princeton, NJ: Princeton University Press, 2012.

Lowen, Rebecca S. *Creating the Cold War University: The Transformation of Stanford*. Berkeley: University of California Press, 1997.

Lucker, Andrew M. *V.O. Key, Jr.: The Quintessential Political Scientist*. New York: Peter Lang, 2001.

MacLean, Nancy. *Democracy in Chains: The Deep History of the Radical Right's Stealth Plan for America*. New York: Penguin, 2017.

Mazuzan, George T. *The NSF: A Brief History*. General Publication, NSF8816, 1994. http://www.nsf.gov/about/history-publications.jsp.

McCaughey, Robert A. *International Studies and Academic Enterprise: A Chapter in the Enclosure of American Learning*. New York: Columbia University Press, 1984.

McClosky, Herbert, and John H. Schaar. "Psychological Dimensions of Anomy." *American Sociological Review* 30, no. 1 (1965):14–40.

McCoy, Charles, and John Playford, eds. *Apolitical Politics: A Critique of Behavioralism*. New York: Thomas Y. Crowell, 1967.

McGoey, Linsey. *No Such Thing as a Free Gift: The Gates Foundation and the Price of Philanthropy*. London: Verso, 2015.

Merelman, Richard. *Pluralism at Yale: The Culture of Political Science in America*. Madison: University of Wisconsin Press, 2003.

Merton, Robert K., and Paul K. Hatt. "Election Polling Forecasts and Public Images of

Social Science: A Case Study in the Shaping of Opinion among a Strategic Public." *Public Opinion Quarterly* 13, no. 2 (1949): 185–222.

Miller, James G. "Toward a General Theory for the Behavioral Sciences." *American Psychologist* 10, no. 9 (1955): 513–531.

Miller, Warren E. "APSA Oral History Interview." In *Political Science in America: Oral Histories of a Discipline*, edited by Michael A. Baer, Malcolm E. Jewell, and Lee Sigelman, 231–247. Lexington: University Press of Kentucky, 1991.

Mishler, William. "Trends in Political Science Funding at the National Science Foundation." *PS* 17 no. 4 (1984): 846–857.

Moore, Matthew J. "Political Theory Today: Results of a National Survey." *PS: Political Science & Politics* 43, no. 2 (2010): 265–272.

Moore, W. E. "Donald Ramsey Young, 1898–1977." *ASA Footnotes* 5, no. 6 (1977): 12.

Morison, Robert S. "Foundations and Universities." *Daedalus* 93, no. 4 (1964): 1109–1141.

Moses, Bernard. *Spain's Declining Power in South America, 1730–1806*. Berkeley: University of California Press, 1919.

———. *The Spanish Dependencies in South America: An Introduction to the History of Their Civilization*. 2 vols. New York: Harper, 1914.

National Parks Service. Overview of the Panama-Pacific International Exposition park site, 2015. https://www.nps.gov/goga/learn/historyculture/ppie-palaces.htm.

National Science Foundation. *Federal Funds for Science*. Washington, DC: National Science Foundation, 1952–1961.

Needell, Allan A. "Project Troy and the Cold War Annexation of the Social Sciences." In *Universities and Empire*, edited by Christopher Simpson, 3–38. New York: New Press, 1998.

Nelkin, Dorothy. *The University and Military Research: Moral Politics at MIT*. Ithaca, NY: Cornell University Press, 1972.

O'Connor, Alice. "The Politics of Rich and Rich: Postwar Investigations of Foundations and the Rise of the Philanthropic Right." In *American Capitalism: Social Thought and Political Economy in the Twentieth Century*, edited by Nelson Lichtenstein, 228–248. Philadelphia: University of Pennsylvania Press, 2006.

Odendahl, Teresa. *Charity Begins at Home: Generosity and Self-Interest among the Philanthropic Elite*. New York: Basic, 1990.

Oren, Ido. *Our Enemies and US: America's Rivalries and the Making of Political Science*. Ithaca, NY: Cornell University Press, 2003.

Osborn, Frederick. "To What Extent Is a Science of Man Possible?" *Scientific Monthly* 49, no. 5 (1939): 452–459.

Osborne, Thomas, and Nikolas Rose. "Do the Social Sciences Create Phenomena? The Example of Public Opinion Research." *British Journal of Sociology* 50, no. 3 (1999): 367–396.

Owens, Larry. "MIT and the Federal 'Angel': Academic R & D and Federal-Private Cooperation before World War II." *Isis* 81, no. 2 (1990): 189–213.

Parmar, Inderjeet. *Foundations of the American Century: The Ford, Carnegie and Rockefeller Foundations in the Rise of American Power*. New York: Columbia University Press, 2012.

The Philippine Public Schools at the Panama-Pacific International Exposition. San Francisco: Marnell and Co., 1915. Full text available at https://catalog.hathitrust.org/Record/009569275.

Pollock, James K. "The Primacy of Politics." 1950 APSA Presidential Address. *American Political Science Review* 45, no. 1 (1951): 1–17.

Pollock, James K., and Samuel J. Eldersveld. *Michigan Politics in Transition: An Areal Study of Voting Trends in the Last Decade*. Ann Arbor: University of Michigan Press, 1942.

Pollock, James K., et al. *British Election Studies, 1950*. Ann Arbor, MI: G. Wahr , 1951.

Pooley, Jefferson D. "A 'Not Particularly Felicitous Phrase': A History of the 'Behavioral Sciences' Label." *Serendipities: Journal of the Sociology and History of the Social Sciences* 1 (2016): 38–81.

Rajaee, Farhang. *Kenneth W. Thompson, the Prophet of Norms: Thought and Practice*. New York: Palgrave Macmillan, 2013.

Ranney, Austin. "Committee on Political Behavior, 1949–64, and the Committee on Governmental and Legal Processes, 1964–72." *Items* 28, no. 3 (1974): 37–41.

Ravecca, Paulo. *The Politics of Political Science: Re-writing Latin American Experiences*. New York: Routledge, 2019.

Rawls, John. *A Theory of Justice*. Cambridge, MA: Harvard University Press, 1971.

Reckhow, Sarah. *Follow the Money: How Foundation Dollars Change Public School Politics*. Oxford: Oxford University Press, 2013.

———. "More than Patrons: How Foundations Fuel Policy Change and Backlash." *PS: Political Science & Politics* 49, no. 3 (2016): 449–454.

Reich, Rob. *Just Giving: Why Philanthropy Is Failing Democracy and How It Can Do Better*. Princeton, NJ: Princeton University Press, 2018.

Riecken, Henry. "Underdogging: The Early Career of the Social Sciences in the NSF." In *The Nationalization of the Social Sciences*, edited by Samuel Z. Klausner and Victor M. Lidz, 209–225. Philadelphia: University of Pennsylvania Press, 1986.

Riley, John W., Jr. "The Status of the Social Sciences, 1950: A Tale of Two Reports." In *The Nationalization of the Social Sciences*, edited by Samuel Z. Klausner and Victor M. Lidz, 113–120. Philadelphia: University of Pennsylvania Press, 1986.

Robin, Ron. *The Making of the Cold War Enemy: Culture and Politics in the Military-Intellectual Complex*. Princeton, NJ: Princeton University Press, 2001.

Rockefeller Foundation. *Annual Reports*. New York: Rockefeller Foundation, 1950, 1952, 1961.

Roelofs, Joan. *Foundations and Public Policy: The Mask of Pluralism*. Albany, NY: SUNY Press, 2003.

Rogin, Michael Paul. *The Intellectuals and McCarthy: The Radical Specter*. Cambridge, MA: MIT Press, 1967.

Rohde, Joy. *Armed with Expertise: The Militarization of American Social Research during the Cold War*. Ithaca, NY: Cornell University Press, 2013.

———. "Pax Technologica: Computers, International Affairs, and Human Reason in the Cold War." *Isis* 108, no. 4 (2017): 792–813.

Ross, Dorothy. *The Origins of American Social Science*. Cambridge: Cambridge University Press, 1991.

Sarf, Hal. *Masters and Disciples*. Berkeley, CA: Center for Humanities and Contemporary Culture & Regent Press, 2002.

Schiesl, Martin J. *The Politics of Efficiency: Municipal Administration and Reform in America, 1800–1920*. Berkeley: University of California Press, 1977.

Schmidt, Jeff. *Disciplined Minds: A Critical Look at Salaried Professionals and the Soul-Battering System that Shapes Their Lives*. Lanham, MD: Rowman & Littlefield, 2000.

Schrecker, Ellen W. *No Ivory Tower: McCarthyism and the Universities*. New York: Oxford University Press, 1986.

Schudel, Matt. "Political Intellectual Pendleton Herring, 100." *Washington Post*, August 20, 2004, national edition, B06.

Schwartz-Shea, Peregrine, and Dvora Yanow. "'Reading' 'Methods' 'Texts': How Research Methods Texts Construct Political Science." *Political Research Quarterly* 55, no. 2 (2002): 457–486.

Scott, Peter Dale. *Coming to Jakarta: A Poem about Terror*. New York: New Directions, 1989.

Seabury, Paul. "'Reconstitute' Universities?" *Freedom at Issue*, September-October, no. 3 (1970): 1–2, 13–15.

Sears, Robert R. "Donald George Marquis." *American Journal of Psychology* 86, no. 3 (1973): 661–663.

Seidelman, Raymond, with the assistance of Edward J. Harpham. *Disenchanted Realists: Political Science and the American Crisis, 1884–1984*. Albany, NY: SUNY Press, 1985.

Seybold, Peter. "The Ford Foundation and the Triumph of Behavioralism in American Political Science." In *Philanthropy and Cultural Imperialism: The Foundations at Home and Abroad*, edited by Robert F. Arnove, 269–303. Bloomington: Indiana University Press, 1982. First published 1980 by G. K. Hall (Boston).

Simpson, Christopher. *Science of Coercion: Communication Research and Psychological Warfare, 1945–1960*. New York: Oxford University Press, 1994.

Slaughter, Sheila, and Gary Rhoades. *Academic Capitalism and the New Economy: Markets, State, and Higher Education*. Baltimore: Johns Hopkins University Press, 2004.

Smith, Mark C. *Social Science in the Crucible: The American Debate over Objectivity and Purpose, 1918–1941*. Durham, NC: Duke University Press, 1994.

Social Science Research Council. *Annual Reports*, 1944–1961. New York: SSRC.

Solovey, Mark. "Project Camelot and the 1960s Epistemological Revolution: Rethinking the Politics-Patronage-Social Science Nexus." *Social Studies of Science* 31, no. 2 (2001): 171–206.

———. "Riding Natural Scientists' Coattails onto the Endless Frontier: The SSRC and the Quest for Scientific Legitimacy." *Journal of the History of the Behavioral Sciences* 40, no. 4 (2004): 393–422.

———. *Shaky Foundations: The Politics-Patronage-Social Science Nexus in Cold War America*. New Brunswick, NJ: Rutgers University Press, 2013.

———. *Social Science for What? Battles over Public Funding for the "Other Sciences" at the National Science Foundation*. Cambridge, MA: MIT Press, 2020.

Somit, Albert, and Joseph Tanenhaus. *The Development of American Political Science: From Burgess to Behavioralism*. New York: Irvington, 1982.

SSRC Committee on Analysis of Pre-Election Polls and Forecasts. Report on the Analysis of Pre-Election Polls and Forecasts. *Public Opinion Quarterly* 12 (Winter, 1948–1949): 599–622.

Stadtman, Verne A. *The University of California, 1868–1968. A Centennial Publication of the University of California.* New York: McGraw-Hill, 1970.

Stivers, Camilla. *Bureau Men, Settlement Women: Constructing Public Administration in the Progressive Era.* Lawrence: University Press of Kansas, 2000.

Stone, Harold A., Don K. Price, and Kathryn H. Stone. *City Manager Government in the United States: A Review after Twenty-Five Years.* Chicago: Public Administration Service, 1940.

Stonor Saunders, Frances. *The Cultural Cold War: The CIA and the World of Arts and Letters.* New York: New Press, 1999.

Storing, Herbert J., ed. *Essays on the Scientific Study of Politics.* New York: Holt, Rinehart & Winston, 1962.

Stouffer, Samuel, Carl I. Hovland, Arthur A. Lumsdaine, Fred D. Sheffield, Social Science Research Council, US Army Information and Education Division. *Studies in Social Psychology in World War II.* 4 vols. Princeton, NJ: Princeton University Press, 1949–1950.

Strauss, Leo. "An Epilogue." In *Essays on the Scientific Study of Politics,* edited by Herbert J. Storing, 305–327. New York: Holt, Rinehart & Winston, 1962.

Teles, Steven M. *The Rise of the Conservative Legal Movement: The Battle for Control of the Law.* Princeton, NJ: Princeton University Press, 2008.

Thompson, Kenneth W. "Toward a Theory of International Politics." *American Political Science Review* 49, no. 3 (1955): 733–746.

Trow, Katherine Bernhardi. *Habits of Mind: The Experimental College Program at Berkeley.* Berkeley, CA: Institute of Governmental Studies Press, 1998.

Truman, David B. "Disillusion and Regeneration: The Quest for a Discipline." *American Political Science Review* 59, no. 4 (1965): 865–873.

Tussman, Joseph. *Experiment at Berkeley.* New York: Oxford University Press, 1969.

Vaughn, Shannon K., and Shelly Arsenault. "The Public Benefit of Benefit Corporations." *PS: Political Science & Politics* 51, no. 1 (2018): 54–60.

Vitalis, Robert. *White World Order, Black Power Politics: The Birth of American International Relations.* Ithaca, NY: Cornell University Press, 2015.

Waldo, Dwight. "Political Science: Tradition, Discipline, Profession, Science, Enterprise." In *Political Science: Scope and Theory, Volume 1, Handbook of Political Science,* edited by Fred I. Greenstein and Nelson Polsby, 1–130. Reading, MA.: Addison-Wesley, 1975.

Walker, Jack L., Jr. *Mobilizing Interest Groups in America: Patrons, Professions, and Social Movements.* Prepared for publication by Joel Aberbach et al. Ann Arbor: University of Michigan Press, 1991.

Watson, M. S. *Chief of Staff: Prewar Plans and Preparations.* United States Army in World War II series. Washington, DC: Center for Military History, United States Army, 1950.

Wertheim, Stephen. "Reading the International Mind: International Public Opinion in Early Twentieth Century Anglo-American Thought." In *The Decisionist Imagination:*

Sovereignty, Social Science, and Democracy in the 20th Century, edited by Daniel Bessner and Nicolas Guilhot, 27–63. New York: Berghahn, 2019.

Whitaker, Ben. *The Foundations: An Anatomy of Philanthropy and Society*. London: Eyre Methuen, 1974.

Wildavsky, Aaron. "On Being a Department Chair." *PS: Political Science & Politics* 25, no. 1 (1992): 83–89.

Winters, Jeffrey A. *Oligarchy*. Cambridge: Cambridge University Press, 2011.

Winters, Jeffrey A., and Benjamin I. Page. "Oligarchy in the United States?" *Perspectives on Politics* 7, no. 4 (2009): 731–751.

Wolin, Sheldon. "Political Theory as a Vocation." *American Political Science Review* 63, no. 4 (1969): 1062–1082.

———. *Politics and Vision: Continuity and Innovation in Western Political Thought*. Boston: Little, Brown, 1960.

Wolin, Sheldon, and John H. Schaar. *The Berkeley Rebellion and Beyond: Essays on Politics and Education in the Technological Society*. New York: Random House, 1970.

Wormser, Rene A. *Foundations: Their Power and Influence*. San Pedro, CA: Covenant House, 1993.

Young, Donald R. "Techniques of Race Relations." *Proceedings of the American Philosophical Society* 91, no. 2 (1947): 150–161.

INDEX

Note: page numbers followed by *t* refer to tables. Those followed by n refer to notes, with note number.

academic freedom, 3
Adcock, Robert, 10, 51, 233n73
African Studies Association, 175
Allport, Gordon, 70–71, 168, 208n64
Almond, Gabriel, 65, 66, 73
American National Election Studies
(ANES) data set
calls for defunding of, 180
as political science's claim to scientific
legitimacy, 180
as product of Michigan's SRC study of
1952 election, 45
success of, 131
American Political Science Association
(APSA), vii, 65, 69, 124, 159,
177–178
American Soldier, The (Stouffer et al.),
34–39
academic reception of, 39
analysis of data for, 36–37
audience for, 38
Carnegie involvement in, 27
continuity of personnel working on,
36
and credibility of social science, 34, 38
funding for, 35–36
government handover to SSRC, 35–36
as interdisciplinary project, 38–39
military's negative response to, 37
number of authors, 39
reasons for SSRC postwar
responsibility for, 38–39
as SSRC-Carnegie cooperation, 34–35
as SSRC project, 27, 34

use of Army's Research Branch data,
34–36
American Voter, The (Campbell et. al.)
Campbell's support for SSRC
involvement, 47
Carnegie's unwillingness to fund later
stages of, 86
funding of, 44–45, 82, 86, 110, 200n96
influence of, 44–45
methods of, as not fully accepted,
86–89
as product of Michigan's SRC, 86
and survey research legitimacy, 89
ANES. *See* American National Election
Studies data set
area and international studies
disputes about methodology, 175–176
foundations' funding of, 4, 14, 143–
145, 175
Arendt, Hannah, 92, 100
Army Information and Education
Division
Carnegie funding for, 35, 195–196n50
Osborn as head of, 24, 34, 35, 38
Army Information and Education
Division, Research Branch
and *The American Soldier,* 34–35
origin of, 35
Osborn's support for, 35
Young and Dollard's work at, 24, 29, 38
Army Special Operations Research Office
(SORO), 12
Association for Asian Studies, 175
Association for Political Theory (APT), 177

Ball, Terence, 75–76
Barrow, Clyde, 173, 177–178
Barrows, David, 135–137
behavioral science
    as amorphous until late 1950s, 69–70,
        73, 75
    current support for, 51
    focus and goals of, 51, 52–53
    and interdisciplinary projects, funding
        for, 53
    new approaches of, 51–52
behavioral science, rise of
    foundation funding and, 6–9, 18–19,
        50–54, 69–76, 77
    historians on, 50, 52, 73–76
    as key development in political
        science, 51
    and linking of government,
        foundations, and academia, 72–73,
        209n71
    and marginalization of political
        theory, vii
    in political science vs. psychology or
        sociology, 52–53
    political scientists on, 70–73, 77
Berelson, Bernard
    on CASBS, 61, 206n38
    and Ford BSP grants, 57–58, 63, 65,
        67, 68, 145, 207n54
    on Ford control of SSRC, 33
    and Ford funding of political science,
        54
    and Ford's BSP, termination of, 55–56,
        76–77
    vision for future of behavioral science,
        77
Berkeley, Ford BSP grants to, 140–143
    creation of new entities by, 143
    delay in using, 58–59
    impact on political science
        department, 139–140
    planning for use of, 140–142
    power of faculty funded by, 144
    size of, 230n32
    university as recipient of, 145
    university commitment to continue
        programs, 59, 62

Berkeley, Rockefeller LAPP grant (1956),
        97–99, 144
    concerns about lack of clear focus of,
        97–98
    department's broad guidelines on use,
        145–146
    fields designated for support, 145,
        165, 230n39
    impact on political science
        department, 165
    as incentive to prioritize research, 146
    influence on institution, 100, 101
    research projects supported by, 146
    size of, 230n37
Berkeley, Rockefeller LAPP grant (1961)
    centrifugal forces created by, 139–140,
        150–151
    and faculty drawn away from
        teaching, 150
    faculty reluctance to teach abroad,
        98–99, 146
    faculty seminars funded by, 98–99,
        147–148, 150–151
    field-crossing in projects funded by,
        146, 150
    funding of faculty work in Africa,
        Asia, and Latin America, 97–99,
        138, 147, 165–166, 172
    influence on political science
        department, 98–99, 100, 165–166
    overseas faculty's political roles,
        149–150
    and political theorists' efforts to leave
        political science department,
        150–157
    size of, 230n37
    turn to focus on comparative politics,
        146
Berkeley, University of California
    Board of Educational Development
        (BED), 154–155, 190n45
    and government postwar funding,
        11–12
    Graduate School of Public Affairs,
        151
    Lawrence Radiation Laboratory, 11–
        12, 138–139

postwar research focus, 14–15, 16,
    138–139
Reconstitution Movement, 157–159,
    163–164
Study Commission recommendations,
    155–157
unrest and experimentation of 1960s,
    153–159
wartime research boom at, 138–139
Berkeley Center for the Integration of
    Social Science Theory, 14, 59, 141,
    165, 238n117
Berkeley Institute for International
    Studies (IIS), 143, 165
Berkeley Institute for Social Science (ISS),
    14, 59–60, 143
Berkeley ORUs
    end of foundation funding and, 165
    establishment of, 14
    influence on political science
        department, 134
Berkeley political science department
    and behavioralism, debate on, 143
    Board of Educational Development
        and, 155
    characteristics vs. Michigan, 134
    departmental history, 137–138
    departure of public administration
        faculty, 151
    founding of, 135
    impact of foundation grants on, 8, 13,
        134, 139–140, 164–165, 172
    influence of US imperial projects on,
        135
    internal conflict of 1960s, 134
    ISS as threat to, 59–60
    limited influence of ORUs on, 134
    political theorists' critiques of
        department, 135
    postwar pursuit of grant funding, 139
    views on arrival of behavioral
        sciences, 142
Berkeley political science department,
        and international and area studies
    departure of faculty, 151
    as focus of early department
        members, 135–138

Ford Foundation funding of, 14,
    143–145
founding of centers for, 134–135, 151
racial component of early work,
    137–138
Berkeley political science department,
        political theorists' efforts to create
        separate department, 150–157
    available evidence on, 152–153
    faculty views on, 233n74
    as ill-fated, 165, 166–167
    justification for, 166
    larger context of, 153–159
    obstacles to, 152
    origin of idea and early supporters,
        153
    planned curriculum for, 156–157
    precedents for, 151, 152
    reasons for, 176
    Study Commission recommendations
        and, 156
    unrest following failure of, 159
Berkeley political science department,
        postwar growth and change in, 8,
        13, 138–140
    faculty reactions to, 164
    foundation grants and, 139–140
    and influx of young faculty, 139
    new courses added, 139
Berkeley political science department,
        student unrest of 1960s, 159–164,
        166
    Graduate Association of Students
        of Politics (GASP) protests and,
        162–163
    and militant tactics, 163, 237nn111–
        112
    pamphlet criticizing department
        (1968), 161–162
    SLATE Supplements criticisms,
        160–161
    strikes and sit-ins, 162–163, 236–
        237n107
Berkeley Survey Research Center (SRC),
    14, 15, 59, 141, 165
Berman, Edward, 144, 148–149
Blumer, Herbert, 59, 60, 238n117

Bromage, Arthur, 121–124
BSP. *See* Ford Foundation Behavioral
    Sciences Program
Buchanan, Norman S., 81, 87, 210n7,
    211n9
Burdick, Eugene, 140–143, 146, 165

Campbell, Angus, 44, 45, 85. See also *The
    American Voter* (Campbell et al.)
Carnegie Corporation
    and *The American Soldier*, funding of,
        35, 36
    and *The American Voter*, funding of,
        44–45, 82, 86, 110, 200n96
    Cox Committee and, 45–46
    creating and sustaining of particular
        academic orientations, 106
    creation of network of academics
        and policy makers focused on
        Asia, Africa, and Latin America,
        144–145
    funding of area and international
        studies associations, 175
    funding of Miller seminar on data
        analysis, 71
    grants to Harvard, 192n17
    patronage of social sciences, prewar,
        4–5
    postwar struggle for influence over
        SSRC, 33–34, 79, 195nn46–47
    strategic funding of social science
        projects to attract federal funding,
        26
    support for behavioral science, 6, 23–
        25, 47–48, 53, 169
    support for creation of new ORUs,
        169
    and supporting academic
        infrastructures, creation of, 79
Carnegie partnership with SSRC to
        promote behavioral sciences, 23–
        24, 25, 26
    Carnegie's muting of its role in, 23–24,
        48, 49
    cultivation of allies and patrons, 48
    figures involved in forming, 24, 192n15
    five major projects, 27, 34, 48

founding of behavioral science
    programs, 69
history of, 28
influence of, 28, 49
influence on federal policy-making as
    goal, 48
lack of publicly promoted program,
    48–49
and legitimacy of behavioral science,
    78–79
promotion of Carnegie ideas under
    SSRC banner, 26, 28, 47–48, 78–79
push toward support of behavioral
    sciences, 169
reshaping of SSRC for, 29–33, 47, 48
and social science as non-ideological,
    26
tense relationship before 1945, 28–29
CASBS. *See* Center for the Advanced
    Study of the Behavioral Sciences
Caucus for a New Political Science, 162,
    177–178
Center for the Advanced Study of the
    Behavioral Sciences (CASBS)
    attractiveness to scholars, 61
    Burdick at, 141–142
    Ford grants for residencies at, 63, 65
    founding with Ford grant, 28, 61, 106,
        141
Chase, Stuart, 39. See also *The Proper
    Study of Mankind* (Chase)
Cold War, and political science, 6, 7, 12,
    55, 148–149, 231–232n56
Columbia University, 97
Committee of Trustees on Defense,
    Welfare, and Recreation
    Experimental Programs (Osborn
    Fund), 35, 195–196n50
Conference for the Study of Political
    Thought (CSPT), 176
conference on political behavior (Ann
    Arbor, 1949)
    Carnegie involvement in, 27, 43
    contributors to, 43–44
    goals for, 34, 43–44
    and rise of behavioral science, 74
    as SSRC project, 27, 34, 43

Converse, Jean, 5, 110
Converse, Philip, 45, 106–107, 114
Cox Committee investigations, 23, 45–46, 190–191n2
Crane, Robert T., 28–30, 121–122

Dahl, Robert, 60, 65, 67, 71–73, 77, 93, 207n54
Deane, Herbert, 85, 90, 91, 95
DeVinney, Leland C., 41, 81–82, 86–88, 90, 211n13, 213n29
Dollard, Charles
    and *The American Soldier*, 34, 37, 38
    background of, 29, 38
    and Carnegie-SSRC partnership, 24–25, 30–31
    on Ford Foundation blunders, 194n42
    on Herring as head of SSRC, 31
    plan for Carnegie social science program, 37–38
    on polls of 1948 failures, 41
    as president of Carnegie Corporation, 17, 28
    pressure on SSRC to pursue Carnegie agenda, 28–29
    and *The Proper Study of Mankind,* 39, 40–41, 197–198nn76–77, 197nn70–72
    on SSRC as propagandist for behavioral sciences, 23–24, 47
    and SSRC study on 1948 polls, 42
    wartime work, 24
    on work for Carnegie Corporation, 17

Easton, David, 66, 73, 93, 95
Eberstadt, Ferdinand, 24, 31
Eldersveld, Samuel
    appointment as chair of Michigan political science department, 122–123
    association with political behavior study, 133
    career of, 113, 221n42
    connections with ORUs outside department, 129
    criticism of Pollock's chairmanship, 129
        as early participant in large funded projects, 106–107
    and federal funding for Michigan's SRC, 111
    Ford grant to, 64, 65, 206n45
    and Michigan political behavior program, 13, 16, 113–117, 132, 219n26
    outside funding of, 13
    power to influence department policy, 106–107
    relationship with Pollock, 118–119, 221n42
election of 1952. *See* Michigan's Survey Research Center, study of 1952 election
Essays on the Scientific Study of Politics (Storing, ed.), 67–68, 207n54
Eulau, Heinz, 65, 66, 70, 71–72, 77
Experimental College (Berkeley), 154, 234n81

Farr, James, 73–74
Ford Foundation
    areas of political science funding, 50
    and CASBS, founding of, 28, 61, 106, 141
    centrifugal forces created at Berkeley, 139–140
    and Cold War University, creation of, 55
    creation of particular academic orientations, 106
    early plans for grants, 229n25
    effect of grants on political science, 50, 55, 144
    founding and support of area and international studies associations, 175
    founding of ORUs at UC Berkeley, 14
    grant to SSRC for behavioral research, 32
    international and area studies centers created by, 14, 143–144
    later grants for international and area studies, 14, 143–145

Ford Foundation, *continued*
  and Michigan ISR/SRC workshops,
    218n15
  older foundations' criticisms of, 33,
    194n42
  Pollock's hope for traditional public
    service emphasis from, 126
  postwar struggle for influence over
    SSRC, 33–34, 79, 195nn46–47
  program areas, 54
  and Reece Committee, 68
  role in creating network of academics
    and policy makers focused on
    Asia, Africa, and Latin America,
    144–145
  size of political science funds, 49, 50,
    53, 55, 170
  Study Commission, Odegard and, 139
  support for Asian studies, 230n34
  support for behavioral science, 169
  support for creation of new ORUs,
    169
  and supporting academic
    infrastructures, creation of, 79, 170
Ford Foundation Behavioral Sciences
    Program (BSP), 54–62
  and accelerated development of
    behavioral science, 61
  boosting of behavioral sciences, 27, 50
  and broad appeal of programs, 62–63,
    68
  delays in grantees' use of money,
    58–59
  ending of, 144
  endowment of CASBS, 61
  founding of behavioral science
    programs, 6–7, 53, 69–77
  funding of psychologists and
    sociologists over political
    scientists, 54
  grants for CASBS residencies, 63, 65
  grants for training in statistics, 60,
    205n35
  grants to individuals, 64, 206n43,
    206n45
  grants to universities rather than
    departments, 145

  grant to critics of behavioralism,
    66–68
  improving relations with humanistic
    disciplines as goal of, 67
  as initiatory, 55–56, 58
  interdisciplinary focus, influence of,
    62–63
  lack of grantee expertise and, 59
  large grants to universities, 63
  and military and corporate patronage,
    hope to attract, 56, 57
  public promotion of projects, 48, 49
  and reform implications of social
    science, 56
  shaping of many academic disciplines,
    77
  shaping of political science agenda,
    6–7, 50, 54–58, 61–70, 76, 77
  shaping of social science, 55–56
  significance of program name, 55–58
  termination of, 55–56, 76–77
  transformative mission of, 60
  unsolicited grants designed to create
    new programs, 58–62
  work with SSRC, 60–61
  See also Berkeley, Ford BSP grants to
Fosdick, Raymond, 80, 210n6
Foundation Center, The, 192n11
foundations
  academics' excitement in 1950s about
    funds from, 70–71, 168
  allies' magnification of power, 4
  conservative and libertarian, 179
  and constraints of tax-exempt status,
    1–2
  consultation among, 25, 192n11
  control of grant recipients by, 105,
    130–131, 132, 168, 170
  creating and sustaining of particular
    academic orientations, 106, 132,
    170
  eventual drying up of funds, 168–169
  and federal funding, arrangements for,
    4–8, 26, 32, 56, 57, 63, 170–171
  impact on departments and
    universities, 106, 168, 169, 173–
    174, 175, 177–181

influence on public policy, 2
partnerships with administrators and
    faculty required for success of,
    171
perpetuation of newly-created
    programs, 170–171
and postwar federal patronage of
    social sciences, 4–8
power of, presented as apolitical, 1,
    2–3
rise of behavioral science as response
    to funding by, 6–9, 18–19, 50–54,
    69–76, 77
role in creating network of academics
    and policy makers focused on
    Asia, Africa, and Latin America,
    144–145
shaping of political science, 3–4, 6–9,
    14, 17–19, 50, 54–58, 61–70, 76,
    77, 171–172, 174–175
as silent partners in US foreign policy,
    148–149
as "third sector," 2–3
Free Speech Movement (FSM), 153–154,
    160

Gaither, H. Rowan, 57, 73
Gardner, John, 44, 45, 46, 200n96
Geiger, Roger, 11, 108
GI Bill, 15
government funding of research,
    and postwar rise of research
    universities, 11–13
government funding of social sciences
    and commercialization of research,
    179, 239n15
foundations' arrangements for, 4–8,
    26, 32, 56, 57, 61, 63, 170–171
postwar drop in, 55
and rise of behavioral science, 72
Graduate Association of Students of
    Politics (GASP), 162–163
graduate students
    criticisms of Berkeley department
    made by, 161–163
increased need for, with ORUs, 12, 14,
    15–16

Michigan's SRC research
    infrastructure as draw for, 110
ORUs' attractive funding for, 16
postwar federal and foundation
    funding, 15–16

Haber, William, 114, 122
Hardin, Charles, 67, 207n55
Harvard University, 97, 192n17
Herring, Pendleton
    and Ann Arbor Conference (1949),
        43, 44
    background of, 31–32
    and behavioral science, funding for,
        53
    and Carnegie-SSRC partnership to
        promote behavioral sciences, 24–
        25, 26, 28, 29, 32, 48
    and Cox Committee, 46
    as former Carnegie officer, 26
    and government and corporate
        patrons for social sciences, pursuit
        of, 26, 32, 57
    as head of SSRC, 26, 31–32, 42, 47–48
    and Michigan's new behavioralist
        program, 119
    and Michigan's SRC study of 1952
        election, 46
    promotion of behavioral sciences, 6
    and Public Opinion Quarterly, 42
    and rise of behavioral science
        research, 53
    and SSRC-initiated projects, 33, 43
    and SSRC's Committee on Political
        Behavior, revival of, 43, 44, 199n87
    and SSRC study on 1948 polls, 42
    and SSRC turn to behavioralism, 122
    and survey methods, support for,
        26–27
    ties to government, foundations, and
        academia, 72
    wartime work, 24
histories of political science, on influence
    of broad cultural currents, 9–10

ICPR. See Inter-university Consortium
    for Political Research

ICPSR. *See under* Inter-university
    Consortium for Political Research
Institute for Government Studies, 226n1
Inter-university Consortium for Political
    Research (ICPR)
    data trove controlled by, 131, 174–175
    and foundation funding, 174
    founding of, 217–218n13
    government funding, 131
    ICPSR rename, 217n5
    impact on Michigan political science
        department, 113, 174
    large amount of funding, 108
    Michigan's survey research
        infrastructure and, 110
    NSF funding for, 110
    power of funded faculty to influence
        departmental policies, 108
    success of, 15, 131
    summer training program, 111, 174
ISR. *See* Michigan's Institute for Social
    Research
ISS (Berkeley Institute for Social Science),
    14, 59–60, 143

Jacobson, Norman
    and behavioralism debate at Berkeley,
        143
    critique of Berkeley political science
        department, 166
    and Experimental College, 154
    on future of political theory, 95
    Miller and, 142
    and Rockefeller grants, vii, 97, 146
    and separate Berkeley political theory
        department, 233n74
    views on arrival of behavioral
        sciences, 142

Kerr, Clark, 13, 14, 139, 140–143, 145
Key, V. O., Jr., 44, 53, 73, 83–86, 101,
    212n22. See also *Southern Politics*
    (Key)

LAPP. *See* Rockefeller Foundation Legal
    and Political Philosophy program
Lasswell, Harold, 65, 67, 71, 73, 207n54

Lawrence Radiation Laboratory, 11–12,
    138–139
Lazarsfeld, Paul, 43, 67
Lowen, Rebecca, 65–66

Marquis, Donald
    background of, 56
    and Ford grants to individuals, 64–65,
        206n43
    Herring and, 57
    and planning for Ford's BSP, 56,
        192n15
    ties to Ford Foundation, 57
    ties to government, foundations, and
        academia, 72
    vision for future of behavioral science,
        77
McClosky, Herbert, 92, 93, 142
Merriam, Charles, 73–74
methodological critiques
    and intellectual cul-de-sacs, 178
    no definite political remedies
        suggested by, 177–178
Michigan, University of
    and government postwar funding,
        11–12
    ORUs, establishment of, 14
    PhD program in political behavior,
        69
    as postwar research university, 14,
        15, 16
Michigan, and Ford Motor Company's
    Willow Run
    acquisition of, 11–12
    continuation of wartime research
        agenda, 109
    as organized research unit (ORU), 12
    University income derived from, 109
Michigan model
    ascendance of, 107, 114
    success of, 86, 88
Michigan political science department
    and funding for traditional *vs.* ORU
        scholars, 111, 218n20
    and government classified research,
        129–130
    and ICPR, 13, 15

impact of foundation grants on, 13,
    171–172
and lack of large funded projects in
    1950s, 106–107
Miller and Eldersveld's critique of
    public service emphasis of, 117–
    118
and political theory, importance of,
    114–115
postwar growth and change in, 8
purpose of political science as issue
    in, 107
speeches at 50th anniversary party,
    125, 224nn63–64
and Survey Research Center, impact
    of, 8, 13, 14
Michigan political science department,
    new behavioralist program
connection to political theory as
    strategic selling point, 114–117
as driven by faculty, not foundations,
    132
early avoidance of conflict with
    department, 117
faculty hired in, 114
focus on ORUs outside department,
    129
foundations as partner in, 171–172
growth of, 108–113
introduction as modest new program,
    107, 113
lack of sustained opposition to, 107
patronage necessary for, 132
power of funded faculty to influence
    department policy, 106–107, 108,
    109–112
replacement of public service model,
    107, 128–129
shedding of connection to political
    theory, 115–116, 219–220n29
takeover of department, 107, 112,
    113–117, 133, 216–217n4
transition to, depicted in Pollock's
    retirement dinner tributes, 124–
    125, 127–128
transition to, depicted in speeches
    about Bromage, 123–124, 223n62

Michigan political science department,
    traditional public service model,
    119–128
career patterns shift away from,
    120–121
current difficulties in grasping, 119–
    120
and devaluing of faculty public
    service, 120–121
flight of adherents to other fields,
    119–120
important figures in, 121–126, 222–
    223n53
Miller and Eldersveld's critique of,
    117–118
postwar marginalization of, 13
postwar research economy and, 120,
    122
Progressive Era and, 121, 128–129
replacement by new behavioralist
    program, 107, 128–129, 133
transition away from, under Bromage,
    123–125
Michigan Politics in Transition (Pollock
    and Eldersveld), 118
Michigan's Institute for Social Research
    (ISR)
and Campbell's *American Voter*
    project, 87
concerns about direction of, 87–88
and federal funding, 110
and foundation funding, 108–112,
    174
founding of, 109
as postwar source for career
    advancement, 120
power of funded faculty to influence
    departmental policies, 106–112,
    119
RCGD as part of, 109
sponsors of, 109
SRC as part of, 109
success of, 131
summer workshops, 110–111
University income derived from, 109
wartime research units folded into,
    109

Michigan's Survey Research Center (SRC)
  and *The American Voter*, 86, 110
  and cost of large-scale behavioral
    research, 76
  early lack of University influence, 46
  early work by, as not fully accepted, 86
  election studies of 1960, 86
  faculty funded by, power to influence
    departmental policies, 63, 108,
    109–113
  and federal funding, 111
  foundation funding, and influence
    over research, 111, 130–131
  government-funded classified
    research, 130
  impact on political science
    department, 8, 13, 14
  institutions funding early work by,
    86–87
  large amount of funding, 108, 111,
    218n20
  origin in World War II research, 109
  as part of Michigan's ISR, 109
  research infrastructure of, as draw for
    scholars, 110, 217n12
  Rockefeller funding of, 79, 82, 86, 87,
    101
  role similar to graduate school, 111
  study of 1952 election, 27, 34, 44–49,
    132, 201n108
  summer workshops, 110–111
Miller, Warren
  and *The American Voter*, 45
  association with political behavior
    study, 133
  at Berkeley, 142
  on classified research, benefits of,
    129–130
  as early participant in large funded
    projects, 106–107
  and federal funding for Michigan's
    SRC, 111
  focus on ORUs outside department,
    129
  Ford grant to, 65
  Jacobson and, 142
  and Michigan political behavior

  program, 13, 16, 108, 113–117,
    132, 133
  outside funding of, 13
  and political theory, 116, 220–221n35
  and power of ORU-affiliated political
    scientists, 15, 106–107, 108, 109,
    110, 119
  on public service model of political
    science, 117–118
  relationship with Pollok, 118, 119
  and rise of behavioral science
    research, 53
  seminar on data analysis (1954), 71
  "Some Thoughts on Classified
    Research," 129–130
  ties to government, foundations, and
    academia, 72
Minerva Initiative, 179
MIT, Center for International Studies
  (CENIS), 73
Mobilizing Interest Groups in America
  (Walker), 105–106
Moses, Bernard, 135–137, 227n5, 227n6

National Bureau for Economic Research,
  Rockefeller Foundation support
  for, 81
National Defense Education Act
  (NDEA), 15, 16, 111
National Institutes of Mental Health,
  25–26
National Municipal League, 120
National Science Foundation (NSF)
  Accountable Institutions and Behavior
    and Security and Preparedness
    programs, 180
  and ANES data set, 45
  drying up of funds for political
    science from, 168
  establishment of, 31–32
  funding for ICPR, 15, 110, 131
  funding for Michigan's SRC, 111
  funding for political science, 25–26,
    179–180, 239n17
  postwar research at, 5
  social sciences funding in 1950s, 126
  support for behavioral sciences,

foundations' role in securing, 63, 171
and support for social sciences, 31–32
National Security Act of 1947, 24
NDEA (National Defense Education Act), 15, 16, 111

Odegard, Peter, 54, 139, 145, 229n20
organized research units (ORUs)
    at Berkeley, establishment of, 12, 14
    financial power over university departments, 16
    and graduate students, attractive funding for, 16
    impact on political science departments, 8, 13, 14, 16
    at Michigan, establishment of, 12, 14, 15
    postwar rise, government funding and, 12–15
    power of funded faculty to influence academic departments, 15, 107, 109–112, 119
    size of funding by, 108
    staff's freedom to focus on research, 15
    success of, 15
    survey research infrastructure built by, as draw for scholars, 110
Organski, A. F. K., 114, 130, 217n12
Osborn, Frederick
    and The American Soldier, 34, 36, 37
    background of, 34
    and Carnegie funding of Information and Education Division research, 35
    and Carnegie-SSRC partnership to promote behavioral sciences, 24
    as former head of Army Information and Education Division, 24, 34, 35, 38
    and Herring as head of SSRC, 31
    and linking of foundations and government, 73
    as propagandist for behavioral sciences, 24–25
    on SSRC conservatism, 29
    wartime work, 24

Paff, Joe, 66, 234n76
Panama Pacific International Exposition (1915), 137
Park, Richard, 122, 146
Parmar, Inderjeet, 144, 175
Parsons, Talcott, 192n15, 194–195n44
political action, patrons' control of, 105
political science
    dependence on universities, 3
    development in universities, 11
    epistemological fracture of, 177–178
    foundations' shaping of, 3–4, 6–9, 14, 17–19, 50, 54–58, 61–70, 76, 77, 171–172, 174–175
    inward-focused discourse in, 3
    studies on foundations, as limited, 2–3
    See also Berkeley political science department; Michigan political science department
political science, postwar
    Cold War focus of, 6, 7, 12, 55, 148–149, 231–232n56
    defense-related projects, effects of, 12–13
    and need for graduate students, 12, 14, 15–16
    orientation toward national clients, 12–13
    and ORUs, 12, 13–15
    viewed as undeveloped field by other social scientists, 46–47, 54
political theory and philosophy
    broad understanding of, in 1950s, 92
    defense of humanist tradition, 176
    efforts to connect to empirical social sciences, in 1950s–1960s, 92–93
    history of marginalization, vii
    professional associations, reasons for, 176–177
    and remaking of political science discipline, 92
    Rockefeller Foundation's effort to expand bounds of, 92–93, 96–97
    and Rockefeller LAPP program, 90, 91–92
Pollock, James Kerr
    career of, 125–126, 224n66

Pollock, James Kerr, *continued*
  death of, 127
  effort to fund department-linked
    research centers, 112
  Eldersveld and, 118–119, 129, 221n42
  elections as research focus of,
    125–126
  hope for Ford support for public
    service model of political science,
    126
  on Michigan's SRC, 46, 200n106
  Miller and, 118, 119
  resignation as chair, 122, 127
  retirement speeches on transition of
    political science department, 124–
    125, 127–128
  sympathy with behavioralism, 118
  and traditional public service model
    of political science, 124–127, 128
polls of 1948, SSRC study on failure of,
    41–43
  analysis of polling errors, 42
  Carnegie involvement in, 27, 41–42
  contributors to, 42
  credibility of social science as issue
    in, 34
  as defense of survey methods, 41,
    42–43
  general audience for, 42
  impact on public perception, 198n85
  as SSRC project, 34, 41
professional associations
  in area and international studies,
    methodological disputes in, 175–
    176
  foundations' founding and support
    of, 175
  as gatekeepers for funding, 175, 176
  as intermediaries for foundations, 4
Project Camelot, 12
Proper Study of Mankind, The (Chase),
    39–41
  Carnegie involvement in, 27, 39,
    197n70
  Chase as hired writer for, 39,
    197nn71–72
  Chase's leftist politics and, 41

and credibility of social science, 34,
    39, 40–41
  failed polls of 1948 and, 41
  on polling accuracy, 40
  royalties from, 41
  as SSRC project, 27, 34, 39
  success of, 41
public administration, postwar
    marginalization of field, 9, 13. *See
    also* Michigan political science
    department, traditional public
    service model

RCGD (Research Center for Group
    Dynamics), 109
Reconstitution Movement (Berkeley),
    157–159, 163–164
Reece Committee investigation, 23, 68,
    190–191n2
Research Center for Group Dynamics
    (RCGD), 109
research councils, as intermediaries for
    foundations, 4
researchers
  as conduits for funders' influence, 62
  in current funding austerity, 178–181
research in political science
  high cost of data resources needed
    for, 179
  as increasingly tied to particular
    agendas, 179
research universities
  origin in wartime research, 108
  postwar government funding and,
    11–13
  transformation of universities by, 108
  University of Michigan as, 109
Rockefeller Foundation
  and *The American Voter*, 110
  Cold War focus of research funding,
    7
  creating and sustaining of particular
    academic orientations, 106
  effort to expand bounds of political
    theory, 92–93, 96–97
  funding of Michigan's SRC, 79, 82, 86,
    87, 101

grant policies crafted in response to other foundations, 101
grants' effect on academic infrastructure, 100–101
grants to Key, 84
internationally oriented political theory, commitment to, 170
as latecomer to political science funding, 101
and Michigan SRC, funding for, 79
patronage of social sciences, prewar, 4–5
and projects in underdeveloped countries, 91
and public administration programs, 79
role in creating network of academics and policy makers focused on Asia, Africa, and Latin America, 144–145
support for creation of new ORUs, 169
Rockefeller Foundation, and behavioral science
Key's influence on views about, 83, 85–86
postwar funding for, 53
skepticism about, 81
support for, 25, 73–74, 83, 169
Rockefeller Foundation Division of Social Sciences (DSS)
and *The American Voter*, 82, 86–89
and conflicts within political science, 82–83
directors of, 80–81
eclectic approach to funding, 79–81, 100, 101–102, 106, 210n3
and economic research, support for, 81
and fluidity of postwar social sciences, 101–102
policy conflict within, 79
and political theory and philosophy programs, funding of, 79, 80
and postwar political science, influence on, 6, 80

pressure on SSRC to administer political theory fellowships, 93–94
skepticism about behavioral sciences in, 81
and SSRC funding, 25, 79
SSRC's turn from, 30–31
support for behavioral sciences, 73–74, 83
Rockefeller Foundation Legal and Political Philosophy (LAPP) program
academics on advisory committees of, 101
broad understanding of political theory, 92, 95–96, 100, 214–215n57
debate on boundaries of political theory, 94–96
debate on goals of, 90–91
debate on place of political theory, 93–94
debate on rules for grants to individuals, 94–96
diversity of funded projects, 92
divided focus of, 99–100
drift away from political theory focus, 97, 99
fellowships for individuals, 92–97, 132, 214n49
focus of, 82–83
founding of, 89–91
grants' influence on institutions, 96, 98–100
grants to Berkeley political science department, 139–140
notable projects funded by, 100
political theory and philosophy emphasis of, 90, 91–92
and response to communism, 7, 89, 91, 100
SSRC administration of fellowships from, 93–94
SSRC awards by category, 96t
transformative ambitions of, 89
See also Berkeley, Rockefeller LAPP grant (1956); Berkeley, Rockefeller LAPP grant (1961)

Rockefeller Foundation University
    Development Program (UDP)
    as anti-communist program, 148–149,
        231–232n56
    focus on universities in Africa, Asia,
        and Latin America, 146
    political uses of, 149, 166, 231–
        232n56, 232n58
    roles of overseas faculty, 149–150,
        232n58
    See also Berkeley, Rockefeller LAPP
        grant (1961)
Rogin, Michael, 142–143
Rohde, Joy, 179, 188n31, 239n15
Rosberg, Carl, 149, 163, 237n112
Rusk, Dean, 80, 89, 91, 97
Russell, John M., 35, 36
Russell Sage Foundation, 31, 42, 53

Scalapino, Robert, 72, 97, 98–99, 146,
    150
Schaar, John
    career of, 142
    and Experimental College, 154
    on Free Speech Movement, 153–154
    and political theorists' efforts to create
        separate department, 153
    and political theory department at
        Berkeley, 233n74, 234n76
    views on arrival of behavioral
        sciences, 142
Schmitter, Philippe, 149–150
Science, The Endless Frontier (Bush),
    192n15
Science of Coercion (Simpson), 207n59
Scott, Peter Dale, 152, 154–155, 233–
    234n75
Seybold, Peter, 51, 61
Simon, Herbert, 67, 73, 207n54
Singer, J. David, 114, 129
"Social Science at the Crossroads"
    (Eulau), 70–71
social sciences
    association with social reform, 56
    departments' postwar growth and
        change, 8

postwar, and Rockefeller's grant
    strategy, 101–102
postwar concerns about loss of
    government support for, 31–32
postwar move from government to
    universities, 5–6
postwar patronage, early shakiness of,
    25–26
Social Sciences Research Council (SSRC)
    administration of Rockefeller LAPP
        fellowships, 93–94
    and behavioral science, funding for,
        53
    Crane as director of, 121–122
    fellowships for individual scholars
        funded by Rockefeller Foundation,
        92, 96t, 132
    Ford grant for behavioral science
        research, 32
    and Ford grants for statistics training,
        60–61
    foundations' postwar struggle
        for influence over, 33–34, 79,
        195nn46–47
    initiation of its own projects, 33,
        194–195n44
    legitimacy granted by Rockefeller
        funding, 101
    and Michigan's new behavioralist
        program, 119
    as postwar source for career
        advancement, 120
    postwar turn from public service
        model to behavioralism, 122
    promotion of behavioral sciences, 6,
        23–27, 47–48
    Ruml and, 73–74
    turn from area studies to global
        studies, 175–176
    as useful intermediary between
        foundations, state, and academy,
        25
    work with Rockefeller Foundation,
        25, 30–31
    Young's aggressive research program
        for, 30

See also Carnegie partnership with SSRC to promote behavioral sciences
Social Sciences Research Council, Committee on Comparative Politics
and behavioral science research, 53
Rockefeller funding and, 79, 82
as "spin-off" of CPB, 199n91
Social Sciences Research Council, Committee on Political Behavior (CPB)
Carnegie Corporation funding of, 32
and conference on political behavior (1949), 34
founding of, 69
funding for, 41, 43
funding of Michigan SRC study of 1952 election through, 45–47, 200n96
Herring's revival of, 43, 44, 199n87
historians on, 74
influence on academic political science, 43
Key as chair of, 84
work with Ford Foundation, 60–61
Solovey, Mark, 25, 65, 218n14, 239nn17–19
sources, 17–19, 27
Southern Politics (Key), 44, 82, 84, 212n19
SSRC. *See* Social Sciences Research Council; Social Sciences Research Council, Committee on Comparative Politics; Social Sciences Research Council, Committee on Political Behavior
Stanford, Ford BSP grants to, 65–66
statistical analysis in political science, foundations' funding of, 4, 60–61, 205n35
Stern Family Fund, 217–218n13
Stewart, John B., 89, 91, 95
Stokes, Donald, 45, 106–107, 110

Stouffer, Samuel, 34, 35, 36–37, 38, 206n38. See also *The American Soldier* (Stouffer et al.)
Strauss, Leo, 66–68, 92, 207n54
survey research
and *The American Voter*, 89
Carnegie support for, 6, 7, 26, 34–35, 45
Key's views on, 85, 212n22
SSRC study on 1948 polls as defense of, 41, 42–43
See also Berkeley Survey Research Center (SRC); Michigan's Survey Research Center (SRC)

Thompson, Kenneth W.
background of, 81, 146
and Campbell's *American Voter* project, 88
and connection of theory and policy, 146
as director of Rockefeller DSS, 81
and expanded bounds of political theory, 92–93, 97
and Rockefeller's grants to Berkeley, 146, 148
and Rockefeller's LAPP program, 89, 91, 92, 100
skepticism about behavioral sciences, 81, 85–86
Truman, David, 43, 53, 66, 111
Tyler, Ralph, 64, 141

universities
administrators' shaping use of grant uses, 7
as center of political science, 10–11
impact of foundations on, 106, 168, 169, 173–174, 175, 177–181
integration into national political economy, 11
as intermediary for foundations, 4
postwar federal research funding, 11
University of Alabama Bureau of Public Administration, Rockefeller support of, 84

University of California system, postwar
   growth, 138
University of Michigan. *See* Michigan,
   University of

Vitalis, Robert, 10, 173

wealthy elite political power, 1, 2–3
Western Political Science Association
   (WPSA), 162
Wildavsky, Aaron, 151–153, 232n69,
   237n111
Willits, Joseph, 30–31, 80, 85, 91, 93,
   210n6
Wolin, Sheldon
   and behavioralism debate at Berkeley,
      143
   on epic theory, 176
   and Experimental College, 154
   on Free Speech Movement, 153–154
   LAPP funding of, 100
   Paff and, 66
   and political theory department at
      Berkeley, 153, 233n74, 234n76

and Reconstitution Movement, 157–
   159, 164
and Rockefeller-funded seminars,
   150–151
and Study Commission on reforms,
   155
views on arrival of behavioral
   sciences, 142

Young, Donald
   and *The American Soldier*, 34, 36
   background of, 29, 38
   and behavioral science, funding for,
      53
   and Carnegie-SSRC partnership to
      promote behavioral sciences, 24–
      26, 28–30, 38, 48
   departure from SSRC, 31, 42
   and *The Proper Study of Mankind*, 39,
      197n70, 197n72
   research program for SSRC, 30
   and SSRC turn to behavioralism,
      122
   wartime work, 24